Gary,

May "His" Word ne joy &
strength to you every day!

Bill Kirk

Feb 15, 2020

May 12th for message

ENJOY THE JOURNEY

a one year devotional
to encourage your heart
and equip your hands
for service

Bill Kirk

Published by:
Bill Kirk
Clay, New York, USA

In conjunction with:
Old Mountain Press
www.OldMountainPress.com
Old Mountain Press eBook Division
www.oldmp.com/e-book

Copyright © 2018 Bill Kirk
Interior text designed by: Tom Davis
Cover designed by: Dan Dullen and Gregg Johnson

ISBN: 978-0-692-10438-5

ENJOY THE JOURNEY: a one year devotional to encourage your heart and equip your hands for service

First Edition
Printed and bound in the United States of America by Gasch Printing • www.gaschprinting.com • 301.362.0700
10 9 8 7 6 5

In Dedication ...

... To Laura, my wife of 37 years, who went to heaven on September 22, 2016.

... To Robby (Krista) and Bethany (Rory), who have been encouraging their dad for years to put the following messages in print.

... To Duane Durst, Bob Reeves, Esther Terry, Christine Fischer, Paul Mead, Gregg Johnson and Doug DeMent, who all, in the same few days said, "You need to write a book."

... To my brother Bob (Linda), who proof-read every line of every page to help correct my mistakes.

... To Almon Bartholomew, who welcomed me into the New York Ministry Network with open arms after graduating from the University of Valley Forge in 1980.

... To the many friends and leaders who serve God, advance others at the expense of themselves, and have personally invested into my life.

... To my wife Eunhee, who joined me in marriage on December 29, 2017, and has a great desire to see a spiritual awakening in our generation.

... To God most of all, who honors us by allowing us to serve Him and live for what really matters in our earthly journey!

Introduction

In 1963 I suddenly contracted a fever, strep throat, the measles and inflamed joints. After three weeks in Mercy Hospital and being diagnosed with rheumatic fever, my Pentecostal grandparents took me in. For the next two years I sat in a wheelchair and didn't walk one step. Yet, day after day my praying grandparents taught me the scriptures and poured faith into my heart in Leesburg, Virginia. They put something in me that caused me to believe that the Word can really change the human heart. Then in the summer of 1974, my uncle in Tampa, Florida gave me a gospel tract. Ten days later I read the tract while flying home to Baltimore, Maryland. My heart was instantly arrested and convicted. I prayed the sinner's prayer, sensed a new-found joy and walked off the airplane a born-again Christian at the age of 19. Two years later I sensed an overwhelming call to ministry and headed to the University of Valley Forge. Ever since graduation I've had the privilege of seeing God's Word change people from the inside out. You just can't underestimate the life changing power of the gospel!

While God is always doing new and fresh things among us, there is one thing that never changes. What is it? It is the Word of the Lord! It's still the Gospel that is our hope and trust and rest! It's the truth of the Gospel that sets us free! It frees us from ourselves so that, "Many will see and fear and put their trust in the Lord" (Psalm 40:3).

The following 366 messages are expository in nature and God's wisdom to enjoy the journey. My sole desire in preparing them is for your spiritual health and fruit that remains. My constant prayer is that God will use His truth to encourage, guide and prepare you for service. If you are involved in a public teaching or preaching ministry of any kind, the following calendar notes may be of help to you as you plan ahead:

January highlights many truths that encourage the heart and reveal God's deep compassion.

February deals with prayer, giving, grace, and the healthy fear of the Lord.

March includes Psalm 23 and the gifts of the Spirit.

April is completely dedicated to the Easter Season and all that surrounds it.

May (for Mother's Day) covers the praying of Hannah, the praise of Leah, and the courage of Ruth.

June (for Father's Day) looks at Saul, Jonah, David, Paul and Moses.

July looks closely at Ephesians and the Armor of God.

August has my favorite Summer Psalms series and how your heart can be renewed.

September deals with the Outpourings of the Holy Spirit in the Book of Acts.

October highlights Daniel, 1 Peter, and The Seven Churches in Revelation.

November details many of Jesus' healings and the Isaiah series.

December celebrates the Christmas themes that speak to us all.

So, blessed reading as God uses His Word to give you strength for the journey, wisdom to make right choices and ammunition for your preaching arsenal! Blessed reading as you take time to feed your spiritual man! Blessed reading as you keep taking in more than you give out! Blessed reading as you faithfully steward the gifts that God has given you! Blessed reading as you trust in "His" performance and not your own! Blessed reading as you live with **nothing to prove** and **no one to impress!** Blessed reading as you live in light of eternity!

Nuf Sed!
Bill Kirk

January 1
"The God of New Beginnings"

"Abram went **down** to Egypt." (Genesis 12:10).
"Abram went **up** from Egypt." (Genesis 13:1).

Has there ever been a time when you needed to quit looking back and start looking ahead? Have you ever wondered how God was going to help you move forward? Have you ever needed the Lord to "pick you up" and help you to "start over" again? You are not alone!

Just like Abraham was sidetracked down into Egypt (and came back to Bethel), you too can discover that God is "The God of New Beginnings"!

When Abraham was in Bethel, he pitched his tent, built his altar and called upon God. When he was distracted (and wasted time) down in Egypt, he temporarily left his tent, altar and intimacy with God. He focused on the famine instead of the faithfulness of God. Abraham lost his peace and began to fret and worry and pretended to be what he was not (Sarah's brother). He made no spiritual progress in Egypt. Time down in Egypt was simply wasted time!

But, did God cast him away and write him off? Not hardly! So, what about you this New Year's Day? Have you been trusting in your own plans, wisdom and strength? Have you been a little distracted from God's plan and leading in your own life? Have you been wondering if God's grace can help you re-calibrate your direction? Will you consider how God might be drawing you back to Himself? Are you wanting to begin the New Year right? Then remember what Abraham discovered in his journey when he went down into Egypt, but turned around and went back to Bethel. He discovered that:

◆ It's always **too soon** to think it's **too late!**
◆ When life treats you **badly**, God still treats you **good!**
◆ Wherever you are, it doesn't make God **nervous!**
◆ Every setback is a set up for a **comeback!**

What's the message from the text (Genesis 12:1-13:4)? It's pretty clear to me: that God is the God of **New Beginnings** because of the grace of Jesus we have today! So, as you begin the New Year and a new day, why not celebrate what Abraham discovered? Why not rejoice in the fact that God has accepted you in His Beloved Son (Ephesians 1:6)? Why not relax and trust God with the things and people outside of your control? Why not start the year fresh with God because of His great work on your behalf at the cross where Jesus died?

What's the take-a-way from Abraham's turnaround?

No one can go back and have a new start; but you can start right now and have a new ending! Nuf Sed!

God is way ahead of you, so quit your worrying

January 2
"The Day That Worry Died"

"And they asked each other, 'who will roll the stone away?' " (Mark 16:3).

Do you ever worry and fret over things or people outside of your control, or ever have to catch yourself with distracted thinking? I have two words for you – you're normal!

While you may think this text today is an "Easter Message", I assure you that it's a life message! For who is there among us that hasn't been tempted to fret and stew instead of trust and obey? In fact, what worries consume you in your thinking right now? Our text reveals a weakness in us all, because of sin and human tendencies. Our text is clear and to the point.

Four women are walking towards the tomb where Jesus was buried. Mary Magdalene, Mary the mother of James, Salome and Joanna (Luke 24:10). They are walking in the dark (John 20:1) to observe the law of the Sabbath (Luke 23:56). So, sometime after 6 p.m. on Saturday evening (when the Sabbath ended) the women bring spices to anoint the body of Jesus. And, one thing is on their mind; "Who is going to roll away the stone from the door?" In other words, they are consumed with one agonizing concern – who will lift the rock that we cannot lift ourselves?

These are sensible and practical women. They are not hysterical or deceived. They remember the strong men who placed the huge stone to close the tomb and they see their own limitations! Yet, they continue to walk with the spices in the dark – even though their feelings, emotions and circumstances say "You're wasting your time."

Maybe the enemy of your soul has been whispering to you. Maybe you have been tempted to worry over something (or someone). Maybe you are consumed with your own limitations instead of God's great ability. Maybe you are churning inwardly or are anxious in spirit. If so, then notice Verse 4, "And when they looked, they saw." Wow! The women saw that what they worried about had already been addressed by the Lord. They flat out discovered two things; God had gone before them (ahead of them) in the journey, and God did for them what they could not do for themselves.

Can you imagine what the worrying women said to each other on their way to Galilee?
♦ "Can you believe it? We worried all that way for nothing!"
♦ "Can you imagine that we wasted all that time fretting for nothing?"
♦ "Can you beat that. Our anticipated trouble was already taken care of by Jesus!"

While God doesn't always answer our prayers in the way we think He should, and, while there are so many things we do not understand, the message from the worried women is clear:

Worry is accepting responsibility that God never intended for you to carry!
Nuf Sed

"When Chains Fall Off"

"A light shone in the cell…. and the chains fell off Peter's wrists" (Acts 12:7).

I still remember the night that my son Robby sat on the couch and asked me: "Dad, why was James killed and yet Peter was released from prison?" My weak response was Deuteronomy 29:29; "The secret things belong to the Lord." In other words, there are some things that happen to us in this life that are painful – and on this side of heaven we'll never know the reason why.

Provoked to study the context of Robby's question, here's what surfaced from Peter's imprisonment.

1. **Painful things can happen to good people in the perfect will of God!** (V. 1-4) In other words, Herod imprisons Peter to hold him until after the Passover Feast. Why? To present Peter to the Jews in a public display so Herod's popularity will rise even more. What about you today? Maybe you've experienced an injustice, betrayal, or great pain. Maybe you've even asked God "why?" Maybe your heart is filled with questions. I have two words for you – you're normal!

2. **Prayer is not the last thing, but the first thing to put in gear.** I love this response from the early church! "Peter was kept in prison, but the church was earnestly praying to God for him" (V. 5). It's a seemingly impossible request, yet people prayed! Why? Because prayer gets God into focus, prayer is combat against the powers of darkness, and prayer enforces what God intends to bring to pass!

3. **God may not be early, but for sure He's never late!** It's no secret that we don't always appreciate God's timing. "The night before" (V.6) means the night before Peter is to be put to death. In other words, believers are praying and the "deadline" is in the morning. The good news is that delay is not denial, and great reward comes to those who refuse to quit in the place of prayer.

4. **When light comes in, chains fall off!** So, a light shines into the prison, an angel intervenes and Peter's chains are broken! (V. 7) Wow! Take this from the story: there is no darkness where God's light cannot penetrate, no barrier that God cannot cross over and no limit to the power of agreeing prayer! What's my take-a-way?

♦ The devil **can** put people into prison, but the devil **cannot** keep God out of prison! (And)

♦ The only thing that lies outside of the **power of prayer** is that which lies outside **the will of God!**   Nuf Sed!

January 4
"Peter's Revealing Question"

"We have left everything to follow you! What then will there be for us?"
(Matthew 19:27).

Have you ever wondered what causes a person to "feel cheated" or "get sour" in their service for the Lord? Ever wonder what causes a "complaining spirit"? Ever wonder what causes someone (not us of course) to resent authority or abruptly quit or claim that life is not fair? Hark, the revealing question of Peter: "Lord, what's in it for us?"

Jesus responds to Peter's question by giving the parable about the laborers in the vineyard, a parable that teaches us the danger of bargaining with God and beholding other people! It's an incredible response that protects the heart from ever "feeling cheated" in following Jesus. It's truth that frees us from ourselves! Here's the point:

Peter had seen the rich young ruler walk away from Jesus. Peter had compared his possessions with the rulers. Peter's attitude became contaminated because he compared himself with another. And, Peter became dissatisfied (instead of grateful) for what Jesus gave him. So why did Peter feel cheated and begin to complain? Because (for a moment) he forgot what he signed up for when he agreed to follow Jesus. Thus, the parable in response and Jesus' great wisdom speaks to your heart and mine! It's a word that changes us from the inside out, a reminder that produces great joy and protects us from ever feeling cheated. So here are the lessons that produce a healthy soul:

1. The root cause of all complaints is when a person feels like they are not getting what they deserve (and the truth of the matter is, we don't want what we deserve!)
2. If I'm not content with what I have, I'll not be content with what I want!
3. If Calvary is not enough to motivate me where I am, then nothing else will ever be enough where I may go!
4. God is not impressed with the dimension of my work, but with the spirit in which it is done!
5. Merchandising is when I empty other people to enrich myself. Ministry is when I empty myself to enrich other people.
6. A "servant" (DOULOS) Mark 10:44 and (DIAKONOS) Matthew 23:11 is defined as someone who:

   ♦ Advances others at the expense of themself,
   ♦ Cares less who gets the credit,
   ♦ Doesn't need to be "thanked" for their service, and
   ♦ Takes up their cross without complaint.

(My prayer?)

"Lord, help me to be grateful for what I DO have, and never murmur over what I don't."

Nuf Sed!

January 5
"Use it or Lose It"

"Consider carefully what you hear", he continued. "With the measure you use it will be measured to you - and **even more**.
Whoever has will be given more; whoever does not have, even what he has will be **taken from him**" (Mark 4:24, 25).

My heart was instantly arrested when I read the words: "even more" and "taken from". These are words from Jesus about "growing forward" or "sliding backwards". And, who doesn't want to keep growing and become stronger?

While all of us would admit that we only grow because of the work of grace in the heart, we also would admit that we must cooperate with God in the process. That's why Jesus said "Consider carefully what you hear" (V. 24). In other words, there is a relationship between how we hear and how we grow. Or simply, we can bring whatever receptivity we want to the table. And whatever capacity we bring to God, He will fill it up, and in fact, give even more.

Did you hear those words "even more"? They mean two things:
1. What you do with what you hear today, determines what can be given to you tomorrow, (and)
2. If you chose to become stagnant, then more cannot be given to you.

Why is this so important? Because Jesus said, if you stop growing, you risk even losing what you already have. Hence, the words, "Even what he has will be taken from him" (V. 25).

So if we ever stop listening (and **learning**) then we stop **changing**. And, if we stop changing, then we stop growing. And, when we **stop growing**, we create our own **lids** and **ceilings** and end up with **wasted potential**.

How can we be sure we keep growing? By a continual willingness to be teachable, so that humility gives us access to God and wisdom through other people. Lord, help us to never forget the following:

- Only a **fool** knows everything!
- Humility allows us to admit, "we don't have **all** the answers."
- If we broaden our hearts, God can pour more into them!
- God is using us as much as He can, but not all that He could!

And, the take-a-way to remember so we can always be moving forward is:
The biggest room in the world is the room for improvement!

Nuf Sed!

"Against All Odds"

"Jephthah the Gileadite was a mighty warrior….his mother was a prostitute" (Judges 11:1).

Jephthah was the ninth of the thirteen judges. His life and story are recorded in a book (Judges) that is all about weakness, failure and the grace of God. Why Jephthah? To show us that whoever you are, wherever you're from and whatever your background may be – God has a plan that supersedes your past. Just think of the odds that Jephthah was up against!

1. He was **illegitimate** (V.1), the son of a harlot. His father (Gilead) was married to a "strange woman", a Gentile, a common heathen prostitute.
2. He was **rejected** (V. 2) and told he would have no part in his father's inheritance.
3. He was **isolated** (V. 3) and exiled to the land of Tob, a place 15 miles east of Ramoth-Gilead.

So, thus far, here's what I'm learning. Not everyone enters this life with the best advantages; it's possible to be ostracized by your own flesh and blood, and we all have choices in responding to our pain.

And, here's where the story really gets good! While Jephthah is in Tob (A Hebrew word that means good, pleasant, sweet, fair, and beautiful) God is orchestrating a plan all the while. Ammon makes war against Israel, and Israel is in desperate need of a leader. And guess who is invited to lead the battle? That's right - Jephthah! "Then the Spirit of the Lord came upon Jephthah." (V. 29)

So, after 18 years in exile and "on hold", Jephthah is asked to help the very ones who had expelled him from the land. And, because of God's grace and Jephthah's willingness to forgive, we have a great report to read; "He devastated twenty towns" (V. 33).

Jephthah is anointed, victorious and even remembered in Hebrews 11:32-34, how "**weakness was turned to strength**." He shows us that we are not responsible for the heritage we've been **given**, but we are responsible for the one we are **leaving**! We learn that, at times, God's work is **invisible** (18 years "on hold" in Tob) but God is working even when we cannot **see Him**! What's the great take-a-way from Jephthah?

I am not a product of my circumstances, I am a product of my decisions!

Nuf Sed!

January 7
"Therapy from Thessalonica"

"We had previously suffered and been insulted in Philippi as you know, but with the help of our God, we dared to tell you his gospel in spite of strong opposition" (I Thessalonians 2:2).

The founding of the church in Thessalonica took place on Paul's second missionary journey (Acts 17:1-15). Paul ministered there for only a short time and was smuggled out in peril of his very life. Paul sent Timothy to see how things were going and then sent a letter (I Thessalonians) from Corinth in response to Timothy's report. Paul revealed how:

1. He suffered and was mistreated in Philippi.
2. He went to Thessalonica anyway.
3. God helped him to minister in spite of past abuse, insults and opposition.

What leaps off the pages here? The truth that Paul's painful experience in Philippi could have made him hesitate to minister in Thessalonica. In other words, Paul's offense could have been his **"tomb stone"** instead of his **"stepping stone"**. But the gift of forgiveness was medicine to Paul. And, the gift of forgiveness is medicine to you and me as well. So, what enables us to forgive our offenders? Only one thing; understanding that God (in Christ) has forgiven you of every sin when you could not forgive yourself! And, what's the big deal about this forgiveness choice? Glad you asked:

Forgiveness frees us from living as the **victims** of other people's behaviors! It allows us to **build** more bridges than we **burn**! Forgiveness protects us from being **controlled** by what someone else has done and it spares us from carrying around emotional **baggage** that is exhausting!

In fact, Paul's forgiveness in our text reveals that past pain doesn't have to **rob** you of future opportunities. His forgiveness reveals that past offenses have **no authority** to make you critical or cynical, past disappointments have **no power** to keep you from miracles, and past rejections were intended by Satan to sideline you – but intended by God to **prepare** you.

My take-a-way lesson learned from Paul in Thessalonica is this:

The only power that an offense has in your life is the power that you give it!

Nuf Sed!

"Medicine from Martha"

"Lord… if you had been here, my brother would not have died" (John 11:21).

My heart is finding it difficult to move on from yesterday's message; I believe (and feel) that there is so much more to this subject of offense, forgiveness and a healthy soul. So here we go; it's wisdom from the Lord who knows us all so well.

Why is this so important? Because whenever change is necessary, not to change is destructive. And, if bitterness ever takes root in the heart, it has the ability to poison everything else. Poison produces a toxic spirit that defiles and stains everyone it touches. So here's the point of our text:

Martha says (and God has recorded it) three things that are revealing:
♦ "Jesus, if you would have arrived on time…" (V. 21)
♦ "Jesus, I know about Lazarus and the future resurrection." (V. 24)
♦ "Jesus, he already stinks because it's been four days." (V. 39)

Why is Martha expressing her disappointment in Jesus? For two reasons. First, she knew that she had sent the message early enough to Jesus, and secondly, Jesus didn't drop what He was doing and come to the rescue when she thought He should.

In other words, Martha has to choose how she will deal with an unfulfilled expectation and disappointment. Martha (as well as you and me) face the same dilemma in life. We look for the ideal, then when reality hits in a broken world, we have to process life with imperfect people.

And, Martha's context leads me to great truth that is medicine and health to the soul:

Disappointment is something that, if not dealt with properly, will always degenerate into nursing a grudge and keep you living in the past.

So, let's ask God to wash us, cleanse us, and allow His grace to help us live "offense free"! Why not ask God to imprint this take-a-way on all of our hearts:

To the degree that I blame someone else for what's inside of me, to that same degree I cannot be changed and will not be healed!

Nuf Sed!

"Offended at the Offering"

"Why wasn't this perfume sold and the money given to the poor?" (John 12:5).

The past two days we've looked at how Paul moved on from his pain in Philippi and how Martha needed to move on from her unfulfilled expectation. I'm trying to move to a new subject…yet praying the Lord will (again) use His Word to move us forward. The words of Judas in your Bible are so revealing:

The Scriptures tell us that Judas betrayed his loyalty to Jesus. Why? Because Judas was offended and refused to move beyond it. Why was Judas offended? Because he disagreed with a decision Jesus made over the pound of spikenard that Mary poured on Jesus' feet. Judas said it was a waste of money and took issue with Jesus. Jesus told Judas to leave Mary alone. And, Judas became offended with Jesus over the spikenard of Mary. Judas was trapped (deceived) by satan when he disagreed with Jesus. Judas just couldn't handle not getting his own way and satan found an open door. And, instead of letting go of the disagreement and moving on, Judas took offense, became toxic and was filled with negative emotions.

This Holy Spirit account in Scripture begs the questions; how do I respond when someone disagrees with me? How do I process it when I don't get my own way? How long does it take to get over our feelings being hurt?

In Hebrews 12:15, the author writes, "that no bitter root grows up to cause trouble." The Greek word for "trouble" is ENOCHLEO. It's a word that means "to be annoyed, harassed and emotionally agitated by negative thoughts about someone that follows you around wherever you go." This is a picture of Judas. So what's the remedy? It's found in the grace of God (on the cross of Jesus) where everything you need to live is found. And by God's grace, the following principle truths have helped me continually, as together we all die to our flesh daily. Let's call them the "**Seven Victory Take-a-Ways**" to live free from bitterness and enjoy the journey:

1. No provocation ever **justifies** an un-Christian response!
2. A bad attitude makes a person a **prisoner** of their own experience!
3. Unforgiveness is the **poison** we drink while we wait for the other person to die!
4. Resentment is allowing someone you despise to live **rent-free** in the house of your mind!
5. If there is someone you have not forgiven, they **own you!**
6. If you're in pursuit of vengeance, be sure to dig **two** graves.
7. The only part of me that can be offended is that part of me which has not **died** to self!

Nuf Sed!

January 10
"Freedom in Forgiving"

"A man 's wisdom gives him patience; it is to his glory to overlook an offense" (Proverbs 19:11).

The past three days we've made some discoveries; discoveries that teach and reinforce the following truth to enjoy the journey in a broken world:

1. Living with hurt feelings will never motivate us to make right decisions!
2. An enemy in the heart is worse than ten thousand in the field!
3. We dare not (by God's grace) let the wrong choices of others determine who we become!

Why is this subject so important? Because, we can make **excuses**, or we can make **progress**, but we cannot make **both**! In other words, I must come to grips with the truth, that I am responsible. I'm not responsible for what someone else does, but responsible for my response to them. Or, it's okay to be injured but it's not okay to live injured. And, the only way to live "offense free" in the heart – in a world full (100% of us) of imperfect people – is to look to Jesus.

What is forgiveness? It's the cancellation of a debt as if it never existed! How can we be good forgivers? By comprehending what Jesus has done in forgiving us when we could not forgive ourselves. Remember:

♦ Forgiveness is a **command**, not an option!
♦ Forgiveness is a **choice**, not a feeling!
♦ Forgiveness is for **my** benefit, not the benefit of my offender!

The good news is, you are never any more like Jesus than when you are in the process of forgiving someone, because Jesus is always in the process of forgiving us! And, to forgive another is to release them from being "in debt" to you. It means we entrust justice to God instead of seeking it ourselves. Someone once said; when you release a wrongdoer from the wrong against you, you cut a malignant tumor out of your own life. Lord, help us to release the right to get even instead of seeking to get even ourselves. Lord, help us (by your grace) to remember that reliving the negative keeps us **stuck** where we are, and the pain of **letting go** of our offenses is less than the pain of **carrying them** around.

My non-negotiable, never forget, always keep in mind take-a-way is this:

No pain of our past ever justifies misbehavior in the present!

Nuf Sed!

"Caves, Chains and Cemeteries"

"When Jesus got out of the boat, a man with an evil spirit came from the tombs to meet him" (Mark 5:2).

On the front side of this miracle (Mark 4:35-41) Jesus calms a storm. On the back side (Ch. 5:21) Jesus heals a woman with a 12-year chronic illness. In other words, Jesus can control what frightens us in the material world (wind and waves) and Jesus can control what afflicts us in the physical world (illness and ailments). But in our text, Jesus shows us that He can control what's inside of us (the spiritual world). And, the grace of God pours out of this passage and reminds you and me:

I. Wherever I Am – It Doesn't Make God Nervous (V. 1-5)
I love how Jesus highlights this one man's journey to health and wholeness. Notice this man's condition:
- He was fighting strong chains of sin (angry, wild and out of control).
- He was preoccupied with death (living outside of town in a cemetery tomb).
- He was habitually disappointed (no one could cure him and rehab wasn't working).
- He was continually restless (always crying day and night).
- He was hurting himself (cutting himself with stones – to cover up his cry for help).

So, what are you involved in that's hurting you and those who love you?

II. Wherever I Am – God Is Personally Speaking (V. 6-10)
In V. 9, Jesus said, "What is your name?" Didn't Jesus know his name? Of course He did! In the Bible "name" stands for "nature". So the man is being asked to confess the nature of his sin that's enslaving him. In other words, I cannot change what I do not confront. And what I do not confront will continue to control.

III. Wherever I Am – God's Power Breaks Every Chain (V. 11-13)
"My name is legion" (V. 9), refers to thousands in number. So the man is saying, I have many issues, many battles, many struggles, many temptations. Yet, Jesus speaks and frees the man by the power of His word. So, it's not how strong (or weak) you are – it's how strong God is to overcome your weaknesses.

IV. Wherever I am – God Has A Plan For Your Future! (V. 14-17)
"Go home to your family and tell them how much the Lord has done for you" (V. 19).

This guy is sent to Decapolis – the ten cities near the Jordan. Ten Greek towns with Greek gods and temples. Why? To tell his story of what God can do and to be the first seed of a mighty harvest.

So friend, it's not about your past, your background or your history! It's about your future that God has in store (planned) for you! My take-a-way? **Every set-back is a set-up for a come-back!**

Nuf Sed!

"He Knows"

"He called down famine on the land…and he sent a man before them – Joseph, sold as a slave" (Psalm 105:16, 17).

W̱ho was behind it all in Joseph's life? It's pretty clear. **It was God** who called for the famine in the land of Canaan. (V. 16), who directed Joseph to be sold as a slave. (V. 17) and who allowed Joseph to be tied in the "shackles and iron" (V. 18).

What About You?

Maybe you (like Joseph) are in an environment that has **less than ideal** circumstances, have had your plans put **"on hold"** or **"detoured"** in your schedule, have experienced **pain** or **disappointment** in the will of God and are learning to **wait upon the Lord** for answers to prayer.

One thing is for sure; God wants us to remember Joseph and allow what we see to strengthen our own hearts. "Remember God's marvelous works that He has done" (V. 5). What is the wisdom that God wants us to always keep in mind about Joseph?

1. <u>Remember</u>: **God knows ahead of time what you don't need to know!** "He sent a man before them" (V. 17). Joseph has a dream how God will use him, but Joseph doesn't have a clue about the famine in Canaan and the pain ahead; the family betrayal, the boss's wife lying, forgotten for two years in prison, and 13 years "on hold". Yet, God knew it all – and He knows about your tomorrows as well.

2. <u>Remember</u>: **God knows what you can handle so you need not be afraid!** "They bruised his feet with shackles, his neck was put in irons" (v. 18). Wow! Bound and chained after being betrayed and forgotten. Did Joseph crack up! No, in fact, he served those in prison with him. He teaches us that the Lord knows what you can handle.

3. <u>Remember</u>: **God knows how long you need to be where you are!** "Till what he foretold came to pass" (V. 19). To Joseph, God seems to be tardy and lost the whereabouts of Joseph. It's the patience test for Joseph. It's God telling you and me that He is in control of time and you are not forgotten.

4. <u>Remember</u>: **God knows that your inward character is more important than your outward comfort!** "The Lord proved him true" (V. 19b). It's a clear lesson – that what happens in you is more important than what happens to you. In other words, there's value in the climb and there's value in the struggle!

5. <u>Remember</u>: **God knows how to open doors that no one else can open!** "The king sent and released him" (V. 20). So, God motivates the powerful monarch to bring a total stranger out of prison. Know why? To show clearly that:

- God is in **control** when you think man is in control! (And)
- God knows **where** you are, when nobody else knows where you are!

Nuf Sed!

January 13
"Peter's Third Encounter"

"Put out into deep water, and let down the nets for a catch" (Luke 5:4).

Peter's encounter with Jesus here is the third out of seven. The first time (in John 1:42) Jesus calls Peter a rock (or stable person). Jesus was giving Peter a new self-concept and letting him know that He will use him with all of his weaknesses and imperfections. The second call comes in Mark 1:16 when Jesus tells Peter to follow Him and become a fisher of men. The third encounter is in our text, a few months later where Peter has returned to his old habits. Peter has leveled off, cooled off, and gotten off track from the mission. He reveals to us that the tendency of fire is to go out! And Jesus catches Peter off guard.

"Launch out Peter and go back out to fish" (V. 4). Peter's response? "Master, we've worked hard all night and haven't caught anything" (V. 5). In other words; Peter is tired, exhausted, disappointed and knows the best time to catch fish is over. He just doesn't "feel it" and maybe you don't either! Yet, Peter obeys and Jesus fills the net in response to Peter's flexibility and obedience. So why does Jesus perform this miracle and what's the message to you and me? It's wisdom for us all to remember:

1. **To show Peter (and us) that if he lives to catch fish (people) Jesus will take care of him!** Peter's boat was filled to provide the funds to continue on. It's a great lesson for us all – that if we give God what He wants, He will give us what we need!

2. **To show us that our past disappointments do not determine our future opportunities!** Peter had to leave his past unfulfilled expectations behind. So many people crucify themselves between two thieves – the regrets of the past and the worries of tomorrow. What about you? Is there a past experience you need to let go of so you can move forward to future opportunities?

3. **To show us that Ecclesiastes 11:4** is true; "If you wait for the perfect conditions, you will never get anything done!" (TLB). Peter goes back out to fish at the worst possible time to catch fish. Are you waiting for perfect conditions to do what God is calling you to do? Remember: no risk, no reward!

4. **To show us that we must never come to a place where the element of faith is not needed!** It seems foolish to cast the net just a few feet on the other side of the boat. Peter is that close to a miracle and has to make a choice; obey in faith or be stubborn and let his ego get in the way. So what's the take-a-way from Peter's third encounter?

♦ It's not the **level** of your faith, it's the **object** of your faith (Jesus!)

- Humility gives us **access** to God and wisdom from other people!
- Our **progress** in God will go no further than our **obedience** takes us!

Nuf Sed!

January 14
"Redeeming Second Choices"

"When they came to the border of Mysia, they tried to enter Bithynia, but the Spirit of Jesus would not allow them to" (Acts 16:7).

Have you ever had "your plans" changed by "God's plan"? You're in good company!

In our text, Paul is longing to take the Gospel to the Gentiles. He has a plan, a burden, and one thing on his mind; "How wonderful that I'm going to Bithynia to plant a church and reach the lost." And, while Paul is heading full speed toward Bithynia, he experiences a "closed door". It's a closing and unfulfilled expectation that presents Paul with a choice; will I stew in my own juice or trust God with the second choice? And God gives us "**Troas Wisdom**" that pours from the text.

1. Troas Reveals The Health Of "Humility"
What does Paul do when his first choice is ruined and his plan is thwarted? He doesn't become offended or resist. Instead, he humbles himself before God and allows God's grace to go deeper into his heart. Paul refuses to live in the world of "if only".

2. Troas Reveals The Power Of "Faith"
I love the fact that Paul doesn't allow Troas to wreck his faith in the sovereignty of God. I love how Paul believes that God's will is unfolding and His purpose is good. I love how Paul's faith produces a good attitude and doesn't feel sorry for itself! In fact, Paul's faith understands that God may close a door for one of two reasons: to protect you from things you do not know, or, to open a greater door you cannot see.

3. Troas Reveals The Importance Of "Patience"
So, Paul wants to be in Bithynia, is stuck in Troas and has to wait for further instruction. He doesn't push and shove or pout and run ahead - he just waits. And while he waits, he receives the Macedonia call (V. 9) that leads to an incredible (fruitful) ministry. What he thought was an inferior place was the very place that God would get his attention.

4. Troas Reveals The Reward Of "Obedience"
When Paul sees the vision and hears the call, he "Immediately endeavors to head to Philippi, the chief city in Macedonia" (V. 10). The result? Lydia (from the upper class) gets saved (V. 14,15), the slave girl (from the lower class) gets saved (V. 16), and the jailor (from the middle class) gets saved (V. 19). In other words, our progress in God will go no further than our obedience takes us! So, what's the take-a-way from Troas?

♦ Wishing you were somewhere else will **waste** the season where you are!
♦ When you cannot trace God's **hand**, you can always trust His **heart**!
♦ If we knew what God knew, we wouldn't **resent** what God does!

Nuf Sed!

January 15
"Getting up When You Fall Down"

"This is what the Lord says, 'When men fall down, do they not get up?'" (Jeremiah 8:4).

Is that a great question or what? It's a great question in a universal context because all of us have sinned, no one is perfect and everybody falls down. So, here's the setting:

Israel has backslidden, gone off course, grieved God's holiness and spiritually drifted. And the Lord says, **When people fall down, don't they get up again?** In other words:

♦ While we contemplate our regrets – God contemplates our recovery!
♦ While we focus on our weaknesses – God focuses on our potential!
♦ While we remind God of our past – God is already planning our future!
♦ Thomas Edison had 10,000 failures before he created the incandescent light bulb.
♦ Walt Disney was fired from his first newspaper job. The reason? Not enough creativity!
♦ R.H. Macy failed seven times before his store in Manhattan, NY caught on.

There are three questions in Jeremiah 8 for anyone who wants to "rebound":

"Why then have these people turned away?" (V.5).
God makes an appeal here (to Israel and all of us) to humble ourselves and receive correction. It's God's way for us to grow and make progress. It's a warning to save us much self-inflicted pain. Why are these warnings so important? Because:

The more that I resist the calling voice of God, the harder it becomes to hear that voice again! And, the longer I stay where I do not belong, the harder it becomes to exit that place!

"No one repents of his wickedness, saying, 'What have I done?'" (V.6).
Here God makes an appeal to repentance (which allows us to be changed and restored to intimacy with God). And, Godly sorrow is the sorrow I feel for how my sin has grieved God's holiness. So why is repentance so important? Because the more that I mourn over my sin, the more that sin loses its power to govern my life!

"Is there no balm in Gilead; is there no physician there?" (V. 22).
So, the Holy Spirit works humility in our hearts, which leads to repentance, which results in health and wholeness. Gilead is a mountain filled with balsam trees. Balsam trees produce a gum or sap that is used for medicinal purposes. So God (in Jesus) is acquainted with our diseases and is skilled in applying the remedy. In other words, God has ordained it that you come His way – so you can "get up when you fall down." My take-a-way?

"Failure is not final" and God has your rebound in store today!

Nuf Sed!

January 16
"Seven Strikes and You're out – of Prison"

It's hard to believe how Joseph could save the nation in famine and spare his brothers who planned his demise. Just think about his trouble:

1. He was **betrayed** by his brothers (Genesis 37:4,18).
2. He was **enslaved** by the Ishmaelites (V. 28).
3. He was **tempted** by the devil (V. 7).
4. He was **falsely accused** by Potiphar's wife (17-19).
5. He was **imprisoned** by Potiphar (20-21).
6. He was **forgotten** by the butler (40:14,15, 23).
7. He was **ignored** by Pharaoh (41:2).

So, how do you keep from cracking up when you're purchased, sold, ignored, forgotten, lied about and put "on hold"? What protects you from giving in to self-pity and bad memories?

"The LORD was with Joseph." (39:21, KJV) And, the Lord is with you! In fact, when you do well and suffer for it, I Peter 2:19-25 says, God is well pleased with your obedience; the same mistreatment happened to Jesus and it's part of the cross life for those who serve the Lord. In fact, the Lord's presence was so real in Joseph's life that he **Served the prisoners in the ward** (40:4). What's that teach us? It's unmistakable to me - it's just so clear; when people treat you badly, God still treats you good! It's always too soon to think it's too late! And, your present field may be limited (he's in prison) but you are not limited by your field!

Below are four truths that affect me inwardly (over and over) when I meditate upon them. I trust they will become a part of your memory to help in time of need:

♦ "Say not thou, I will recompense evil; but wait on the Lord, and He shall save thee" (Proverbs 20:22, KJV).
♦ "The discretion of a man deferreth his anger, and it is his glory to pass over a transgression" (Proverbs 19:11, KJV).
♦ "Avenge not yourselves, but rather give place unto wrath, for vengeance is mine, I will repay, saith the Lord" (Romans 12:19, KJV).
♦ "Say not, I will do so to him as he hath done to me; I will render to the man according to his work" (Proverbs 24:29, KJV).

So, what's my take-a-way from Joseph's story?
Jesus didn't suffer so that Christians wouldn't have to, He suffered to show us how to go through it!

Nuf Sed!

January 17
"The Father's Kiss"

"But when he was yet a great way off, his father saw him, and had compassion, and ran, and fell on his neck, and kissed him" (Luke 15:20).

I love to see my kids when they come home! I love to hug them, embrace them and kiss them when they walk through the door. Why? Because parents just flat out love their children!

In Luke 15, a father is waiting for his son. The son has journeyed to a far country because he was **impatient** and wanted instant gratification, or his portion of the estate right now. He was **independent** and wanted to be free from his father's control and he was **indulgent**, he wasted his substance on wild living (a true "party animal").

What does the son experience away from his loving father? He spends all that he has, ends up in a pigpen and hits rock bottom. He experiences two noticeable things, he is **deceived**, thinking that something apart from God can satisfy his thirst and he is **enslaved,** since what he wanted now controls his life.

And notice this; the father never chased down the son and begged him to come home. Why? Because until we are in touch with the pain that our sin has caused, we are destined to repeat it!

So what does the father do when the prodigal son returns home? He sees him, has compassion, runs to meet him and kisses him! What's the discovery here? That God is more willing to forgive than we are to ask Him! So much so, that the father gives four things to the returning son.
The **robe**, which signifies the release from all condemnation and the gift of the righteousness of Jesus, the **ring**, which is a mark of dignity and value, the **shoes**, which mean to be restored to liberty and the **calf**, which was sacrificed at public feasts on occasions of great joy.

What's the big deal about the father's kiss? The big deal is, according to Deuteronomy 21:18-21, the rebellious son should have been stoned to death. And, this is all a picture of Jesus and His great love for you and me. And, what does God's mercy reveal in the story? Glad you asked and here's my take-a-way: **The Four Things God Doesn't Know:**

♦ God doesn't know of **any sinner** that He does not love!
♦ God doesn't know of **any sin** that He cannot forgive.
♦ God doesn't know of **any other way** to be forgiven except through the cross of Christ.
♦ God doesn't know of **any better time** to be forgiven than right now.

Nuf Sed

January 18
"Avoiding Lost Potential"

"Let the godly strike me! It will be a kindness! If they correct me, it is soothing medicine. **Don't let me refuse it**" (Psalm 141:5, NLT).

David writes this Psalm and is filled with all kinds of emotions. He says things like: "Please hurry up Lord" (V. 1), "Accept my prayer Lord" (V. 2), "Take control of my speech Lord" (V. 3), "Don't let me drift toward evil" (V. 4). But in V. 5, David makes an incredible request. **"If someone corrects me Lord, don't let me refuse it, for it will be like soothing medicine."**

How's that for a prayer request? **"Lord, don't let me refuse it when someone corrects me for my good."** I think David prays this (and God records it) because we all have **blind spots**, none of us can see the **whole picture**; nobody is an **island** to themself, and, David doesn't want to **waste** his God-given potential.

So what causes us to resist and resent correction? What causes us to despise those who rebuke us? What leads us to "pull back" from those who could be offering "medicine to our souls"? What could rob us from our future potential? The bottom line answer is pride, as opposed to humility.

All of us are prone to reject correction and accountability. Know why? Because:
♦ Fragile egos can't handle it!
♦ Primadonna types won't tolerate it! (And)
♦ The flesh would rather feel good and look good instead of be good and be changed!
In fact, just think of how much potential has been wasted because of pride within our hearts.

Remember the word below, and together let's avoid lost potential:
♦ "Poverty and shame shall be to him that refuseth instruction, but he that regardeth reproof shall be honored." (Proverbs 13:18, KJV)
♦ "He that hateth reproof is brutish." (Proverbs 12:1, KJV)
♦ "He that refuseth instruction despiseth his own soul, but he that heareth reproof getteth understanding." (Proverbs 15:32, KJV)
♦ "Hear counsel and receive instruction, that thou mayest be wise in thy latter end." (Proverbs 19:20, KJV)

My take-a-ways to enjoy the journey?
♦ **When I bury my ego, I can welcome correction! (And)**
♦ **Growth is destroyed when we resent those who correct us!**
Nuf Sed!

January 19
"When Your Vision Becomes Obscured"

"And when neither sun nor stars in many days appeared…all hope that we should be saved was then taken away" (Acts 27:20, KJV).

Haven't we all been there? Those times or seasons when our hearts sank in sadness or despair? And, how do we feel when the storm robs us of perspective for the future? Acts 27:20 gives us a glimpse of reality; "All hope that we should be saved was then taken away" (KJV). So here's the context:

Paul is being transported to Rome as a prisoner. Paul had stood before Agrippa, shared his testimony and appealed to have an audience with Caesar. Festus and Agrippa place Paul in the hands of Julius to be taken as a prisoner to Rome. Paul is on a boat and Festus thinks he's in charge. But, Paul is on a boat because God is always in charge of those in charge over you. Don't ever forget this; **man proposes, but God disposes!**

What happens now in the midst of the calm? "There arose against the boat a tempestuous wind" (V. 14). In other words, when all seemed well, a typhoon blows in. The storm causes the crew to throw all the grain and furniture overboard, and Scripture tells us how the people felt:
"All hope that we should be saved was then taken away" (V. 20, KJV).

Why was hope being lost? Because a storm on the "voyage of life" can obscure our vision and perspective for tomorrow. Just think, the storm was **unexpected.** (Maybe you've encountered a sudden tempestuous wind that's caught you off guard.) The storm was **course changing.** (Maybe your plans have been changed by a "Higher Plan" in recent days). The storm was **exhausting.** (Maybe you are drained, fatigued and emotionally spent).

What was God's Word to Paul and the 276 on board? It's a timely word for you and me: **Be of good cheer, no one will be lost. And, Fear not, you will get where you need to be.**

What comes out of all this trouble? Paul ends up on the island of Melita where the father of Publius is healed when Paul prays for him. And many others were miraculously healed (28:9). What's the take-a-way from this recorded event? Don't miss this:

Something is going on in your life today – but God is also up to something else!

Nuf Sed!

"The Therapy of Prayer"

"Take this cup from me. Yet not what I will, but what you will" (Mark 14:36).

Apart from the crucifixion, Gethsemane was the most intense moment of Jesus' life. It was in Gethsemane where Jesus teaches us how to pray under pressure. And remember; Jesus didn't pray in the garden to escape the pressure. He prayed to be able to endure the pressure and face it head on.

Why is the garden prayer listed in all four Gospels? To teach us how to pray in our gardens of life! Jesus himself was very heavy and exceeding sorrowful (Mark 14:33,34). In other words, Jesus was under "extreme distress" and "intense agony". And, what does Jesus do? He prays! And in His praying, He teaches us how to pray when we face our own "cup" in life. He shows us how not to become cynical or critical when we experience our own garden experiences. Notice how Jesus prays:

Jesus prays with faith! "Everything is possible for you" (V. 36).
Here Jesus acknowledges that the Father has all power and authority to remove the "cup". He acknowledges that God is sovereign and still in control! And this kind of praying protects us from cynicism, bitterness, self-pity and a martyr's complex. It protects from a victim mentality and a "poor me" mind set.

Jesus prays with surrender! "Not what I will, but what you will" (V. 36b).
Here is where Jesus wins the victory at His cup experience. He wins when He prays, "Not what I will". He prays until He conquers something. What is it? When we surrender ourselves to God when there is a cup we cannot change, we receive the power in prayer that we need to embrace the cup we face! Wow! And this kind of praying protects us from anger towards God.

Jesus prays with strength! "An angel from heaven appeared to him and strengthened him" (Luke 22:43).
Jesus knew He would be betrayed, arrested and crucified. And, in prayer, He was made strong, courageous and calm. So, what happened to Jesus while praying in the Garden? The same two things that happen to us in prayer; there was not the removal of the cup, but the **removal of the fear** of the cup. And secondly, there was the **infusion of divine strength** for the upcoming challenge of the cup (crucifixion).

What's the take-a-way to enjoy the journey? It's unmistakable:

In prayer, God puts something within us, that is greater than the pressures outside of us!

Nuf Sed!

January 21
"Changed"

"But we all, with open face beholding as in a glass the glory of the Lord, are changed into the same image from glory to glory, even as by the Spirit of the Lord" (II Corinthians 3:18, KJV).

The last few years I've often prayed, "Lord, I don't want to be stirred, I want to be changed; go deeper, and deeper and deeper into my sinful heart." And, who doesn't want to be changed for the better? Who doesn't know someone that has been wonderfully changed by the grace of God? So how does real genuine change take place?

In II Corinthians 3, Paul addresses a counterfeit gospel. It was a gospel mixture of law and grace, and it was very popular. Why? Because human nature loves to achieve religious goals. So Paul deals with this error head on – because Paul knows that the Law cannot change the human heart! Why can't the Law do what only grace can do? Because the Law was on tables of stone (it was external but had no internal power to change the heart). It wasn't given to save us (its purpose was to show us how much we needed grace). The Law can only condemn us (it cannot free us from a guilty conscience or deliver us from the slavery of sin's power and control).

So, how does God change any of us? It's spelled out by Paul in four words in II Corinthians 3:18.

1. Transparency - "But we all with open face."

"Open face" means we are not like Moses under the old system of Law. Moses covered his face which was symbolic of the Law causing us to be ashamed. Now, we are "open faced" because the obstacle of the Law is removed. So, now we've been invited to unveil our heart and come transparent to the Lord. No need to pretend - but just be real!

2. Focus - "Beholding as in a mirror the glory of the Lord."

A mirror is a symbol of the Word of God (James 1:22-25). When we look into the mirror we see Jesus. When we see Jesus, we are allowing and preparing our hearts to be changed.

3. Transformation – "Are changed into the same image degree by degree."

The word "changed" gives us our English word Metamorphosis. It describes the process that changes an insect from a larva into a pupa and then into a fully mature insect. The change comes from the inside out, not the outside in.

4. Spirit – "Even as by the Spirit of the Lord"

How does God change any of us? We come transparent before God, we search the Word and see Jesus, we become more like the one we worship and gaze upon, and it's the Holy Spirit that changes us into the character and likeness of Jesus! So, don't give up friend! None of us are perfect and we are all in process! And, God will finish what He started in you! What's my take-a-way?

Transparency and repentance are for our good – because Calvary only covers what we uncover!

Nuf Sed!

January 22
"When Life Doesn't Make Sense"

"Naked I came from my mother's womb, and naked I will depart. The Lord gave and the Lord has taken away; may the name of the Lord be praised" (Job 1:21).

In the past few weeks, many tears have been shed. One pastor and friend buried his son (40 years old), another pastor and friend buried his daughter (31 years old) and I buried my beautiful wife Laura (58 years old). All I can conclude is, that in a broken world, things break and no one can escape grief, loss, pain and tears. The question is, how do we respond when life doesn't quite make sense? Thus, the story of Job.

Think for a moment of Job's loss, pain and tears: Job lost his **employment** (his oxen), his **finances** (his sheep), his **transportation** (his camels), his **friends** (his three companions), his **health** (his body broke down), his **encourager** (his wife's support) and Job lost his **offspring** (his children died unexpectedly).

And in the midst of it all, Job became better not bitter! He ran to God instead of away from God! He responded in a way that teaches us how to be comforted by the God of all comfort:

Job Looked Back (To His Birth) "Naked came I out of my mother's womb." Job confesses here; as he looks back, that he came into this world with nothing. He reminds us all that we are only stewards (managers) and that everything in life belongs to God. He helps us to remember (and "Thank God") because all that we are and have above zero is by the grace of God alone.

Job Looked Ahead (To His Own Death) "And naked shall I return." In other words, Job will one-day return to the earth – dust to dust! He's telling us that the mortality rate is 100%; everybody dies! It's the Lord pulling and tugging at our hearts. It's a call to get ready for the world to come. It's a wake-up call, reminding us that we all will leave this temporary system to inherit the eternal.

Job Looked Up (In Faith) "The Lord gave and the Lord has taken away; blessed be the name of the Lord." I love how Job responds to his pain. Instead of blaming God and cursing God – he blesses God and acknowledges that God is good! He "looks upward" and finds comfort, strength, peace and grace to help in time of need.

Job Looked Within (And Stayed Free From A Toxic Attitude) "In all this Job sinned not, nor charged God foolishly." Wow! Job refused to stew in his own juice. He refused to become a victim! He refused to feel entitled, that he deserved a better lot in life. By not charging (or blaming) God, Job allowed God to heal his broken heart. What's the take-a-way from Job's response to his grief and loss?

A bad attitude will make a person a prisoner of their own experience!

Nuf Sed!

January 23
"A Valley Full of Ditches"

"This is what the Lord says: Make this valley full of ditches" (II Kings 3:16).

In II Kings 3, we see the record of Israel at war with Moab. The war is on because the Moabites refuse to pay tribute to Israel since the death of Ahab. Notice what Jehoram does:

In V. 6, he numbers Israel for battle; in V. 7; he asks Jehoshaphat to help him, in V.8 he asks "Which way do we sneak up on Moab?"

What's the problem Israel? "There is no water for the army or the cattle, and panic sets in" (V. 9). Jehoshaphat says, "I know a prophet named Elisha, and he knows how to pray" (V. 11,12). And wisdom is poured out for us all. My three discoveries are:

1. God's Plan for Your Life Can Always Be Trusted! "And Jehoram said, which way should we go up and advance? "And Jehoshaphat said, "The way through the wilderness of Edom" (V. 8). There are two ways to enter the land of the Moabites and gain the victory. The short and most direct route is by going above the Dead Sea. The longer route is by going around the southern point of the Dead Sea. Why is this so interesting? Because the way the Lord led Israel was the longer of the two routes; it had the most difficulties and dangers. So what's up with God taking Israel the long way around? It's wisdom for a healthy soul. The easy way is not always the best way; present disappointments have a long term purpose and God knows more than we do!

2. God Is No Respecter of Persons, Only Our Preparation! "And Elisha said, thus saith the Lord, make this valley full of ditches, for the valley will be filled with water" (V. 16). What's the instruction? Dig some ditches! Why the ditches? Because there is a principle of God here; human responsibility and Supernatural provision or our part on earth and God's part in Heaven. What's the big deal about all this preparing ditches? The big deal is; "If you don't till the land, you will just be chasing fantasies; if you work the land, you will have plenty of bread." (Proverbs 12:1) In other words, we till the land, then God grows the bread! What's God saying to us? It's obvious; it does no good to sow seed in the ground if God does not send rain on the fields; and, it does no good for God to send rain on the fields if we have not first put seed in the ground. In other words, I can't do God's part and God won't do my part!

3. God Is Always Working, Even When You Cannot See Him! "For thus saith the Lord, you will not see wind, neither will you see the rain" (V 17). In other words, you'll have to dig the ditches in faith! "And sure enough on the following morning, water suddenly appeared" (V. 20). In other words, a heavy rain fell in the eastern mountains of Edom (a great distance from Israel's camp). The water filled the valley, came from a distance and Israel never observed the source. What's the discovery? The discovery is; at times God's work is invisible, but God is working even when you cannot see Him! What's the take-a-way today?

God may send you what you need in packages you do not like!

Nuf Sed!

January 24
"Chill"

"And it came to pass, when Pharaoh had let the people go, that God led them not through the way of the land of the Philistines, although that was near; for God said, lest peradventure the people repent when they see war and they return to Egypt" (Exodus 13:17, KJV).

Every now and then I recall the words that my son and daughter said to me when they were teenagers. When they would see me a little uptight, they would sometimes say, "Dad, you need to chill." In Exodus 13-14, the Lord says the same thing to His children. Here's the setting:

Israel has gathered at a place called Succoth on their way to Etham (13:20). And somewhere between Succoth and Etham, God begins leading Israel with a cloud by day and a fire by night. God also leads Israel on a different route than they intended to travel. He knows that the shorter route (full of Philistines) will discourage Israel but **God has information that we are not aware of!**

Israel's next lesson is unmistakable! When Pharaoh reevaluates his release of the Israelites, he assembles his army and overtakes the Israelites in Baalzephon (14:9). Israel is hemmed in on all four sides; on one side is the mountain range of Baalzephon (impossible to cross over), on the other side were the vast sand dunes (where no traveler could survive), before Israel is the deep Red Sea, and behind Israel is an enemy of 200,000 footmen. So how does Israel respond to the unexpected? **Fear;** "And they were sore afraid" (V. 10). **Blame;** "Moses, you led us out here in the wilderness" (V. 11). **Despair;** "It would have been better to serve the Egyptians than to die out here" (V. 12).

Why does God allow this to Israel, and record it in our Bibles? "Now all these things happened unto them for examples, and they are written for our admonition" (I Corinthians 10:11). In other words, the more we learn about Israel, the more we learn how to handle it when in between a rock and a hard place. And here's what to do when you don't know what to do. (Exodus 14:13):

"Fear Not." Fear defined is; *anxiety over a real or possible danger or pain*. It is an unpleasant emotion caused by the belief that someone or something is threatening or dangerous.
"Stand Still." In V. 15, God said "Go forward." In V.13, God says "Stand still." The command to "stand still" is a military term and means; *to stand by until you receive further orders from the Lord.*
"See The Salvation of The Lord." This means to concentrate on God, get God into focus and grasp a long term perspective.

Here's my take-a-way from this glorious account:
Since we all have **Egypts** in life; things of the world the Lord wants to wean

us away from; since we all have **Pharaohs** in life; people the devil wants to use to discourage us and since we all have **Ethams** (detours) in life; seasons when it seems like it's the "long way" in the journey, maybe today the Lord is saying **"chill"** and **"trust"** and **"rest"** in the One who will never leave you nor forsake you! Maybe it's time to fear not, be still, and put your eyes on Jesus!

Nuf Sed!

"Detoured and Distracted"

"And the days of Terah were two hundred and five years: and Terah died in Haran" (Genesis 11:32).

I admit; there are times when I have been distracted! Times while fishing, reading, praying, driving, in conversations, mowing the lawn, listening to a seminar. Our text is about a man who became distracted.

Terah was the father of Abraham, Nahor, Haran and the grandfather of Lot (Genesis 11:26). He is mentioned 11 times in Scripture and his name means "wandering". So what happened to Terah?

First, he received instructions from God to leave Ur of the Chaldees and go into the land of Canaan. He started out well, (Genesis 11:31) journeyed approximately four months and then did something very strange. He turned north of his route to Canaan and traveled 150 miles out of his way. He became distracted and detoured to a place called Haran. Haran was a commercial city located on the Belikh river, 60 miles from the Euphrates River. It was located on a busy caravan road connecting Nineveh, Ashur and Babylon in Mesopotamia with Damascus, Tyre and other cities in the Southwest. Haran was also a center of the Moon God Cult; a place of idolatry, lust, sin and sensuality. It was a place you'd want to get out of – a city to avoid!

So, why did Terah get distracted and sidetracked to Haran? He arrives at Haran at the age of 185. He dies in Haran at the age of 205. His short layover on the way to Canaan turned into a 20-year detour; "Terah lived for 205 years and died while still at Haran" (Genesis 11:32). It's so sad that God said; "Your fathers dwelt on the other side of the flood; even Terah, the father of Nahor, and they served other gods" (24:2). Why did Terah serve other gods?

1. Terah Was Deceived by Sin! Haran was a weakness to Terah and a comfortable place to relax. Yet, Haran became a foothold of the enemy to weaken Terah's heart. Terah's heart was deceived and captured because the will becomes weaker the longer we entertain sin's offer. Remember; the longer we stay where we do not belong, the harder it becomes to exit that place!

2. Terah Wanted the Best of Two Worlds! His relatives made the right choice; "And Abram took Sarai his wife and Lot his brother's son and all their substance that they had gathered, and the souls that they had gotten in Haran; and they went forth to go into the land of Canaan; and into the land of Canaan they came" (Genesis 12:5). But Terah became entangled and attached to the lesser gods of Haran. He ran all the warning signals and ignored the red lights. Remember, the longer we resist the calling voice of God, the harder it becomes to hear that voice again.

3. Terah Entertained Wicked Thinking! He somehow forgot that only

God can satisfy and transform the human heart. He forgot that sin never satisfies the one who sins, always leads to more sin and humiliates the sinner. He somehow traded God's peace for created things. He forgot that your life will always go in the direction of your most dominant thoughts! The take-a-way?

If we would not eat of the forbidden fruit, we must stay away from the forbidden tree!

Nuf Sed!

"John's Fallacy and Forgiveness of Sin"
Part I

"If we say that we have fellowship with him, and walk in darkness, we lie, and do not the truth" (I John 1:6).

The Apostle John wrote I John as a personal letter to several congregations. There is no formal greeting, farewell or personal references to reveal the recipients. This means that every person can read John's letter as though it is written personally to them. In other words, it's a letter just for you – a letter of good news from the heart of God to your heart today.

The purpose of this letter is to reassure believers in their faith and counter the false teachings that were creeping in. The result of the letter is found in V. 4; "And these things we write unto you that your joy may be full." The good news is that overflowing joy will fill your heart to the degree you receive what John has written. And what he has written is life-giving, life-enriching and life-saving. Notice the four great subjects John begins his letter with:

I. The Fallacy of Sin Revealed. "If we say that we have fellowship with God and yet walk in darkness, we lie and do not practice the truth" (1:6). To walk in darkness means to willfully practice sin. It means to claim to belong to God on one hand, yet at the same time go on living in spiritual darkness. False teachers were teaching that the body was evil. They approved the gratifying of every physical lust because the body was going to be destroyed in the grave anyway. The fallacy (or deception) was thinking you could live in the light (and serve God) while at the same time live in darkness (and serve sin). John says, "it's a lie." Or, it's impossible to walk intimately with God while at the same time practicing sin. It just can't happen because "God is light and in Him is no darkness at all" (1:5).

II. The Forgiveness of Sin Received. The good news is, there is an answer to the fallacy and lie that seeks to destroy us all; "But if we walk in the light, as He is in the light, we have fellowship one with another, and the blood of Jesus Christ His Son cleanses us from all sin" (V. 7). To "walk in the light" means to live each day transparently and not conceal anything from the light. It means to run from the darkness and run to the light whenever our sin is revealed. What happens when we yield to conviction? Two things; inner transformation takes place that produces intimacy and fellowship with God and with others (V. 7). Secondly, forgiveness is experienced that results in being cleansed and purified from deep rooted sin. The word "cleanses" denotes a continuous action verb where God frees us from sin continually. Wow! Now that's something to sing and shout about. What's the take-a-way?

To the degree that I am transparent (honest) before God; to that same degree I will be delivered from my own sin!

Nuf Sed!

"John's Fact and Freedom from Sin"
Part II

"If we say that we have no sin, we deceive ourselves and the truth is not in us" (1 John 1:8, KJV).
"If we say that we have not sinned, we make him a liar and his word is not in us" (V. 10, KJV).

I remember the day I was gloriously saved – reading a gospel tract and praying the sinner's prayer on July 10, 1974. I said to myself, "I will never sin again!" The next day I cursed and came to a rude awakening; I still live with my sinful nature, I still have choices, and I still have temptations. The good news is that; there is an answer to the dilemma that we all face every day:

III. The Fact of Sin's Presence
John gives us an encouraging word on this subject; he tells us in V. 8 and V. 10; there is no need to deny our sinful nature and no need to deny our sinful actions. That's right! We are depraved and possess a sinful nature from birth! And, we cannot say that we have never sinned!

This is an encouragement from John to new Christians. Many new believers become discouraged when they see their sin coming to light. Many are surprised and think, "I seem to be more of a sinner than I ever was before." What's going on inside the new believer? It's simply the result of "walking in the light". In other words, our conscience is being educated by the Word and sensitized by the Holy Spirit. It's the process of God peeling off layer after layer after layer of the "old man". So cheer up! Before conversion sin never bothered you. After conversion, the sanctification process continues all the way to glory. So take heart; there are no sinless saints that have reached perfection.

IV. The Freedom from Sin's Power
"If we confess our sins, He is faithful and just to forgive us our sins and to cleanse us from all unrighteousness" (V 9). What's the good news if no one can live in sinless perfection? It's two-fold: **If we confess our sin, God will forgive us!** The word forgive means; *The cancellation of debt and the dismissal of charges.* So, you may struggle with being forgiven, but God doesn't! In fact, if God forgives at all, He must forgive of all – in Christ. (And) **Sin's habit and pattern has been broken!**
"My little children, I write unto you, that you sin not" (2:1). This means that even though we all have a sinful nature; no one has to continue in the slavery of sin! In other words, in Christ we have the power to break from sin's controlling influence and ruling authority in our lives. Perfect - no! But making progress daily – yes! What's the take-a-way from John's Epistle?

God uses imperfect people to share a perfect Gospel, that can liberate anyone from the controlling power of habitual sin! Nuf Sed!

January 28
"Small, Invisible and Powerful"

"Then said he, Unto what is the kingdom of God like?" (Luke 13:18, KJV).

My wife and I had just left Grace Assembly of God in Syracuse, N.Y. to plant a new church in Cooperstown, N.Y. It was our first Sunday in Cooperstown (September 1981) and six people attended our "grand opening" launch day. Some friends said to us, "Why did you do this?" And, "How can you start like this with only six people?" While the early days in planting were not outwardly exciting, we were excited in our hearts. While there were hurdles, setbacks, frustrations and challenges, the Lord did a great work over the next eight years. In the midst of the planting process, the Lord put today's passage in my heart. It protected me from despair and sustained me in trial. It's a word from Jesus to every heart who listens.

Jesus said that the kingdom of God in your life and His church is like two things; "A grain of mustard seed, which is the least of all seeds." And, "A little leaven (yeast) which a woman took." Jesus said that the seed was cast into the ground and the leaven was placed into the meal. And, three powerful truths leap out of the text:

1.God's Work Always Starts Small!
"A grain of mustard seed." (And) "A little leaven which a woman took" (V.19, 21; KJV).
Why is this so encouraging? Because (thanks to the first Adam) we are prone to measure our work and worth by **size** (what's the biggest) **speed** (what's the fastest) and **sound** (what's the loudest). And, the enemy whispers things like: "You're not successful or significant." "Things will never change around here." "Look what's happening over there." Remember friend; the progress of growth in your heart is just as important as the end product itself!

2. At Times God's Work Is Invisible, But God Is Working Even When You Cannot See Him!
The mustard seed was cast into the ground (out of sight). The woman hid the fermented dough in the meal (out of sight). What's the danger? Your frustration between the time when you plant and the time when you pick. When you cannot see all that God is doing and when you do not know what progress is being made.

Did you ever see a shooting star? It is not falling when you see it, but thousands of light years before. Daniel prays for 21 days before the answer is manifested. God heard on day one (Daniel 10).

3.God's Word With Your Faithfulness Always Brings Results! In V. 19, the little seed grew into a great tree and in V. 21, the little leaven multiplied to feed an estimated 162 people. But a man had to sow the seed and a woman had to sow the yeast! So, we can't do God's part and He won't do our part! Oh friend, get this take-a-way and never let it leave your heart:

Discouragement is a lie of the enemy – to blind you in the present of what God is going to do in the future! Nuf Sed!

"It's Okay Not to Know"

"So is the kingdom of God as if a man should cast seed into the ground. And should sleep, and rise night and day, and the seed should spring up and grow, he knoweth not how. For the earth bringeth forth fruit of herself; first the blade, then the ear, after that the full corn in the ear. But when the fruit is brought forth, immediately he puteth in the sickle, because the harvest is come" (Mark 4:26-29; KJV).

I remember like it was yesterday (maybe today) when in between a rock and a hard place. I remember asking in my heart, "God, how will you ever bring resolve to this matter?" I was traveling at the time, overwhelmed with questions with no answers and came across our text. The text leaped into my heart as the Lord talks about sowing seed through active effort and labor, sleeping and resting along the journey and supernatural intervention in response to our sowing.

I believed at the time that I was being faithful to God. Yet, I wasn't "resting" and "enjoying the journey" like I should. I was planting seed, yet something was missing. For whatever reason, I was accepting God's responsibility that He never intended for me to carry. And then, Verse 27 so overwhelmed me that the burden and weight lifted and I was free from anxiety. The light came on and the truth freed me from myself. Here's my discovery on that glorious day:

You Can Live "Anxious Free"!
"And should sleep night and day" (V. 27) means; the farmer scatters the seed, works the land, does his part and then "rests well". In other words, he trusts that God will do His part. So instead of fretting how God is going to do it, he chooses to live "anxious free" because it's in God's hands. What (or who) are you anxious about today?

You can Live With "Joyful Expectation"!
"And the seed will sprout and grow" (V. 27.) The discovery here is, if we faithfully do our part in sowing, God will do His part in growing! If we sow good seed, God will see that it produces good fruit. If we believe that God is true to His Word, we can live with a joyful expectation instead of a fearful disposition. Why? Because, there is no cessation of God's activity even though we cannot see all that He is up to!

You Can Live "Without" All The Answers!
"He knows not how (or doesn't understand) how it happens" (V. 27.) Wow! This means you don't have to have all the answers, know all the solutions or figure out what you cannot see. It means it's okay "not to know" what you would really like to know. I guess since Jesus died and rose again, then He can take care of every lesser matter. My take-a-way?

Like the farmer who sows seed by day and then sleeps well at night, it's best for us to do the same! Nuf Sed!

January 30
"A Well in the Valley"

"As they pass through the valley of Baca, they make it a place of springs;…They go from strength to strength" (Psalm 84:6,7).

Psalm 84 is the diary of a valley walker. The psalmist is heading to Jerusalem because he misses the Tabernacle (or Sanctuary) on Mount Zion. He remembers the awesome presence of God (V. 1), he longs to be in the house of God (V. 2), he pictures himself meeting God at an altar of prayer (V. 3), he misses the song services when God was praised and exalted (V. 4), but in (V.5) he makes an announcement:

"Blessed are those whose strength is in you, who have set their hearts on pilgrimage."

In other words, we all are on a pilgrimage (or journey). And, we all have two choices; we can look back or look ahead, retreat or move forward, hide out or step out! Psalm 84 is wisdom from God to keep us moving forward and not get stuck in a rut. Why is this Psalm so important? Because, if we stand still we will lose sight of God – for God is always moving forward! Grasp God's timely word today, for every season of your life:

God Has A "Duration" For Every Season!
"Who passing through the Valley of Baca (weeping) make it a well" (V.6). Here the psalmist describes his hardship in Baca, but also declares good news. He longs to move beyond where he is and reveals his perspective. What protects him from despair? The two words; "**passing through**" (V. 6). It's the Lord revealing to us that we will pass through every season of regret, every barren place and every valley of tears! Your valley has a duration and will one day cease!

God Has "Strength" For You In Every Season!
"Blessed are those whose strength is in You…they will continue to grow stronger and stronger" (V. 5,7). This means that your strength is being developed by the very things you consider as hardships. It means our hardships can become the barbells and bench presses of your soul. So much so, that God says He will supply "springs and a well" in the middle of your Valley of Baca (V. 6). And this takes the worry out of living, because God's presence will sustain us in every season. When we are tempted to get angry or resentful, God pours out His grace as we humble ourselves before Him. His strength will be equal to your test!

God Has "Contentment" For You In Every Season!
"Better is one day in your courts than a thousand elsewhere" (V. 10). There is a danger that faces all of us on the journey. It's the danger of looking too far down the road at things outside of our control. Why is this a bad idea? Because looking too far ahead produces anxiety, forfeits our present joy and

discredits God – that He knows where you're going and what you'll need! Plan ahead? Yes! But relinquish to God what is outside of your control! My take-a-way?

Happiness is not a place but a state of mind!

Nuf Sed!

"Three Hinges on the Door"

"And Elisha said, I pray thee, let a double portion of thy spirit be upon me"
(II Kings 2:9; KJV).

A great way to end this last day of January is to look at how Elijah ended his last day of earthly life and ministry. How Elijah left a legacy to Elisha speaks volumes to your heart and mine today! In this closing scene of Elijah's earthly life, he visits three places; Gilgal, Bethel and Jericho. Elijah's closing hours will be invested in the young people at the schools of the prophets. Elijah will speak words the Bible school students will never forget.

Is Elijah traveling alone? No, he has a minister in training alongside him named Elisha. What does Elijah tell the trainee? In V. 2, "Stay here, I'm going to Bethel." In V. 4, "Stay here, I'm going to Jericho." In V. 6, "Stay here, I'm going to Jordan."

And, how does Elisha respond? Notice what the trainee says in V. 2, "No, I'm not leaving you." In V. 4, "No, I'm not leaving you." In V. 6, "No, I'm not leaving you."

So, both men travel from Gilgal to Bethel, from Bethel to Jericho and from Jericho to the east side of Jordan. Elijah then takes his mantle, smites the water of Jordan and asks Elisha one final question; **"What can I do for you before I'm taken away from you?"** (V. 9). And Elisha's response reveals the three **hinges on the door** of all spirituality. It's a principle for living as an anointed man or woman of God. It's wrapped up in three words:

Word #1 is **Desire** (To go after God with all your heart). Elisha expresses his desire to Elijah; "Let a double portion of your spirit be upon me" (V. 9). Elisha (after 10 years sitting at the feet of Elijah) never got used to the anointing, never became familiar with God, and never stopped hungering for more of God. Three times Elisha was tested to go no further and all three times he refused to retreat.

Word #2 is **Wisdom** (To tear off the old man of self-reliance). Elisha "Took hold of his own clothes and rent them in two pieces" (V. 12). Know why? Because this was the time for a wise decision to discard his own dependence and depend on the Lord, to get radical with every besetting sin and hindering influence, to live transparent, and wisdom to separate from anything questionable – to move forward.

Word #3 is **Faith** (When you face your un-crossable Jordan Rivers). When Elijah departed, Elisha had to cross back over Jordan alone. And, Elisha asks the famous question; "Where is the Lord God of Elijah?" (V. 14). And, God parts the water to let Elisha cross over. Why is this recorded? To show us that the God of the past is the same God of the present! And, to show us that God's power has not diminished one bit over time. And, to reveal to us that God still honors faith when we face our un-crossable Jordans in life! What's the take-a-way?

Desire will keep us spiritually hungry, wisdom will keep us avoiding sin by focusing on Jesus and faith will keep us believing in the supernatural!

Nuf Sed!

February 1
"The Leveling Effect"

"Be still before the Lord and wait patiently for Him, do not fret" (Psalm 37:7).

Many have called Psalm 37 "The Psalm that calms the soul." Why? Because through David, God silences and hushes what wants to disturb our peace, tranquility and quietness. David is older now (V.25) and speaks from experience – words to enjoy the journey with God! Three resources leap off the pages, resources that have a leveling effect when we are tempted to be agitated.

1. The Power of "Trust" (In times of uncertainty)
"Trust in the Lord and do good" (V. 3). "Trust in Him" (V. 5).
Why are we instructed to **"trust the Lord"**? Because in Verse 1, all of us are tempted to **"fret"** which means; *"To burn, kindle or be incensed."*
So what protects us from "fretting" over people and things outside of our control?

♦ **Trust** in the Lord (V. 3) means to direct your thoughts upward.
♦ **Delight** yourself in the Lord (V.4) means to find your deepest joy in who He is to you.
♦ **Commit** your way unto the Lord (V. 5) means to leave your burdens in His hands.
♦ **Rest** in the Lord (V. 7) means to be still, hold steady and cease from murmurs.

2. The Power of "Patience" (While waiting)
"Be still and wait patiently for the Lord" (V. 7).
Why is this so important? Because all of us are tempted to take matters into our own hands when, "people carry out their wicked schemes" (V. 7). So what is patience anyway? **Patience (longsuffering)** is the grace to suffer long under pressure and adversity. It is the ability to bear with difficult people and circumstances. Patience is the power to endure hardship with a good attitude and the fruit that keeps you steadfast under straining situations.
Patience ("Hupomone" in the Greek) and **Longsuffering** ("Makrothumia" in the Greek) mean: *To remain, to wait, to stay, long-tempered.* "Waiting patiently for the Lord" in this context means to subdue your first human response to take matters into your own hands!

3. The Power of "Contentment" (When looking around)
"Better the little that the righteous have than the wealth of many wicked" (V. 16). What is the greatest thief of contentment? It is envy, which is the feeling of displeasure when witnessing the advantage of another. It's the pain we feel when someone else has something we want. Why is this so damaging? Because envy cannot be grateful for what it has, cannot celebrate the successes of others and cannot rest because of disorder on the inside. The take-a-way?

I can fret and worry, or I can trust and rest; but I can't do both!

Nuf Sed!

February 2
"He Knows Your Story"

"Come, see a man who told me everything I ever did" (John 4:29).

If you've ever wondered what grace looks like or if God's grace is greater than your past, this story is for you! To see Jesus travel through Samaria knowing the Samaritans hated the Jews, stop at a well for an undeserving woman, and then offer forgiveness is love in action. Three things leap off the pages into our hearts:

I. We See the Compassion of Jesus!
The Pharisees had just heard of all the success Jesus was having in winning disciples. This success created some jealousy among John's followers. So Jesus, to avoid division among the new believers, withdraws from Judea and heads north for Galilee. But why travel through Samaria with the long standing feud between Jews and Samaritans? And, what was the feud about? The Samaritans were a mixed race, part Jew and part Gentile. They grew out of the Assyrian captivity of the 10 Northern Tribes in 727 B.C. They were rejected by the Jews because they could not prove their genealogy. The Samaritans established their own temple and worship on Mt. Gerizim.

And yet, Jesus goes through Samaria anyway, for one reason alone: to minister to one undeserving woman and do what no one else can do – reveal the compassion in the heart of the Savior! To show us His mission in reaching someone who is looked down upon and in need of help. To show us what He thinks of us all!

II. We See the Conviction of the Spirit!
While Jesus is on His journey, the woman is on hers as well. She ends up at a well in Sychar and at noon comes out to draw water from a well. Why at noon when the custom is 6 p.m.? Because she doesn't want anyone to see her, confront her and point out her failures. But Jesus knows her story and He knows your story too. Two statements of Jesus "leap out" to me. First, **"Whoever drinks this water will thirst again"** (V. 13). Secondly, **"Go call your husband"** (V. 16).

Jesus is teaching two truths here. First, nothing material of this world can quench the deepest need of the soul, and secondly, until we admit we have a need, there can be no progress in spiritual things. Jesus wants us to confess and respond to the conviction of the Holy Spirit.

III. We See the Change in The Woman!
"Many of the Samaritans from that town believed in him because of the woman's testimony" (V. 39). So Jesus saves, changes and uses this woman in a remarkable way. She goes from a loner to a herald who runs into the city to tell everyone about Jesus. How is this possible? Because if the blood of the cross covers **at all**, it must cover **of all**! The Good News is, we don't have to hide, pretend or run. Why? Because He knows your story and it doesn't scare Him at all. My take-a-way from the well in Sychar?

God is more willing to forgive us our sin than we are to ask him!

Nuf Sed!

"The Midnight Hour of Crisis"

"When this man heard that Jesus had arrived in Galilee from Judea, he went to him and begged him to come and heal his son, who was close to death" (John 4:47).

It's a horrible feeling when someone you love is dying. Watching a family member suffer has a crushing affect upon our hearts. No matter how tough and strong you are, God has created us with the capacity to love, hurt, grieve and feel pain. Our text reveals the reality and the resource in the "midnight hour".

In John 4, Jesus ministers to the Samaritan woman (v.1-30), the Disciples (v.31-38), the Samaritans (v.39-42), and the nobleman and his son (v.43-54). Only John records this event, and it's the first recorded healing of Jesus in scripture. Jesus has come back to Cana where he attended the wedding feast (v.46), and a father makes a 20 mile journey to see this Jesus. Notice:

1. The Faith of the Father.
"The man took Jesus at his word and departed" (v.50). The dad had traveled to Cana and asked Jesus to, "Come and heal his son, who is close to death" (v.47). This royal official from Capernaum thought that his son was going to die, but also believed that Jesus could answer his prayer. And, what does Jesus tell the dad? "You may go. Your son will live" (v.50).

2. The Fever That Was Healed
As the dad was going home, he ran into his servants who had come looking for him (v.51). The servants told the dad, "The fever left him yesterday at the seventh hour" (v.52). So, the dad had spent the entire night "on hold", praying to God for his son. This dad had to agonize alone in prayer, wondering about his son back at home. I call this, "the **Midnight Hour** of Crisis". Why? Because the dad is stuck in Cana, the son is sick in Capernaum, and Jesus is now out of sight! And, everybody will encounter a **"Midnight Hour"**:
♦ A time when you are in the trenches all alone!
♦ A time when no one else can help you but God!
♦ A time when all you can do is wait patiently upon the Lord!

3. The Following of The Miracle
What was the result of this gift of healing in the father's son? The result was "all his household believed" (v.53). The ultimate purpose of the miracle was to witness to God's existence and power, and bring people to follow Jesus Himself. In other words, when the nobleman realized that Jesus could be trusted with his own son, he and his family committed themselves to Jesus. My friends; you can trust this Jesus today with the things and the people outside of your control! The take-a-way?

When fear starts filling your heart (like the dad), faith in Jesus will sustain you in the "midnight hour"!   Nuf Sed!

"The Pharisee, Publican and the Principle"
Part I

"To some who were confident of their own righteousness and looked down on everybody else, Jesus told this parable:" (Luke 18:9).

In this parable, Jesus tells us why some believers never feel rested. He also shows us how to have a gospel centered heart that results in an audience with God in prayer. Here's the context: Two men went up to the Temple to pray (that's normal). The devout Jew observed three prayer times a day; 9 a.m., 12 noon, 3 p.m. People near Jerusalem loved to go to the Temple to pray - the center of their worship.

I. One Was the Pharisee (What's a Pharisee?).

The Scribes and Pharisees had thousands of rules and regulations to keep – but it didn't make them sweet, humble, godly or joyful! In fact, the Scribes were scholars devoted to spelling out the principles set forth in the Law. The Pharisees were a group of laymen who separated from society to carry out all the regulations developed by the Scribes. And, legalism became oppressive and smothering to the spirit. What was the result of legalism? Two things:

♦ Some people felt **unspiritual** (because they couldn't find the power to keep all the rules). The result was frustration (we're bad and others are good).

♦ Other people felt **super spiritual** (because they had mental records of all the rules they were keeping). The result was arrogance (we're good and others are bad).

So, what kind of heart is in a Pharisee?

1. He has an **observatory** attitude. "God I thank you that I am not like other men" (V.11). He tattletales on the Publican (to God) in the prayer meeting.

2. He has a **measuring** mindset. "Or even like this tax collector" (V. 11). He measures his spirituality by someone else's and looks pretty good.

3. He has a **boastful** spirit. "I fast twice a week and I give a tenth of all I get" (V. 12). (Wow.) Fasting was mandatory for the Jewish people once a year on the Day of Atonement, (Leviticus 23:32). The Pharisees fasted twice a week, on Mondays and Thursdays. Mondays and Thursdays were the market days when Jerusalem was full of country people. This gave the Pharisees the largest audience to advertise their spirituality.

What's the discovery? This Pharisee didn't really go to church to pray, he went to inform God how good he was, how much he deserved, and how many laws he kept. What's the legalistic Pharisee teach us? Legalism is trusting in **my works** instead of Christ's work. Legalism is trying to **gain God's favor** through my good behavior. Legalism is an assumption that my performance can be leveraged against the wrath **that my sin** deserves.

What's the take-a-way from the praying Pharisee? It's clear:

I can't by my works, deeds or behavior build up enough funds to pay my debt (only the Gospel can satisfy what I owe!)

Nuf Sed!

"The Pharisee, Publican and the Principle"
Part II

"But the tax collector stood at a distance. He would not even look up to heaven, but beat his breast and said, God have mercy on me, a sinner" (Luke 18:13).

Yesterday we read about the praying Pharisee who was boastful, proud and yet unrestful, Why? Because there are always three joy stealing feelings inside of legalistic people:

1. **Fear -** that you won't do enough good things for God to love you.
2. **Arrogance** - that you have done enough good so God must love you.
3. **Failure** - that you've sinned too much and made too many mistakes.

Why can't a legalistic person ever be joyful? Because legalism is all about me, not about God. Legalism has to **defend** itself, **explain** itself and **justify** itself. Legalism makes you approval hungry, feeds the "disease to please" and does the right things for the wrong reason. So, how does this second praying man (the Publican) approach God in V. 13?

"He stood **afar off** to the side." Why? Because he was embarrassed by his sin (he felt unclean).

"He wouldn't **lift up his eyes.**" Why? Because he knew that God knew all about his sin.

"He **smote** his breast." Why? Because he was grieved about his sin offending God.

"He **pleads** for mercy." Why? Because he doesn't want what he really deserves.

"He calls himself a **sinner.**" Why? Because he realizes his good deeds can't pay the debt for his sin and make him acceptable to God. In other words, this guy understands that anything we experience in life that is better than hell is sheer grace, and undeserved!

So why does Jesus teach us with a contrast of these two men in church? In order to drive home a glorious truth; that there's nothing of value I can bring to God to deserve His salvation and approval. Salvation is a gift, not a paycheck for being good. The gospel is our only hope because there is **nothing** we can do to earn God's favor or deserve His goodness. And this truth protects us and heals us so that we can enjoy the journey with a "gospel centered" heart. How?

1. A gospel centered heart understands that we are **sinful** beyond belief yet **loved** beyond measure!
2. A gospel centered heart understands, it's the **object** of my faith, not the **level** of my faith.
3. A gospel centered heart understands that my **good** is not good

enough to make God love me, and my **bad** is not bad enough to make God hate me.

4. A gospel centered heart becomes less and less impressed with my **self** and more and more impressed with **Jesus**!

5. A gospel centered heart can succeed well (it won't go to our head in arrogance) and can suffer well (it won't go to our heart and play the victim card)!

6. A gospel centered heart doesn't think more of itself or less of itself! The take-a-way?

The gospel brings rest to our hearts, allows us to enjoy the journey and frees us from the comparison trap in having to measure up to someone else!

Nuf Sed!

"The Pharisee, Publican and the Principle"
Part III

"I tell you that this man, rather than the other, went home justified before God. For everyone who exalts himself will be humbled, and he who humbles himself will be exalted" (Luke 18:14).

The past two days we discovered how the Publican was justified (God heard his prayer that depended upon the grace of God). The Pharisee left the temple with the same cold heart. Why? Because; "Everyone that exalts himself shall be abased." And, "Everyone that humbles himself shall be exalted."

What's the Principle? The Pharisee missed the boat, the bus, the train and the cab. He told God about all the sins he didn't commit, thinking that God was now obligated to him on the basis of what he didn't do. He told God about all the good he did do (thinking that God was impressed by the observance of certain rites, rituals and ceremonies).

The Publican went home justified before God because he offered no self-proclaimed righteousness. He placed all his hope on the righteousness of another; Jesus.

What's it all mean to us? It means that I can **stop pretending**; I can embrace my flaws and failures, I don't have to be defensive when I'm corrected and I don't have to fake it, hide or pretend that I have it all together. And, I can **stop proving** myself. You can rest in His resume, not yours. You can overcome the stress of being driven to prove or promote yourself. You don't have to dress or drive to be noticed, and you don't have to stretch the truth or exaggerate to "wow" anybody. Why not? Because your concern is not "will anyone think less of me?" You can rest because the gospel reminds you of what God thinks of you!

In other words, grace invites us to draw near to God; to be changed from the inside out. This translates into joyful living and enjoying the journey. Why? Because:

♦ I do not feel **entitled** because the reality is we all deserve death, yet God's grace has given us what we don't deserve! This truth produces a **grateful spirit**.

♦ I do not feel **exempt** from difficulties and disappointments in life because the cross proves there is nothing that God cannot ask of us. This truth produces a **contented spirit**.

♦ I do not feel **elite** since we are sinners, only made holy by the work of another; Jesus! This truth produces a **humble spirit**.

What's my take-a-way? **When you do not feel entitled, exempt or elite, you can enjoy your days because life is not all about you! And, I will only be content when I truly understand what I deserve. And, what I deserve is wrath, but what I've been given is grace, love and forgiveness.**

Nuf Sed!

February 7
"A Giving Spirit"
Part I

"Each man should give what he has decided in his heart to give, not reluctantly or under compulsion, for God loves a cheerful giver" (II Corinthians 9:7).

People who enjoy the journey love to give! And, here's the reason why. Paul is writing to the Corinthian believers. The Corinthians had promised a love offering for the impoverished saints in Jerusalem. A year had gone by so Paul reminds them to keep their commitment. Paul wants the offering to strengthen all the churches (as the Gentiles give to the Jewish congregations across the sea). So, Paul uses the Macedonian churches as an example of how to give. I discover:

1.Giving Always Begins In The Heart!
"In the midst of a very severe trial, their overflowing joy and their extreme poverty welled up in rich generosity" (II Corinthians 8:2).
Some believers had lost their jobs, hit rock bottom destitution and were banned from the trade guilds for not bowing down to idols. And yet, people were giving in spite of their poverty. In fact,"beyond their ability" (V. 3) means they gave and refused to allow their circumstances to hinder their generosity. And, **"praying as with much entreaty that we would receive the gift"** (V.4), means they were so eager to give that they begged Paul to receive their offering. **"And they exceeded our expectations: They gave themselves first of all to the Lord, and then by the will of God also to us"** (V. 5). This means the believers surrendered their hearts to the Lord when they gave. It means the people used the occasion of the offering to rededicate their hearts and possessions to Jesus.

2.Giving Understands God's Grace!
"For you know the grace of our Lord Jesus Christ, that though he was rich, yet for your sake he became poor, so that you through his poverty might become rich" (II Corinthians 8:9). Here Paul reveals true spiritual (Gospel) motivation. He tells us to just look at Jesus and understand what He's done for us. He is saying; when we really see what God has done for us, it just isn't hard to give back to God! In other words, if Jesus sacrificed to save me eternally, then I can sacrifice something temporally. This is "Grace Giving" – when you remember God gave us His Son!

3.Giving Is A Matter Of Faith Not Income!
"As it is written: 'He who gathered much did not have too much, and he who gathered little did not have too little'"(II Corinthians 8:15). This is reference to the miracle of mana in Exodus 16:18. No matter how much manna the Jews gathered each day, there was always enough to supply the need. God was saying; gather what you need! Share what you can! Don't hoard it up or else it will rot. The lesson is; God will see to it that you will never lack; if God took care of Israel, He will take care of you! The take-a-way? **We shovel it out, God shovels it in, and His shovel is bigger than our shovel!**

Nuf Sed!

February 8
"A Giving Spirit"
Part II

4. Giving Carries Its Own Reward!
"Remember this: Whoever sows sparingly will also reap sparingly, and whoever sows generously will also reap generously" (II Corinthians 9:6).

Paul tells us here that spiritually mature people know the law of the farmer. What is it? We reap in measure to what we sow! We don't sow to obligate God; we just sow and know that God honors our obedience to His truth. Our motive is love, but our reward is in proportion to our generosity. Remember; in heaven we'll be rewarded for what we gave, not for what we received. And, the law of the farmer teaches us; **we reap after we sow and we reap more than we sow!**

5. Giving Carries The Fragrance of Deep Joy!
"Each man should give what he has decided in his heart to give, not reluctantly or under compulsion, for God loves a cheerful giver" (II Corinthians 9:7).
Paul tells us here, not to give out of duty or obligation. He instead teaches us to give with a smile! The Greek word for "cheerful" is Hilaron which gives us our English word "hilarious". Cheerful giving loves to give for two reasons; it understands what God has given in Christ and it wants others to experience what it has found in Jesus. My wife often said, "Takers may eat better but givers will sleep better." It's no secret that givers are happier than takers!

6. Giving Carries A Spirit of Heartfelt Gratitude!
"Thanks be to God for his indescribable gift" (II Corinthians 9:15).
This is the real motivation for all giving. What is it?
♦ Gratitude for God sending us His Son!
♦ Gratitude for His Son dying for my sins (in my place)!
♦ Gratitude for allowing me to participate in His great work!
And, this gratitude translates into extreme generosity. It produces a generous spirit that loves to support God's work and bless other people. It never resents giving tithes and offerings. Why? Because:
♦ The tithe is **mathematically** a tenth. (Genesis 28:22)
♦ The tithe is **scripturally** a command. (Deuteronomy 14:22)
♦ The tithe is **spiritually** a blessing. (Malachi 3:10)
♦ The tithe is **emotionally** a joy. (Acts 20:35)

What's the take-a-way from a New Testament giving spirit?
♦ **Loving never empties the heart and giving never empties the purse! And,**
♦ **God has given us two hands; one to receive with and the other to give with!**

Nuf Sed!

February 9
"Sufficient Grace"
Part I

"But he said to me, 'My grace is sufficient for you, for my power is made perfect in weakness.' Therefore, I will boast all the more gladly about my weaknesses, so that Christ's power may rest on me" (II Corinthians 12:9).

Paul had founded the church in Corinth (Acts 18:1-18) and when problems arose after his leaving, he sent Timothy to address them. When matters grew worse, Paul made a painful visit, wrote a "severe letter" that was delivered by Titus and finally received word that the problems had been solved. It was then that he wrote the letter of II Corinthians.

Paul wrote this letter to encourage the church to forgive a troublemaking member, to explain his change of plans, to encourage the church to give a "relief offering" and to declare how God's grace is sufficient in every season of life.

The key word in II Corinthians is **"encouraged"** or **"comfort"**. The Greek word means, *"Called to one's side to help."* It's a verb used 18 times in Paul's letter – to reveal your resources in the midst of whatever you face. Today we'll look at how Paul was **privileged** and yet **broken**.

I. Paul Was A "Privileged Man" (V. 1-6) He was blessed with visions and revelation (V. 1), he was blessed with going to heaven (V. 2) and he was blessed with hearing unspeakable words (V. 4). Can you imagine this? Just think of Paul's experience. He saw Jesus exalted at conversion (Acts 9:23), he saw a vision of Ananias coming his way (Acts 9:12), he had a vision when called to the Gentiles (Acts 22:17), he was called in a vision to Macedonia (Acts 16:9), encouraged in Corinth by a vision (Acts 18:9-10) and assured in a storm by an angel (Acts 27:23). He overheard divine secrets in heaven that impacted him forever. And yet, in all of this…

II. Paul Was A "Broken" Man. (V. 7,8) "There was given me a thorn in my flesh (V. 7) and "three times I pleaded with the Lord to take it away from me" (V. 8). The word **"thorn"** means; *"A sharp stake used for torturing"*. Paul's thorn was some type of affliction that brought pain and distress to him. It was used of God to protect his ego from becoming inflated. The thorn was a blessing in disguise to a fruitful and productive ministry.

The word **"buffet"** means; *"To beat or strike with the fist"*. The tense of the verb means that Paul's pain was constant or recurring. No wonder he prayed three times! The discovery here?
1.God permitted satan to afflict Paul which kept Paul from becoming proud and boastful!
2.God trusted Paul not to get bitter and blame God for robbing him of pleasure and comforts.

3.God didn't answer Paul's request for the removal of his thorn, but God did do something else!

So, what's the take-a-way thus far? Great spiritual experiences are to **draw attention to God**; never to ourselves! When God doesn't answer our prayers like we think He should; remember that **He has information that we are not aware of!** Your troubles in life will either be your **tombstone** or your **stepping stone**, it all depends on how you respond!

Nuf Sed!

"Sufficient Grace"
Part II

Yesterday we learned how Paul was a **privileged** and **broken** man; today discover how Paul was a **supported** man. See what God provides for you to enjoy the journey!

I. "My Grace Is Sufficient For You." While Paul was hoping for a "yes" answer to his thorn being removed, God answered Paul's prayer in a different way. Paul was allowed to keep what was pricking and distressing him. What about you? Do you have any thorns that are sharp, painful or cutting at your heart? If so, here's the Good News:

♦ The word **"grace"** means: *"Divine support"* and *"provision as needed"*.
♦ The word **"sufficient"** means: *"Never in shortage of"* and *"never running out"*.

When you put the two together like Jesus did, Jesus is saying two things:
1. "I will not only be your divine support and provision", but
2. "I will prove to be sufficient (or) never in shortage of what you need at the time you need it."

II. "My Power Is Made Perfect In Weakness." But aren't we supposed to be self-sufficient, self-assured, self-confident and self-made? Jesus is saying here; the strength which I give is manifested when My people feel their weakness. In other words:

♦ It's not imparted to those who feel they are strong and have no need of divine help.
♦ It's not poured out to those who believe they can make it without God.

"My strength is made perfect in weakness" means that when I am conscious I am feeble, and when I know my flesh is weak, and when I acknowledge I am zero without God, it's then and only then that Jesus manifests His power to uphold you (and) imparts His strength to sustain you!

III. "I Will Boast About My Weaknesses." This doesn't mean that Paul preferred pain to health or had some "poor me" martyr's complex. It means Paul discovered that; the grace of God was proving sufficient day after day, his weakness was being replaced (or compensated) by God's strength, and the presence of God was more than adequate for what he had to endure.
This means that Paul (in prayer) received God's strength to glory (and not resent) his infirmities.

IV. "So That Christ's Power May Rest Upon Me."
♦ "The power of Christ" refers to the enablement of the Holy Spirit.
♦ "May rest upon me" means to "pitch a tent" or "overshadow".

So Paul is saying two encouraging truths (and promises):
1. We have access to the fresh grace that God pours out. (And)

2. We have access to the very provision which enables us "to glory in infirmities."

We don't glory *for* our infirmities (that's foolishness). Instead, we glory *in* (or in the midst of) our infirmities. How? Because God's grace will assist and support you through every season!

My take-a-way? **There is no reason to fear the future when you know that God's sufficient grace will always be equal to your task!**

Nuf Sed!

February 11
"The Potter's Wheel"
Part I

"And the vessel that he made of clay was marred in the hand of the potter: so **he made it again** another vessel" (Jeremiah 18:4, KJV).

Jeremiah (known as the weeping prophet) ministered during the final years of Judah's history (from 626 to 580 B.C.). He prophesied Judah's destruction, yet also announced that Judah would be restored through the coming Messiah. He faithfully warned of Babylon's victory, but Judah refused to accept his warnings. His purpose was to warn Judah that her sins would result in chastisement from the North (The Babylonians). And, his ministry appeared totally unsuccessful as the nation declined until Judah was taken captive by Babylon in 586 B.C. Even though Jeremiah was threatened with death, rejected by those he served, cast into a dungeon and cursed the day he was born, he was prompted by God to go down to the potter's house in the Valley of Hinnom. Why? Because God had a message for then, and for now!

I. The Making of the Vessel (V.1-3)
"I went down to the potter's house, and, behold, he wrought a work on the wheels" (V.3).

Manufacturing pottery was a major industry in Jeremiah's day. Jeremiah had seen the potter's house many times. On this day, God gives a special message to Jeremiah, Israel, you and me. Here's what Jeremiah sees in front of him; the potter sits between two stone wheels that are joined by a shaft. He turns the bottom wheel with his feet, working the clay on the top wheel as the wheel turns. Jeremiah sees the clay resisting the potter's hands; he sees the vessel (ruined from resisting) yet the potter keeps on working. How does this apply to you and me? Judah was resisting the hands of the Potter, rejecting the Law of God and choosing idols contrary to God. And, the nation was made up of individuals like you and me. In other words, you and I have the choice to yield or resist the hands of the potter. The good news is the Master Potter knows what He's doing in your life. Remember:

- The Potter has a **choice**; he can leave the clay alone untouched, or make out of it a vessel of beauty. So the Lord could leave us alone and untouched or make us vessels of honor.
- The Potter has **tools**; he uses the wheel to spin, hands to press, instruments to slice away rough edges. So the Lord allows you to be pressured at times in ways you cannot understand.
- The Potter has **wisdom**; he has a wise purpose in mind for every vessel on the wheel. So the Lord has a unique purpose for your life and mine.
- The Potter has **patience**; he takes his time, spins the wheel, ever patient in forming each individual vessel. So the Lord is ever patient with us, always changing us, but never discarding us.

"He wrought a work on the wheels" (V.3) is awesome! The Hebrew word for "wrought" is *ASAW* which means: *To fashion, to prepare, to trim, to advance, to finish.* What's the take-a-way?

The Potter like the Master Vinedresser is never so close than when He is pruning His beloved!

Nuf Sed!

February 12
"The Potter's Wheel"
Part II

"But the pot he was shaping from the clay was marred in his hands; so the potter formed it into another pot, shaping it as seemed best to him" (Jeremiah 18:4).

Yesterday we learned how the Potter is never so close, than when He is making a vessel for His glory. It is His plan to form, fashion, prepare and finish His work on the wheel. And, you and I are the work on the Potter's wheel. And, God knew what He was getting into when He made you.

II. The Marring of the Vessel Is Recorded:
(V. 8) "If that nation I warned repents of it's evil."
(V. 10) "If it does evil in my sight and does not obey me."
(V. 15) "My people have forgotten me."

In other words, Judah was resisting God's will, rejecting God's call to repentance, worshipping idols, living for vain things and refusing to confront what needed to change. In fact, their frustration was so intense that she said, there is no hope, so we'll just have to walk after our own devices. Or, "Since our sin has been so bad for so long, we might as well just give up." But wait a minute! Did God give up? Did He throw the vessel away? Did He say, "Just forget it"? No, not even close. Verse 4 says, **He made it again**. And you are tempted to think; "I've been marred too long." "I've sinned too much." "I've tried to change in the past." "I've promised God before and failed."

Yet, God says, "And if that nation I warned repents of its evil, then I will relent and not inflict on it the disaster I had planned" (V. 8). Do we really serve a "He made it again God"? Is God really the God of the second chance? Never forget this; God is removing the grit and base materials that will crack the vessel in the fire. He is preparing you on the wheel, so that you can survive in the fire. And, lest you be deceived or despairing, remember the kiln and furnace secrets:

- Clay in the furnace requires just the right **preparation**. God is preparing you today for service.
- Clay in the furnace requires just the right **oven**. God has you right where you belong.
- Clay in the furnace requires just the right **heat**. If it's too cold, the clay won't get hard; if it's too hot, the clay will be destroyed.
- Clay in the furnace requires just the right **timing**. The potter knows exactly when to take the vessel from the heat in the oven.

And remember, vessels were placed in the furnace so that no one single clay pot could touch another. Why not? Because if any two vessels fused together in the fire, both would be ruined. In other words, it's not the church congregation God is dealing with as a **group**, it's you and me **alone** that God is making on the wheel for His glory!

III. The Message from the Potter's Wheel? The take-a-way is clear:
God approves of fresh starts and no failure is final when God is in the picture!

Nuf Sed!

"A Safe Deposit"

"So then, those who suffer according to God's will should commit themselves to their faithful Creator and continue to do good" (I Peter 4:19).

I love how the Lord wants us to enjoy the journey and live anxious free. You just have to appreciate God's wisdom to help us live without fretting and panic.

Peter is writing here to believers who are suffering. His purpose is to encourage those going through affliction, pain and disappointment. Peter mentions suffering 16 times by using eight different Greek terms. It's a relevant word for both then and now! Notice the strength that pours out of Chapter 4:12-19:

◆ In V. 12, how not to be surprised that being a Christian doesn't grant us immunity from pain in this life.

◆ In V. 13, how it is an honor to partake of the pain that comes by taking up our own cross.

◆ In V. 14, how the Holy Spirit will "rest" upon us (or refresh and strengthen us in times of ridicule and insult).

◆ In V. 16, how suffering the right way will attract others to Jesus.

◆ But in V. 19, how to trust God (and overcome anxiety) by doing two things:

1. Commit Ourselves!
When Peter says "Commit themselves to their faithful creator" (V.19), he uses a banking term. The word "commit" means to "deposit" or "entrust". It means that we can entrust ourselves to the Lord for safekeeping. It means we can trust the Lord to deliver us from (or deliver us in) whatever pain that suffering may cause, and, this takes the worry out of living! This helps us rest and not fret over tomorrow! This helps us to plan ahead – but not live ahead! This frees us from trying to control people or things outside of our control!

2. Remember God!
What makes it possible to deposit (or trust) ourselves and our future to God? By remembering that God is our "Faithful Creator" (V. 19). The word "Faithful" means the Lord can be counted on to keep His promises to you. The word "Creator" means; if the Lord has power to oversee nature and His creation, He will certainly oversee those who belong to Him. In other words, if the Lord can keep the earth rotating on its axis at 23.5 degrees without our help, He can surely be responsible to care for you and me. What's the take-a-way from this word written to those facing uncertainties in Peter's day and today?

◆ **God has an unblemished track record and is worthy to be trusted! (And)**

◆ **It is an insult to God to doubt what He has said!**

Nuf Sed!

"Sadness into Gladness"

"In bitterness of soul Hannah wept much and prayed to the Lord" (I Samuel 1:10).

"Then she went her way and ate something, and her face was no longer downcast" (V. 18).

Hannah's story is one that helps us all. It's a true account of how God (through prayer) brings change within our hearts. Hannah was the wife of Elkanah and soon-to-be mother of Samuel. She was barren, and having no children was considered by society as a punishment from God. Her story reveals how God changes people who want to be changed.

We all have two choices when we hurt: we can become victims and look for pity or we can grow and move forward through the ministry of prayer. Discover how Hannah was changed by God!

I.Hannah's Sadness and Tears
The cause of Hannah's brokenness is listed in Scripture. She was barren with no children (V. 5). She was verbally abused (V. 6,7). She was neglected by her insensitive husband (V. 8). She was misunderstood by Eli the priest (V. 13,14). She was seemingly forgotten by God (V. 15). And her pain is revealed in V. 7, as she wept and could not eat. Maybe, like Hannah, you've had an unfulfilled expectation, were verbally abused, suffered neglect from an insensitive spouse, been misunderstood or seemingly forgotten by God. Notice what Hannah does.

II. Hannah's Supplication And Travail
In I Samuel Ch. 1, Hannah's family makes the annual trip to the tabernacle. The family goes to Shiloh to worship, 15 miles from home. While everyone else is eating and enjoying the festival, Hannah goes to the tabernacle to unburden her heart to God in prayer. She can retaliate against Peninnah, Elkanah and Eli (and get bitter) or she can be healed in prayer (and see her pain become a stepping stone instead of a tombstone.) Her choice? She prayed and wept sore (V. 10), continued praying (V. 12), and poured out her heart to the Lord (V. 15). And, Hannah's praying teaches us all that:

♦ Prayer requires no special formula or method (V. 13). She pondered in silent prayer.

♦ Prayer releases our problems over to God. She released her burdens and travelled home.

♦ Prayer recovers our joy and peace. She went her way, "and was no longer sad" (V. 18).

III. Hannah's Song And Transformation
After Hannah prayed, was healed and gave birth to Samuel, we find her singing! What did God do in Hannah's heart in the therapy of prayer? She

worships and sings victoriously because:

♦ God provides us with salvation (2:1), and God makes no mistakes (V.2).
♦ God understands us fully (V.3) and, God will make all the wrong things right (V. 10).

So, all of this and more takes place in Hannah – because she took her pain to the Lord in prayer! The take-a-way?

What happens "in" us is far more important than what happens "to" us!

Nuf Sed!

"Put Your Sword Away"

"Put your sword back in its place", Jesus said to him, "for all who draw the sword will die by the sword" (Matthew 26:52).

Noe of us are exempt from temptation and all of us have to deal with our reactions to people. And, Jesus gives us a healthy lesson to enjoy the journey more fully.

The arrest of Jesus and the severed ear are listed in all four gospels. (Matthew 26:51, Mark 14:47; Luke 22:50, John 18:10). The event records the last miracle Jesus performs before His death. It follows a season of prayer in Gethsemane, a mob coming along with swords and clubs, a kiss from Judas and a question from the disciples: **"Lord, should we strike with our swords?"** (Luke 22:49). And, before Jesus can even answer the question, Peter cuts off the ear of Malchus and is rebuked by Jesus with: **"Put your sword back in its place...for all who draw the sword will die by the sword."** (Matthew 26:52). So, Peter draws his sword and begins to slash away. He forgets that its only himself and ten disciples against a mob of Roman soldiers. He then cuts off Malchus' ear in haste and is rebuked by Jesus. Why was Peter in trouble?

Peter was **impatient**, which means; "showing annoyance because of delay, not willing to wait for something to happen." Peter asked, "Lord, shall we smite with the sword?" (v. 49). He never waited for an answer from Jesus. He simply spoke and sliced.

Peter was **impulsive,** which means; "A sudden inclination without conscious thought; moving without thinking carefully first." Peter wasn't' thinking about the multitude behind the servant he injured. His unholy zeal caused him to leap before he looked.

Peter was **impetuous**, which means "Moving with force or violence, acting furiously, rash, rushing". Peter is fighting flesh with flesh. He is trying to accomplish something the wrong way. Peter never thought how his one act could have cost the lives of the other ten disciples.

What's the lesson in this recorded account in all four gospels? I see two:

1.There is Peter, who cuts off the ear with unholy zeal.
♦ Have I cut off any ears lately (and hastily reacted from my flesh)?
♦ Have I engaged in carnal warfare with carnal means?
How busy we keep the Lord putting on ears, that we in our fleshly zeal cut off.

2. There is Jesus, who heals what someone else has severed in a hasty outburst.
♦ Jesus shows us how to forgive someone who doesn't deserve it (and)
♦ Jesus shows us that He can heal you from what someone else may have

done to you!

Today you may feel like **undisciplined Peter** or **underserving Malchus**, but Amazing Grace rescued and restored them both! The take-a-way from the sword?

No provocation ever justifies an unchristian response! And, if you have a short fuse, you can be sure that someone will light it.

Nuf Sed

"Prayer's Reward"

"I pray that out of His glorious riches He may strengthen you with power through His Spirit in your inner being" (Ephesians 3:16).

Paul is writing here to the believers in Ephesus, the chief city of Asia Minor. He's writing from prison and, an incredible prayer for believers comes from his lips. He "bows his knees" in prayer (v. 14) and reveals he is earnest, contrite and desperate. He prays, "to his Father" (V. 14) which means he is praying to the God who hears His children and who answers prayer. I love what Paul prays for; it's good for you and me, as it was for the believers in Ephesus.

I. Next Level Praying Provides "Strength" For The Inner Man. (V. 16) The word "strengthen" means "To be made strong, to be made tough and to be able to endure." The word "power" means, "Force, energy and might." The words "inner man" refer to the deepest part of our heart, soul and being. How does God strengthen us? "By His Spirit" (V. 16). So God pours out His Spirit, "out of His glorious riches" (V. 16) – which means there is no shortage with God and no limit to what He supplies.

II. Next Level Praying Provides "Wisdom" To Make Right Choices (17) "That Christ may dwell in your hearts by faith, that ye being rooted and grounded in love" (V. 17) KJV. The word "dwell" means to be at home with, to rule and reign and to control and guide. It means that God will dwell, rule, reign and call the shots in the center of our wills. It means as we pray, we will be conscious of His presence and sensitive to His direction for us. And, this helps us to be "rooted" (firm), and "grounded" (solid) and unshakable in an unpredictable world.

III. Next Level Praying Provides "Encouragement" In Every Season (V.15, 19) "May have power together with all the saints, to grasp how wide and long and high and deep is the love of Christ" (V.18). How can we be sure of God's faithfulness in every season of life? Because God's love (in Christ) is:
♦   **Wide** – Covering the breadth of our entire experience in life.
♦   **Long** – Enough to cover the entire length of life on earth.
♦   **High** – Or rising to the heights of your greatest joy.
♦   **Deep –** And able to reach the very depths of our despair.

IV. Next Level Praying Provides "Faith" For Your Impossible Mountains (V. 20) "Now unto Him who is able to do…
♦   **Exceeding** – which means to surpass and go beyond our requests.
♦   **Abundantly** – which means to overflow with more than enough.

♦ **Above** - which means to go over and above any need we present to God! In other words, God is provoking us to believe and prove Him and see what He can do!

The take-a-way?

It is a compliment to God when we ask Him to do what only He can do!

Nuf Sed!

"Pure in Heart"
Part I

"Above all else, **guard your heart**, for it is the wellspring of life" (Proverbs 4:23).

"My son, give me **your heart** and let your eyes keep to my ways" (Proverbs 23:26).

"Who may ascend the hill of the Lord? Who may stand in His holy place? He who has clean hands and a **pure heart**" (Psalm 24:3,4).

A believer once told me that the devil is on a chain. I responded by saying, "Then it must be a long chain because he seems to get around to everybody." My point was; none of us are immune from temptation and all of us have to be vigilant to keep our hearts clean. And, while only Jesus can forgive us and cleanse us, we must cooperate in the process. And here's the reason why.

The heart is our source of life, the seat of our inner man. The heart includes our desires, affections, will, motives and emotions. The heart, in essence, is the inward spiritual nature of man.

Why is it so important to guard, watch and protect our hearts? Because, "It is the wellspring of life" (Proverbs 4:23) which means:

1. The human heart has main arteries which carry blood from the heart to the rest of the entire body. The heart must not be injured or we suffer.

2. The fountains and wells of the East were watched over with special care. If the enemy could taint the well with poison, victory was automatic. The water was the life source and it all flowed from the well.

3. Our own heart is such a function, that if it be tainted, the streams that flow out will be tainted as well.

4. Our bodily parts do not pump blood to the heart, but the heart pumps blood to each part of our body. So, our hands do not cause us to sin; they simply act out what's in our heart. Everything **we do** (our hands) is an extension of what **we are** (in our heart).

The Hebrew text for Proverbs 4:23 conveys the clear thought that we must keep close watch over our hearts because that is the place where God speaks to us. Or, from within our hearts come Divine direction for our lives. In other words:

♦ If we fail to guard our **heart**, we will be unable to discern God's **will** when He speaks to us.

♦ If we allow our heart to be cluttered with **weeds**, we will miss the **direction** God wants to give us.

♦ If we fail in our heart (what we **are**) we will fail with our hands (what we **do**).

The take-a-way?

If our character is impure – then our vision of Jesus is impaired!

Nuf Sed!

"Pure in Heart"
Part II

"Blessed are the pure in heart, for they will see God." (Matthew 5:8)

The word "pure" in Matthew 5:8 comes from the Greek word Katharos which means:
♦ Without mixture
♦ Without division
♦ Without defilement

The words "see God" in V. 8 are not referring to eternity, but refer to this present earthly journey right now. So Jesus is saying:
♦ To the extent that our heart is undivided, to that extent we will experience the **leading** of the Lord (or)
♦ Jesus can only reveal Himself to those who are walking in **singleness** of heart.

While Jesus loves us the same on our worst days and best days, there are consequences when we allow sin to remain:
♦ Adam and Eve were forgiven, but they still were never allowed back into the garden again.
♦ Moses was forgiven, but he was not allowed to enter the Promised Land.
♦ David was forgiven, but he suffered dearly because of the consequences of sin.

I can't help from remembering God's word to Joshua when Achan was hiding his sin:
"I will not be with you anymore unless you destroy whatever among you is devoted to destruction" (Joshua 7:12).
"You cannot stand against your enemies until you remove it" (V.13)So Achan teaches us:

1. **Concealing sin does not erase sin**. Achan hid the stuff, but couldn't hide his sin.
2. **Sin will never allow you to suffer alone.** Achan's whole family suffered because of his sin.
3. **The consequences of sin may be delayed, but never ignored.** There was a "season of time" that seemed to tell Achan, "You got away with it."
4. **What is committed in secret will be exposed in public.** Achan sinned alone, but the whole congregation would eventually know it.
5. **The sting of sin is sharper than its pleasure**. Achan's pain far outweighed his pleasure.
6. **To delay in repenting is to hasten God's anger.** While Achan

delayed and covered up, the wrath of God was kindled.

7. **To conceal any sin is to lose God's help in battle**. God emphatically declared, "I won't be with you anymore, until you address the sin that is among you." (V. 12)

What's the "Good News" in all of this? The good news is, our hearts can be purified and made strong! How does God purify our hearts and lead us forward?

♦ God deals with us about sin (that's conviction) John 16:8
♦ We respond and agree with God (that's confession) Psalm 139:23
♦ The result is something glorious (that's cleansing) I John 1:9

The take-a-way? **Transparency leads us forward, hiding sin leads us backward!**

Nuf Sed!

"The Fear of the Lord and its Reality"
Part I

1. "Let all the earth **fear** the Lord" (Psalm 33:8).
2. "The **fear** of the Lord is the beginning of knowledge, but fools despise wisdom and discipline" (Proverbs 1:7).
3. "The **fear** of the Lord - that is wisdom" (Job 28:28).
4. "Now **fear** the Lord and serve Him with all faithfulness" (Joshua 24:14).
5. "O **fear** the Lord ye His saints, for there is no want to them that **fear** Him" (Psalm 34:9, KJV).

The Fear of The Lord Is Described In Four Ways:

1. **<u>Leviticus 10:1-3</u>**
   Nadab and Abihu offered profane fire before the presence of the Lord. The word "profane" means: "Showing disrespect or contempt for sacred things." It means to become familiar with (and treat what God calls holy as if it were common). Nadab and Abihu were careless and approached God as if He were common. God reveals to us here that irreverence cannot survive and make progress in the presence of a Holy God. It was service on the outside, but disobedience on the inside.

2. **<u>I Samuel 6:19,20</u>**
   The Ark of God was the Presence Chamber of God in the Old Testament. The Philistines couldn't handle God's holiness and sent the Ark away to Bethshemesh. The ark was received with shouts of joy at a frivolous church gathering. And, when the people opened the Ark to look in 50,070 men were instantly smitten dead. Why? Because no one can really approach God in frivolity, familiarity and looseness.

3. **<u>Isaiah 6:1-3</u>**
   Isaiah gets a glimpse of the atmosphere in heaven. He sees the Lord and the angel's response to the Lord. What's the one description that reduces Isaiah to the fear of the Lord? (V. 3) "Holy, Holy, Holy is the Lord of Hosts."

4. **<u>Acts 5:1-16</u>**
   Ananias and Sapphira sold land and pretended to give the proceeds to the Lord. They were exposed for lying to God and smitten with death. The result was, "And great fear came upon all the church...and many signs and wonders were wrought among the people" (V. 11,12)
   The take-a-way? The "Fear of the Lord" is:
   1. The response of my **will** to the holiness of God.
   2. An **attitude** within me that produces a trembling heart.
   3. A **transparency** that is void of all pretense and pretending.
   4. A steadfast **disposition** that takes God extremely serious in every area of my life.   Nuf Sed!

February 20
"The Fear of the Lord and Humility"
Part II

"By humility and the fear of the Lord are riches, honor and life." (Proverbs 22:4; KJV).

Yesterday we discovered that the fear of the Lord is a steadfast disposition that takes God extremely serious in every area of our lives. Today we'll look at what humility is and what humility does. Notice the Scriptures:

1. "For everyone who exalts himself will be humbled, and he who humbles himself will be exalted" (Luke 18:14).
2. "Humble yourselves before the Lord, and he will lift you up" (James 4:10).
3. "Humble yourselves, therefore, under God's mighty hand, that he may lift you up in due time" (I Peter 5:6).
4. "A man's pride brings him low, but a man of lowly spirit gains honor" (Proverbs 29:23).
5. "When pride comes, then comes disgrace, but with humility comes wisdom" (Proverbs 11:2).

What Is Humility?

1. It is an inward condition that gives us proper <u>view</u> of God, others and ourselves.
2. It is recognizing my inability to accomplish anything for God apart from His <u>grace</u>.
3. It is allowing the Holy Spirit to <u>replace</u> all arrogance, conceit, fear, worry, self-preoccupation, self-promotion, and self-vindication.

♦ "A man can receive nothing except it be given him from heaven" (John 3:27; KJV).

♦ "What do you have that you did not receive?" (I Corinthians 4:7).

Some Inventory Questions To Grow By:

1. Do I have any desire to impress other people?
2. Do I have any desire to prove my own importance?
3. Do I ever feel pain when my enemies are praised?
4. Do I justify (or cover) my own faults?
5. Do I desire any revenge on those who have offended me?
6. Do I need to be "thanked" for my service to feel good about myself?
7. Do I find it difficult to do the "little unseen" things?
8. Do I allow God and others to speak into my life?
9. Can I admit that I don't have all the answers?
10. Am I passionate about growing beyond previous boundaries?
11. Can I submit to the authorities that God has placed in my life?
12. Can I support the team when I don't get my own way?

The take-a-way? **Stay low to the ground and you won't have far to fall!**

Nuf Sed!

February 21
"The Fear of the Lord and Humility"
Part III

"The meek also shall increase their joy in the Lord" (Isaiah 29:19, KJV).

25 WAYS THAT HUMILITY WILL "LESSEN STRESS" IN YOUR LIFE

1. Humility allows you to ask for **help** (because you never reach the place of knowing it all!)
2. Humility will allow you to build a **team** and value the strengths of those around you!
3. Humility will free you to accept the way that God has gifted you (and have no need to compete or **compare** with someone else!)
4. Humility frees you from the stress of seeking **approval** (and having to prove yourself).
5. Humility finds its **validation** vertically (in Jesus) so you don't have to shop for it horizontally (in people)!
6. Humility delivers you from self-display and the **desire** of seeking preferential treatment.
7. Humility spares you much pain because you can receive **correction** and instruction!
8. Humility promotes **health** because you can serve God without feeling cheated!
9. Humility results in a **calm** spirit that spares you from impulsive activity!
10. Humility allows you to fear the Lord so you can say "no" without feeling **guilty**!
11. Humility keeps you from being **detoured** by the narcissism and egotism of others!
12. Humility keeps you **balanced** after someone expresses their disapproval of you!
13. Humility allows you to **forgive** after being wounded, offended, or betrayed!
14. Humility frees you from carrying **secret** sin that needs to be confessed and repented of!
15. Humility overcomes the **fear** of getting close to those who could hurt you!
16. Humility overcomes self-consciousness which is the feeling of being observed yet not **approved**!
17. Humility protects you from **blaming** others for your own unhappiness!
18. Humility can **rejoice** (instead of envy) the successes of those around you!
19. Humility crucifies the desire to seek **credit** for what God and others have done!
20. Humility allows you to answer your critics with your **life** instead of

your words!

21. Humility leaves you still feeling okay when you do not meet everyone else's **expectations**.
22. Humility allows me to let others make **mistakes** (as well as take the risk to confront in love when necessary).
23. Humility helps me see the **truth** about myself.
24. Humility will allow me to clean the church bathroom without passive aggressive behavior toward the person who **promised** to do it.
25. Humility helps us not to say "I told you so" when someone realizes they were **wrong**.

The take-a-way is – that humility basically….
♦ Saves you time! ♦ Welcomes new ideas! ♦ Purifies your motives!
♦ Conserves your energy! ♦ Increases your wisdom! ♦ Promotes your health!
♦ Protects your integrity! ♦ Attracts God's favor! ♦ Leaves you content!

Nuf Sed!

"The Fear of the Lord and Authenticity"
Part IV

"Now therefore, **fear the Lord** and serve Him in **sincerity** and in **truth**" (Joshua 24:14, KJV).

For the past three days we've looked at the reality, reason and reward of "Fearing the Lord". Nothing (in my opinion) conquers hypocrisy like the fear of God. After all, the fear of God is a guardrail at the top of the cliff-instead of a hospital at the bottom.

In this final devotional of four messages on this subject, I want to pray and agree with you. I want us to pray together that we will fear the Lord, walk in humility and avoid hypocrisy like the plague. And, God will honor us as we align ourselves with His purpose, His truth, and really set us free. Before we pray, remember what a hypocrite is and remember what we are avoiding:

"For what is the hope of the **hypocrite**, though he hath gained, when God taketh away his soul?" (Job 27:8, KJV).
"The joy of the **hypocrite** is but for a moment" (Job 20:5; KJV).
"The **hypocrite's** hope shall perish" (Job 8:13).
"Thou **hypocrite**, first cast out the beam out of thine own eye; and then shalt thou see clearly to cast out the mote out of thy brother's eye" (Matthew 7:5; KJV).

"Do not do as the **hypocrites** do in the synagogues and in the streets, that they may have glory of men" (Matthew 6:2; KJV).

The English word **"hypocrite"** comes from the Greek word Hupokrites which means: An actor under an assumed character, a deceit, and acting under a feigned part. So a hypocrite:
♦ Is someone (like a stage player) who feigns to be what he is not.
♦ Is someone who appears to be virtuous without possessing the reality.
♦ Is someone who says one thing but does another.
♦ Is someone who isn't in private what they are in public.

Hypocrite: when there is any difference between my sincerest moment before men and what God knows to be the reality – to that degree I am a hypocrite, not transparent, insincere and not walking in the fear of the Lord!!!

"Lord, help us to be real, genuine and authentic! Help us to remember that the greatest liberty in life is having nothing to prove and no one to impress. Lord, because of your grace and our standing with you, help us to walk in humility, the healthy fear of God and run from hypocrisy. We ask this earnestly, in Jesus' name, Amen!" My take-a-way?

What a waste of time it is – to ever pretend to be something we are not!
Nuf Sed!

"One Thing Is Needed"

"Only one thing is needed. Mary has chosen what is better, and it will not be taken away from her" (Luke 10:42).

I once heard a preacher say, "No one can do enough for others if they are always surrounded by others." And, that's what we learn in Luke 10:38-42. Jesus clearly teaches us; we do not need more time, we simply need to choose!

In Luke 10, Jesus enters the village of Bethany, a suburb two miles outside of Jerusalem. He visits the home of Martha whom He thought much of (John 11:5). Martha owned a large house where she hosted Jesus and the disciples. She was also caring for her younger sister Mary and her brother, Lazarus. And, here's the truth that sets us free to enjoy the journey day by day:

I. Mary's Devotion Is Admirable
Mary of Bethany is seen three times in Scripture:
♦   In John 11:32 (Sharing her burden at the feet of Jesus).
♦   In John 12:3 (Pouring out her worship at the feet of Jesus).
♦   In Luke 10:39 (Listening to the Word at the feet of Jesus).
In First Century Judaism, it was highly unusual for a woman to be accepted by a teacher as a disciple. But Jesus overcomes every objection and obstacle, and swings the door wide open. He invites you and me to come in and sit down. Remember; Mary could have chosen to sit in the back or off to the side. But Mary was hungry and "heard His word" which means she was attentive!

II. Martha's Distraction Is Avoidable
"But Martha was distracted by all the preparations" (V. 40). The Greek word for distracted means: To twist and to be drawn here and there. And, what happens when we get distracted from Jesus' feet? "Martha, Martha…you are worried and upset about many things" (V.41). Martha became anxious and troubled, which means she was agitated, ruffled, disturbed and stirred up. Why? Because she was distracted from what Mary was doing.

III. Jesus Directions Are Advisable
"Only one thing is needed and Mary has chosen what is better" (V. 42). So, Jesus tells Martha (and you and me) three things in V.42:
♦ "One thing is needful." ♦ "Mary has chosen that good part." ♦ "I'm not telling her to move."

What's the message here? Not that Martha had too much work to do, but that she allowed her work to interfere with her intimacy with God. She became distracted on the outside and "pulled apart" on the inside. The message is: "One thing" is needed above every other thing in your life and mine. And, that **"one thing"** is the **"main thing"** that our spirituality is built upon – closeness to Jesus! What's the take-a-way from Martha's house?

Failure to pray will forfeit what prayer was meant to do!

Nuf Sed!

February 24
"No Attention Please"
Part I

"As he taught, Jesus said, "Watch out for the teachers of the law. They like to walk around in flowing robes and be greeted in the marketplaces; and have the most important seats in the synagogues and the places of honor at banquets" (Mark 12:38,39).

Something in all of us likes to win! We love to watch and root for our team to come out on top. It might be the Super Bowl, World Series, NBA Finals, Stanley Cup, boxing, NASCAR, swimming, bowling, golf, etc. But in Jesus' day, there were none of these contests. So how were people entertained? They loved to listen to the Rabbi's debate one another. Intellectual volleys went back and forth, a verbal ping-pong match of words. So here's the context of Mark 12:38-40:

The crowd had gathered around Jesus in the temple courts. It was Tuesday before His death on Friday. Jesus had just won five debates (Mark 11:27-12:37). So after trouncing the religious hypocrites, Jesus says, Watch out for people who like these six things! And in Mark 12:38-40, Jesus gives us six telltale signs of a healthy "gospel centered" person. We'll cover three today and three tomorrow. It's incredible wisdom for a spiritually healthy heart:

1.The "Flowing Robe"

In Jesus' day, "flowing robes" were to attract attention. In our day, it's showing how cool and hip we can dress to impress people with our attire. The key here is the intent of the wearer of the clothes. The issue is, do I want to impress people or do I want to develop a hunger for God in people? Do I want attention or can I serve when no one is looking? So #1, a gospel centered heart can serve with joy regardless of the attention it receives.

2. The "Love to be Greeted"

In Jesus' day, some people loved to be greeted in the marketplace to be recognized and feel important. They loved to be "thanked" and "noticed" and greeted by others to feed their ego. They just had to be stroked to feel valued and needed. So discovery #2 is this; a gospel centered heart needs no recognition to be motivated or validated!

3.The "Best Seats in the Synagogue"

In Jesus' day, many people used their gifting and talent to show off. These were people who sought for a following to draw people to themselves, instead of pointing people to the unseen God. This person fed on being envied and admired. Whereas the "flowing robe" person wanted attention and the "marketplace greeter" needed recognition, this person wanted the credit for themselves. Discovery #3 is; a gospel centered heart can defer praise to others, and seeks no following for itself. What's the take-a-way from Jesus' warning in all of this?

To the extent that man is seen – God isn't!   Nuf Sed!

February 25
"No Attention Please"
Part II

"And for a show make lengthy prayers." (Mark 12:40)

Yesterday we discovered three things about gospel centered (healthy) people:
♦ They can serve with joy regardless of the attention they receive,
♦ They need no recognition to be motivated, and
♦ They defer praise to others instead of seeking a following for themselves.
Today, three other signs of a healthy heart (to really enjoy the journey):

4. The "Place of Honor at Banquets"
This warning was given by Jesus because some people actually felt entitled to sit next to the host at every feast. They felt they deserved to be treated better than others. They wanted to be elevated and have other people wait on (serve) them. They thought that leadership was about being on top with everyone serving them (instead of working your way to the bottom to support everyone else). They forgot that none of us are elite (above anyone else) because all of us are sinners and only made holy by the work of another (Jesus). Discovery #4 is: A gospel centered heart never feels cheated and needs no "thank yous" to serve the Lord!

5. The "Devourer of Widows' Houses"
In Jesus' day, some leaders took advantage of other people. They thought they deserved more; therefore, they shifted from a giver to a taker. Unethical behavior replaced trusted behavior. Merchandising replaced ministry. A generous heart was replaced by a greedy heart. Today we call them charlatans; Jesus called them "devourers of widows' houses." They forgot that givers are happier than takers! They teach us Discovery #5: A gospel centered heart is grateful and full of extreme generosity.

6. The "Show Off with Lengthy Prayers"
In Jesus' day, people would mask their shallowness. They covered up their lack of private prayer with public "lengthy prayers". They pretended to be spiritual and boasted of their piety. They didn't pray in secret, but loved to pray in public. Their main concern was "What do others think of me?" They just had to advertise their devotion! Discovery #6? A gospel centered heart never needs a public audience to participate in spiritual disciplines.

What's the take-a-way?
♦ **The greatest liberty in life is having nothing to prove and no one to impress! And,**
♦ **No one can lift up themselves and Jesus at the same time!**
Nuf Sed!

"Not Me"
Part I

"Then you will know the truth, and the truth will set you free. They answered him, 'We are Abraham's descendants and have never been slaves of anyone. How can you say that we shall be set free'?" (John 8:32,33).

Have you ever been confronted or questioned and respond with, "Who, me?" or "Not me" or "No way."? If so, you're on a boat with many passengers! There really is nothing new under the sun!

In John 8, Jesus has just spoken His great words of forgiveness to the woman caught in adultery. The Pharisees then tell Jesus, "Your testimony isn't valid" (V. 13) and "Who are you?" (V. 25). Jesus responds with that often quoted verse: "The truth will set you free" (V. 32). So why did Jesus say this and what does it mean to you and me today?

Jesus is addressing certain hearers who think they're okay, but Jesus knows they're really not okay. They have a false security and Jesus (out of love) bursts their bubble of self-confidence. With deep compassion, Jesus reveals great truth that protects us, and spares us much regret:

I. Jesus Reveals the Danger of Spiritual Pride!

When Jesus confronts the proud spirit of Jewish independence, His audience is insulted. The people were offended at the suggestion that freedom from the slavery of sin was something they didn't already possess. And, their false sense of confidence was pushing them away from Jesus instead of pulling them closer to Jesus. So much so, that the listeners said, "We are not illegitimate children" (V. 41). Or, we're not children of fornication, we're not like those Samaritans who descended from an unholy union between Jews and the heathen. Can you hear their response because of spiritual pride?

♦ "We are not guilty like those unspiritual Samaritans."
♦ "We are not bad on the inside like other people."
♦ "We are not in need of repentance and godly sorrow, No sir, not me!"

II. Jesus Reveals the Power of Biblical Truth!

The word "truth" (that frees us from ourselves) is powerful in V. 32. It refers to the Word of God and Jesus (who is the life and power behind the Word). Why does Jesus say that we must "know" the truth? Because truth exposes lies, and until the truth is known, people will live under the servitude (slavery) of sin: "The god of this age has blinded the minds of unbelievers, so that they cannot see the light of the gospel of the glory of Christ, who is the image of God" (II Cor. 4:4). Why is it so important that we be exposed to truth? Because truth has power; power to liberate us from a carnal nature that steals our peace, our joy and our future.

What's the take-a-way?
♦ **Humility gives us access to God who is truth** (and)
♦ **Truth leads us to justification (right standing) and sanctification (right living).** Nuf Sed!

"Not Me"
Part II

"We are Abraham's descendants and have never been slaves of anyone. How can you say that we shall be set free?" (John 8:33,34).

Yesterday we discovered the danger of spiritual pride and the power of Biblical truth. Today's good news is that the Lord has liberated us from sin's control.

III. Jesus Reveals the Slavery of Sin's Dominion!

I love how Jesus responds to our excuses and makes truth simple to understand in V.34:

♦ Whoever still practices sin is enslaved to sin and is out of control.

♦ Whoever refuses to admit their condition, will default to care more about their appearance than their true state of being.

Why does Jesus confront his audience with their sense of pride, comparison and false security? Because you cannot change what you do not confront and, what you do not confront will continue to control you! This is why Jesus loves to show us ourselves, tell us the truth about ourselves and confront our inconsistences! The good news is; Jesus alone can break the law of controlling sin in our nature! He alone can satisfy and transform our sinful hearts!

IV. Jesus Reveals the Wisdom of "Long-Term" Choices

"Now a slave has no permanent place in the family, but a son belongs to it forever" (V.35).

Jesus is making a comparison here that everyone can understand. The "slave has no permanent place" means: a servant who works in the house, works but is never the heir of the house. So, being an offspring of Abraham is great, but it is only a short term privilege. In other words, a servant with a job in a house is good, but it's only temporary! And, being a child of Abraham (a Jew) is good, but it's only temporary.

"But the Son abides forever" means that you can have a nice job and a nice house, but still be in bondage to sin! And, you can boast of a religious upbringing, but still be in bondage to sin! On the other hand, you can connect with God and abide with the Son forever! In other words, we can make a wisdom choice that affects us in two ways;

1. We can serve God now, and experience freedom from controlling sinful habits by the help of the Holy Spirit today, and,

2. When we die, we can experience the joy and reality of eternal life in the presence of Jesus.

And, here's what's so amazing about this text; at first, everyone is hostile to Jesus. But by V. 30, many put their faith in Him! Why? Because the truth has the power to liberate us and change our hearts where change is needed! The take-a-way?

Faith in God's Word (truth) has the power to change anything in our hearts that needs to change! Nuf Sed!

"The Curse and its Cancellation"

"Christ redeemed us from the curse of the law by becoming a curse for us, for it is written: cursed is everyone who is hung on a tree." (Galatians 3:13)

Have you ever felt unworthy, and that you just didn't measure up to God's expectation? Have you ever felt condemnation that comes from the accuser of the brethren? Have you ever wondered if every sin you've ever committed has really been forgiven? I have two words for you; you're normal!

Paul founded the churches in Galatia and believers had embraced the message of justification by faith. Then, false teachers invaded the church. They taught that salvation was by faith and by works. They were in danger of bringing believers into bondage to the Law of Moses. So, Paul wrote Galatians to magnify God's grace, and the freedom that results from knowing the truth. Paul gets his point across with three non-negotiable truths.

I. The Problem Of The Curse

What is the "curse of the law" in V. 13? It is the sentence of condemnation which the Law pronounced on us because of sin. It is you and me guilty and needing to face punishment as law-breakers. It is against us because none of us can fulfill its obligations! It means, we can't be good enough to keep all the Law, we are guilty before God and we cannot earn salvation.

II. The Pain Of The Curse

"The Scripture declares that the whole world is a prisoner of sin." (3:22) which means:

♦ "Shut up as a prisoner in solitary hopelessness."
♦ "Confined as a criminal in unescapable confinement."
♦ "In bondage to a debt that we could never repay."

In other words, without grace we are in bondage to sin, addicted to sinful behavior, cannot conquer our sinful nature and are unable to change our own hearts. Why is the Law so painful? Because it shows us where we fail, come up short and condemns our guilty conscience.

III. The Payment Of The Curse

"Christ redeemed us by becoming a curse for us" (V. 13). The dilemma is: God is holy and just and thereby must punish sin (and we've all sinned). The answer is: if God's holy law can be satisfied, then God can exercise mercy towards those who trust in the One who satisfies His law. The good news is: Jesus has "redeemed us from the curse of the Law" (V. 13) which means:

♦ He has bought us back (as a master bought a slave out of slavery).
♦ The word "redeemed" in the Greek means: "to buy a slave for the purpose of freeing them".

How did Jesus do this? By "being made a curse for us" (V. 13) which means: all of our sin was laid on Him, He paid the penalty I deserved and God has accepted His righteous sacrifice as our substitute for sin. The take-a-way?

God (In Christ) has removed every accusation against you!

Nuf Sed!

February 29
"Worry Free Living"

"Therefore I tell you, do not worry about your life, what you will eat or drink, or about your body, what you will wear" (Matthew 6:25).

It's no secret that many people crucify themselves between two thieves. What are the thieves? The regrets of the past and the worries of tomorrow! My questions are:

♦ Does it really bring glory to God to fret over things outside of your control?
♦ Is it any profit at all to mortgage your present by fretting over the future?
♦ Do you really want to forfeit your health by carrying burdens that God never intended for you to carry?

I. God Gives Us The Plan For Worry Free Living:

"Do not worry about your life, what you will eat or drink, or about your body, what you will wear" (V. 25). Jesus isn't telling us to be careless or slothful. He is telling us not to allow our temporal needs to dominate our thinking because that will cripple our effectiveness in life. When Jesus says, "Is not life more important than…" (V. 25), He is telling us something profound. He is saying; if God has given us life (or our breath) which is the greater miracle, won't He take care of the other needs which are the lesser of the two miracles? Life from God is so much more than food, and drink and clothes!

II. God Gives Us The Picture For Worry Free Living:

♦ Look at the **birds** (V. 26). In other words, the birds of the air are fed by the hand of God, have no anxiety over the future and sing, sing, sing.
♦ Look at **yourself** (V. 27). You cannot get taller by worrying over your height, neither can you increase your length of life by worrying about it.
♦ Look at the **lilies** (V. 28). Lilies never fret or worry about their beauty and yet they soon fade away. So how much more will God take care of His children?
♦ Look at the **unbeliever** (V. 32). Unbelievers have a reason to fret and worry, but you have a Heavenly Father who knows the needs of all His children!

III. God Gives Us The Promise For Worry Free Living:

"But seek first His Kingdom and His righteousness and all these things will be given to you as well" (V.33). This means, that if we put God's interests first in our hearts, He will see to it that we are provided with everything that's needed in the journey! So why increase your burdens today by borrowing trouble from tomorrow? It just makes no sense at all!!!

The take-a-way?
If we live to please God today, we can leave every tomorrow with Him as well.

Nuf Sed!

"The Joy of Godly Sorrow"
Part I

"Godly sorrow brings repentance that leads to salvation and leaves no regret, but worldly sorrow bring death" (II Corinthians 7:10).

Have you ever wondered what the difference is between "Godly Sorrow" and "The Sorrow of the World?" There is a huge difference, a difference that every spiritually healthy person has to know to enjoy the journey.

Paul founded the church in Corinth, had to return and make a painful visit when problems arose, sent Timothy to provide some leadership and then wrote II Corinthians. Paul's purpose was to encourage the church to forgive the members causing trouble, to remember the needs of the saints in Judea and to explain his authority as an apostle. It's a great story of how believers were restored through godly sorrow and genuine repentance.

I love how Paul's heart is revealed in our text. In V. 8, he tells us how he didn't enjoy the confrontation. Paul had proclaimed the truth, the truth went to work and many believers were convicted. In V. 9, Paul rejoices; not because members felt guilty and sorrowful, but because their sorrow led to repentance. In V. 10, Paul speaks of two kinds of sorrow:

I. The "Sorrow of the World" (V. 10)

This is sorrow that a person feels when they are guilty, get caught, and feel ashamed or disgraced. Paul said this sorrow "worketh death" in V. 10, which means its only concern is the sadness over being found out. In other words, this sorrow is only a sorrow because of the consequences being experienced. Why does this sorrow produce death? Because this sorrow results only in remorse, regrets, depression and defeat. It leads to resentment, anger, bitterness and more rebellion. It leaves us unchanged, void of a clear conscience and still bound by sin. It doesn't lead any higher than my own self-preoccupation and self-preservation.

II. "Godly Sorrow" (V. 10)

Godly sorrow is that sorrow in the heart because of the Holy Spirit's conviction. It is sorrow that comes from agreeing with God about my sin. It is sorrow because I know that my sin has offended God. And, what does this sorrow produce? Whereas "Worldly sorrow" is only sad because of the consequences of sin, Godly sorrow sees it's sin against God and thereby wants to leave it. Worldly sorrow is preoccupied with how I feel; Godly sorrow is preoccupied with how God feels. The sorrow of the world leads me nowhere but to myself. Godly sorrow leads me to the next step in the process of change. And, that step is repentance, where my heart is changed and my life is renewed by the awesome grace of God. What's the take-a-way from II Corinthians 7:10?

"Godly Sorrow" is a gift that protects us from self-destruction and leads to lasting change! Nuf Sed!

March 2
"The Joy of Godly Sorrow"
Part II

"Godly sorrow brings repentance" (II Corinthians 7:10).
"See what this godly sorrow has produced in you; what earnestness, what eagerness to clear your yourself" (V.11).

Yesterday we discovered the difference between "godly sorrow" and the "sorrow of the world". Now, look at the fruit (or result) of true godly sorrow. Paul said, "Godly sorrow brings repentance" (V. 10). So, what is repentance and why is it necessary to enjoy the journey?

Repentance is not remorse. Remorse is a human feeling that never graduates beyond guilt, regret and the consequences of human behavior. Repentance sets us free because it cries out to God for mercy and discovers the grace of God in daily living. Let's be clear:

♦   Repentance is the fruit (or result) of godly sorrow.
♦   Repentance is my response to godly sorrow.
♦   Repentance is a sorrow for sin with a desire to forsake it.
♦   Repentance is a change of mind and heart.
♦   Repentance results in a change of heart, revealed by a change in conduct.
♦   Repentance is always a change for the better. In fact, there is nothing negative (not one thing whatsoever) about repentance!

When Paul says that repentance "leaves no regret" (V. 10), he is saying a lot. In fact, he uses two words (V. 11) that speak to us all.

1.   The word "carefulness" means: haste, speed and eagerness. It means that the Corinthians went to work immediately to remove themselves from sin which had been allowed to exist.

2.   The word "clearing" means: apology for what had been done. It means that the Corinthians "cleared themselves' or accepted responsibility for their part so that God could do His part. The Corinthians teach us a great lesson here; to the extent that I agree with God about my sin, to that same extent I will experience the power of God that leads to change! Again I say, there is not one negative thing about genuine biblical repentance!

A Simple Illustration

1.   A traveler learns that he is on the wrong train (conviction).
2.   The traveler is disturbed at his discovery and annoyed (godly sorrow).
3.   He leaves the train at the first opportunity and boards the right train (repentance).
4.   Thus, his change of mind (and practical response) allows him to get where he is supposed to go). The take-a-way?

True Godly sorrow causes me to regret that I haven't felt sorry enough to repent of what I need God to change in my heart!

Nuf Sed!

March 3
"Contented Sheep"

"The Lord is my shepherd; I shall not be in want. He makes me lie down in green pastures, he leads me beside quiet waters" (Psalm 23:1,2).

We've all heard the 23 Psalm and millions have memorized it perfectly. Why? Because the message speaks to the heart; personally, specifically and individually from the heart of God. The contents of this great passage reveals two main realities:

♦ The watchful care of Jesus as our Great Shepherd, and,
♦ The resulting assurance that we have as one of His sheep. And Scripture gives us three resources why we are able to rest content as sheep of "His" pasture:

1. "The Lord is My Shepherd" (Is The Reason of Contentment)
From Carmel to Gilead, Hermon to Paran, and all over the green hills of Canaan, sheep covered the land. David then contemplates and discovers that as He cares for the four legged animals under his watch, so the Lord is caring for Him. As David takes great pain to provide for his sheep, so the Lord has taken great pain to care for David. And this produces contentment in the heart. David knows that the One who created the earth, numbered the stars and knows how many hairs are upon every head – is his personal Shepherd. And, this all wise Shepherd is caring and watchful of those who belong to Him. The sheep in Psalm 23 are you and me.

2. "I Shall Not Be In Want" (Is The Rest of Contentment)
This truth means that, Jesus as our Shepherd, will provide all that is needed for His own. "I shall not be in want" means that we will never lack His expert care or His divine provisions.
Remember: "do not want" would only cover our present. But "shall not be in want" covers all of your tomorrows. And this promise brings great rest to the soul.

3. "He Makes Me Lie Down In Green Pastures; He Leads me Beside Quiet Waters" (Are The Resources of Contentment)
♦ **"Lie Down"** means the Shepherd addresses our fears so we can be calm and free from agitation.
♦ **"Green Pastures"** means the Shepherd provides the food in His Word to sustain and grow the soul.
♦ **"Still Waters"** means the Shepherd will pour out refreshing streams of living water to satisfy our thirst.
With resources like these, is there any reason why we should live agitated and unrestful? With a Shepherd like this, is there any excuse to fret and stew over people and things outside of your control? With a Shepherd this caring, do we really need to pace the floor and worry? I hardly think so and I think you will

agree! The take-a-way?

It is an insult to God when we fail to trust Him with every detail of our lives, our needs and our future! Nuf Sed!

March 4
"Restored Sheep"

"He restores my soul" (Psalm 23:3).

If anybody knew what it meant to be "restored", it was David. He had committed adultery with Bathsheba, had her husband Uriah murdered, and covered it all up until he was confronted by Nathan. David had also restored many sheep as a shepherd. He knew from "hands on" experience, how important it was to help his sheep get back on their feet. And, God uses David to speak to us all about the ministry of restoration.

I. The Need For Restoration Is Clear!

Sheep in the field would often become "cast". This is a term used to describe a sheep that is turned over on its back, and can't get back up by itself. Without the shepherds help, the sheep will die. Why? Because gasses build up, cut off the blood circulation to the extremities and the cast sheep become easy prey to cougars and coyotes. This is why the shepherd agonizes when one sheep is missing. The vulnerable sheep become cast for three primary reasons:

♦ **Too much wool**: and when the fleece becomes too long, it gets heavy and hinders the sheep from moving around.

♦ **Too much weight**: and when the sheep become too fat, it is not agile on its feet. This causes the sheep to lose the center of gravity and easily fall over on its back.

♦ **Too much wandering**: and when the sheep thinks the grass is greener outside of the shepherd's care, it strays into dangerous territory where predators await.

II. The Reality Of Restoration Is Available!

The Hebrew word for "restore" in Psalm 23:3 is SHUWB which means:
To start again, to recover, to rescue, to release, to bring home, to pull in, to change, to refresh, to fetch back, to retrieve, to restore, to return as before.

The three New Testament Greek words for restore in Luke 19:8, Hebrews 13:19, and Galatians 6:1 mean: To give again, to reward, to restore, to repair, to frame up, to reverse the course, to reconstitute, to mend, to join together, to set back into place. For David, in Psalm 23:3, the Lord "restoring his soul" means:

1. The Lord revives my spirit again!
2. The Lord causes my life to return!
3. The Lord renews my strength!
4. The Lord excites me to new effort!
5. The Lord brings me back from wandering!
6. The Lord turns me in the right direction!
7. The Lord restores to purity what was stained by sin!

So, what's the take-a-way? Its unmistakable:

If you've wandered out of bounds, God has your rebound in store and God gets glory when you are restored to His intimate care! Nuf Sed!

"Guided Sheep"
Part I

"He guides me in paths of righteousness for His name's sake" (Psalm 23:3).

The opposite of guided is misguided, and I don't know of anyone on earth who wants to be misled down the wrong path. The good news for every believer is: God has promised to speak to, lead and direct those who want direction. For instance:

♦ "I will instruct you and teach you in the way you should go" (Psalm 32:8).
♦ "His sheep follow Him because they know His voice" (John 10:4).

So, when it comes to the voice of God and being led by God, what is most important? What should we consider? How can we tell if it's the Lord or not? The following guidelines from scripture have really helped me to enjoy the journey:

♦ **Remember first of all: it is God's intention that we know His will.**
"Therefore, do not be foolish, but understand what the Lord's will is" (Ephesians 5:17).
This means that we don't have to guess about important things, trust in fortune cookies, rely on palm readers or lean on someone else to prophesy over us. You can know God's will for yourself!

♦ **It is more important to hear what God is saying than for God to hear what you are saying!**
"So Eli told Samuel, go and lie down, and if He calls you, say, "Speak Lord, for your servant is listening" (I Samuel 3:9).
"The Lord came and stood there, calling as at the other times, "Samuel! Samuel!" Then Samuel said, "Speak, for your servant is listening" (V. 10).In other words, we need God's instruction more than He needs our instruction! Here are seven practical guidelines to discern and know the voice of God:

1.It is a familiar voice! When sheep hear the shepherd in the field, they know his voice. When you sense God's leading in your life, it will be comprehendible and understandable. And, the more we grow in the Lord (Hebrews 5:14) and exercise our spiritual senses, the more we can discern the Holy Spirit's leading.

2.It is a personal voice! God called Adam by name. Jesus called Zacchaeus and Bartimaeus by name! And Jesus knows your name as well. In other words, be careful of those who use the "God told me" card and tell you God's will for your life. Why be careful? Because people are human and fallible. People are imperfect and make mistakes. Remember this: someone may confirm something that God has been dealing with you about already. But never regulate your major life decisions to what someone else is telling you to do. A personal prophesy should be "confirming" in nature not "direction giving" in nature. The take-a-way?

Discovering God's will for your own life is much too important to entrust to anyone else besides your Great Shepherd! Nuf Sed!

March 6
"Guided Sheep"
Part II

"He guides me in paths of righteousness for His names sake" (Psalm 23:3).

Yesterday, we discovered how the voice of God is a **familiar** voice and a **personal** voice. Today we'll learn more about how the voice of God is discerned in your own personal life. Here are some practical guidelines to know the voice of God:

3. It is an inner voice! It's not normally an audible voice or handwriting on the wall. God's leading most likely will not be in a vision or at a burning bush experience. The temptation in Pentecost is to have a flare for the dramatic, extol the flamboyant and sensationalize. Yet, the voice of God is often an inner voice of impression or an inner voice of conviction, comfort, or calling. Remember Elijah in I Kings 19:11,12 – how he discovered the Lord (Not in the wind, earthquake or fire) but in a still small voice. The lesson? It doesn't have to be nonsense to be spiritual, weird to be anointed or flashy to be God!

4. It is a recurring voice! God called Samuel three times in I Samuel 3:3-8. This teaches me that I don't have to fret and worry about missing the will of God. It means, if we are open to do God's will, He will speak again and get our attention. This should encourage you greatly!

5. It is a voice in accord with the Word of God! Never ever forget this: God will never tell you to do something that is contrary to His Word. If it's something commanded or forbidden in Scripture, God will not change His mind. You have His will in your hands – in the Bible!

6. It is a voice associated to the voice of love and peace! The devil condemns, confuses and causes conflict. God is not the author of strife, division, deception, disorder or harm. God never intimidates or manipulates, but He leads us! And, if God is leading you, you will have peace ruling your heart (Colossians 3:15) and feel led not pressured.

7. It is a voice that results in the glory of God! "He guides me in paths of righteousness for His name's sake" (V.3) means:
♦ The end result of God's leading will be right living and lasting fruit (paths of righteousness).
♦ The end result of God speaking and leading will be that His name is extolled, magnified and lifted up in your life!

The take-a-way?
Discerning and obeying the voice of God's leading will bring glory to God and bear fruit that remains!

Nuf Sed!

March 7
"Fearless Sheep"

"Even though I walk through the valley of the shadow of death, I will fear no evil, for you are with me" (Psalm 23:4).

I will never forget how my wife, Laura, responded to her brain tumor, surgery, ICU and the last 22 days of life on earth. Night after night she asked me to play her a gospel song. She would sing along, whisper how she wanted to see Jesus, and never once expressed any fear. She lived without fear during the most fearful 22 days of her life. Her valley was her pathway to higher ground.

In Psalm 23:4, David refers to the season when sheep begin the long trip to the high country. The only way to the sheep's food supply (on the higher hills) was through the valleys around the mountains. The sheep would encounter rivers, snow, storms, sleet, hail, poisonous plants, drought and predators. But the purpose of every valley was to lead the sheep to higher ground. The purpose of every detour and delay was to ultimately get the sheep to a higher level. And, the truth is, valleys come to everyone who is climbing to "higher ground". And, the devil wants to use our valleys to sour us, and stop us from making progress. He wants us to become fearful instead of fearless. It's his intention that our valleys be our tombstone; it's God's intention that they be our stepping stone. And, here's what gives you great assurance - and takes away all fear:

1.There is Progress In The Journey!
The word "walk" in V. 4 denotes movement and steady advancement. It means the Shepherd is advancing you through every valley path. It means that God is leading you someplace, taking you somewhere, and making progress in ways you cannot see.

2.There Is Freshness In The Journey!
During the summertime journey, it gets hot, dry and wearisome. The sheep will experience intense thirst, and yet will make a discovery. What is it? It's great to live on the mountaintop, but the water flows in the valley. The sheep discover that God supplies what is needful and refreshment is at hand.

3.There Is Wholeness In The Journey!
Another reason the shepherd takes his flock to higher ground (through the valley) is this: the best meadows and richest food source is along the stream banks and in the low ravines. And, why are the sheep not afraid of evil? Two reasons:
- ♦ The shepherd never takes the flock where he has not already gone beforehand, and
- ♦ "Thou art with me" (V. 4, KJV) means the Shepherd goes with us every step of the way!!!

The take-a-way today?
"Through the valley" means, you don't stay, stop or sour in the valley – because God will finish what He started in you! Nuf Sed!

"Comforted Sheep"

"Your rod and your staff, they comfort me" (Psalm 23:4)

Just in case you ever feel that God doesn't comfort much anymore, remember:

♦ "You, O Lord, have helped me and **comforted** me" (Psalm 86:17).
♦ "I even I am He who **comforts** you" (Isaiah 51:12).
♦ "As a mother comforts her child, so will I **comfort** you" (Isaiah 66:13).
♦ "Blessed are those who mourn, for they will be **comforted**" (Matthew 5:4)
♦ "Who **comforts** us in all our troubles" (II Corinthians 1:4).

The word "comfort" comes from the Greek word PARAKLEO which means: To console, to come along side of, to advocate for, to be present, to encourage, to entreat and to call near. How does the Great Shepherd comfort His sheep today? David said, this ministry takes place in two ways. The shepherd in the Middle East carried two pieces of equipment to tend to his sheep:

♦ The Rod
The rod was a sapling carved to fit the shepherd's hand. It was an extension of the shepherd's hand and stands for power, strength and authority. It speaks to us of the Word of God. The shepherd's rod was used for three primary reasons:

1. For Protecting and Defending!
The shepherd used the rod to drive off predators and defend against coyotes, wolves and cougars. So the Word of God defends and protects you in the journey.

2. For Examining and Searching!
The shepherd used the rod to open the fleece, examine the skin and search for trouble. So the Word of God searches us and exposes what needs to be addressed in our hearts.

3. For Discipline and Correction!
The shepherd would hurl his club at misbehaving sheep who drifted or got too close to danger. So the Word of God will correct us and lead us in the way of righteousness.

♦ The Staff
The staff was a long slender stick with a hook on one end. It is a picture of compassion, concern, feeling and affection. The shepherd's staff was used for three primary reasons:

1. **For Guiding** the sheep down the path and through open gates. So the Holy Spirit leads us along and guides to the right paths to take.
2. **For Lifting** – the shepherd would use his staff to lift a sheep out of a dangerous place, back to higher ground. So, the Holy Spirit revives

us, refreshes us and lifts us to new levels.

3. **For Drawing** – the shepherd used his staff to draw his sheep unto himself. So, the Holy Spirit draws us back to Jesus when we are prone to go astray. What gives us great comfort today? The Word and the Spirit which protects, examines and corrects us; as well as guides, lifts and draws us. The take-a-way?

The Shepherd is never so near, than when He is tending your heart and mine!

Nuf Sed!

March 9
"Anointed Sheep"

"You prepare a table before me in the presence of my enemies. You anoint my head with oil; my cup overflows" (Psalm 23:5).

In this text, David speaks as a sheep of the Lord, but also as a shepherd. As a shepherd, David reflects on how he cares for his sheep. As a sheep, David reflects on how the Lord cares for you and me. This text is an awesome revelation of how much our Shepherd loves His sheep.

1.There Is The Table In The Journey!
The table is the high range where sheep feed in the summer. It is the table of meadows, vegetation and provision. For you it means that God has prepared a "feast of provision" on your journey of life. It means you can rest free from a worried mind, because the Lord has made provisions for the needs of every sheep. God is telling us clearly here that you can trust Him.

2.There Is The Timing In The Journey!
God tells us that the table is prepared "before" us. This reminds us that the Shepherd would always go beforehand to prepare the table meadows for his sheep. He would check for poisonous weeds, coyotes, wolves, bears, cougars and danger. David tells us here that the Lord sees ahead of us and already knows the things that take us by surprise. It's a message to our hearts that Jesus has the answers before we even ask the questions.

3.There Is The Tranquility In the Journey!
Where does God provide His table? In the presence of your enemies! Remember now, sheep had many enemies; there were predators, cliffs, droughts, storms, poisonous weeds, etc. And yet, the Shepherd provided the table in the midst of them all. What is David saying here? That even in the midst of his own enemies, he found a divine calmness and tranquility regardless.
- Saul became jealous and tried to kill David.
- Goliath intimidated Israel and tried to bring fear into David.
- Absalom was rebellious and thought he could overthrow his father, David.

Yet, in the midst of it all, David found that his external foes could not prevent him from internal peace. Why? Because he was anointed with oil till his cup overflowed! Shepherds in the field poured oil on the head of a sheep. This oil would protect the sheep from tormenting insects like bot flies, nasal flies, deer flies, ticks, mosquitos, gnats, bugs, etc. Without the oil, the sheep would be tormented, restless and even panic under distress. This anointing with oil had to be repeated over and over again. A fresh application was the only answer for the sheep.

So, are there any flies or insects bugging you at home, at work, at school, or somewhere else? Are you losing sleep because of something that torments your mind, thoughts and peace? If so, then allow the Lord to anoint you with fresh oil in His Presence. Come apart and allow His presence to fill your cup to overflow and "run over". The take-a-way?

Anointed sheep are peaceful sheep in the midst of a hectic, disordered and chaotic world!

Nuf Sed!

March 10
"Enduring Sheep"

"Surely goodness and love will follow me all the days of my life, and I will dwell in the house of the Lord forever" (Psalm 23:6).

You have to love how David ends Psalm 23! He has written from the standpoint of a sheep, and rehearsed how his Great Shepherd has been so faithful. David testifies that the Lord has made it possible to be a contented sheep, restored sheep, guided sheep, fearless sheep, comforted sheep, anointed sheep – and finally an enduring sheep! Why is David so grateful? Because he has experienced the Great Shepherd's faithfulness in every season of life. David concludes his Psalm with a revelation that makes it possible for every sheep of God's pasture to endure.

I. David Testifies Of God's Personal Care!
"Surely goodness and love (mercy) will follow me."
David testifies here that the Great Shepherd has been good and merciful every step of the way!

- In goodness; the Shepherd supplied all that was needed in every season.
- In mercy; the Shepherd loved the sheep even when it strayed, wandered and stumbled.
- In goodness; God never left David in need of anything.
- In mercy; God removed David's sin and didn't give him what he really deserved.

This causes David to rejoice from his heart! He looks back and can see it now! He remembers how God brought blessing out of brokenness, progress out of painfulness and healing out of hurt. He flat out rejoices in God's personal care, because the Shepherd was working all things together for good in ways that David could not see.

II. David Testifies of God's Steadfast Consistency!
"All the days of my life" means that God has a plan and that plan will be fulfilled in your life. As David reflects back, he concludes the following:
- His times really are in God's hands (Psalm 31:15) and,
- His steps really are ordered of the Lord (Psalm 37:23).
So much so, that David recollects his past and can find no fault with God in any season of life. David's words, "All the days of my life" mean that we have a guarantee that God will never fail in the future. And, this takes the worry out of living! "All the days" means that there is never one day in your life that God takes off or quits as your Shepherd!

III. David Testifies of God's Unwavering Commitment!
"I will dwell in the house of the Lord forever" doesn't mean a literal building. It means that David wants to dwell (or live) in such a way that God's favor will rest upon him. David wants to live close to the Shepherd! He wants to

dwell in the presence of God! He wants to remain in the place of intimacy and usefulness. He doesn't want to come and go or be a weekend Christian. He only wants to dwell (or stay real close) and never wander off from the table of the Lord. Don't you want to feel the same way David did? I do as well! The take-a-way?

The door is open for you and me to be as close to Jesus as we want to be!

Nuf Sed

March 11
"The Spirit of Prayer"

"And pray in the Spirit on all occasions with all kinds of prayers and requests. With this in mind, be alert and always keep on praying for all the saints" (Ephesians 6:18).

In Paul's prison epistles, he writes to the believers in Ephesus. Among other subjects, Paul tells us how to be strong in the Lord and stand firm. As Paul covers the armor of God in Ephesians 6, he ties it all together with the final piece of spiritual clothing. What is it? It is the spirit of prayer; how Pentecostal praying holds all the other armor in place. It's a revelation of how prayer is the spiritual air that soldiers breathe, the atmosphere of a winning army. Discover how clear Paul is when it comes to winning the battle in prayer.

I. The Pattern of Prayer
"Praying always with all prayer and supplication" (6:18, KJV). To "pray always" means to be ready to pray at all times. It means to live in a spirit of prayer, an attitude of prayer and to have a mind stayed upon God. It means to be careful not to be anywhere, with anyone, doing anything that would hinder prayer on that occasion. Why is this so important, not to be caught off-guard? Because you'll be alert in battle, steady in a crisis and continually aware of God's presence. You'll be sensitive to divine opportunities as well, and you'll also love perpetual communion with the Lord. The words "all prayer" refer to an attitude of fellowship with God in prayer; the words "all supplication" refer to prayer for specific needs. It's this kind of prayer that keeps us strong.

II. The Power of Prayer
"...In the Spirit" (V. 18). What does it mean to pray "in the Spirit"? It means:
♦   Under the influence of the Holy Spirit.
♦   With the assistance of the Holy Spirit.
♦   Energized by the Holy Spirit.
Paul is teaching us that the Holy Spirit is our helper in prayer and He enables us to pray beyond just our natural ability. Paul said in Romans 8:26; "The Spirit himself intercedes for us with groans that words cannot express". And, in V. 27: "The Spirit intercedes for the saints in accordance with God's will". This means that we can pray in our own language and pray in other tongues as well – all to be more effective in the place of prayer.

III. The Perseverance of Prayer
"With this in mind, be alert and always keep on praying" (V. 18). The word "always" means to persevere in prayer without giving up or giving in to discouragement. It means to be earnest, determined and committed to the ministry of prayer. And, what is Paul's one great prayer request? Not for release from prison or pain, but for boldness "to make known the mystery of

the gospel" (V. 19). Wow! Paul's one concern is that the gospel gets out and sets people free! So what does Paul's praying in prison teach us? It's pretty clear and it's our take-a-way:

⟨ **Your present field may be limited but you are not limited by your field!** ⟩

Hallelujah!

Nuf Sed!

"Undeserved and Unexpected"

"Jesus entered Jericho and was passing through. A man was there by the name of Zacchaeus; he was a chief tax collector and was wealthy" (Luke 19:1,2).

Jesus is passing through Jericho on His way to Jerusalem, to die and rise again. And, on this day, one man gets far more than he bargained for! The man is a tax collector and a supervisor of tax collectors. He is looked upon as a traitor to his own people. Why? Because he was collecting taxes of his own people and transmitting them to the Roman Government. The Jews hated being taxed by Rome. They were looking for a messiah to deliver them from the power of Rome. And, Zacchaeus was becoming wealthy by oppressing his own people. He was despised, rejected and avoided because of his tax occupation. He was an outcast to many, but loved by Jesus!

I. Zacchaeus Was Curious Inside!
"He wanted to see who Jesus was, but being a short man he could not because of the crowd. So he ran ahead and climbed a sycamore fig tree to see Him, since Jesus was coming that way" (V. 3,4).

Zacchaeus has a choice that we all have in life: allow his obstacles and pain to be his tombstone or his stepping stone. He could have said things like:
♦ "My past history of stealing tax money is too much for Jesus to forgive."
♦ "My past neglect of spiritual things is too much for Jesus to deal with."
♦ "My past pain, rejection and abuse is too much for Jesus to overcome."
Instead, he takes a chance and discovers what everyone discovers who comes to Jesus. He discovers that Jesus is not intimidated by your past, your pain, your fears or your reputation.

II. Zacchaeus Was Called By Name!
"When Jesus reached the spot, he looked up and said to him, Zacchaeus, come down immediately; I must stay at your house today" (V. 5).
♦ This was a **personal call** (Jesus called Zacchaeus by name). And, He knows you by name.
♦ This was an **affectionate call** (Jesus went to his house just to spend time with him).
♦ This was an **urgent call** (Jesus said "immediately" because He didn't want Zacchaeus to miss his opportunity).
♦ This was an **accepted call** (Zacchaeus humbled himself and came down the tree).

III. Zacchaeus Was Changed Forever!
"Look Lord, here and now I give half of my possessions to the poor" (V. 8). "Jesus said to him, today salvation has come to this house" (V. 9). Wow! Undeserved and unexpected grace comes to the heart and house of

Zacchaeus. How can this be? Because, no one is so good that they don't **need** the grace of God and no one is so bad that they can't **receive** the grace of God! The take-a-way?

The tug you feel in your heart to draw near to God will be met with open arms, extravagant grace and ready forgiveness!

Nuf Sed!

March 13
"Lord Have Mercy"
Part I

"But because of His great love for us, God, who is rich in **mercy**, made us alive with Christ even when we were dead in transgressions" (Ephesians 2:4). "He saved us, not because of righteous things we had done, but because of His **mercy**" (Titus 3:15). *Thank You Lord!*

I can still hear my grandmother saying this phrase, "Lord, have mercy". While I didn't know what she meant at the time, I would learn in 1974 what mercy is and how much I needed it. And, nothing has changed because all of us need mercy or we are forever lost!

The Hebrew word for mercy in the Old Testament is KHEH-SED which means "favor". The Greek word for mercy in the New Testament is EL-EH-EH-O which means, "to have pity on by Divine Grace". The question is, how can I have favor with God when God is holy and I am sinful? How can God's wrath against my sin be replaced by His mercy? What removes my guilt, condemnation and feelings of unworthiness? What allows me to have access to God and enjoy the power of a clean conscience? Today and tomorrow we'll look at the God of mercy.

I. The Container (Was The Ark)
In the Old Testament, God revealed His mercy to Israel with the Ark of the Covenant. This Ark was the throne of God and God said he would meet and commune with Israel there (Exodus 25:22). The Ark was a wooden box 4 feet long, 2 ½ feet wide and 2 ½ feet high; it was the presence chamber of God throughout the years the Tabernacle was in existence. It was the place where God's visible brightness (or Shekinah) was dwelling in the Holy of Holies. The other five pieces of furniture in the Tabernacle were empty pieces if the Ark was not there. Wherever Israel travelled, Israel was to carry the Ark (symbolic of the presence of God dwelling in their midst).

II. The Contents (Were A Witness Against Us)
In the Ark of the Covenant were three articles that speak to us all: "This Ark contained the gold jar of manna, Aaron's staff that had budded, and the stone tablets of the covenant" (Hebrews 9:4).

♦ **The Jar of Manna** (Exodus 16)
   This was a reminder to Israel of their grumbling and desire to go back to Egypt.
♦ **The Rod of Aaron That Budded** (Numbers 16)
   This was a reminder to Israel of Korah's rebellion. Aaron's rod reveals **failure in service for God**. We've all rebelled at times and failed to obey the promptings of the Holy Spirit.

♦ **The Broken Tablets** (Exodus 32)
This was the broken Law of God because of Israel's failure when they danced a jig to the golden calf. The broken Law reveals **failure in relationship with God.** And, we've all broken the Law of God and need a savior to pay the penalty we deserved. The take-a-way?
No one is so good that they do not need the mercy of God!

Nuf Sed!

"Lord Have Mercy"
Part II

"When Christ came as high priest of the good things that are already here, He went through the greater and more perfect tabernacle that is not man-made" (Hebrews 9:11).

Yesterday we learned how God instructed Israel to build the Ark of the Covenant and put three things in the box: The Jar of Manna, Aaron's Rod and The Broken Law. Why did God give this instruction? It's clear from Deuteronomy 31:26: "Take this Book of the Law and place it beside the Ark of the Covenant of the Lord your God; there it will remain as a witness against you". In other words, the Ark with the Broken Law was a witness of two things:

♦ The Law testified of the righteousness and holiness of God. And,
♦ The Law testified of the sins and backsliding of Israel, wrapped up in three words:

Word #1: Holiness which means God is holy in character and nature (and without fault).

Word #2: Sinfulness which means we've all been marred by sin and disturbed the personal relationship between God and ourselves.

Word #3: Wrath which means God's holiness and our sinfulness demands satisfaction of the violated law of God.

♦ To excuse sin means that God would cease to be God.
♦ To not punish sin means that God becomes unholy.
♦ So, to remedy the past, cover our sin and assure us of God's favor is the initiative of God. Why do we need His mercy? God shows us with the mercy seat that covered the Ark.

III. The Covering (Was The Mercy Seat)

1. The law condemned us because we broke the law when Adam sinned.
2. God said, place the mercy seat over the ark, so that I won't see the broken law.
3. Cover the ark with pure gold and place all of your past failures in the wooden box.
4. Tell the priest to enter into the Holy of Holies and sprinkle blood on the mercy seat.
5. The golden mercy seat (with blood) will reveal how the holiness of God is vindicated (or satisfied) by the death of Jesus.

"Whom God hath set forth to be a propitiation through faith in His blood to declare His righteousness for the remission of sins that are past" (Romans 3:25, KJV). The word **"propitiation"** in Romans 3:25 is the Greek word for **"mercy seat"**. It means **"covering"** with a sacrifice. The "**mercy seat**" with blood teaches us that God can pardon our sin because of the blood of another. Who is the other? It is Jesus (Hebrews 9:12).

♦ The word "propitiation" also comes from the Latin word PROBE which means "**near**".

♦ So, the word means "**to bring together, to bring near, to reconcile and to make favorable**".

It Means: We've been brought near to God, have had our sins atoned for ~~(covered)~~ and now have favor with God because of the blood sacrifice of another!!! The take-a-way?

If you are haunted by your past – put it in the box!

Nuf Sed!

Not covered! That would be something you had to continue doing like in OT. Instead, He took all our sin; past, present, future upon Himself by becoming the perfect sacrifice... the ONLY ONE that could remove our sin forever!

"No More Blame Game"
Part I

"As he went along, he saw a man blind from birth. His disciples asked him, Rabbi, who sinned, this man or his parents, that he was born blind?" (John 9:1,2).

At the end of John 8, Jesus' enemies were furious! Why? Because Jesus had just claimed to be God and said that He even existed before Abraham. The Jews then attempted to stone Jesus, but Jesus hid Himself and slipped through the crowd. As Jesus walked along, He was looking for an opportunity to reveal His Father's compassion and healing power. And, four very noticeable events take place in this encounter. We'll cover two today and two tomorrow.

THE AGONY OF PAINFUL EXPERIENCES. "He saw a man blind from birth" (V. 1). This man born blind from birth was sitting by the roadside begging. He is the only blind person in the gospels who is said to have been born blind. He is well known to the locals and regarded as a nuisance to the general public. He can contribute nothing to community life and nobody back home believes that he will ever be changed. Yet, Jesus saw this one person in a crowd of many! Jesus observed this man with a condition that no one could cure. He views this man as one who needed His gift of healing. Jesus knew what was going on inside of the man and, he knows what's going on inside of you as well! Maybe you are struggling and asking the question, "Why me Lord?" Just maybe, you are asking questions and answers don't seem to be at hand. If so, you're normal! That's right, you're normal!

THE ASKING OF THE DISCIPLES. When the disciples see Jesus they ask Him, "Rabbi, who sinned, this man or his parents, that he was born blind?" In other words, they ask Jesus, why did this happen? Or, whose fault is it; who's to blame? The disciples asked this because the popular doctrine of the day was, all suffering in this life has its origin in some particular sin in the person suffering, or it is the parent's fault that God has visited the son with this blindness and affliction.

The disciples here have fallen into the "blame game" and the "why game". Have you ever been tempted to do this? It's not that unusual you know. In Judges 6:13, Gideon asked, "Lord, if you are with us, then why are we in all this trouble?" And, in Job 8:6, Bildad said, "Job, if you were upright and pure, you wouldn't be going through all of this." In Acts 28:4, when Paul was bitten by a poisonous snake, the island people said, "He must be a murderer and God is getting vengeance."

So, how do we escape the blame game that leads to nowhere? By understanding Hebrews 5:8; "Although He was a son, He learned obedience from what He suffered." So who sinned, Jesus or His Father? Neither one, that's right, neither one!

The take-a-way?

God has made it possible to move beyond the asking stage and the blame game! (so don't miss tomorrow's read)   Nuf Sed!

"No More Blame Game"
Part II

"Neither this man nor his parents sinned, said Jesus, but this happened so that the work of God might be displayed in his life" (John 9:3).

The disciples had asked Jesus who was to blame for a man being born blind. Jesus responds here with a mild rebuke because unwholesome thinking will cripple us all. Poor thinking will ruin our days and not allow us to enjoy the journey. Notice the Lord's response.

I. THE ANSWER FROM JESUS. In response to the disciple's question Jesus says four things that are incredible wisdom to lead us forward. It's wisdom to enjoy the journey.

"Neither this man nor his parents sinned" (v. 3) means, in a broken world (fallen because of sin) things break. In an unpredictable world, we will never understand it all. In a world full of questions, we will never have all the answers. Jesus is saying here, that if you keep questioning and blaming you'll become angry, frustrated and depressed. You will then eventually slide into a victim mentality that feels cheated in life.

"This happened so that the work of God might be displayed in his life" (V. 3) means; God wants to reveal His nature in this opportunity. He wants to show us that He can heal the sick, meet the need and has the answer at hand.

"We must do the work of him who sent me" means; Jesus wants to demonstrate the mercy and nature of God's power. He must convey to the onlookers how much His father loves humanity. He wants you to know today – how much He cares for you when you don't have answers to your questions. He wants you to know, that you are the object of His attention.

"I am the light of the world" means; as the sun dispels darkness each day, so Jesus will push out all the works of darkness in your life. In other words, Jesus can lead you from questioning and blaming – to trusting and receiving fresh grace. If you're finding this hard to believe, notice:

II. THE ANOINTING FROM JESUS. "He spit on the ground, made some mud with the saliva, and put it on the man's eyes" (V.6). Why did Jesus cover the very eyes that He wanted to be able to see? Jesus wanted to evoke hope, expectation and faith in the man. He wanted the man to expect a cure from Jesus. He wants to teach us as well, that it's not the level of our faith; it's the object of our faith! Did you notice that the man obeyed Jesus, washed in the pool and received his sight? It's a lesson about how Jesus can change what needs to be changed – in our bodies or in our hearts. What's the take-a-way?

I can waste my time blaming and questioning God, or I can enjoy my days trusting His plan and receiving His grace. (the first choice makes me sour, the second choice makes me sweet.) Nuf Sed!

March 17
"I Saw the Lord"

"In the year that King Uzziah died, I saw the Lord seated on a throne, high and exalted, and the train of his robe filled the temple" (Isaiah 6:1).

Would you like to remain calm in a crisis? If you would, then this text is for you! Isaiah 6 has a specific setting to understand; King Uzziah had reigned for 52 years of prosperity, then suddenly dies. He had been victorious in war and successful in industry. Ominous clouds were gathering in the north and threatening Judah. So, Isaiah is facing some anxious days ahead, and takes his thoughts and enters the sanctuary. As he stands with the priests for the temple ceremonies, he looks through the open doors. Smoke from the incense altar was ascending before the veil of the temple. And, on this day, an encounter takes place that speaks to you and me.

I.Isaiah Sees Something!
On this ordinary day at work in the temple, Isaiah gets a glimpse of Jesus. What does Jesus look like?
♦ He is exalted – high and lifted up and reigning over everything that touches your life.
♦ He is holy – as angelic beings (seraphs) cover their faces and feet and bow down in reverence. This picture of Jesus goes to work in Isaiah's heart. It leads Isaiah (and us) to reverence, awe, humility and deeper spirituality. It speaks to us about drawing closer to the Lord with honor, respect and a deep sense of gratitude.

II.Isaiah Says Something!
"Woe is me, I cried, I am ruined. For I am a man of unclean lips" (V. 5).
When Isaiah sees Jesus, he is reduced with an overwhelming conviction of his own unworthiness. He is pierced in the heart because of his own sin. Compared with other people, he could pat himself on the back. But compared to Jesus, he comes up short and is melted, broken and humbled! He sees himself as he really is and knows it's time for change.

III.Isaiah Hears Something!
What does he hear after he prays "Woe is me"? Isaiah hears the Lord's response, "Your guilt is taken away and your sin atoned for" (V. 7). This means there is forgiveness and freedom for anyone who confesses their sin to God. This means we can have a new beginning, right standing with God and a clear conscience. It means, God has the power and ability to welcome you and treat you as if you've never sinned. Why? Because Jesus has taken your place at the cross and paid the debt you could not pay! In fact, after Isaiah's confession and repentance, the Lord re-commissioned him to service. In other words, God wasn't finished with Isaiah, and God is not finished with you! He has your rebound in store; all because of His grace and mercy. He waits for

you to humbly acknowledge His sacrifice to give you right standing with God! The take-a-way?

Your sin can never outweigh God's grace and God invites you now to be forgiven and cleansed as white as snow!   Nuf Sed!

"Malachi's Danger Signals"
Part I

"I have loved you, says the Lord, but you ask, how have you loved us?"
(Malachi 1:2)

It's no secret that a guardrail at the top of the cliff is better than a hospital at the bottom. Malachi's message is a guardrail to warn us and protect us from possible danger ahead. What's the setting and context?

Malachi is writing to the Jews who have returned from captivity. His message will prepare God's people for great ministry under Ezra and Nehemiah. But the ministry was in danger. Why?
♦ Worship had degenerated into mere routine (without passion).
♦ Spiritual leaders had become discouraged after the Temple rebuilding.
♦ People were becoming tired, weary, impatient and cynical.
And, God raises up Malachi to awaken us all by listing six "danger signals" to be aware of in the journey:

Signal #1. When Grace Turns Into Law (and we begin to question God's love towards us).
"Was not Esau Jacob's brother? The Lord says, yet I have loved Jacob." (1:2) Israel has become cynical and says to God, "How have you loved us?" The Lord says here, even though Jacob was a schemer, "Yet I still loved Jacob." In other words:
♦ Even though Jacob's name means "cheater and deceiver", and
♦ Even though Jacob was stubborn and full of himself, and
♦ Even though Jacob didn't deserve God's grace and patience,
Yet God loved Jacob (which means). "Quit thinking that I'm against you because of your past." And, "Quit questioning my love because of your hardships and detours." In other words, God loved undeserving Jacob and God loves you just the same!

Signal #2. When Joy Turns Into Weariness (and we offer God less than our best).
"You place defiled food on my altar." (V.7)
"I will accept no offerings from your hands." (V. 10)
"You say, what a burden." (V. 13)
What's the danger here? The danger is to become weary in well doing, let the fire go out in our hearts and offer God less than our best! The joy of ministry had turned to weariness and joylessness. Has joy departed from your heart?

Signal #3. When Busy Turns Into Too Busy (and we neglect those closest to us).
"The Lord no longer pays attention to your offerings. Why? Because you have

broken faith with the wife of your marriage covenant." (2:13,14)
What's Malachi's warning? Neglecting the sacredness of your marriage vow, ignoring the turmoil at home and refusing to put your spouse before anyone else. This is the heart of God expressed towards married couples, how much He desires us to be "one flesh", united and together in spirit. In fact, God tells us He doesn't regard our offerings or tears if we neglect those at home. Wow!

What's the take-a-way so far?
There is danger ahead when we cannot receive God's love for us, lose the joy of our salvation or ignore the turmoil behind closed doors!

Nuf Sed!

"Malachi's Danger Signals"
Part II

Yesterday we discovered the first three "danger signals" listed by Malachi. We learned how important it is:

♦ To experience the embrace of the love of God,
♦ To allow God to restore the joy of our salvation,
♦ To honor our marriage vows and love our spouse wholeheartedly.

Today? Three lies from the evil one that signal to us that it's time to allow God to bring change:

Signal #4. When Rest Turns Into Resentment (and we lose our merciful spirit).
"You have wearied the Lord with your words. How have we wearied him you ask? By saying, all who do evil are good in the eyes of the Lord, and He is pleased with them or where is the God of Justice?" (2:17) The people became discontent, sour and murmuring. Why? Three reasons:

♦ What the people thought should be quickly judged by God wasn't taking place.
♦ People were upset with how gracious and merciful God was being with other people.
♦ There was an impatient spirit because God wasn't working on their timetable. In fact, the people became toxic because they thought that God was being too kind and patient with people who didn't deserve it. They accused God of not being just, being too slow to act and complained that God was "too gracious." I wonder how many times I've done the same!

Signal #5. When Stewardship Turns Into Ownership (and we keep what we should give).
"Will a man rob God? Yet you rob me. But you ask, how do we rob you? In tithes and offerings." (3:8). What's the danger here? When we become tightfisted and act as owners instead of stewards! When we forget that givers are happier than takers! When we forget that:

♦ Giving Reflects the Nature of God! (John 3:16)
♦ Giving Brings Joy Beyond Measure! (Acts 20:35)
♦ Giving Proves God's Power in Your Life! (Malachi 3:8-10)
♦ Giving On Earth Bears Fruit for Eternity! (Matthew 6:20)
♦ Giving Is Sowing Seed for a Future Harvest! (II Corinthians 9:6)
♦ Giving Helps Meet the Needs of Other People! (Romans 12:13)

Signal #6. When Zeal Turns Into Indifference (and we think that our labor for the Lord is in vain).
"You have said harsh things against me, says the Lord. Yet you ask, what have we said against you? You have said, it is futile to serve God" (3:13,14). To me

this is the greatest of all the dangers. People were actually saying; "There is no profit in serving God." "Our labor is in vain", and "There's no difference between living for God or living for yourself." How foolish it is when we forget the difference between being enslaved by sin versus being captivated by Jesus.

So what's the answer to Malachi's warning and our dilemma? **"Return to me"** (3:7) and we will see the Lord, **"Rise with healing"** in His wings! The take-a-way from Malachi?
When we return to the Lord, we will be renewed in His presence beyond our wildest dreams!

Nuf Sed!

"Paul's Final Words"

"At my first defense, no one came to my support, but everyone deserted me. May it not be held against them" (II Timothy 4:16).

Many people have said, that it's not what you accomplish in the ministry and in life, but it's who you become in the process. And, who we become is determined largely by the choices that we make. In II Timothy 4, Paul reveals some choices that he made that allowed God to use him in a great way. They are insights that produce a healthy heart to last the long haul and enjoy the journey. They are in the Scriptures to speak to us individually. They are God's Word (His voice) to your heart as you process life in every season. What does God say to us through Paul's final letter to his beloved assistant Timothy? It's wisdom to enjoy the journey:

1.God Knows That We Can't Do Life Alone!
In V. 9, Paul tells Timothy to hurry up and visit him. In V. 11, Paul asks Timothy to bring Mark along as well. The example of Paul is clear; he never reached a place of not needing other people! He never isolated himself out of fear of being wounded. He just flat out loved to work and do life with other people. Paul teaches us that we can run faster alone, but farther together!

2. God Knows That Your Heart Will Be Broken!
Paul is so transparent in V 10 and 14 when he says that Demas deserted him and Alexander the metal worker did him much harm. Paul is telling Timothy, and us, some valuable lessons:
♦   People will let you down and disappoint you in life.
♦   Not everybody that you start with will you end with.
♦   It would be nice if everybody liked you, but it's not necessary for God to use you.

3.God Has An Escape Hatch From Internal Destruction!
"No one came to my support but everyone deserted me. May it not be held against them" (V. 16). What protected Paul from carrying an offended and wounded spirit? It was forgiveness! Forgiveness is the willingness not to hold you in debt to me. It frees us from living as the victims for other people's behaviors. It protects us from a toxic disposition!

4.God Reserves Some Secrets Only For Himself!
"I left Trophimus sick in Miletus" (V. 20) means, that a faithful worker got sick. Paul prayed for sure, but healing didn't come for Trophimus. Why are some healed and others are not? No one knows because some things are just plain unexplainable! They are secret things; things we must leave in the eternal chambers of heaven! And, lest you ever be tempted to worry, remember how Paul encouraged Timothy: "No one came to my support" (V. 16), "But the

Lord stood at my side and gave me strength" (V. 17). What's the take-a-way from Paul's final words?

- **When you cannot trace God's hand, you can always trust His heart, and,**
- **God is with you when no one else is!**

Nuf Sed!

"Escaping the Great Deception"
Part I

"When I surveyed all that my hands had done and what I had toiled to achieve, everything was meaningless, a chasing after the wind; nothing was gained under the sun" (Ecclesiastes 2:11).

Last week when I checked out of my Hampton Inn motel, I was offered a "Happy Bag". In the brown paper bag was a bottle of water, a muffin, a piece of fruit and a fruit bar. On the outside of the bag was a bright round sticker that said, "Happy Bag". Can happiness really be found in a paper bag? Solomon thought so, and he came up empty. Clearly, he tells us that there is a true and false happiness to be aware of in the journey. His two-part confession is an incredible story of how to avoid the "Great Deception". He shows us the reality of what life is truly all about:

I. Everybody Is Born With A Desire To Be Happy!
Solomon wants to be happy! In pursuit of happiness, he travels down the following four different roads:

♦ **Laughter Lane**
"Laughter, I said, is foolish. And what does pleasure accomplish?" (V.2) Solomon's desire leads him to surround himself with happy people. He thinks that if he can just hear a lot of jokes and funny people, he will be happy. If he can watch comedy central 24 hours a day, all will be well. And what does he discover? He discovers that jokes and comedians grow stale and do not satisfy. They distract for a moment, but have no power to satisfy inwardly. They come up short and cannot change the "happenings" of life. Laughter Lane just doesn't work, so Solomon tries…

♦ **Alcohol Avenue**
"I tried cheering myself with wine" (V. 3). Solomon now pulls out the bottle for happiness. What happens next? He ends up with an empty bottle and an empty life. Why? Because the same pressures that existed before he numbed his mind were there when the effects wore off. Solomon then tries…

♦ **Workaholic Highway**
"I undertook great projects; I built houses for myself and planted vineyards. I made gardens and parks" (V. 4). How did Solomon attempt to fill his emptiness? He became a workaholic! Yet great construction and architectural projects couldn't' satisfy his thirst for happiness. Solomon then tries…

♦ **Entertainment Expressway**
"I bought male and female slaves…I also owned more herds and flocks than anyone in Jerusalem…I amassed silver and gold…I acquired men

and women singers, and a harem as well" (V. 7,8). Solomon became the ultimate party animal! Wine, women, song, dance, sexual excitements and he still comes up empty. Why? It's the take-a-way from Part I:

Enjoyment in life without God is only entertainment, and you cannot live on entertainment and enjoy the journey!

Nuf Sed!

"Escaping the Great Deception"
Part II

"Yet when I surveyed all that my hands had done and what I had toiled to achieve, everything was meaningless, a chasing after the wind; nothing was gained under the sun" (Ecclesiastes 2:11).

What did Solomon's travel down "Pleasure Parkway" bring him? It brought him the realization of this one truth: **everybody can find true happiness – in God alone!** In other words, Solomon comes to a great conclusion in his pursuit of happiness. After every party (when the wine, women and song were over) he was empty. Why was he empty? He confesses in V. 11: **"Nothing was gained under the sun."** In other words, Solomon realizes the disconnect between life on earth and the life to come! That's why he says things like this: "Nothing was gained under the sun" (V. 11), "The fool walks in the darkness" (V. 14), "This too is meaningless" (V. 15), "In days to come both will be forgotten" (V. 16), and "I hated all the things I had toiled for" (V. 18).

What did Solomon discover at the end of his life? He discovered what God wants us all to discover: "For without him (God) who can eat or find **enjoyment**? (V. 25). "To the man who pleases him, God gives wisdom, knowledge and **happiness**, but to the sinner he gives the task of gathering and storing up wealth to hand it over to the one who pleases God" (V. 26).

Here is Solomon's Great Discovery: we all have eternity in our hearts because we've been made in the image of God. We all were created to have fellowship with God, and without this we are empty and unsatisfied. We all live with only one of two world views: we live with an **"under the sun"** world view (which Solomon tried) or, we live in a **"relationship with God"** world view.

In other words, if you live for what's under the sun without God, you lose in this life and in the life to come, but, if you live for God's purpose, you get to enjoy this life now and life eternally. In other words, if you try to live now without God, you lose now and you lose later! But if you live in relationship with God, you win now and you win later! The take-a-way wisdom discoveries from Ecclesiastes 2?

♦ **To live under the sun (or only for the immediate) is to destroy your purpose for existence.**
♦ **To live without God is to invite many idols to fill a void that only God can fill.**
♦ **To aspire for only what's under the sun will produce a hamster on the wheel that is never content, satisfied or restful!**

Nuf Sed!

"Restoring Wounded Soldiers"

"Brothers, if someone is caught in a sin, you who are spiritual should restore him gently. But watch yourself, or you also may be tempted" (Galatians 6:1).

I truly believe that our spirituality is revealed:
♦ By the degree of peace we have in a storm.
♦ By the way we forgive those who offend us.
♦ By our daily choices in spiritual disciplines.
♦ By our response to advice and correction.
♦ By how we deflect all glory to God, and praise to others.
♦ By how we respond to those who fall or fail!

Paul gives us some practical wisdom to restore a wounded soldier. He reminds us that:
I. The fallen are a part of kingdom living!
"If someone is caught in a sin" means: to be taken by surprise or unexpectedly. It refers to a believer who suddenly trips on the journey. It is a revelation that we all face temptation and no one is exempt from satan's prowl against us.
II. The fallen need our help, not our criticism!
"Restore him gently" means, to set the broken bone back in its proper place. This means that spiritual people seek to mend and heal, while carnal people seek to exploit and condemn. Paul is saying that we are responsible to care for the fallen as our own case at hand. In other words – help them as you yourself would want to be helped!
III. The fallen require three spiritual responses! Notice the language in the KJV:
♦ **Meekness Within:** "Restore in a spirit of meekness" (V.1) which refers to gentleness and humility. Whereas the proud condemn to elevate themselves, the humble are gentle because they're aware of their own fallibility.
♦ **Sincere Examination:** "Considering yourself" (V.1). The Greek word for "consider" here is SKOPEO where we get our word microscope from. It means "to look intensely at yourself when another falls".
♦ **Personal Responsibility:** "Let every man prove his own work" (V.4) and, "Bear his own responsibility" (V.5). Here Paul is telling us to test our own motives and attitude. He's telling us to: exercise compassion (as opposed to censorship), pull people up (instead of pushing them away), remember how God (in Christ) has forgiven us of all, and avoid shaming people (because God has forgiven and wants to restore and make whole).

The take-a-way?
The fallen need our help, so let's treat them the way that we ourselves would want to be treated! Nuf Sed!

"Do the Wicked Really Prosper?"
Part I

"For I envied the arrogant when I saw the prosperity of the wicked" (Psalm 73:3).

Have you ever felt like God was not being fair? Have you ever compared yourself to people around you? Have you ever been angry over perceived injustices? Have you ever wondered if the scales of life would balance out in the end? If you have, you're in good company.

Psalm 73 was written by Asaph, a man of intense worship and expressive feeling. He was a member of the tribe of Levi, wrote Psalms 50, 73-83 and was put in charge of the music that was performed at the Tent of Meeting before Solomon built the great temple in Jerusalem (I Chronicles 6:39). But, there was just one problem; Asaph couldn't enjoy the journey in life because he was looking at the people around him. He was feeling cheated in life as he viewed the ungodly prospering nearby. So God takes him on a journey and gives us a message that is loud and clear. It's a message that will change us from the inside out. Notice the process that produces great contentment:

I. Asaph Looks "Beside" Himself (V. 1-12)
"But as for me, my feet had almost slipped: I had nearly lost my foothold" (V. 2). Why was Asaph losing confidence in God and slipping in his faith? It was because he was focused on three things about the wicked around him:
♦   **Asaph was upset at their "prosperity"** (V. 3-5)
"I saw the prosperity of the wicked" (V. 3) means, they seem to "have no struggles" (V. 4), seem to be "free from the burdens common to man" (V.5), and seem to be exempt from the afflictions of the righteous.
♦   **Asaph was upset at their "pride"** (V. 6-9)
"Pride is their neckless" (V. 6), they have more than they could wish for (V. 7), they wouldn't give God the credit for what they had (V. 8), and they felt superior to those who lived for God (V. 9).
♦   **Asaph was upset at their "popularity"** (V. 10-12)
"Their people turn to them and drink up waters in abundance" (V. 10) which means the people drink it all in and ask for more. They even say, "Does God know who I am and what I've got?" How does Asaph respond to all that he sees nearby?
II. Asaph Looks "Inside" Himself (V.13-15)
And bemoans himself by saying, "Surely in vain have I kept my heart pure" (V. 13). In other words, Asaph feels like God is being unfair and overlooking some things! But wait…the story is about to change! The take-a-way?

Whenever you begin to feel that serving God is in vain, it's time to remember - there's always a bigger picture!   Nuf Sed!

March 25
"Do the Wicked Really Prosper?"
Part II

"I entered the sanctuary of God; then I understood their final destiny" (Psalm 73:17).

Asaph has just expressed his loss of confidence in God because the wicked were proud, prosperous and popular. He even feels like his service for God is in vain (as he watches the unbelievers party on). So, what do you do when you feel like your service for God might be in vain or unnoticed? You do what Asaph did; you get alone with God until the light comes on, and you settle it once and for all. And, what did God reveal about the wicked that Asaph had been envying?

III. Asaph Looks "Outside" Of Himself and Discovers: (V. 16-22)
♦ **The wicked stand in slippery places** (V. 18) or, They have no sure foundation, footing or anchor to hold onto!
♦ **The wicked are heading for destruction** (V. 18) or, Their end is in view of God and now in view to Asaph.
♦ **The wicked are prosperous, but it's only temporarily** (V. 19) Because, in a moment they can lose it all and become filled (consumed) with terror.
♦ **The wicked are living only a dream** (V. 20) Because, the unsaved person doesn't realize: their life is only an image (there is no reality to it). How is Asaph changed forever? He does what all of us must constantly do:

IV. Asaph Looks "Ahead" of Himself (V. 23-28)
After Asaph goes into the sanctuary and gets a glimpse of the end for the wicked (V. 17); he confesses his foolishness and ignorance (V. 22). He may not have prosperity, applause or a trouble-free life, but look what Asaph does have:

♦ He has the **presence** of God with him! "I am always with you" (V. 23).
♦ He has the **guidance** of the Lord! "You guide me with your counsel" (V. 24)
♦ He has a **future** with the Lord! "And afterward you will take me into glory" (V. 24)
♦ He has **strength** from God to do His will! "God is the strength of my heart" (V. 26)
♦ He has **fellowship** and **security** with God! "It is good to be near God; I have made the Sovereign Lord my refuge" (V. 28)

The take-a-way from Asaph?

- The prosperity of the wicked is not real prosperity from God's point of view.
- It's not what we accumulate down here, but what we send ahead that really matters.
- Whenever you are tempted to envy someone else, remember, there's always a bigger picture!

Nuf Sed!

"The God of Jacob"
Part I

"Then the man said, your name will no longer be Jacob, but Israel, because you have struggled with God and with men and have overcome" (Genesis 32:28)

I love those two words above, **"struggled"** and **"overcome"**. Why? Because Jacob illustrates how the flesh wars against the Spirit, and how God can subdue our hearts when we surrender all to Him. Truth be known, there is a little bit of Jacob in all of us!

In our context of Genesis 32, Jacob has arrived at his most critical moment in life. He is about to face Esau whom he had cheated out of his birthright years before. Jacob is now at Jabbok where he will experience a great spiritual change. At Jabbok, Jacob will see the Lord, become a broken man, die to his self-life, leave with a limp in his walk, and have his name changed from Jacob to Israel.

So, how does Jacob prevail with God? How does God change Jacob from the supplanter and deceiver to "Israel the Prince"? The process is highlighted in Ch. 32, and it speaks to your heart and mine today. Notice how God worked from His side and how Jacob cooperated with God:

1.Jacob Was Left "Alone" (V. 24)
The family and the servants were sent over the brook. Jacob's plan was to guard against a possible night attack from his brother. God had orchestrated this night "alone" to be a turning point in Jacob's life. Why is solitude not so bad at all? Hosea gives us a glimpse:
"I will lead her into the desert and speak tenderly to her." (Hosea 2:14)
It was in solitude that God worked with Jacob, Moses, David, and Elijah. And, it is alone that God will work with you and me as well! In fact:
- Solitude is a place of freedom (to hear those Divine Whispers from God).
- Solitude (in the dark nights of life) allows God to work an inner transformation.
- Solitude allows you to reorient your life so that your words can be few and full.
- Solitude teaches us how to overcome impulsiveness and hurriedness.

2. Jacob Was In "Pain" (V. 24)
While alone, the Lord appeared in the form of man to wrestle with Jacob. Jacob resisted because he felt he could still manage his life without God. Jacob's carnal self tried to resist what God wanted to deal with. And, what did God do? He dislocated Jacob's thigh to overcome Jacob's self-reliance and teach us all a lesson. It's the take-a-ways so far:
- **The sooner we surrender our will, the better off we'll be!**
- **The sooner we say yes to God; the less time we will waste!**
- **The sooner we relinquish control to the Lord, the quicker God can change what needs to be changed!** Nuf Sed!

"The God of Jacob"
Part II

"The Lord Almighty is with us; the God of Jacob is our fortress." (Psalm 46:7)
"Blessed is he whose help is the God of Jacob" (Psalm 146:5)

Why is it so encouraging that the God of Jacob is our help? Because if God could change Jacob, then this same God can change us! Yesterday, we discovered from Jacob's "night of change", that he was **left alone** and was **experiencing pain**! Today, see the completed process of change in Genesis 32:24-30.

3. Jacob Was Desperate (V. 26)

"I will not let you go unless you bless me." Before the dislocated thigh, Jacob said, "leave me alone." After the dislocated thigh (when Jacob was a broken man) he says, "I will not let you go." The discovery here is clear; we must cooperate with God and be earnest in our desire to be changed. In other words, persevering prayer is costly but the prize is worth the price! Jacob flat out refused to quit in his seeking – and thereby aligned himself with God in prayer. Prayer is alignment; it is placing ourselves, positioning ourselves and preparing ourselves to be changed by God.

4. Jacob Was Honest (V. 27)

"The man asked him, what is your name? Jacob, he answered." Didn't the Lord know his name? Of course he did! Then why did God ask him his name? To see if Jacob would admit he was Jacob and confess to all that his name stood for; sham, fraud, cheater and deceiver. So, Jacob then answered (confessed) to all that his name stood for. What's the lesson? That our effectiveness in prayer will never rise above our willingness to come transparent before the Lord.

5. Jacob Was Changed (V.28)

"Your name will no longer be Jacob, but Israel." Why the dramatic change? Because Jacob finally acknowledged his "Commander in Chief." "Israel" means "Prince with God" and his new name indicated Jacob's submission to God. And what happens when we surrender to God? "Then he blessed him there" (V. 29) which means:

♦ A sense of approval comes to Jacob's heart (and)
♦ A sense of awe and God's presence sweeps over his soul.

Jacob's scheming and worry over Esau turned into blessing beyond description. What's the take-a-way?

♦ **Heart change only comes to those poor in spirit!**
♦ **Deliverance from sin is birthed in humility!**
♦ **If we cover up, we dry up!**
♦ **Calvary only covers what we uncover!**

Nuf Sed!

March 28
"The Baptism in the Holy Spirit"

"All of them were filled with the Holy Spirit and began to speak in other tongues as the spirit enabled them" (Acts 2:4).

The Baptism in the Holy Spirit is a work of God within the believer where you are energized for service in God's kingdom. This baptism is clearly taught in Scripture:

1. In Acts 2:4 on the day of Pentecost.
2. In Acts 8:17, 18 Simon saw believers baptized in the Holy Spirit.
3. In Acts 9:17, Paul was baptized in the Holy Spirit.
4. In Acts 10:45,46 the Gentiles received the baptism at the house of Cornelius.
5. In Acts 19:9, while Paul was on his second missionary journey, some disciples in Ephesus were baptized in the Holy Spirit and spoke in other tongues.

On all five occasions (over a 30-year period) believers were baptized in the Holy Spirit and spoke in tongues as the Spirit flowed through them.

Is the Baptism in the Spirit for me?
♦ "I am going to send you what my Father has promised; but stay in the city **until** you have been clothed with power from on high" (Luke 24:49).
♦ "For John baptized with water, but in a few days **you will** be baptized with the Holy Spirit" (Acts 1:5).
♦ "And these signs **will accompany** those who believe; in my name they will drive out demons; they will speak in new tongues" (Mark 16:17).
♦ "Whoever believes in me as the Scripture has said, streams of living water **will** flow from within him. By this he meant the Spirit, whom those who believed in him were later to receive" (John 7:38,39).
♦ "When Paul placed his hands on them, the Holy Spirit came on **them**, and they spoke in tongues and prophesied" (Acts 19:7).
♦ "I would like **every one of you** to speak in tongues, but I would rather have you prophesy" (I Corinthians 14:5).
♦ "The promise is for you and your children and **for all** who are far off, for all whom the Lord our God will call" (Acts 10:39).
The take-a-ways?
♦ **The Baptism in the Holy Spirit gives the believer his or her "prayer language" to use daily in personal prayer.**
♦ **The Baptism in the Holy Spirit opens the door for God to use you (if He chooses) in the gift of tongues in a public service.**

Nuf Sed!

"The Gifts of the Spirit"

"Now about spiritual gifts brothers, I do not want you to be ignorant" (I Corinthians 12:1)

It's quite clear from Scripture that God wants us to be aware and alert concerning the gifts of the Holy Spirit. It's not gifts or fruit, and it's not fruit or gifts, it's both fruit and gifts of the Spirit that build healthy people and healthy churches. I Corinthians 12, 13 and 14 are God's instruction to us about the Gifts of the Holy Spirit. Three distinct lists give us understanding and wisdom.

I. The Support (or Leadership) Gifts - Ephesians 4:11
Apostles, Prophets, Evangelists, Pastors, Teachers.
♦ These five gifts are for establishing and the maturing of the local church. They are public in nature and have to do with the ministry of the Word of God.

II. The Service (or Motivational) Gifts – Romans 12:6-8
Mercy, Teaching, Prophecy, Giving, Exhortation, Serving, Administration
♦ These seven gifts are for service, outreach and function on a more personal basis.

III. The Sign (or Manifestation) Gifts – I Corinthians 12:7-10
Word of Wisdom, Faith, Prophecy, Word of Knowledge, Healing, Tongues, Discerning of Spirits, Miracles, Interpretation of Tongues.
♦ These nine supernatural manifestations are gifts for the edification and strengthening of the local church through individual members.
♦ They are supernatural and spontaneous in nature.

Scripture is very clear that the gifts of the Spirit are not natural endowments and are not for promoting human personalities. They are expressions of God's presence and power to bring glory to His name alone. They are God's way of getting His work done (to edify the entire church body). They are resident in the Holy Spirit (and manifested through believers). They are distributed according to God's will (not ours). And, they always point people to Jesus (never to ourselves). Many have asked, "What is the most important spiritual gift?" That's easy to answer – it's the one that's needed at the time! Some have wondered if the gifts of the Spirit were manifested in the Old Testament. Seven of the nine were in operation. The gift of tongues and the interpretation of tongues followed Pentecost in the New Testament. Below are Old Testament references:

1. **The Word of Wisdom** – Solomon (I Kings 4:29-32)
2. **The Word of Knowledge** – Elisha (II Kings 4:25-27)
3. **Discerning of Spirits** – Saul's servant (I Samuel 16:14-15)

4. **Faith** – Joshua (Joshua 10:12-14)
5. **Miracles** - Elijah (I Kings 17:17-24; 18:38)
6. **Healings** – Isaiah (II Kings 20:5)
7. **Prophecy** – Balaam (Numbers 23:24)

One thing is clear in Scripture; it is God's will that we be open to and make room for the Holy Spirit to do His work. We dare not grieve the Holy Spirit (Ephesians 4:30) for fear of abuse or disorder. The take-a-way?
God's will for us is to "Eagerly desire spiritual gifts" (I Corinthians 14:1)

Nuf Sed!

"Praying in the Spirit"

"But you dear friends, build yourselves up in your most holy faith and pray in the Holy Spirit" (Jude 20).

One of the glorious results of the Baptism in the Spirit is, we receive a new prayer language. This prayer language enables us to pray more effectively even when our natural mind doesn't know what to pray for. Below are five great benefits of praying in other tongues.

1.Praying In The Spirit Allows You To Speak Directly To God:
"For anyone who speaks in a tongue does not speak to men but to God. Indeed, no one understands him; he utters mysteries with his spirit" (I Corinthians 14:2)
- Praying in tongues in your private devotions is speaking directly to God.
- It is communicating in your born-again spirit with the Lord.
- You can pour out your heart to God from your innermost spirit in prayer.

2.Praying In The Spirit Edifies The Prayer:
"He who speaks in a tongue edifies himself, but he who prophesies edifies the church" (V. 4).
- This refers to tongues without an interpretation; it is personal and private prayer.
- Paul testified of this blessing in V.18, "I thank God that I speak in tongues."
- This praying edifies, strengthens, builds up and lifts your inner man.

3.Praying In The Spirit Enables You To Be A More Effective Intercessor:
"We do not know what we ought to pray for, but the Spirit himself intercedes for us with groans that words cannot express. And he who searches our hearts knows the mind of the Spirit, because the Spirit intercedes for the saints in accordance with God's will" (Romans 8:26,27) which means:
- The Holy Spirit is our helper in prayer!
- The Holy Spirit knows what the mind and the will of God is!
- The Holy Spirit enables us to pray effectively apart from our natural ability!

4.Praying In The Spirit Leads You To More Intimate Worship:
"I will sing with the Spirit" (I Corinthians 14:15).
- Praying in tongues will increase your desire to worship, to praise and to exalt the Lord.
- You'll be lifted to higher realms and deeper levels of personal worship.
- You'll overcome the thief and robber of your "pent up potential" to worship from your heart.

5.Praying In The Spirit Makes Jesus More Real To Your Heart:
"But I tell you the truth, it is for your good that I am going away. Unless I go away, the Counselor will not come to you; but if I go, I will send him to you" (John 16:7).

♦ Praying in the spirit increases our sensitivity and awareness of God's presence.

♦ This praying develops our consciousness of His ever present comfort and help.

What's the take-a-way?

The Holy Spirit is your greatest helper to a better prayer life.

Nuf Sed!

"Abuses Are Corrected in Corinth"

"So if the whole church comes together and everyone speaks in tongues, and some who do not understand or some unbelievers come in, will they not say that you are out of your mind?" (I Corinthians 14:23)

God has given us I Corinthians 14 in the Scriptures because Paul encountered problems in the church. The Corinthian Christians were being baptized in the Holy Spirit. They began to pray in tongues regularly in their daily devotions. But, when they came into the public worship service, their enthusiasm led to disorder and confusion. Their prayer language was authentic, but the manner they were using it was out of place. It became an exhibition instead of ministry. Paul reveals two aspects for the use of praying in the Spirit (in tongues) (I Corinthians 14:2,3).

♦ There is the use of tongues when in personal prayer and devotion (V. 2), and,

♦ There is the gift of tongues to be exercised publicly in a worship service (V. 3).

The Corinthians needed instruction for four reasons:

1.There was too much speaking in tongues out loud in the public gatherings.
> "So if the whole church comes together and everyone speaks in tongues…will they not say that you are out of your mind?" (I Corinthians 14:23)

♦ So, God says, limit the public gift of tongues to three in any single meeting:
> "If anyone speaks in a tongue, two or at the most three should speak, one at a time, and someone must interpret" (V. 27).

2.There was speaking in tongues in the assembly without the interpretation:
> "How will anyone know what you are saying? You will just be speaking into the air" (V. 9).

♦ So, God says, there must be an interpretation so that all may benefit (V. 28).

3. There were those who claimed that their inspiration was beyond criticism (V. 29-31).
♦ And God says that the utterance should be judged by those in the meeting:
> "The others should weigh carefully what is said" (V. 29).

4. There were some Corinthian Pentecostals who spoke in tongues out of order and claimed that they "could not help themselves." (V. 28, 30)

- God says not so, and, "The spirits of prophets are subject to the control of prophets" (V. 32). Which Means:
- The gift of tongues is not to interrupt.
- The gift of tongues is not disorderly (too soft that all can't hear or too loud that it scares).
- The gift of tongues is limited to three in any one service.
- The gift of tongues is to edify, encourage and comfort the believers gathered (V. 3).
- The gift of tongues will be a sign to the unbeliever (V. 22) and draw them.

The take-a-way?

If we fail to teach and allow the real because we fear the unreal, we limit the working of the Holy Spirit (and both fanaticism and formalism can kill).

Nuf Sed!

"The Triumphal Entry"
Part I

"The crowds that went ahead of him and those that followed shouted, 'Hosanna to the Son of David! Blessed is he who comes in the name of the Lord! Hosanna in the highest!'" (Matthew 21:9)

The Triumphal Entry took place at Passover season. Thousands of Jews would come to the Holy City (Jerusalem) to celebrate the deliverance of Israel from bondage in Egypt. It was at this time that Jesus would fulfill prophecy that the Lamb of God be crucified. And, Palm Sunday reveals three awesome things about Jesus.

I. Palm Sunday Reveals The "Passion" Of Jesus!

"As he approached Jerusalem and saw the city, he wept over it" (Luke 19:41). Jesus was on the road from Bethany to Bethpage, then on to Jerusalem. The road is 2,600 feet in elevation with a breath-taking view of Jerusalem. Jesus looks at the city and says, "If you, even you, had only known on this day what would bring you peace" (V. 42). So Jesus sees the people, draws near to them, and weeps for them. Why did Jesus weep tears on this day? Because Jesus was broken over the lost opportunity in Jerusalem. He knew that the people could have been saved, healed and restored. Yet, they missed the One who came to save them. The good news today is, Jesus sees you and draws near to minister to your heart at this present moment. He feels today what He felt then, and He passionately cares for you!

II. Palm Sunday Reveals The "Priority" Of Jesus!

"Jesus entered the Temple area and drove out all who were buying and selling there. He overturned the tables of the money changers and the benches of those selling doves" (Matthew 21:12). Why was Jesus so upset in the Temple? Because He wanted three things in His house:

Jesus wanted a pure heart (and removal of carnal distractions). The court of the Gentiles was turned into a place where people could exchange money and purchase sacrifices. But what began as a service for visitors had turned into a big business venture. Dealers were charging exorbitant prices and people couldn't compete with them. The missionary place turned into the market place as merchandising took the place of ministry.

Jesus wanted a praying heart (of alignment). "My house will be called a house of prayer" (V. 13). This is praying that gives evidence of our absolute dependence upon God. It is aligning ourselves with His purposes. It is preparing an atmosphere of prayer where we unite in worship, praise, petition, intercession and intimacy. There is still great power in the place of prayer!

Jesus wanted a powerful heart (where ministry takes place). "The blind and the lame came to Him at the Temple and He healed them" (V. 14). Palm Sunday teaches us that people should feel welcome in the house of God and people should find help in the house of God! The atmosphere of expectancy really is the breeding ground for miracles! The take-a-way thus far?

Palm Sunday is a revelation of just how much Jesus wants to meet you in the place of prayer!

Nuf Sed!

April 2
"The Triumphal Entry"
Part II

"Early in the morning, as he was on his way back to the city, he was hungry. Seeing a fig tree by the road, he went up to it but found nothing on it except leaves" (Matthew 21:18,19).

Yesterday we discovered that Palm Sunday reveals #1: The **Passion** of Jesus, and #2: The **Purity** of Jesus. Today, see how...

III. Palm Sunday Reveals the "Purpose" of Jesus!
When Jesus entered Jerusalem, the people responded with enthusiasm: "Hosanna in the highest" (V. 9). In fact, V. 10 records; "When Jesus entered Jerusalem, the whole city was stirred." So much so, that garments were taken off and spread before Jesus, palm branches were waved in a victory salute, and praise without reservation took place. Why all the fuss? Because, when a general was victorious on foreign soil, he was welcomed with an official parade. If he slew at least 5,000 of the enemy and gained new territory, he was honored with a procession. The general rode in a golden chariot while the priest would burn incense in his honor. The people would shout the general's name with joy. The general would display his captured enemies. It was a gala celebration in honor of the one who conquered and triumphed. In this context, Israel was praising because they believed that Jesus would defeat the Romans and set Israel free.

The Morning After: Jesus had lodged out in Bethany (v. 17) and the next morning He returned into town (V. 18). When He returns back into Jerusalem, He reveals to us that worship is more than shouting and dancing. He reveals that He has a purpose for us all!

The Morning Lesson: As Jesus entered back into the city, (V. 18) tells us that "He was hungry". And "Seeing a fig tree by the road, he went up to it but found nothing on it except leaves" (V. 19). Jesus then spoke and the fig tree withered away. The fig tree symbolized Israel as a nation. Just as the tree had leaves but no fruit, so Israel had a show of religion but no practical spirituality. Now, Jesus wasn't angry at the tree. He simply used the tree to teach us His purpose for you and me. What is it? Leaves usually indicate the presence of fruit, but this wasn't the case. In fact:

Leaves can make a lot of **noise** in the wind, but it's **fruit** that gives life to someone else. Leaves can make a lot of **motion** but it's **fruit** that sustains and strengthens people. Leaves can cover a lot of **space**, but it's **fruit** that reveals the true condition of the tree. So what's the take-a-way?

♦ **If my worshiping doesn't affect my walking, then it's not worship acceptable to God!** _fruitful_
♦ **Worship that doesn't end in obedience is a dead end street. (It's nothing but leaves).** Nuf Sed!

April 3
"The Alabaster Box"
Part I

"While he was in Bethany, reclining at the table in the home of a man known as Simon the Leper, a woman came with an alabaster jar of very expensive perfume, made of pure nard. She broke the jar and poured the perfume on his head" (Mark 14:3).

One of the first signs of a grace filled heart is generosity. Why? We simply want to give, because we realize how much God has given to us!

The setting before us reveals the spirit of true devotion. It takes place in Bethany (where Jesus raised Lazarus from the dead). It takes place in the house of Simon the Leper during a dinner meal. It takes place with Mary, the sister of Martha and Lazarus. Today, notice the box; tomorrow, notice the burial!

Inside of Mary's box was a vase, or flask, of perfume. These containers were made at Alabastrom in Egypt and used to contain costly ointments. They would be broken and the contents poured out. In Mary's box was ointment of spikenard or nard, a perfume made from the root of a plant found in India. While there was an inferior (cheaper) oil used for anointing, Mary's oil was used by kings and worth one year's wages. Her act was an act of extravagant love and true devotion.

What happens when Mary sacrifices her love to Jesus? "Those nearby rebuke her harshly" (V. 5). But Jesus said, "leave her alone" (V.6) and, "She did what she could" (V. 8). So, the selfish onlookers scold and growl. But Jesus commends and admires her. Remember; the hypocrites will always reveal themselves by the way they respond to the sacrifice of others! You'll hear things like, "Who do they think they are?" or, "Why do they have to give so much anyway?"

Now, why does Jesus tell us to remember Mary's giving forever?

1.Extravagant love is **individual** devotion! Mary didn't send a servant; she ministered to Jesus herself. Her giving was not out of custom, tradition or duty – but out of love. She didn't let someone else do her giving for her.

2.Extravagant love is **public** devotion! Mary anointed Jesus in the presence of the assembly. She wasn't afraid to express her love publicly. She gives in front of man, but not to be seen of man!

3.Extravagant love is **sacrificial** devotion! Mary could have poured out a flask of the cheaper oil but she didn't. Instead, she tangibly expresses that Jesus is worth (and deserving) of all she has.

4. Extravagant love is **remembered** devotion! When Jesus said Mary's gift would "be told in memory of her" (V. 9), He was saying that our giving is recorded and will never be forgotten. The take-a-way?

May what was said of Mary be said of you and me, "She has done what she could."

Nuf Sed!

"The Alabaster Box"
Part II

"She did what she could. She poured perfume on my body beforehand to prepare for my burial" (Mark 14:8).

Yesterday we saw how Mary broke her alabaster box and demonstrated a heart full of generosity. Today we see why she did what she did. What was her motive for what she did?

"She poured perfume on my body...**to prepare for my burial"** (V. 8).

Why did Mary pour out the perfume on Jesus? Because she had a sense that Jesus was soon to die. She had an awareness (a discernment) that the cross was just ahead. She wanted Jesus to know that she understood and that He was not alone in the mission. Remember: the Jews used spices and ointments to wrap up the bodies of their dead before burial. So, Mary teaches us some awesome lessons to live by:

1. If Mary and the disciples are going to minister to Jesus, they must do it now!
2. The poor will always be present on earth to help, but our privilege to serve Jesus will not always be available!
3. Now is the time to seize upon, because no one gets a second chance to do life over again.

This is why Jesus memorialized Mary's gift. He is teaching us that our faith is revealed by our sacrifice and that He remembers what you do in His Name.

FIVE ILLUSTRATIONS
1. There is a bird in South America called the "Me-Me" bird. The only sound it ever makes is "Me-Me-Me-Me".
2. Two bodies of water are fed by the same Jordan River; the Sea of Galilee and the Dead Sea. The Sea of Galilee is full of fish, life and vegetation. The Dead Sea is full of salt and is fruitless and lifeless. Why? Because Galilee gives what it receives while the Dead Sea keeps all that it gets.
3. When you go to the beach and squeeze sand in your hand; the tighter you squeeze, the smaller the handful of sand becomes.
4. The closed fist is the sign of a stingy person. The open hand is the sign of a giving person.
5. Look at a farmer with his hand in his pouch for seed to be sown. If he's going to sow seed, he has to let it go or it will never reproduce. If he keeps it to himself, nothing will ever grow.

WHY DO I WANT A MARY SPIRIT? Because:
Giving helps to destroy my envy and covetousness! (Philippians 2:13), enlarges my heart with God (Matthew 6:21), and proves God's power in my life! (Malachi 3:8-10) The take-a-way?

The more grateful we are for God's grace, the more generous we will be with our gifts!

Nuf Sed!

April 5
"The Lord's Supper"
Part I

"The Lord Jesus, on the night he was betrayed, took bread and when he had given thanks, he broke it and said, this is my body, which is for you; do this in remembrance of me" (I Cor.11:24).

"Then he took the cup, gave thanks and offered it to them, saying, drink from it, all of you. This is my blood of the covenant, which is poured out for many for the forgiveness of sins" (Matt. 26:28).

Two observations have saddened me during times of communion services. On one hand, I've seen it rushed through at the beginning of a service to get to the Word. On the other hand, I've seen it hurriedly tacked on at the end, to get out the door. When Jesus served communion with his disciples in his final hours, I believe it was meaningful, sobering and life-changing (not a tradition, duty or quick religious exercise).

Paul the apostle gives us incredible instruction for partaking of communion in a "worthy manner". He addresses the subject because abuses had crept into the church. In other words, what was intended by God to strengthen the body was weakening the body. What did Paul deal with?

1. A **Sour** Spirit; as division among believers was noticeable (V. 18).
2. A **Shallow** Spirit; as childlike behavior was present (V.19).
3. A **Selfish** Spirit; as some ate the food while others went hungry (V. 21).
4. A **Silly** Spirit; as some got drunk before communion (V. 21).
5. A **Self-Righteous** Spirit; as pride caused some to "despise" and look down upon others who were perceived as less spiritual than themselves (V. 22).

How sad it is to read about the Corinthians at the table of the Lord. Just imagine what Paul is addressing: cliques had developed where people ate and excluded others. Some brought food early to eat alone, and not be bothered with other people. Some were mixing the love feasts along with Holy Communion. Some were feasting and reveling and then simply rushing into the Lord's Supper. In short, the Corinthians had lost the sacredness of the Table of the Lord! The consequences were clear to Paul and his heart was broken over what was happening. Why?

♦ What God intended for power, turned into pollution.
♦ What God intended for healing, turned into heresy.
♦ What God intended for edification, turned into entertainment.
♦ What God intended for ministry, turned into a mess.

What's the take-a-way when the awe and conviction of communion degenerates into a loose and formal exercise?

We shame the Lord and His church, whenever we lose the sacredness and reverence of the Table!

Nuf Sed!

April 6
"The Lord's Supper"
Part II

"This do in remembrance of me" (I Corinthians 11:24).

Yesterday we learned why Paul addressed the Corinthian Church about communion. He faced a problem head on, because the church had turned the communion service into a carnival atmosphere. Today let's look at God's intention for a real, genuine, authentic communion service.

I. Communion Is A Time Of "Remembrance".
"This cup is the new covenant in my blood; do this...in remembrance of me" (V. 25).

Jesus would no longer be with his disciples, so he takes this last opportunity to remind them of all he would do for them. He uses bread and a cup to symbolize His broken body and sinless blood. The key word is "remembrance". It's a word that means: "To strike deep into the heart", and, "To leave a vivid impression". So, communion is a memorial (a continued reminder) to recall in a deep and vivid manner the passion, sacrifice, and cost to remove our sin. To "remember" means to allow the Holy Spirit to strike deep into our hearts the event of Christ's death for sin.

II. Communion Is A Time Of "Expectation"
"For whenever you eat this bread and drink this cup, you proclaim the Lord's death until he comes" (V.26).

So, we not only look back (in remembrance) but we look ahead in expectation of a glorious return. In other words, according to I Thessalonians 4:13-18, there will be:
- ♦ A resurrection (as the dead in Christ will rise first).
- ♦ A rapture (as we'll be caught up together in the clouds).
- ♦ A reunion (as we are reunited with loved ones and Jesus).

III. Communion Is A Time Of "Examination".
"A man ought to examine himself before he eats of the bread and drinks of the cup" (V. 28).

To "examine" means: to search your own heart, to judge your own sin, and to confess that sin to the Lord. It means that self-examination will prepare us for true spiritual communion with the Lord. And, if we fail to take this seriously, many will be weak, sick and die prematurely (V. 30).

IV. Communion Is A Time Of "Respect".
"When you come together to eat, wait for each other" (V. 33).
The word "wait" (tarry) means communion is a time to look beside you and see the Lord's body (His Church). It means to honor and respect those who sit nearby. So, communion is a time to demonstrate unity in the congregation,

a time to appreciate those nearby! The take-a-way from this text? **A real communion service will change our hearts for the better!**

Nuf Sed!

"The Place Called Calvary"
Part I

"When they came to the place called the skull, there they crucified him" (Luke 23:33).

Is there any more moving Scripture, or truth, in the Bible than Luke 23:33? It's hard for me to believe there is! Who was crucified? Jesus, the Son of God! Where was Jesus crucified? On a hill called "the skull" (or in Latin, Calvaria, where we get the name Calvary). Whose idea was the crucifixion? It was God's idea:

"It was the Lord's will to crush him and cause him to suffer...the Lord makes his life a guilt offering" (Isaiah 53:10).

So, Calvary was not an afterthought of God! Calvary was not a death planned solely by evil men! Calvary was conceived by God, the foreordained place where God's Son should die as the Savior of the world:

♦ "The lamb that was slain from the creation of the world" (Revelation 13:8).

♦ "He was chosen before the creation of the world, but was revealed in these last times for your sake" (I Peter 1:20).

♦ "For he chose us in him before the creation of the world to be holy and blameless in his sight" (Ephesians 1:4).

In other words, as the Old Testament Passover lamb was "foreordained" several days before it was killed (Exodus 12:3,6), so Christ our Passover Lamb was foreordained as well, "Promised before the beginning of time" (Titus 1:2).

The **good news** is, Calvary did not usher in a new religion some 2,000 years ago. Calvary is simply the historical manifestation of the eternal purpose of God. The **bad news** is, crucifixion was the most horrible of deaths. Just think of...

1...The pain from the spikes driven through Jesus' hands and feet.

2...The weight of His body pulling against the spikes as the cross was lifted.

3...The scourged back and His stick-beaten head.

4...The crown of thorns driven into His scalp.

5...The blood flowing down his face and lacerated back.

6...The hot sun, dry mouth, and nakedness.

7...The mocking, ridicule, spitting, punching, taunting and rejection.

Yet, Jesus paid it all as His family and friends looked on. Why? One reason:

"I live by faith in the Son of God, **who loved me and gave himself for me**" (Galatians 2:20).

Jesus endured the cross because He loves you like no one else will ever love you. The take-a-way? **You are highly valued by God, because of what it cost to obtain your salvation!** Nuf Sed!

"The Place Called Calvary"
Part II

"When they came to the place called the skull, there they crucified him" (Luke 22:33).

Yesterday we discovered that Calvary was not an afterthought of God! It was God's plan to rescue us from sin before the creation of the world! But what exactly happened when Jesus died at the place called Calvary? His **"O.A.T.H."** says it all:

I."O"ur Debt Was Paid In Full!
"God made him who had no sin to be sin for us, so that in him we might become the righteousness of God" (II Corinthians 5:21).

"So Christ was sacrificed once to take away the sins of many people" (Hebrews 9:28)

When it comes to our salvation, three truths must be understood: first, all of us have sinned and broken the Law of God. Second, none of us can pay for our own sin. Thirdly; God is holy, we are sinful and our iniquities have separated us from God. Genesis 3 describes our dilemma:

Our first parents sinned in the garden and became aware of their naked conscience. They tried to cover themselves with leaves, excuses and blame – to no avail. They couldn't pay their debt for sin, so God took the initiative. He took the skins from an animal sacrifice to cover the sinners. Why? To make provision for man's redemption. The innocent creature died to cover the guilty. This was a type (or shadow) of Jesus, where a sacrifice was made to cover the conscience of the guilty. It's a beautiful picture of Jesus, paying our debt in full.

II. "A" Door Was Opened Into God's Presence
"And he is the propitiation for our sins; and not for ours only, but also for the sins of the whole world" (I John 2:2, KJV).

The word "propitiation" means "mercy seat". It means, "to make favorable and bring near". It's a picture of Jesus at Calvary, solving the problem by removing the obstacle that kept us away from God. In other words, we can now "draw near" in intimate fellowship with the God of the universe.

"For through him we both have access to the Father by one Spirit" (Ephesians 2:18).

"We have confidence to enter the Most Holy Place by the blood of Jesus, by a new and living way opened for us through the curtain, that is, his body" (Hebrews 10:19).

Oh, beloved, is there any other place so sacred as the place called Calvary? The take-a-way?

Your debt has been paid and the door has been opened; so, there is no guilt or distance against you any longer!

Nuf Sed!

April 9
"The Place Called Calvary"
Part III

Yesterday we discovered that our debt has been paid and a door has been opened into God's presence. This took place at Calvary! What else took place on this hill far away?

III. "T"he Law Against Us Was Satisfied
"Since we have now been justified by his blood, how much more shall we be saved from God's wrath through him" (Romans 5:9).

Since God is holy and we are sinful, God demands just payment for sin. And, since none of us can satisfy God's just demand, we need a perfect sacrifice to turn His wrath away from us. The good news is, Christ at Calvary has met the demands of God's Law. In other words, (now get this):
♦ God can be gracious without being unjust (and)
♦ God can be just without being ungracious. In other words,
If God were not **just**, there would be no **demand** for His son to die. If God were not **loving**, there would be no **willingness** for His son to die. The good news is: "Christ redeemed us from the curse of the law by becoming a curse for us" (Galatians 3:13) which means; Jesus satisfied the Law that was against us when He was made a curse for us: and all of our sins were laid on him!

Now, since Christ's death is the basis for our righteousness, perfection and justification; we have obtained this glorious righteousness and a right standing with God. As Paul said; "Not having a righteousness of my own that comes from the Law, but that which is through faith in Christ" (Philippians 3:9).

IV. "H"elp Over Sin's Dominion Was Secured!

"He himself bore our sins in his body on the tree, so that we might die to sins and live for righteousness" (I Peter 2:24).

To **"live for righteousness"** (V. 24) means that when Jesus died;
♦ He broke sin's power to control us any longer! And,
♦ He offers us access into His strength to practice the following:
"Count yourselves dead to sin" (Romans 6:11)
"Do not let sin reign in your mortal body" (V. 12)
"For sin shall not be your master" (V. 14)

The take-a-way from Calvary? (It's really clear:)
Our debt was paid in full!
A door was opened into God's presence!
The Law against us was satisfied!
Help over sin's dominion was secured!

Nuf Sed!

April 10
"The Burial by Joseph
(God's Promises Kept)"
Part I

"Later, Joseph of Arimathea asked Pilate for the body of Jesus" (John 19:38).

The burial of Jesus is one of the most fascinating events recorded in Scripture. If you've ever doubted the wisdom, timing or ability of God to keep his promises, this text is for you. You will be amazed at how the Lord works out all the details in "His time", to see His plans fulfilled!

There were two groups of people involved in the burial of Jesus; Roman soldiers (V. 27-31) and Jewish believers (V. 38-42). The Roman soldiers were permitted by Pilate to set a guard at the tomb. The guard would put an official Roman seal on the stone in place. The two believers nearby were Nicodemus and Joseph of Arimathea. These two men were led by God to give Jesus a decent burial, in fulfillment of biblical prophecy (that they did not know about).

Notice how each gospel writer adds to the account:
♦ Matthew says that Joseph was a rich man and used his own tomb (Matthew 27:57-60).
♦ Mark says that Joseph was an honorable counselor (Mark 15:42-46).
♦ Luke says that Joseph was a good man (Luke 23:50-53).
♦ John says that Joseph worked with Nicodemus (John 19:38-42).

Look How God Keeps His Promises!
I. The Unbroken Bones Of Jesus
"When they came to Jesus…they did not break his legs" (John 19:31,33)

Why didn't the soldiers do what they were commanded to do? Because God always keeps His word: "Do not break any of the bones" (Exodus 12:46). "They must not…break any of its bones" (Numbers 9:12). "He protects all his bones, not one of them will be broken" (Psalm 34:20)

II. The Pierced Side Of Jesus
"One of the soldiers pierced Jesus' side with a spear" (John 19:34).

The Roman soldiers were not supposed to pierce the crucified. Soldiers would hasten the death of criminals by smashing their legs with iron mallets. This made it impossible for the victim to push up with their legs to get air for breathing. So, why the piercing of Jesus? Because God always keeps His Word: "They will look on me, the one they have pierced" (Zechariah 12:10).

III. The Grave of Jesus
"At the place where Jesus was crucified, there was a garden, and a new tomb" (John 19:41).

Bodies of the crucified were normally thrown into a trench field. Why was

Jesus buried in a rich man's new tomb with spices from Nicodemus? Because God is always true to his promises:

"He was assigned a grave with the wicked and with the rich in his death" (Isaiah 53:9).

The take-a-way from the bones, piercing and grave of Jesus?

God always keeps His word so He can be trusted with every area of your life!

Nuf Sed!

"The Burial by Joseph (God's Providence Revealed)"
Part II

"Taking Jesus' body, the two of them wrapped it, with the spices, in strips of linen. This was in accordance with Jewish burial custom" (John 19:40)

The burial of Jesus teaches us great lessons about the providence of God. It shows us how God is at work behind the scenes (and working in your life even when you cannot see him).

The **"who"** in this event were Joseph of Arimathea and Nicodemus. Joseph was a wealthy member of the Sanhedrin (the 71-member Jewish council). Nicodemus was a wealthy member of the Council as well. The **"what"** has to do with what they did. Joseph furnished the linen bandages and his own new tomb. Nicodemus provided the spices of myrrh and aloes. The **"how"** is what reveals the awesome providence of God.

The English word **"providence"** comes from two Latin words: **"pro"** which means **"before"** and **"video"** which means **"to see"**. The providence of God in your life means that God **"goes before you"** to prepare the path for you to walk in. And, that God **"sees ahead"** and orchestrates events that you know nothing about.

Remember: the providence of God had to be at work because the burial could not be a "decision of the moment".

1. Joseph had to prepare the garden tomb **beforehand.** ✓
2. Joseph had to prepare the tomb **near** where Jesus would die.
3. Joseph and Nicodemus would have to obtain a large quantity of spices beforehand, because the shops were **closed** for Passover.
4. The entire preparatory work had to be done with skill and **secrecy**.
5. The two men had to be hiding **nearby** when Jesus died (so that Joseph could appeal to Pilate and Nicodemus could guard the body until the official release of it).

Why did the plan have to be calculated (in the providence of God with the crucifixion)? Because there was only a three-hour window of opportunity. Jesus died at 3 pm on Friday. Friday was the preparation for the Sabbath day. The Jewish Sabbath began at 6 pm on Friday and went to 6 pm on Saturday.

In other words, these two disciples had only three hours to work because work was forbidden on the Sabbath. Jewish law also stated that no burial of the dead could take place on the Sabbath. Thus, if Jesus was not buried quickly (within these three hours) the Romans would have dumped His body on the trash heaps and prophecy would not have come true. The take-a-way?

♦ **God is always at work in unseen ways in your life!**
♦ **God is always one step ahead in ways unknown to us!**
♦ **God is always able to overrule what evil men have planned!**
♦ **God is always orchestrating your future, so you can rest well today!**

Nuf Sed!

April 12
"The Burial by Joseph
(God's Principles Rewarded)"
Part III

How was Joseph of Arimathea changed from a secret (fearful) disciple to one of courage and boldness? He was changed by what he experienced at the cross: The words of Jesus upon the cross, the darkness that came over the land, the earthquake that shook the ground, the veil that was supernaturally torn, and the prophesies that were fulfilled before his eyes.
Question: How can embracing the cross change you and me for the better? **(Notice the character change of Joseph of Arimathea)**

1. Joseph was a **responsible** man; he was a counselor, senator and member of the Sanhedrin (the ruling body of Israel).
2. Joseph was a **good** man; he was moral in his character and he was esteemed and responsible as a leader.
3. Joseph was a **spiritual** man; Mark records that Joseph was "waiting for the kingdom of God." (15:43), which means Joseph experienced a spiritual, life-changing blessing, and accepted God's reign and authority in his life as a believer.
4. Joseph was a **giving** man; he had not purchased the tomb for himself (since a wealthy man would not choose to be buried near a place of execution). He had purchased and prepared the tomb ahead of time out of love for the Savior to fulfill Bible prophecy.
5. Joseph was a **decisive** man; he "had not consented to their decision and action" (Luke 23:51). In other words, Joseph voted against the Sanhedrin's plan to condemn Jesus.
6. Joseph was a **courageous** man; he actually braved the threat of Pilate's reaction in asking for the body of Jesus. Joseph even risked the discipline of the Sanhedrin who could have expelled him (a harsh reaction from his friends). Yet, Joseph openly took the body of Jesus from the cross and openly cared for His body at the risk of great danger.
7. Joseph was a **faith-filled** man:
When Joseph heard Jesus' final words, he went to work by securing Jesus' body. He then wrapped the body in linen, covered it with spices and laid it in his own tomb. He even forfeited his participation in the Passover feast, because no one could do so after being defiled by touching a dead body.

Why was there such courage and dedication from this former "secret disciple"? Because Joseph believed that Jesus truly was the Lamb of God, would keep His word and rise again!

The take-a-way? **You can rest assured that your faith and dedication will be rewarded one day, because all believers will see the Risen Savior face to face!**

Nuf Sed!

"The Resurrection Prelude"
Part I

"From the sixth hour until the ninth hour darkness came over all the land" (Matthew 27:45).

When Jesus was crucified, He said **seven things**:
1. "Father, forgive them for they do not know what they are doing" (Luke 23:34).
2. "I tell you the truth, today you will be with me in paradise" (Luke 23:43).
3. "Dear woman, here is your son", and to the disciple, "Here is your mother" (John 19:26,27).
4. "My God, my God, why have you forsaken me?" (Mark 15:34)
5. "I am thirsty" (John 19:28).
6. "It is finished" (John 19:30).
7. "Father, into your hands I commit my spirit" (Luke 23:46).

When Jesus was dying on the cross, He said seven things, and God the Father did four things. What did the Father do and why?

♦**"From the sixth hour, until the ninth hour, darkness came over all the land."** (Matthew 27:45)

Calvary was a busy place! Soldiers blaspheming, elders scoffing, by-passers jeering, plus the priests, scribes and robbers reveling and repenting. Jesus had uttered His first three words between 9 am and noon. Then suddenly, the land becomes dark when you least expect it (high noon). Why the darkness? Because darkness in Scripture is a symbol of judgement (Isaiah 5:30, Joel 2:30, Amos 5:20; Zephaniah 1:15; Acts 2:30; II Peter 2:17; Revelation 6:12). Darkness meant the judgement of God upon our sin, the wrath of God against sin Jesus was carrying, and symbolic of the darkest day in human history when God's Son died for your sin and mine.

♦**"At that moment the curtain of the temple was torn in two from top to bottom"** (Matthew 27:51).

In the temple, the Holy of Holies was the presence chamber of God. Only once a year, on the Day of Atonement, could the high priest enter this chamber. The room outside of the Holy of Holies was called the Holy Place. Between the two rooms hung a thick curtain separating all humanity from the presence of God. When Jesus died, the Father supernaturally tore the curtain. Why? To let us know that God has accepted the substitutionary sacrifice on our behalf. The torn curtain is God telling us two things:

1. We all need a Savior and can only be saved through the righteous sacrifice of God's Son, and,
2. God is now inviting everyone to approach Him through the work of our Great High Priest -Jesus!

What's the take-a-way?
God has judged your sin (in Jesus), invites you now to have intimate fellowship with His son, and there is no more guilt or condemnation to those who are in Christ Jesus!

Nuf Sed!

April 14
"The Resurrection Prelude"
Part II

"The earth shook and the rocks split" (Matthew 27:51B).

Yesterday we looked at the first two supernatural acts of God when Jesus died. They were; 1. The darkness upon the earth at noon, and, 2. The curtain that was torn in the temple. Today, notice the third and fourth acts of God and what they mean to you and me.

♦ **"The earth shook and the rocks split"** (Matthew 27:51B).
The earth shaking and the rocks splitting was a clear message to those nearby. The earth shook because the weight of our sin was placed back on the earth's Creator. The earthquake was a thundering from heaven to pronounce the fatal blow to satan's kingdom. The earthquake was to strike awe and reverence in us. It was telling us all that God will have the last say. God was saying to us, **"at attention"**.

♦ **"The tombs broke open and the bodies of many holy people who had died were raised to life. They came out of the tombs, and after Jesus' resurrection they went into the holy city and appeared to many people"** (Matthew 27:52,53)
So, why the opened graves and the resurrected saints appearing to many people in Jerusalem?
1. The resurrection here is symbolic of Christ's **victory over death.**
2. The resurrection is prophetic of **all believers** who will **rise again** one day.
3. The resurrection proves that Jesus **is the Savior** as He said.
4. The resurrection of those who "appeared to many" in Jerusalem means that we **will know each other** in our glorified bodies (when we appear to each other).

The Father's Four Messages At Calvary?
♦ **Darkness** from noon to three means:
  Our sin was judged at Calvary and Jesus took what we deserved!
♦ The **torn veil** means:
  We are invited and welcome into the very presence of God for intimacy and fellowship!
♦ The **earthquake** means:
  Satan's kingdom has been dealt a fatal blow!
♦ **Resurrected saints** means:
  Death has been conquered and Jesus is alive!!!

The take-a-way?
Heaven will be wonderful and we will know each other as we are known!
Nuf Sed!

"The Resurrection of Jesus"
Part I

> "Always remember that Jesus Christ, a descendant of King David, was raised from the dead. This is the Good News I preach" (II Timothy 2:8 NLT).

That Christ rose from the dead is a historical fact.

- ♦ **David prophesied that Jesus would rise from the dead.** "You will not abandon me to the grave, nor will you let your Holy One see decay" (Psalm 16:10).
- ♦ **Jesus Himself said that He would rise from the dead.** "For as Jonah was three days and three nights in the belly of a huge fish, so the Son of Man will be three days, and three nights in the heart of the earth" (Matthew 12:40).
- ♦ **Peter's message was the resurrection.** "We are witnesses of everything…they killed him, but God raised him from the dead on the third day" (Acts 10:39;40).
- ♦ **Jesus Himself testified that He actually died and rose again.** "I am the Living One; I was dead, and behold, I am alive for ever and ever" (Revelation 1:18).
- ♦ **There were 13 separate sightings of Jesus after he was risen from the dead.**

1. Mary Magdalene
2. The women returning from the tomb
3. Peter
4. The disciples on the Emmaus Road
5. The apostles
6. Seven by the lake of Tiberius
7. James at Bethany
8. Paul near Damascus
9. Stephen near Jerusalem
10. Paul in the temple
11. 500 believers in Galilee
12. A multitude at His ascension
13. John on the Isle of Patmos

So, why did Paul tell Timothy in II Timothy 2:8, "Remember that Jesus Christ rose from the dead"?

Empty

I. The empty tomb reveals that your salvation is paid for!

"He was delivered over to death for our sins and was **raised to life** for our justification" (Romans 4:24) means: Jesus' death was a reality, a payment for our sin, and made it possible for God to forgive us. "Raised to life for our justification" means: Easter is the seal and guarantee that God's justice has been satisfied. The empty tomb means that God the Father has accepted the sacrifice of God the Son. In other words, if our substitute had not fully paid the debt for sin, Jesus would still be under the power of death. Easter proves that you can live free from all condemnation!

II. The empty tomb renews in us a "lively hope"!

"Praise be to the God and Father of our Lord Jesus Christ! In his great mercy, he has given us new birth into a living hope **through the resurrection of Jesus Christ** from the dead" (I Peter 1:3). After the crucifixion, Peter was downcast and despondent. But now Peter has "joy unspeakable" (I Peter 1:8). What transformed his heart? It was Easter Sunday, when God birthed in Peter a "lively hope". This phrase "lively hope" means; a hope that is certain, vibrant, substantial, powerful and sustaining in every season of life! It means that God gives every believer an internal assurance that we too will be resurrected one day!!! The take-a-way?

The resurrection of Jesus produces a shout that is beyond our earthly vocabulary!

Nuf Sed!

April 16
"The Resurrection of Jesus"
Part II

"Always remember that Jesus Christ, a descendant of King David, was raised from the dead. This is the Good News I preach" (II Timothy 2:8).

Yesterday we discovered the first two reasons why Paul told Timothy to never forget the resurrection: The empty tomb reveals that your salvation is paid for and the empty tomb renews in us a lively hope. Today, we have three more reasons to remember that Jesus rose from the dead.

III. The empty tomb means that you have a High Priest interceding for you!

"Christ Jesus who died, more than that, who was **raised to life**, is at the right hand of God and is also interceding for us" (Romans 8:34).

How does this truth encourage you? How does Easter lift your spirit? It's simple; Jesus lived on earth like you and me, and knew sorrow, heartache, pain and infirmity. So, when we embrace the empty tomb, and realize that Jesus has power over death, then we can believe that every issue smaller than death is under His control as well. In other words, if Jesus could deal with death victoriously (which is the greater issue), then surely He can intercede and give you grace for every other issue in your life. Easter means that Jesus is your faithful High Priest, and He is touched with the feelings of your infirmities. In fact; "the Spirit of him who raised Jesus from the dead…will also give life to your mortal bodies through His Spirit who lives in you" (Romans 8:11).

IV. The empty tomb removes all fear of dying!

"To live is Christ, and **to die is gain**" (Philippians 1:21).
"We are confident, I say, and would prefer to be away from the body and **at home with the Lord**" (II Corinthians 5:8).
"He died for us so that, whether we are awake or asleep, we may **live together with Him**" (I Thessalonians 5:10).

When your body dies, some "soul sleep" does not await you. You go home, you see Jesus, you have it far better and await your resurrected body at the Lord's return. Until you receive your new body, you live with Christ in heaven. Easter means that there is no fear of dying for the Christian!

V. The empty tomb reassures you of your own resurrection!

"If we have been united with Him like this in His death, we will certainly also be **united with Him** in His resurrection" (Romans 6:15).

Yes, friend, you will be in heaven with a brand-new body! You will be raised with a glorified (non-material) body! You will come out of the ground, will be seen again, and "and so we will be with the Lord forever" (I Thessalonians 4:17). Your body that is buried in weakness will be changed and raised in eternal glory.

The take-a-way?
While on earth we have a High Priest to help us; in death, we'll have a High Priest to receive us!

Nuf Sed!

April 17
"The Resurrection of Jesus"
Part III

"Always remember that Jesus Christ, a descendant of David, was raised from the dead. This is the Good News I preach" (II Timothy 2:8)

The past two days we've learned that the Empty Tomb:
♦ Reveals that your salvation is paid for!
♦ Renews in us a Lively Hope!
♦ Reminds us of our interceding High Priest!
♦ Removes all fear of dying!
♦ Reassures us of our own personal resurrection!

Today we'll look at the final two reasons why we should remember the resurrection:

VI. The empty tomb revives us to live a consecrated life!
"And if the Spirit of him who **raised Jesus from the dead** is living in you, he who raised Christ from the dead will also give life to your mortal bodies through his Spirit who lives in you" (Romans 8:11).

The Greek word for "give life" means; to quicken, to make alive, to renew, and, to cause to live. In other words, the same Spirit that raised Jesus from the dead (in His resurrection) is the same Spirit that revives us to live a consecrated life. How do we know this? Because Romans 8:11 is followed by 8:12 which says: "Therefore, brothers, we have an obligation – but it is not to the sinful nature, to live according to it." So, because the Holy Spirit raised Jesus from the dead:
♦ We are debtors to live for God's purposes.
♦ We are debtors to deny the sins of our flesh.
♦ We are debtors to break with everything that is questionable.

VII. The empty tomb rescues us from future judgement!
"And to wait for his Son from heaven, whom he **raised from the dead** – Jesus, who rescues us from the coming wrath" (I Thessalonians 1:10).

The wrath to come is the final judgment that awaits the unsaved person. Remember; there is only one bad thing about the resurrection. What is it? Not everyone will enjoy it! Notice the following:

"There will be a resurrection of both the righteous and the wicked" (Acts 24:15).

"Multitudes who sleep in the dust of the earth will awake; some to everlasting life, others to shame and everlasting contempt" (Daniel 12:2).

"For a time is coming when all who are in their graves will hear his voice and come out – those who have done good will rise to live, and those who have done evil will rise to be condemned" (John 5:28,29).

The take-a-way is undeniable:
"In a flash, in the twinkling of an eye, at the last trumpet…the dead will be raised imperishable, and we will be changed" (I Corinthians 15:52)

Nuf Sed!

"Easter Evening"
Part I

"On the evening of that first day of the week, when the disciples were together, with the doors locked for fear of the Jews, Jesus came and stood among them and said, "Peace be with you!" (John 20:19)

The news of Jesus' resurrection was spreading far and wide. The disciples didn't believe the first reports (Thomas even demanded proof of Jesus being alive). Yet, lives were being transformed as they encountered the risen Christ.

Jesus made five appearances on the day of His resurrection:
1. To Mary Magdalene (John 20:11-18)
2. To other women (Matthew 28:9 & 10)
3. To Peter (I Corinthians 15:5)
4. To the two Emmaus Road disciples (Luke 24:13-32)
5. To Jesus' disciples, minus Thomas (John 20:19-25)

Our text (John 20:19) is so revealing. It surrounds the day on which John, Peter and Mary Magdalene had visited the sepulcher early in the morning. It was now evening of the **"first day of the week"** (the evening of Jesus' resurrection). It was a Sunday evening meeting where great ministry took place. I notice three things:

I. The Volume of Fear Displayed
"The disciples were together, with the doors locked for fear" (V. 19).

Why were the disciples fearful? Because they dreaded the rulers who had put Jesus to death, they found themselves in a season of transition, and they were uncertain about their tomorrows. They had just experienced sorrow and disappointment, and unfulfilled expectations had left them wounded and deflated.

Fear is the feeling of anxiety caused by the presence of perceived danger, evil or pain. Fear is a feeling of apprehension which can lead to irrational action. Worry is the brother of fear. Worry is the committee meeting going on in your head. Worry is the opposite of faith. Worry is praying to yourself. Worry is accepting responsibility that God never intended for you to carry. In fact, fear and worry produce nothing good at all. They polarize our faith, paralyze our spiritual growth and presume that God is unaware of what's going on around us. Fear and worry are tools of the enemy to steal our joy and peace in the journey. What about your heart today?
- Is there anything that is causing fear in your heart?
- Are you facing any uncertainties like the Lord's disciples?
- Have unfulfilled expectations dented your spirit or caused anxious thoughts?

If so, then God has good news for you! The take-a-way?

- **The Lord is seldom early, but for sure He's never late! (and)**
- **He already knows what you need before you get where you're going!**

Nuf Sed!

April 19
"Easter Evening"
Part II

"Jesus came and stood among them and said, "Peace be with you!" (John 20:19)

II. The Visitation of Jesus
What did Jesus have to get through so that His disciples could see Him? Closed doors! Why did Jesus walk through the closed doors that were locked?
- ♦ To show us that our limitations (doors) do not limit Jesus.
- ♦ Our impossibilities(doors) do not intimidate Jesus.
- ♦ Our obstacles (doors) do not have to keep Jesus on the outside.
- ♦ Our fears and worries (doors) are not strong enough to keep Jesus from us.

I love what Jesus didn't do when He walked into the meeting:
- ♦ He didn't rebuke the disciples for hiding behind closed doors.
- ♦ He didn't resist them because of their fears.
- ♦ He didn't upbraid them because of any unbelief.
- ♦ He didn't scorn them for their insecurities and low spirits.

Why didn't Jesus jump all over them for their sadness while processing their disappointment? Because Jesus knew that we can believe in the resurrection and yet still struggle in this earthly environment! He knows that we all face things that will test us, surprise us, and weary us in some way!

How did Jesus enter the meeting place on Easter Evening? He came in **"on time"** when the disciples were in need. And, He came **"on through"** the doors that were closed to keep everyone out. Why this visitation? To show us something:
- ➤ Jesus knew where they were, and He knows where you are!
- ➤ Jesus knew what they needed; and He knows what you need!
- ➤ Jesus knew how to get through the door; and He can get through every door and objection that you might offer!

You might offer objections to Jesus (reasons why you can't enjoy the journey). But remember!
1. Doors are made to swing open!
2. Doors are made to travel through!
3. Doors are made to see Jesus enter in and bring change where change is needed!

In other words:
There is not one door in your life that can keep Jesus out if you want Him to come in. And, There is not one door in your life that Jesus can't get through to minister to your heart!!!

The take-a-way?

Your objections to progress are God's opportunity to prove Himself strong!

Nuf Sed!

"Easter Evening"
Part III

"After He said this, He showed them His hands and side. The disciples were overjoyed when they saw the Lord." (John 20:20)

The past two days we've seen how the disciples were full of fear on Easter Evening, and how Jesus walked through a locked door unexpectedly. Today, we'll see what Jesus did when He surprised the disciples huddled together in uncertainty.

III. The Victory on Sunday Evening.
What did Jesus do when He came into the meeting on Easter evening? He did three things that speak volumes to us. What He did should help us to enjoy the journey as we follow Him.

◆ Jesus ministered "peace".
"Peace be with you." (v.19)
"He showed them His hands and side." (v.20)
The very first thing Jesus said when He appeared to the disciples was something that brought a calming influence. Jesus said something: "Peace be with you". And Jesus did something: "He showed them His hands and side". The wounds displayed by Jesus were evidence of two things:
1. The price for your salvation has been paid! (and)
2. You indeed can have peace with God today!

In other words, at Calvary Jesus made it possible to have **peace with God**, and in the Easter meeting Jesus offered the **peace of God!** The Greek word for peace is Eirene and means: Order, harmony, security, quietness, and tranquility. So...
- ◆ Peace is tranquility and assurance in your inner man.
- ◆ Peace is security in the midst of life's unexplainables.
- ◆ Peace is that fruit of the Spirit which guards your heart (feelings) and your mind (thinking).

◆ Jesus ministered "pleasure." [Purpose]
"As the Father has sent me, I am sending you" (v.21)
These were the same disciples that forsook Jesus and fled and miserably failed Him. What's the message in this text? The message is, God is the God of the second chance! Also, that God has a job for you to do, can redeem your past failures, and isn't finished with you yet!

◆ Jesus ministered "power."
"He breathed on them and said, 'receive the Holy Spirit'" (v.22)
This was not the baptism in the Spirit, but a special anointing even before the

day of Pentecost. This was a pledge or guarantee of what was to soon follow. This is Jesus telling us that if we will evangelize as He says, He will empower us to do His will! The take-a-way?

You never need to fear if you follow in His steps!

Nuf Sed!

"Condemnation Gone for Good"
Part I

"For just as through the <u>disobedience</u> of the one man the many were made sinners, so also through the obedience of the one man the many will be made <u>righteous</u>" (Romans 5:19). *Thank You Lord!*

Have you ever wondered why so many believers are defeated by condemnation? Why is it that so many Christians feel unworthy to approach a Holy God? How can the accuser of the brethren be so effective when he has been dealt a fatal blow (at the cross and resurrection)?

Paul clearly outlines the basis and byproduct of our justification. This truth will truly set you free!

I. The Guilt of Sin Is Clear (Romans 5:12-14)

"Therefore, just as sin entered the world through one man, and death through sin, and in this way death came to all men, because all sinned" (Romans 5:12).

Here we learn that sin came into the world by one man, and death was the consequence. The whole world was condemned because of Adam's choice to disobey God. And, disobedience by Adam placed you and me under condemnation and death. Was it fair for God to condemn the whole world just because of one man's disobedience? It was not only fair, but it was wise, gracious and compassionate on God's part. Why? Because, by condemning the entire human race through one man (Adam), God was then able to save the human race through One Man (Jesus). In other words, we all are racially united to Adam and his deed affected us all. Because we were lost in Adam (our racial head) we can now be saved in Christ (the Head of the New Creation). So, here is the dilemma we found ourselves in before the Second Adam (Jesus), Romans 5:12-14:

Death came to us as the result of disobeying the Law of God. There was no law from Adam to Moses, yet people still died. The cause of death can only be one thing, the disobedience of Adam. When Adam sinned, he died, as well as all of his descendants (Genesis 5). This occurred when the Law had not yet been given. Thus, we must conclude that they died because of Adam's sin. That's the point of Romans 5:12: "Sin entered the world through one man, and death through sin, and in this way death came to all men, because all sinned".

This makes it clear that we don't die because of our own acts of sin, otherwise babies would not die. We die because we are united racially to Adam. The good news found on the next page is "for as in Adam all die, so in Christ all will be made alive" (I Corinthians 15:22).

The take-a-way?

The first step to enjoy the journey of life is to admit: We all were born sinners and we all need a Savior!

Nuf Sed!

"Condemnation Gone for Good"
Part II

"But the gift is not like the trespass. For if the many died by the trespass of the one man, how much more did God's grace and the gift that came by the grace of the one man, Jesus Christ, overflow to the many" (Romans 5:15)

When I read Romans 5, one word stands out above all others: It's the word **"GIFT"** (v.15,16,17)

II. The "Gift" reveals God's Provision (Romans 5:15-18)
The "gift" followed many trespasses and brought justification" (Romans 5:16).

In this context, Paul reveals and compares the difference between what Adam did and what Jesus did. The following three truths should bring joy to your heart and a shout of gratitude to your voice. Notice the three comparisons:

♦ Adam's Offense vs. Christ's Gift (v.15)
The word offense or trespass in (v.15) means "fall". It refers to the fall, or first sin of Adam. It is the fall from obedience to condemnation. The word "gift" refers to the free gift of life that Christ brings to us all. This word "gift" means: **"Without merit on our part, and bestowed on the undeserving"**. It means that we were spiritually dead under the dark and gloomy reign of death. But now, we are found in the abounding mercy of God. Oh, what a gift indeed!

♦ The Effect of Adam's Sin vs. The Effect of Christ's Obedience (vs.16)
"The gift followed many trespasses and brought justification" (v.16)

Paul makes it clear, here, that Adam's sin brought judgment and condemnation upon us all. When Adam sinned, he was declared unrighteous and condemned (so were we). But now in Christ, there is a change! Christ's work on Calvary has made us righteous, brought justification and set us free. In other words, Christ at Calvary has more than counterbalanced for the ills introduced by the sin of Adam. Praise God!

♦ The Reign of Adam vs. The Reign of Christ (v.17)
"How much more will those who receive God's abundant provision of Grace and of the gift of righteousness reign in life through the one man, Jesus Christ" (v.17).

Because of Adam's sin, death reigned. Yet, because of Christ's obedience, we now "reign in life" through Christ Jesus (which means:)

Our Spiritual reign is far greater than Adam's earthly reign because: We are free from all guilt, condemnation, and Adam's curse – because of the work of another (Jesus)!

The take-a-way?

We are so sinful that Jesus had to die for us, yet we are so loved He was glad to die for us!

Nuf Sed!

"Condemnation Gone for Good"
Part III

"The law was added so that the trespass might increase. But where sin increased, grace increased all the more". (Romans 5:20)

The past two days we've looked at two truths that Paul wanted to convey in Roman's 5: First, all of us are guilty of sin because of Adam, and secondly, Adam's sin has been addressed by God's great gift of Jesus. Today we'll discover the result of God's Grace and what it means in your life.

III. God's Great Grace Over Sin (v.20,21)

Paul tells us (in this text of Romans 5) why the law was given by God. It was given to show us that we couldn't keep it and that we needed grace. What exactly did the law accomplish? It revealed our sin, brought it to light and crowds us to Christ. In other words, the law made our sins increase in our sight, and, the law was effective in declaring us guilty. The good news is, "Where sin increased, grace increased all the more". (Romans 5:20) Which means:

- ◆ The pardoning mercy of the Gospel triumphs over sin!
- ◆ The super bounding Grace of God is sufficient for every sin of your past!
- ◆ When God declares you righteous, you are righteous and justified in His sight!

This all means something glorious:

- ◆ It has nothing to do with your feelings! (However punishing they may be at times)
- ◆ It has nothing to do with your sin! (However bad your acts of disobedience have been)
- ◆ It has nothing to do with your past! (However long you lived in sin)
- ◆ It has nothing to do with your efforts (However hard you work and labor to please God)

Why? Because it is God's grace that has cleared you, declared you righteous and made it possible to "reign in life" in Christ Jesus. In fact, God's grace was so effective in paying the debt that you could not pay, God has declared the following:

- ▪ "As far as the east is from the west, so far has he removed our transgressions from us" (Psalm 103:12)
- ▪ "I even I, am he who blots out your transgression, for my own sake, and remembers your sins no more" (Isaiah 43:25)
- ▪ "You will tread our sins under foot and hurl all our iniquities into the

depths of the sea" (Micah 7:19)
- "Their sins and lawless acts I will remember no more" (Hebrews 10:17)
- "Though your sins are like scarlet, they shall be as white as snow" (Isaiah 1:18)

The take-a-way?
If you ever feel unworthy, inferior or second class as a believer, you are declaring that the blood of Christ is not sufficient to satisfy God's justice and cover your sin!

Nuf Sed!

April 24
"The Crucified and Risen Life"
Part I

"For we know that our old self was crucified with Him so that the body of sin might be done away with, that we should no longer be slaves to sin." (Romans 6:6)

In Romans 5, we discovered that where sin abounds, grace much more abounds! Now in Romans 6, Paul unveils the crucified life that brings great joy and lasting fruit. Why is Paul so anxious for us to grasp the truth of Romans 6? Because, this truth leads us from death to life and power over sin. And, unless we know these truths, we can't put our faith in them and live them out day by day and enjoy the journey! What Paul reveals is all wrapped up in four words:

I. "Identify'"
"Count yourselves dead to sin but alive to God in Christ Jesus." (Romans 6:11)

Romans 6:1-4 was written so that we could identify with our crucified and risen Lord. This identification involves two pictures:

♦ Christ's Death:
"All of us who were baptized into Christ Jesus were baptized into His death." (v.3)

To be "baptized into Jesus' death" means, Jesus was put to death, died to sin, carried our sin to His cross and died to abolish sin's power to rule your life. It means that Jesus was crucified to destroy the ruling principle of sin to govern and control your life any longer. It means that Jesus slew sin's power to call the shots in your life.

♦ Christ's Resurrection:
"As Christ was raised from the dead through the glory of the Father, we too may live a new life." (v.4)

To **"live a new life"** means that Jesus came out of the tomb, left behind what sin did to Him and broke sin's power to enslave us. In fact, if the power of sin was not broken and God's justice was not satisfied, Jesus would still be in the grave. The resurrection means Jesus died to break sin's power to rule us and He rose again to enable us to walk in newness of life. This means that we (as believers) are the benefactors of His provision. We can be tempted to sin but cannot be forced to sin. Why? "The body of sin" (v.6) has been destroyed and we are free indeed. Tomorrow, it gets even better!

The take-a-way?
As Jesus left the grave behind, so you can leave behind whatever would keep you from reaching your fullest potential!   Nuf Sed!

"The Crucified and Risen Life"
Part II

"For we know that our old self was crucified with Him so that the body of sin might be done away with, that we should no longer be slaves to sin." (Romans 6:6)

Yesterday, we learned that Paul was anxious for us to receive the liberating truth of Romans 6. Why? Because it's truth that frees us from ourselves! And, Paul's great message is wrapped up in four words. We've covered word number one, which is **Identify**. Today, it gets better:

II. "Crucify"
"Our old self was **crucified** with Him." (v.6)

What does it mean, "our old self was **crucified**"? The term "old self" is used by Paul to describe our sinful, corrupt, and former nature before we were renewed. The term "crucified" means: slain, subdued, and rendered powerless to rule. In Galatians 2:20, Paul said, "I have been crucified with Christ" and "I live by faith in the Son of God." "I live by faith" means:
- I place confidence in what Jesus has done!
- I look to Him for all the strength that I need!
- I trust in Jesus to quicken me and assist me in resisting temptation!

III. "Mortify"
"If ye through the Spirit do mortify the deeds of the body, ye shall live." (Romans 8:13, KJV)

The word **"mortify"** means: to put to death, subdue, and destroy the strength of sin. It means to destroy the strength of sin as it attempts to master our bodies. It means that the "potential" for resisting sin is God's part, but the "practice" of resisting sin is our part. The only way that we "put to death" sin when it comes knocking at our hearts, is to trust in Jesus while we feed our spiritual man to be strong day after day. And, prayer, the word, humility, and obedience are choices to cooperate with God.

IV. "Glorify"
"For ye are bought with a price, therefore, **glorify** God in your body, and in your spirit, which are God's." (I Corinthians 6:20, KJV).

The following four questions help guide us to "glorify" God:
- Is what I am doing beneficial to me spiritually, mentally or physically? (I Corinthians 6:12)
- Is there anything that has me under its power? (6:12)
- Is what I am doing harmful or offending anyone else? (8:13)
- Does what I am doing glorify God? (10:31)

Paul is so clear about this when he says:
"So whatever you eat or drink or whatever you do, do it all **for the glory of God**." (I Cor. 10:31)

The take-a-way?
The more that we trust in what Jesus has done, the more joyfully we will submit and present ourselves to Him!

Nuf Sed!

April 26
"Victorious Christian Living"
Part I

"Those who live according to the sinful nature have their minds set on what that nature desires; but those who live in accordance with the Spirit have their minds set on what the Spirit desires." (Romans 8:5)

In Romans 7, Paul confessed his struggle between the flesh and the Spirit. Yet in Romans 8, there is a burst of praise from Paul's lips. Why? Because he has found the answer to his dilemma and spiritual struggle. He's fully aware of his sinful nature, but more fully aware of the resurrected Jesus. He's received a word from God that lifts the level of joyful living for us all. The word in Romans 8 is so clear, and reveals three absolutes:
- We get a new nature at the new birth! ✓
- We still have to deal with the old fallen nature of Adam!
- We have the Holy Spirit to help us overcome our propensities towards evil!

Romans 8 really is the Christian's Declaration of Independence! And, here are the reasons why:

I. You Have Power Over The "Voice" of Sin!
"Therefore, there is now no condemnation for those who are in Christ Jesus." (v.1)

Paul's song of victory begins with this declaration: The voice of accusation against you has been silenced! In other words, to those who are "in Christ Jesus", you are no longer under the penal consequences of sin, the Divine displeasure over sin, the judicial anger from sin, or the separation from God because of sin. In other words, even though you are not perfect (no one is on earth) sin has no legal right to condemn you any longer. Why? Because Jesus has removed God's wrath against you by placing that wrath upon Himself! What this means to you is:
- There is rest and liberty for every believer!
- There is joy and freedom for every Christian!
- There is no fear for anyone forgiven!
- There is a conscience that is relieved!

...all because your acquittal is sealed and your favor with God is assured. This means, God loves you on your best days, the same as on your worst days – because of Jesus. And, His opinion and approval of you is the only one that really matters!

So, when the voice of the accuser whispers in your ear, just remember what it means to be "in Christ Jesus"!

The take-a-way?
If you do not live "with" approval from God, you will live "for" approval from people which is a dangerous place to be.

Nuf Sed!

April 27
"Victorious Christian Living"
Part II

"Because through Christ Jesus the law of the Spirit of life set me free from the law of sin and death." (Romans 8:2)

In Romans 8:1, we learned that we have power over the "voice" of sin. In v.2, Paul tells us this:

II. You Have Power Over the "Law" of Sin!

What exactly is the "Law of sin and death"? The "Law of sin and death" is the rule and reign of sin that results in death. Because of what Jesus has done on the cross, two things now make it possible for you to enjoy the journey:

♦ You are free from the law (or energy and power of sin that leads to death).
♦ You can now live in the Spirit of life in Christ Jesus, which means: you live in the energy and power of the Holy Spirit (which produces life).

The "Law of the Spirit of life" (v.2) means:
1. The same spirit and energy and life in Jesus – is now the same spirit, energy, and life in you!
2. The same energy and power that raised Jesus from the dead – now fills believers to live the Christian life on earth!
3. The same energy and power that brought Jesus out of the grave – is now the same energy and power that brings us out of the tomb of sin and low living.

"Set me free from the law of sin" means:
You have been liberated to a new life of power, obedience and joy! You are now free to choose to please God in your words, thoughts, motives, attitudes, and actions. You have been risen indeed from death to life because of a new law "of the Spirit."

I Agree that:
We are all capable of sin. We all live in a corrupted body. We all possess the stain of sin in our nature. But, we have all been delivered from the "law of sin" that seeks to rule our members. How are we delivered? By the "law of the Spirit in Christ Jesus." This new power now rules over the old power. This new law now supersedes the old law that is bent towards sin! What's the take-a-way?
If you are "in Christ", the law of the Spirit has freed you from (and overpowered) the former law of sin!   Nuf Sed!

"Victorious Christian Living"
Part III

"For what the law was powerless to do in that is was weakened by the sinful nature, God did by sending his own Son in the likeness of sinful man to be a sin offering. And so he condemned sin in sinful man." (Romans 8:3)

In Romans 8:1,2, we discovered how God has given you power over the **"voice"** of sin and the **"Law"** of sin. In v.3, Paul makes it clear that:

III. You Have Power Over The "Rule" of Sin!

The key phrase here in v.3 is this: "**Condemned sin in sinful man**" (which means:) Before salvation we were in slavery to the rule and reign of sin (in bondage to an internal dictator that ruled the day). But at the cross, Jesus **"condemned sin"** for all who believe in Him (which means):

- ◆ Jesus abolished the ruling principle of sin to call the shots in your life (and)
- ◆ Jesus delivers those "**in Him**" from the ruling authority of sin.

In other words, sin still exists as an influence and can still hurl its fiery darts of the lust of the flesh, lust of the eyes and the pride of life! But, in Christ, we are dead to sin and have the freedom to obey the promptings of the Holy Spirit moment by moment.

IV. You Have Power Over The "Urge" of Sin!
"That the righteousness of the law might be fulfilled in us, who walk not after the flesh, but after the Spirit." (Romans 8:4, KJV)

- ▪ In v.1, there is no condemnation (guilt) before God!
- ▪ In v.2, the Spirit that raised Jesus now lives in you!
- ▪ In v.3, Jesus condemned sin in the flesh and delivered us from the rule of sin to control us!
- ▪ Now in v.4, we have the response to all of God's provision in the cross:

"Who walk not after the flesh, but after the Spirit" (which means:)
1. We feed the impulses and urges of the Holy Spirit!
2. We focus on the things that strengthen our Spiritual man!
3. We fill our minds with things that fuel our spirituality!
4. We forsake whatever would weaken and pollute our inward man!

The take-a-way?
The nature that we feed is the nature that will rule!   Nuf Sed!

April 29
"Victorious Christian Living"
Part IV

In light of all that God has provided in the death, resurrection, and ascension of Jesus, Paul shows us how to respond and cooperate with God. I love the words of Paul in the KJV:

"For to be carnally minded is death; but to be spiritually minded is life and peace." (Romans 8:6)

"They that are in the flesh cannot please God." (v.8)

"We are debtors, not to the flesh, to live after the flesh." (v.12)

"If ye live after the flesh, ye shall die." (v.13)

What does all of this mean? It means:

V. You Have Power Over The "Ways" of Sin!
In other words, here's how we respond to being born again and "quickened" by the Holy Spirit. We accept responsibility and understand that we are "debtors." The word "debtors" means: 1. to be obligated to, 2. to owe, 3. to be bound by duty. It means that we accept the responsibility of saying "NO" to every fleshly intrusion that comes our way.

And, we say "yes" to every opportunity to feed our spiritual man. This means that we choose to cooperate with God, which allows Him to destroy the strength of sin to dominate our lives. In other words, the more we submit to God in absolute surrender, the more that God's Spirit can break the power of sin in our lives. And, what is the reward for obedience to the will of God?

"Those who are led by the Spirit of God are sons of God." (Romans 8:14)
To be "led by the Spirit" means:
- ♦ To be carried along and supported in every season.
- ♦ To be guided along as God goes ahead of you.
- ♦ To be directed on a specific course.
- ♦ To be willingly led and ~~controlled~~ by the Holy Spirit.
  influenced

The verb for "Led by the Spirit" means: "willingly led". It refers to our cooperation. It means that the Holy Spirit will lead, guide, direct and ~~control~~ the person who is yielded to God's Spirit.

The Take-a-way from this text?

In light of what it cost to be free from sin's control, how can we not say "yes" to anything that God would ask of us?   Nuf Sed!

"Living Above Sin's Dominion"
Part I

"Do not offer the parts of your body to sin, as instruments of wickedness, but rather offer yourself to God, as those who have been brought from death to life; and offer the parts of your body to him as instruments of righteousness." (Romans 6:13)

It's no secret to any of us, that no one will live holy who doesn't cooperate with God in the process! The Scriptures cannot be any more clear than this:

- **"Present your bodies** a living sacrifice, holy, acceptable unto God, which is your reasonable service." (Romans 12:1, KJV)
- **"Yield yourselves** unto God, as those that are alive from the dead, and your members as instruments of righteousness unto God." (Romans 6:13 KJV)
- **"Submit yourselves** therefore to God. Resist the devil, and he will flee from you." (James 4:7, KJV)

So, what are the parts of our body that we can yield to God? What exactly do we present to God so that he can control and use and purify us from sin's influence?

"Seven Members We Can Yield to God"
(as instruments of righteousness)

1. My Mind:

"Whatever is true, whatever is noble, whatever is right, whatever is pure, whatever is lovely, whatever is admirable – if anything is excellent or praiseworthy, think about such things." (Philippians 4:8)

Here we begin with our thought life. This is you and me placing our thinking under God's control, because evil thoughts will germinate and grow. Remember: Every evil thought is sin in its embryo stage! And, sin that is destroyed in our minds will not become a part of our history. It really is possible to <u>meditate</u> on wholesome thoughts that result in life and peace.

"Take captive every thought to make it obedient to Christ." (II Corinthians 10:5)

2. My Eyes:

"The eye is the lamp of the body. If your eyes are good, your whole body will be full of light." (Matthew 6:22)

This is a powerful reminder: That seeds are planted in our hearts <u>through the "eye gate"</u>. And, what we gaze upon we become like over time. This is instruction and a warning from Jesus: To be on guard and be careful of what

Eye gate

we read, watch on T.V (or computer) and what we feed upon. David was wise when he said, "I will set before my eyes no vile thing" (Psalm 101:3).

The take-a-way?

We are what we eat in the physical and the spiritual realm!

Nuf Sed!

"Living Above Sin's Dominion"
Part II

"Offer the parts of your body to Him as **instruments of righteousness**."
(Romans 6:13)

Yesterday, we looked at our mind and our eyes; how important it really is to feed on wholesome things. Today, what else can we present to God so that He can work great grace in our hearts?

3. My Ears:
I consecrate my ears to the Lord, by not listening to garbage, language or conversations that poison and defile my heart. I turn a deaf ear to gossip, whispering, slander and evil reports. I set boundaries to avoid what does not build my spiritual man.
"A wicked man listens to evil lips; a liar pays attention to a malicious tongue." (Proverbs 17:4)

4. My Tongue:
I consecrate my influence over others through my speech unto the Lord. I ask the Lord to keep my heart pure, so that what flows out will edify (not defile) anybody. I ask the Lord to control my tongue and speak only what is in accordance with His will.
"May the words of my mouth be pleasing in your sight." (Psalm 19:14).

5. My Hands:
These I dedicate to God, to work, acquire, give and serve. I consecrate them to God so that all of my possessions and energy remains available to build His Kingdom. I reach one hand up to God and the other out to man – to bring the two together. I use my hands to serve the Lord!
"Whatever you did for one of the least of these brothers of mine, you did for me." (Matthew 25:40)

6. My Feet:
My feet represent my walk, ways, steps, and path that I travel. Consecrated to God, my feet take me where God wants me to go. They go where God is leading, with the companions God has chosen for me, and avoid the places that would cause me to stumble.
"Make level paths for your feet and take only ways that are firm. Do not swerve to the right or the left; keep your foot from evil." (Proverbs 4:26,27)

7. My Heart:
The center of my physical man is the heart, the place where all blood flows in and out. So my heart in the spiritual realm is the center (seat) of all affections and desires. If my heart is tainted and stained, the streams that flow out will

be stained as well. So today I choose to humble myself before God and refuse to harbor anything that will interfere with my intimacy with Jesus.

"Above all else, guard your heart, for it is the wellspring of life." (Proverbs 4:23)

The take-a-way?

God will bless and use what I present to Him; God will not use what I refuse to give Him!

Nuf Sed!

"Elijah's Meltdown"
Part I

"Elijah was afraid and ran for his life…he came to a broom tree, sat down under it and prayed that he might die. 'I have had enough, Lord,' he said, 'Take my life.'" (I Kings 19:3,4)

You are normal! That's right, normal! You heard me right, you are normal, normal, normal! If you've ever had low resources, encountered criticism, had delays to answered prayer, or wondered about your next steps – you're normal, and a little bit like Elijah. Who is this man named Elijah?

Seven wicked kings led up to Elijah's appearance. They were Jeroboam, Nadab, Bassha, Elah, Zimri, Omri, and the worst of all, Ahab:

"Ahab did more to provoke the Lord, the God of Israel, to anger than did all the kings of Israel before him." (I Kings 16:33)

Ahab (and wife) lived in pagan worship and built an altar and a temple for Baal in Samaria. And, in the worst of times, God raised up a man from Tishbe (in the mountains of Gilead) named Elijah. What does God call Elijah to do? He calls him to pronounce the judgment of God through a drought. Having announced the drought, God then used Elijah to teach us some marvelous lessons to be spiritually strong and enjoy the journey. The lessons are both powerful and practical in your daily life!

1. In Cherith, Elijah discovers that obedience to God is rewarded with provisions from God! (I Kings 17:1-7)
The Lord told Elijah to turn eastward, hide in the Kerith Ravine, and water would be provided to drink, as well as ravens would deliver food everyday (v.3,4). "So he did what the Lord had told him" (v.5). And guess what? "The ravens brought him bread and meat in the morning and in the evening" (v.6). What's the discovery? That <u>God sent</u> – as Elijah **went!** Why? Because Elijah **trusted** the Lord and **obeyed** the Lord. And, during the three and a half years of drought, Elijah always had food and water. What's the message to your heart today? Your prayers with God will go no further – than your obedience takes you!

2. In Zarephath, Elijah discovers that <u>when it's time</u> to move, you never <s>have to worry</s> about your next assignment! (v.8-16)
"Go at once to Zarephath… I have commanded a widow in that place to supply you with food" (v.9). Zarephath was over <u>100 miles away</u> from Cherith and Elijah would have to trust God to go before him, and provide his needed food from a poor widow that was planning to soon die. Elijah trusted God with this next assignment and made a great discovery (now hear this): The God who led you where you are – is the same God who will feed and provide in your next season of life! The take-a-way so far?
It's not the size of your need, it's the size of your God that is most important!
Nuf Sed!

May 3
"Elijah's Meltdown"
Part II

"What do you have against me, man of God? Did you come to remind me of my sin and kill my son? (I Kings 17:18)

Yesterday, we learned two great lessons from Elijah's story:
1. God provides in the places where He sends us, and,
2. There is always a "next" with God when our present assignment changes. Today, we'll see more practical lessons as the story unfolds:

3. Criticism is a normal part of servant leadership! (v.17-24)

After the miracle with the jar of oil, the widow's son became ill and she blamed Elijah. What did Elijah do? He asked for the son, prayed for him, and God restored his body with the gift of healing. Elijah's response of calmness speaks to us all today. What's the lesson?

♦ No provocation ever justifies an unchristian response!
♦ Answer your critics with your life and not your words!
♦ Every misbehavior of another is a revelation of a deeper need and an unspoken request for prayer!

Here we learn the reality of Proverbs 12:16, "A fool is quick tempered, but a wise person stays calm when insulted" (N.L.T).

4. God is Responsible to Defend His Own Name! (I Kings 18:1-40)

"Call on the name of your God, and I will call on the name of the Lord. The god who answers by fire – he is God." (18:24)

At the showdown on Mount Carmel, God proved Himself and honored Elijah's faith. It's a great lesson and reminder to our hearts that faith still moves mountains.

"'Answer me, O Lord, answer me, so these people will know that you, O Lord, are God'...then the fire of the Lord fell." (v.37,38). It's unmistakable what God is teaching us here:

♦ The atmosphere of expectancy is the breeding ground for miracles! (and)
♦ If we prostrate ourselves before the Lord, we will never be prostrated before the enemy!

5. Elijah reveals that God honors those who persevere in prayer! (41-46)

"'There is nothing there,' he said; seven times Elijah said, 'Go Back.'" (v.43)
As Elijah prayed for rain, his prayers seemed ineffective. In fact, his servant proclaimed, "There is nothing there" (v.43). But the seventh time around, "The servant reported a cloud as small as a man's hand is rising from the sea" (v.44). What's the message to your heart in this today?

You may be in between the time of sowing and reaping in prayer, but God is working even when you cannot see Him. So, in the midst of processing your unfulfilled expectations, remember this (it's the take-a-way):

♦ **God honors those who refuse to give up in prayer!**
♦ **God, who sees in secret, will reward you openly!**

Nuf Sed!

May 4
"Elijah's Meltdown"
Part III

"All at once an angel touched him and said, "Get up and eat." (I Kings 19:5)

Elijah will now face the wrath of Ahab's wicked wife, Jezebel. She sends word that she's going to have the prophet killed. She could have sent an executioner, but Elijah's death would have unified God's people and inspired them even more. Her real desire was to scare the prophet out of town, all to prevent him from rallying the faithful. And, God records Elijah's steps to teach us more valuable lessons.

6. Elijah discovers that running from your problems doesn't solve your problems! (19:1-3)

The Lord had sent Elijah to Cherith, Zarephath and Carmel – but the Lord never sent him to run out into the wilderness by himself. Elijah traveled 85 miles on foot to the southern border of Judah (v.3), another day's journey into the wilderness (v.4) and is filled with fear and intimidation. Scared and fearful, Elijah becomes distracted from the vision he received from the Lord. If vision is a picture of the future that produces passion in us today, what has been robbing you and impeding your progress? What is it that has put fear in your heart? What scares you and keeps you from launching out in "next steps"? What problems are you ignoring and refusing to deal with?

7. Elijah discovers that he is not superman and we all have limitations! (v.4)

"I have had enough, Lord" (v.4). The prophet who called fire down from heaven is now totally spent and fully depleted! Weariness, despair and fatigue have set in. In total exhaustion, Elijah prays a foolish prayer of quit and "no more". And what does God do? He feeds him! Maybe you are like Elijah. Maybe God is calling you to rest, slow down, take a break and come apart. Just maybe, you need to get control of the calendar, get quiet and still before God, get away and learn to rest, and get God's will for you (not everybody else's).

8. Elijah then discovers that "who he is" is more important than what he does! (v.5-9)

After Elijah ate and fell asleep, the Lord "came back a second time" (v.7) and strengthened Elijah enough to travel "forty days and forty nights" (v.8). Wow! God didn't condemn Elijah for his meltdown; instead He ministered strength and a new beginning! Why? Because God was not shaken by Elijah's weakness nor finished with Elijah's service! And friend, who you are is more important than what you do! And, God is still the God of new beginnings; He is still the "lifter up of our heads" (Psalm 3:3). The take-a-way?

Elijah thought his best was behind him, but he learned that it's always too soon to think it's too late!

Nuf Sed!

May 5
"Elijah's Meltdown"
Part IV

"Elijah was afraid and ran for his life." (I Kings 19:3)
"I am no better than my ancestors." (v.4)
"He went into a cave." (v.9)
"What are you doing here, Elijah?" (v.13)

Cave discoveries can be good! And, alone in the cave, Elijah makes a discovery that speaks to us all. This discovery is helpful because all of us are tempted to do what Elijah did. What was it?

9. Elijah discovered that comparing yourself with others is foolish and a total waste of time! (v.4-10)
On one hand, Elijah says he quits because "I am no better than my ancestors" (v.4). On the other hand, Elijah boasts that he is the zealous one and "the only one left" (v.14) serving God. When Elijah compares himself with others, he speaks foolishly because of two reasons:
Looking at those who "seem" to be more blessed than you will cause you to feel **inferior** and **jealous**!
Looking at those who "seem" to be less blessed than you will cause you to feel **superior** and **prideful**. (And neither one is of the Lord!!!)
So, what's the healthy way to live? Understand that in Jesus, you have approval and identity. And, if you live **with** approval (from God) you will not live **for** approval (from men).
10. Elijah discovers the joy of handing off the baton! (II Kings 2:1-14)
"The Spirit of Elijah is resting on Elisha." (v.15)
The final hours on earth for Elijah are very revealing. What's he doing? He's seen visiting the three ministry training centers in Bethel, Jericho, and Jordan. Why? He wants to encourage the young people as they prepare for ministry! I love this! Elijah is thinking about his succession plan with Elisha, and beyond Elisha. He is investing his life (and time) in those who will follow him. He wants to reproduce after Christ's kind and leaves us a great example.

What about you today? Who are you mentoring or coaching forward? Who are you bringing alongside of you? Who are you making room for? Who are you handing off the baton to? Who are you investing in that will bear fruit when your season is behind you?

Don't you love how God takes Elijah from a meltdown to a mentor? The take-a-way?

If God has committed to finish His work in you (Philippians 1:6), why would you ever give up on yourself?

Nuf Sed!

"Anxiety Overcome"
PART I

"Do not be anxious about anything, but in everything, by prayer and petition, with thanksgiving, present your requests to God. And the peace of God, which transcends all understanding, will guard your hearts and your minds in Christ Jesus." (Philippians 4:6,7)

If anybody had a reason to worry and be anxious, it was Paul in prison. He was writing to a church that was having some anxious moments as well:

1. There was division among the preachers (1:15,16)
2. There was persecution (1:18,19)
3. There was a dispute going on (4:2)
4. There were some self-centered members (2:3,4)
5. There were false teachers coming in (3:2,3,18,19)

And yet Paul says, "Do not be anxious about anything" (4:6). The word "anxious" means "to be pulled in different directions." So, how does God protect us from being pulled in many directions? How does God preserve us from being robbed of His perfect peace? How does God provide calmness and security in the middle of an unpredictable journey? Here's how:

"In everything by **prayer** and **petition**, with **thanksgiving**, present your **requests** to God" (v.6). The answer is a good prayer life, so that God's peace can rule our hearts. And, God gives us four words that reveal how real prayer is the answer to restless and anxious living:

I. "Prayer": "In everything by prayer" (v.6)
This word for prayer means to give time to worship and devotion. It refers to those moments set apart for fellowship with God. It means to draw near to the Lord for intimacy and communion.

II. "Petition": "...and petition" (v.6)
This word "petition" (or supplication) means to feel a deep need to pour out your soul to God. It means to cry out to God, lay your need before God and place that need into the hands of God. It refers to transferring what's on your heart, over to the heart of God.

III. "Thanksgiving": "...with thanksgiving" (v.6)
This word for thanksgiving refers to a spirit of gratitude for all that God is to us. It is our response to His care, ability, and willingness to minister to His children. It is an expression of confidence in advance of God's involvement. It is an expressed, heartfelt appreciation for our Father who cares!

The Take-A-way so far?
You can worry or you can pray – but you won't do both!

Nuf Sed!

May 7
"Anxiety Overcome"
Part II

"And the peace of God, which transcends all understanding will guard your hearts." (Philippians 4:7)

Yesterday we looked at the first three words that Paul used to describe healthy praying. Today, notice the fourth and last word, and see the consequence of a healthy prayer life.

IV. "Requests": "…Present your requests to God" (v.6)
This word "requests" is not a general attitude of prayer, but a specific and definite target. It means that we can be detailed with God and that God wants to hear our specific requests. And, how often do we pray this way? "In **everything**" (v.6) which means:
- ♦ To **"pray"** continually in a spirit and attitude of communion and devotion.
- ♦ To **"petition"** whenever you feel the need to pour out your heart to God.
- ♦ To offer **"thanksgiving"** and gratitude to God, who cares for His children.
- ♦ To make **"requests"** to God as you live to do His will on earth.

What is the result of praying like this?
"The peace of God…will guard your hearts and your minds in Christ Jesus." (v.7).
This word "peace" means something awesome! It means to be tranquil in your inner man as the result of committing things to God in prayer. It means to be calm and secure because God is in control. This peace is a fruit of the Spirit, which leaves you in harmony and at rest on the inside.
And, what is the great reward of having His peace? It "will guard your hearts and your minds in Christ Jesus" (v.7). The word "guard" means that God's peace will:
1. Garrison about and protect you
2. Shield you against anxieties
3. Fend off the fiery darts that seek to pull your mind in many directions.

What does God's peace guard? (Two things:)
- ♦ Your **heart** (which means your **feelings**)
- ♦ Your **mind** (which means your **thinking**)
The reality is, people without the peace of God seem to be emotionally up and down. It becomes hard to think clearly and makes us vulnerable to be consumed by outward things. When peace is absent, it's just harder to enjoy

the journey. The answer? A good prayer life where we understand: It's not the level of our faith, it's the object of our faith – Jesus!

The take-a-way?

One of the best things you can do for you each day, is just be still and quiet in the presence of God in prayer!

Nuf Sed!

"David's Emotional Ups and Downs"
PART I

"So Achish called David and said to him: 'As surely as the Lord lives, you have been reliable…but the rulers don't approve of you. Turn back and go in peace.'" (I Samuel 29:6,7)

In I Samuel 29, David was preparing for battle. David and his 600 men were supporting King Achish. The Philistine commander became nervous and ordered David to leave and go home. David responds in v.8 with the question, "What have I done?" And in v.11, David leaves without an attitude and heads home to Ziklag. What does David discover when he arrives home after three days of travel? He is devastated as he sees:

♦ The Amalekites left Ziklag in smoking ruin.
♦ All the property and cattle had been stolen.
♦ Worst of all, David's family and 600 men had been kidnapped.

As we closely read the details that God gives us in Scripture, truth leaps off the pages! I call it revelations (or lessons) from Ziklag – that protect us from the enemy lies. Remember: it's truth that frees us from ourselves. Here's my Ziklag discovery to enjoy the journey!

1. Closed Doors Can Be a Favor from God to You!

"Send the man back" (1 Samuel 29:4). What happens to David (unexpectedly)? He is rejected in battle, told to get out of town and is mistreated while doing good. Why was this a blessing in disguise? Because David had no idea, that back home at Ziklag, he was desperately needed. In other words, David's closed door was God's appointed way to change David's direction (for his good). This is a clear reminder to us all, that God always sees the bigger picture. So, if your heart is tempted to despair, remember:

♦ "As for God, His way is perfect" (Psalm 18:30)
♦ "He has made everything beautiful in its time" (Ecclesiastes 3:11)

2. Disappointments in Life Are a Part of The Journey!

"So David and his men wept aloud until they had no strength left to weep." (I Samuel 30:4)

The Bible is filled with people who wept tears from pain and loss. The good news is, your tears are not wasted, because leaky heads don't swell! In fact, pouring out your heart to God will allow God to heal your broken spirit and make you a "wounded healer" for others. And, faith in God's character in times of pain will protect you from yielding to self-pity, developing a martyr's complex and fainting by the wayside. Our response to our disappointments will either help us or hurt us!

The take-a-way?

When you go through a dark tunnel on a train, you don't jump off; you just sit still and trust the engineer! Nuf Sed!

"David's Emotional Ups and Downs"
PART II

"David was greatly distressed because the men were talking of stoning him; each one was bitter in spirit." (I Samuel 30:6)

Here are three more revelations (lessons) from Ziklag to enjoy the journey:

3. Criticism is Normal for Those Who Serve!
What happens when David's men become distraught over their loss? They begin to talk of stoning him (v.6). What's the lesson?
- No one will agree with you all the time!
- No one can meet everyone's expectations all the time!
- No one has to live with the "disease to please"!

God help us all to be slow to react (Proverbs 14:29), soft in our response (Proverbs 15:1), searching the Scriptures (Psalm 119:23), and seeking you in prayer (Psalm 109:4). Lord help us to practice this: "The Lord will fight for you; you need only to be still" (Exodus 14:14).

4. Encouragement from Others Can Only Go So Far!
"…but David encouraged himself in the Lord his God" (I Samuel 30:6, KJV)
What's the lesson from David refusing to stay down forever? There comes a time when we must move on with our feelings, get back in the fight, and let God be our source of affirmation, validity, comfort and joy! What does God teach us right here? That God (in prayer) will do what no one else can do, and put something inside of us that is greater than what is around us!

5. The Holy Spirit Still Leads Those Who Seek God in Prayer!
"And David inquired of the Lord, 'Shall I pursue this raiding party? Will I overtake them?'" (v.8)
How did David respond to his critics? He humbled himself in prayer and refused to take up an offense! He sought the Lord and His wisdom! He did not repay evil with evil! He practiced the principle of "delayed response." He allowed humility to turn his offense into a gift! He (in prayer) heard from God and received the direction that he needed: "Pursue them…you will certainly overtake them and succeed in the rescue" (v.8).

Maybe you are in between a rock and a hard place. Just maybe, you need wisdom from above for direction and decisions. Why not get alone, be still, and shut out all the noise and distractions. Why not quietly listen for that still small voice of leading or confirmation? I firmly believe that God will lead you one step at a time! The take-a-way?

While encouragement from others can only go so far, you can always encourage yourself in the Lord!

Nuf Sed!

"David's Emotional Ups and Downs"
PART III

"Two hundred men were too exhausted to cross the ravine." (I Samuel 30:10)
Four final lessons from Ziklag – to your heart today. Don't miss these four:

6. What You Have Is Enough When God Is in It! ✓
When David set out with 600 soldiers to recover what was taken, something unexpectedly happened. The extra traveling proved too much for one third of the team. Two hundred of the six hundred dropped out, refused to continue, and stayed behind. But little is much when God is in it! So, remember this when you lose a friend or people walk away:

- ◆ Five loaves and two fish can still feed a multitude!
- ◆ A little oil in a jar can keep on burning!
- ◆ Gideon's small army won an unforeseeable victory!

7. God Still Works in Unconventional Ways!
"My master abandoned me when I became ill three days ago." (v.13)
How did God lead David into the enemy's camp? Through an Egyptian man lying in a field who was sick, hungry, weak, and abandoned! In other words, God provided for David through a total stranger. God provided what David needed, but at least David was doing his part and marching forward. Remember this: If you do what you can do, God will do what you cannot do. What a discovery here, that big doors can swing on little hinges!

8. Givers Are Happier Than Takers!
"The share of the men who stayed with the supplies is to be the same as that of him who went down to battle." (v.24)
In v.22, some of David's men said that the 200 men who stayed behind should receive nothing from the victory spoils. But David blessed those who couldn't go with him in battle:

- ◆ He was patient with those who were extremely exhausted!
- ◆ He was generous and willing to give and share and bless!
- ◆ He was supportive of those who had stayed behind! (And he teaches us that givers are always happier than takers because we shovel it out, God shovels it in, and His shovel is bigger than our shovel!)

9. Every Set-Back Is a Set-Up For A Comeback!
"David was King in Hebron over the house of Judah" (II Samuel 2:11)
Wow! In I Samuel 29, David was rejected by Aphek and told to go home. In chapter 30, David was broken, criticized, weeping, and in despair. In II Samuel 2, David is anointed king. What are the take-a-ways for you to remember from this?

The past is no indication of your future opportunities!
The devil is a liar and God is not finished with you yet!

Nuf Sed!

May 11
"Responding to the Unexpected"
Part I

"She went up and laid him on the bed of the man of God, then shut the door and went out" (II Kings 4:21).

Have you ever heard the following statements?
♦ **What happens in you is more important than what happens to you!**
♦ **Life is 10% of what happens to us and 90% of how we respond!**

Our text today is a great lesson and illustration of how to respond to the unexpected. Elisha travels through Shunem and befriends a wealthy woman there (v.8). The woman takes notice of Elisha's character and tells her husband, "I know that this man who often comes our way **is a holy man of God**" (v.9). Elisha is given a guest room to stay in whenever he visits her city (v.10,11). Elisha then prophesies to the woman, "About this time next year, you will hold a son in your arms" (v.16). The woman gives birth to a son as Elisha said (v.17), and the son becomes very ill one day (v.19) and dies in his mother's arms (v.20). Notice how the Shunamite woman responds:

1. She Goes "Up" To Elisha's Room!
"She went up and laid him on the bed of the man of God" (v.21).

Why did she go up to the prophet's chamber? Because the room where Elisha stayed represented the presence of God to the mother. It was where Elisha prayed and talked with God. It was a choice to focus on God's provision, not just the problem. She didn't curse God, blame anybody or forget who gave her the child in the first place. The woman flat out looked **"up"** to God, and placed her expectation with the Lord. What's the lesson in this so far? The lesson is, prayer is the first step in every crisis we encounter. Why? Because:

♦ Prayer will allow us to focus on the Lord and bring God into the picture.
♦ Prayer will spare us from feverish activity and calm our spirit.
♦ Prayer will align our hearts with the heart of the Lord.
♦ Prayer will protect us from rash decisions.
♦ Prayer will allow God to speak to us in our spirit.
♦ Prayer will keep us connected to our Wisdom Source.

What else happens when we **"go up"** in the place of prayer and faith? We remind ourselves of what God has already spoken to us in His word:
"Your God **reigns**" (Isaiah 52:7).
"Who works out everything in conformity with the purpose of **his will**" (Ephesians 1:11).
"As for God, his way is **perfect**" (Psalm 18:30).
"I was young and now I am old, yet I have **never** seen the righteous forsaken" (Psalm 37:25).

"He has made everything beautiful in **its time**" (Ecclesiastes 3:11).
So what about you today? Do you need to "go up" and get alone with God and quiet your heart? Do you need to pause and listen quietly for clear directions?

The take-a-way?

The gospel means that I can rest and trust in God's Sovereign plan, for He is always for my good!

Nuf Sed!

May 12
"Responding to the Unexpected"
Part II

"'Everything is all right', she said" (II Kings 4:26).

Yesterday, we saw how the Shunamite Woman responded to the shocking news of her son dying. When the son became ill and died, the mom immediately went up to the prophet's chamber. Why did the mom take the child into Elisha's room? Because the room represented the presence of God. It was the room where Elisha prayed, talked with God, and got God into focus. So, what did the mother do after she entered the prophet's room of prayer?

2. She "Goes Down" and Places Her Son on The Bed!
"She went up, and laid him on the bed of the man of God" (v.21).

This is one of the hardest things to do for so many people. Why? Because we so often want to hang on and be in control! But the woman sets an example for us:
♦ She places her burden down so that God can work!
♦ She relinquishes responsibility over to God!
♦ She commits her need into the hands of God!
♦ She believes that God is bigger than she is!
♦ She knows that God can do what she cannot!

Remember friend, worry is accepting responsibility that God never intended for you to carry! Not only does she "go down", notice what else she does:

3. She "Goes Out" and Shuts the Door Behind Her!
"She went up and laid him on the bed of the man of God, then shut the door and went out" (v.21).

Let's be honest here, don't we want to leave the door open, hold onto the door and stay by it? Don't we have a hard time releasing what we cannot control? Don't we want to "stand by" and see what might (or might not) happen? How can the Shunamite mother shut the door and go find Elisha for help? Because...
♦ She believed that God could work a miracle.
♦ She believed that the God of Elisha was alive.
♦ She believed that faith still moves mountains.

In fact, she believed so much in the faithfulness of God, that she said, "Everything is all right" (v.26) to Elisha when she found him at Mount Carmel (v.25). I love this true story in the Word of God. Why? Because it teaches us that God can keep us balanced, stable, and on solid footing in the midst of life's challenges. Why not pray with me today, that God will help us to Go Up, Go Down, and Go Out when we face our impossible mountains? Why not trust instead of worry? Why not relinquish what is outside of your control? The take-a-way?

"Everything is all right" (v.26), means, it is well, it is well, it is well with my soul!   Nuf Sed!

May 13
"The Praying of Hannah"
Part I

"Then she went her way and ate something, and her face was no longer downcast." (I Samuel 1:18)

Maybe no other person in Scripture reveals to us the therapy of prayer like Hannah does. Just think of this; she goes from: **"In bitterness of soul Hannah wept much and prayed to the Lord"** (v.10) to this: **"Her face was no longer downcast"** (v.18). This is an incredible story of how God takes us from sadness to gladness – in prayer. *The only thing she did was pray.*

Who was Hannah? She was the wife of Elkanah and soon to be mother of Samuel. What was her dilemma? She was barren, and having no children was considered by society a punishment from God. Was her unfulfilled expectation painful? "In bitterness of soul, Hannah wept much" (v.10).

Why is Hannah's story in Scripture? Because pain is real, and we all have two choices:
1. We can stuff our tears, which causes us to carry pain and be pitied (or)
2. We can be changed by God through the ministry of prayer. Notice Hannah's pain:

1. She was barren with no children (v.5)
In a male-centered society where the focus was on producing an heir to the family name, to be barren was to fail the family. Hannah was an object of reproach and scorn.

2. She was verbally abused (v.6,7)
Peninnah continued to provoke her and torment her, telling her that, "You're barren because God is punishing you for some sin."

3. She was neglected by her husband (v.8)
Elkanah asked her, "Why are you crying? Why aren't you eating? Why are you depressed? You have me; isn't that better than having kids?" This insensitivity further increased Hannah's pain. (She was unable to tell her troubles to her husband).

4. She was misunderstood by Eli the priest (v.13,14)
When Hannah prayed from her heart without words, Eli accused her of being intoxicated (v.14) (he misjudged her). "How long will you keep on getting drunk? Get rid of your wine." *Evidently a habit to cope.*

5. She was seemingly forgotten by God (v.15)
Hannah replied to her accuser this way in v.15: "I am a woman who is deeply troubled. I have not been drinking…I was pouring out my soul to the Lord."

If you've ever prayed like Hannah, you're normal:
"O Lord Almighty, if you will only look upon your servant's misery and remember me" (v.11). Hannah's pain caused her to weep and to lose her

appetite (v.7,10). The good news is, if you have an unfulfilled expectation, suffered from abuse or neglect, live with an insensitive spouse, have been misunderstood, or feel forgotten by God – God has your rebound in store! This season will pass and prayer with God will protect your heart. On the next page learn how God turns our pain into praise through the ministry of prayer. The take-a-way?

God knows that where you are, is not where you're going to stay!

Nuf Sed!

The Praying of Hannah"
Part II

"Then Hannah prayed and said; "My heart rejoices in the Lord." (I Samuel 2:1)

Our text today is a beautiful picture of how God (in prayer) can change our hearts. The setting and the message is clear and direct:
Hannah's husband makes the annual trip with his family to the tabernacle. The family travels to Shiloh to worship and offer peace offerings 15 miles from home. Everyone is eating, drinking, and enjoying the festival. Yet Hannah (in the crowd), is in bitterness of soul. What does she do? She goes into the tabernacle to unburden her heart to God in prayer. In other words, it's make or break time! Hannah can dwell on her problem and carry the weight of her sorrow, or she can unburden her heart to God in the secret place. It's one of two choices:

1. Retaliate against Peninnah, Elkanah, and Eli (or)
2. Draw near to the One who can heal a broken heart. *God*   *De'.*

In other words, Hannah's pain will be her stepping stone or her tombstone! Her pain will make her better or bitter! Her pain will make her sweeter or make her sour. Her pain will leave her like the first Adam in the garden or like the second Adam on the cross.

So what did Hannah do? She did the right thing: *chapt. 2*
♦ She, "Prayed to the Lord." (v.10)
♦ She, "Kept on praying to the Lord." (v.12)
♦ She, "Was praying in her heart." (v.13)
♦ She said, "I was pouring out my soul to the Lord." (v.15)

And, how Hannah prayed teaches us valuable lessons about praying and healthy living.

1. Prayer Requires No Special Formula or Method! *Also I Cor 14 with mind – fruitful without mind is Spirit*
Hannah prayed spoken prayers and unspoken prayers. Her "lips were moving but her voice was not heard" (v.13). She pondered in silent prayer and connected with God. What does this mean to you? It means that you can speak a prayer, think a prayer, or sing a prayer (sitting, kneeling, standing, driving, wherever)! What matters is that you experience the therapy of true prayer.

2. Prayer Releases Our Tensions Over to God!
When nothing seemed to be going right, Hannah prayed. She released her problems over to God and returned home. She placed her expectations in

God's hands. This teaches us that prayer turns over to God what is outside of our control. It reveals that God (in prayer) can heal our heart when we relinquish things. Prayer releases burdens so that you can smile again and enjoy the journey. The take-a-way?

As Hannah poured out her heart (in prayer), God poured in His Grace to heal!

Nuf Sed!

May 15

"The Praying of Hannah"
Part III

"My heart rejoices in the Lord…for I delight in your deliverance." (I Samuel 2:1)

Yesterday we learned how prayer requires no special formula or method, and that prayer releases our tensions over to God. Today, we'll cover the last two lessons from Hannah's praying and the consequence of a good prayer life.

3. Prayer Renews Our Trust in The Sovereignty of God!

In prayer, Hannah was able to walk away with confidence that God had heard her and was at work. Her fears somehow turned to trust. Her fretting turned to faith. Somehow (in prayer) God revealed to Hannah that He was aware, alert, and was working all things together for her good. Somehow Hannah was assured that God's way is perfect and He makes no mistakes.

4. Prayer Recovers Our Joy and Peace!

Hannah reveals that prayer has an amazing effect on our insides and outsides. She shows us how God (in prayer) turns our sorrows into hopefulness. She reveals how prayer changes us before it ever changes our situations. We learn from Hannah how God recovers our joy and peace as we transfer over to God what is outside of our control. I love the revelation of I Samuel 1:18: **"Then she went her way and ate something, and her face was no longer downcast."**

And, what exactly happened after Hannah prayed silently, was healed inwardly, and gave birth to Samuel? In chapter II, we see her singing joyfully to the Lord. What is her song about? It's about truth that God wants you and I to never forget. It's truth that helps to take us from sadness to gladness.

♦ God delivers us from sin to salvation! (v.1)
♦ God makes no mistakes! (v.2)
♦ God understands you fully! (v.3)
♦ God will take care of you! (v.9)
♦ God will make all the wrong things right! (v.10)

"The bows of the warriors are broken, but those who stumbled are armed with strength." (v.4)

How was Hannah "armed with strength" (v.4)? She emptied herself of herself in prayer! And God filled her with Himself. The take-a-way?
♦ **Pain and tears are a normal part of life!**
♦ **Prayer is available for everyone to participate in!**
♦ **God is the One who turns sadness into gladness!**

Nuf Sed!

May 16
"The Courage of Ruth"
Part I

"Where you go I will go, and where you stay I will stay. Your people will be my people and your God my God." (Ruth 1:16)

Ruth is a love story that takes place during the dark ages of Judges. It's a picture of God's grace at work today, even in the midst of decay and despair. It's a revelation of God's providence at work in the lives of Naomi, Ruth, and Boaz. It's a book that begins with tears and ends in triumph; it begins with a funeral and ends with a wedding; it goes from Ruth being empty to finding fullness in her kinsman – redeemer.

The story revolves around a famine in the land and a respectable family. Elimelech was the husband, Naomi was the wife, and Mahlon and Chilion were their two sons (who would marry Orpah and Ruth).

And God speaks to us in three specific ways!
I. The Crisis of Naomi (1:1-13)

Dilema

"In the days when the judges ruled, there was a famine in the land, and a man from Bethlehem in Judah, together with his wife and two sons went to live for a while in the country of Moab." (1:1)

Detour

♦ **Notice the Detour in The Road!**
Mom and Dad made a poor choice when they left for Moab. Moab had refused to allow Israel passage through its territory when Moses led Israel to Canaan. Moab was a product of the flesh (born to Lot through incest with his daughter). The Moabites were immoral and the enemy of the people of God. And, Elimelech and Naomi were detoured from Bethlehem to Moab. In other words, they chose the path of least resistance and looked towards the land of Lot instead of the God of Abraham.

Decision

♦ **Notice the Decision to Return!**
"She left the place where she had been living and set out on the road that would take them back to the land of Judah." (1:7)

Here we learn that Naomi was willing to change her mind and change direction. She lost her husband, two sons, and is now willing to leave Moab for Bethlehem. She heads towards home and brings her two daughters-in-law to the fork in the road. Orpah and Ruth now have to make a choice for themselves!

The take-a-way?
♦ **As God is the God of a second chance for Naomi, so God is the God of a second chance for you!**
♦ **Naomi's discovery then, is your wisdom now -There is no bread, no blessing, and no benefit outside the will of God!**

Nuf Sed!

"The Courage of Ruth"
Part II

"Orpah kissed her mother-in-law goodbye, but Ruth clung to her" (Ruth 1:14).
"Your sister-in-law is going back to her people and her gods" (v.15).

Yesterday we saw the crisis of Naomi, how she left Moab after her husband's death and headed for Bethlehem. We learned that God is the God of a second chance (for Naomi, and for you and me).

Today, God speaks to us through:

II. The Curse of Orpah (1:14,15)
"At this they wept again. Then Orpah kissed her mother-in-law goodbye" (v.14).
Three widows were left behind (desolate and destitute). Naomi somehow hears that the famine in Israel is over, and she starts for home. Naomi wants her two daughters-in-law to stay in Moab where they might find security and provision (v.8). Naomi knew the attitude of the Israelites towards a Moabite (Orpah and Ruth). Naomi didn't want any more hardships to come to Orpah and Ruth. So, Naomi pleads with Ruth and Orpah to return to Moab instead of traveling back to Bethlehem. And, Orpah chooses differently than Ruth.

Orpah started out well; she "prepared to return home" (1:16). She traveled a distance with Naomi and Ruth, and "set out in the road that would take them back to the land of Judah" (v.7). She even promised Naomi that, "We will go back with you to your people" (v.10). She was also full of outward affection:
♦ She lifted her voice (but words are not enough)
♦ She wept passionate tears (but tears are not enough)
♦ She kissed Naomi (but emotions are not enough)

And, the Scripture says that Orpah went **"back to her people"** and back to **"her gods"** (v.15).

In other words, Orpah looked at Moab (and the temporal goods back at home) and looked at Bethlehem (where Jehovah Jireh cared for His covenant people). In other words, Orpah made a choice to go backwards, leave God's plan for her life and forfeit her legacy and so much more. Why?
♦ She chose the pleasures of Moab over the pleasures of God.
♦ She chose the path of least resistance.
♦ She chose the pursuit of earthly things and missed what God had in waiting.
The take-a-way?

Only one life will soon be past; only what's done for Christ will last!
Nuf Sed!

"The Courage of Ruth"
Part III

"Look," said Naomi, "your sister-in-law is going back to her people and her gods. Go back with her." (Ruth 1:15)

Can you believe this offer from Naomi to Ruth? Naomi pleaded with Ruth to do what Orpah had done (go back to Moab and serve "other gods"). But what did Ruth do? "When Naomi realized that Ruth was determined to go with her, she stopped urging her" (v.18). Remember, Orpah leaving made it easier for Ruth to leave. Orpah's quitting made it easier for Ruth to quit. Orpah's turning made it easier for Ruth to turn. Yet, Ruth would not leave Naomi and made a choice to return to Bethlehem. The question is, why did Ruth make the right decision and how does it speak to us today?

1. Ruth based her decision upon **"faith,"** not sight!
She knew exactly what was in Moab, but had no idea of what lay ahead in Bethlehem.
2. Ruth based her decision upon **"conviction,"** not emotion!
Orpah cried and kissed and hugged Naomi, but Ruth made a decision of her will (a commitment deep down inside).
3. Ruth based her decision on what was **"right,"** not what was convenient!
There was no job offer in Bethlehem, and no promise of security. There was no guarantee of her being welcomed there, nor any visible reward awaiting her.
4. Ruth based her decision upon **"God's"** approval, not her friend's approval!
She wasn't moved by the possibility of Orpah's rejection, and didn't care if ten years of friends in Moab rebuked her or not. Ruth flat out wanted to please God more than anyone else.
5. Ruth based her decision upon **"finality,"** leaving no room for hesitation!
"Where you die, I will die" (v.17) were the words of Ruth. In other words, she didn't adapt to the gods of Moab, but made a decision for the eternal over the temporary. Ruth saw beyond the here and now – to the future.

Does it really pay to serve God and live for the world to come? Remember:
♦ Ruth was used in the lineage of <u>Jesus</u>.
♦ Ruth was <u>provided</u> for when she returned to Bethlehem.
♦ Ruth was given a <u>husband</u> (Boaz).
♦ Ruth was eternally rewarded for her <u>obedience</u> to God.

The take-a-way?
If you do God's will it doesn't matter who doesn't like you; if you don't do God's will, it doesn't matter who does like you!

Nuf Sed!

"The Praise of Leah"
Part I

"She conceived again, and when she gave birth to a son she said, "This time I will praise the Lord." (Genesis 29:35)

God said through Solomon, "Hope deferred makes the heart sick, but a longing fulfilled is a tree of life" (Proverbs 13:12). If anyone ever illustrated this, it was Leah. Her story is one of pain (from "Hopes Deferred") to praise (from Hopes Relinquished"). It's a story recorded by God to teach us valuable lessons.

Why is this so important? Because of three major reasons:
1. No one in life can escape pain, disappointment, and being hurt (unfulfilled expectations come to everybody)!
2. Setbacks, rejection, and hopes deferred have the potential to make us cynical, fearful, joyless, and sour!
3. God has a way to change us all from the inside out to "enjoy the journey" day by day! Here's the conflict:

In Genesis 29, Jacob married Leah, then married Rachel one week later. The sad news in Genesis 29:30 is that Jacob, **"loved Rachel more than Leah."** So, Jacob served Laban for seven years to obtain Rachel for his wife. On the wedding night, Laban puts Leah in the nuptial tent instead of Rachel. Jacob marries Rachel a week later, and Rachel is loved but Leah is second fiddle. And, God records this to show us three clear lessons:

I. Leah's Pain Was Real!
Is there anything worse than being single and wanting to be married? Yes, it's being married to someone who doesn't like you! What's the good news for Leah (and you and me in a time like this)? The good news is:

"The Lord saw that Leah was not loved." (v.31)
In other words, the Lord knew all about Leah and He knows all about you! He knew that Leah was unloved, carrying pain, and living with "hopes deferred." The good news is, the Lord is drawn to those who hurt! Why? Because God is the God of all comfort, and His nature is one of compassion. So, if you're in a season like Leah, take courage and remember:
♦ If you have any "hopes deferred," you're normal!
♦ If your dreams have been put "on hold," you're normal!
♦ If unfulfilled expectations have touched your life, you're normal!

The take-a-way?
Jesus didn't suffer so that Christians wouldn't have to; He suffered to show us how to go through it!

Nuf Sed!

May 20
"The Praise of Leah"
Part II

"Surely my husband will love me now." (Genesis 29:32)

Yesterday we learned how pain touched Leah after she married Jacob. Why? Because Jacob, **"loved Rachel more than Leah"** (v.30). We also discovered that, **"The Lord saw that Leah was not loved"** (v.31).

Today is about how Leah processed her pain and her desire to win her husband Jacob.

II. Leah's Process Was Learned!

What did the Lord do for Leah in her "hopes deferred" season?

"When the Lord saw that Leah was not loved, he opened her womb, but Rachel was barren. Leah became pregnant and have birth to a boy. She named him Reuben, for she said, 'It is because the Lord has seen my misery. **Surely my husband will love me now'''** (v.31,32).

Leah gives her husband a first born son and thinks:

"If the Lord can open my womb, surely He can open Jacob's heart." And how did Jacob respond? He still didn't love her. Next step? She gives birth to a second son, Simeon (v.33). Jacob still doesn't love her. Next step? She gives birth to a third son, Levi (v.34). And, what does Leah say?

"Now at last my husband will become attached to me, because I have borne him three sons" (v.34).

Yet Jacob's heart still did not desire her. What was Leah learning? Many things:

♦ You cannot make another person love you!

♦ The more you pressure someone, the more frustrated you will become!

♦ Putting all your hopes in someone else's love, can interfere with your relationship with God!

♦ Placing your expectations in the Lord will protect you from adding to your disappointments!

What was God teaching Leah? He was showing her that her "hopes deferred" were being used for a higher purpose. What was it? The Lord was wooing Leah to himself! The Lord was wanting to do something deeper in her heart. What was it? It was to shift Leah's hope from Jacob to Himself! It was to show us today where real rest and freedom comes from. And, that rest comes from trusting in the finished work of Jesus-above every other expectation in life! How was Leah changed from the inside out? Get ready for it tomorrow!

The take-a-way?

God may allow what we really don't like, to ultimately give us what we really, really need!

Nuf Sed!

"The Praise of Leah"
Part III

"She conceived again, and when she gave birth to a son she said, 'This time I will praise the Lord.' So she named him Judah" (Genesis 21:35)

Did you notice the two words, "this time" (v.35)? Remember, when Rueben was born, Leah said, "Surely my husband will love me now" (v.35). When Levi was born, Leah said, "At last, my husband will become attached to me because I have borne him three sons" (v.34).

III. Leah's Praise was Therapy and Healing!
What changed in Leah? It's obvious in the text because Judah's name means "praise":

♦ She became aware that while she was not loved by Jacob, she was still loved by God!
♦ As her fourth pregnancy drew near to completion, she drew nearer and nearer to God!
♦ As Leah shifted her hopes from Jacob to the Lord, her soul slowly began to change!
♦ When Leah looked higher than her husband, an inner beauty began to grow and she became a woman at rest!
    And, so it is with us! For when Jesus becomes more beautiful than useful, something happens and we change for the better!

"This Time I Will Praise the Lord" (v.35) means:
1. Worship teaches us **to practice God's presence** in every season!
2. Worship **makes us sensitive** to God's voice and Divine whispers!
3. Worship **opens our heart** to the love of God!
4. Worship **clears our mind** of those lesser and trivial things!
5. Worship **overcomes our insecurities** as we give God first place!
6. Worship **reminds us** of God's character and goodness!
7. Worship **nourishes our souls** and quickens us inwardly!
8. Worship **helps us relinquish** what is outside of our control!
9. Worship **stills the anxiousness** in my flesh!
10. Worship allows God to **renew our strength** and increase our faith!

The take-a-way?
Placing our expectations in the Lord will protect us from having to be first, having to be right, having to be liked, and having to be noticed!

Nuf Sed!
Psalm 62:5 "... for my expectation is from Him."

"The Praise of Leah"
Part IV

"There Abraham and his wife Sarah were buried, there Isaac and his wife Rebekah were buried, and there **I buried Leah**." (Genesis 49:31)

I love these words of Jacob on his deathbed. It's an account of how Jacob buried Leah in the ancestral place of honor. It's a testimony of how God had beautified Leah when she began to praise and worship God. It tells us that Leah found fulfillment in God Himself. It's a reminder that, when Leah delighted herself in the Lord, something happened and something changed.

♦ The negative effects of grief and rejection were healed.

♦ The love and joy of life returned.

♦ The pain of misplaced affection vanished away.

Notice Leah's Progressive Journey:

Child #1 was Reuben (which means:) "See a son that God has given"
Leah began to recognize (in Reuben) that all good things come from God. Reuben was a witness to Leah that God was causing all things to work together for her good. Leah was learning that she could complain, murmur, and have a pity-party, or she could trust in the unseen hand of God.

Child #2 was Simeon (which means:) "God hears my prayers in affliction"
Simeon was a constant reminder to Leah that her present field was limited, but she was not limited by her field. She could pray anywhere, at any time, regardless of her feelings and affliction.

Child #3 was Levi (which means:) "A joining companion"
Levi was a constant reminder that God has joined us to Himself, and that He is in the middle of the valley with us. Indeed, God is the God of the hills and He is the God of the valleys.

Child #4 was Judah (which means:) "Praise"
Judah was a constant reminder that something happens inside of us as we praise and worship God. Judah teaches all of us that we can focus on ourselves and dwell on the past, or we can lift up our eyes to Someone who is higher and "over all."

Is this the Gospel or what?

♦ Isn't Jesus a Son that was given to us?

♦ Isn't Jesus our high priest that hears us in prayer?

♦ Isn't Jesus with us and will never leave us?

♦ Isn't Jesus the object of our constant praise, who brings wholeness and meaning to life?

The take-a-way?
Leah started out in pain, but ended up in honor. This means your present season is only just a season!

Nuf Sed!

May 23
"Praying in Agreement"

"I tell you the truth, whatever you bind on earth will be bound in heaven, and whatever you loose on earth with be loosed in heaven. Again, I tell you that if two of you on earth agree about anything you ask for, it will be done for you by my Father in heaven. For where two or three come together in my name, there am I with them" (Matthew 18:18-20).

While prayer is a mystery, it is also a mighty force in seeing God's will done on earth. While prayer is intimacy, union, communion and connection with God – it is also a powerful way to unite with others in battle. In other words, one snowflake isn't much by itself, but it takes a bulldozer to move them when they cooperate!

I can still remember my grandparents taking me to church and pushing my wheelchair to the altar. Why? They had people unite in prayer that I would be able to walk again. For two years, they had people unite together in faith, that God would heal their grandson. And, after rheumatic fever left me unable to walk for two years, united prayer prevailed on my behalf. Here's what Jesus says about the ministry of uniting together as one:

I. You Have "Authority" In Prayer!
"Whatever you bind on earth will be bound in heaven" (v.18).
The Greek word for "bind" is (DEO) and it means to restrain, to hold back, and to prevent. It means that Jesus has delegated authority to us to act on His behalf. Why? So that we can restrain and frustrate Satan's activity and evil intentions. It's a call to arms to enforce the victory of the cross on planet earth.

II. You Have "Power" In Prayer!
"If two of you on earth agree" (v.19).
Jesus teaches here that there is accumulated power in united praying! He teaches us that we can be mighty in prayer alone, but mightier in prayer with someone joining us. Here we learn that when we couple our faith with the faith of others, there is power to see spiritual breakthroughs.

III. You Have "Confidence" In Prayer!
"For where two or three come together in My Name, there am I with them" (v.20).
To pray "In My Name" means to pray in harmony with God's will, and in faith on His merits, not our own. It means that we are to pray in "His Name," so that we can accomplish His purpose here on earth. And, what happens (in prayer) when we focus on God's will and not our own? Jesus said, "There am I with them" (v.20), which means: Jesus is present to enforce and give strength to our petitions. Oh, what confidence we have in prayer! Let's always remember this:

♦ We have authority (in prayer) to bring Jesus into the arena of standing against the powers of evil!

♦ We have power (in prayer) when we unite together with like-minded believers!

♦ We have confidence (in prayer) because we trust in His Name and not our own works and merits!

The take-a-way?

It's not the "level" of your faith (in prayer), it's the "object" of your faith (in prayer) – Jesus!

Nuf Sed!

May 24
"Uzziah's Undeniable Message"
Part I

"He sought God during the days of Zechariah, who instructed him in the fear of God. As long as he sought the Lord, God gave him success" (II Chronicles 26:5).

A good friend of mine once worked as a crusade director for a well-known evangelist. One day, my friend asked the evangelist why so many of his peers had fallen from grace. The evangelist looked him straight in the eye and said, "They prayed until they got there." This is the story of Uzziah's rise and fall. He prayed until he got there!

Uzziah was chosen by the people to reign after the death of his father (Amaziah). When Solomon died, Israel split into two Kingdoms – the Northern Kingdom called Israel, and the Southern Kingdom called Judah. Uzziah took the throne as Judah's tenth King in 791 B.C. and reigned for 52 years. He was so effective that Isaiah felt it a calamity when Uzziah died (Isaiah 6).

I. Uzziah's Fame: (What were his deeds?)
1. He restored the key coastal city of Eloth (v.2).
2. He lived obedient and pleased the Lord (v.4).
3. He sought the Lord as a teenager and became a great young man of prayer (v.5).
4. He defeated the Philistines and rebuilt the cities (v.6).
5. He destroyed Israel's long time enemy (v.7).
6. He received gifts from the Ammonites (v.8).
7. He continually became stronger and stronger (v.8)
8. He led the great construction projects in the capital city (v.9).
9. He became an extensive cattle breeder (v.10).
10. He built fortresses to protect the livestock (v.10).
11. He maintained farmers and vine-dressers upon the mountains and in the fields (v.10).
12. He organized and armed the great military forces (v.11-15).

"His fame spread far and wide, for he was greatly helped until he became powerful" (v.15).
What's the greatest danger of being successful in what you do? What's the greatest peril when all is going well? What's the greatest way to default and lose God's favor, support, and blessing?

"But after Uzziah became powerful, his pride led to his downfall" (v.16).
As long as Uzziah sought the Lord, God made him to prosper. But, when Uzziah became ensnared by the bareness of a "too busy" life, something happened. What was it? He allowed his work to squeeze God right out of his

heart. He drifted away from seeking God. He went on momentum and put his life on "cruise control." His character didn't keep pace with his accomplishments. His branch life became larger than his root system. He flat out drifted away from God and pride filled the void that Uzziah had created.

The take-a-way?

♦ **When we are too busy to pray, we are busier than God intends us to be!**

♦ **We never need more time – we simply need to choose!**

Nuf Sed!

May 25
"Uzziah's Undeniable Message"
Part II

"As long as he sought the Lord, God gave him success" (II Chronicles 26:5).

Yesterday we learned what happened when Uzziah put his work before his walk. We learned that if sin cannot make you bad, it will try to make you busy – too busy for God! We discovered that Uzziah allowed his busyness to squeeze God right out of his heart. What happened when Uzziah began to go on momentum?

II. Uzziah's Familiarity (His Danger Is Revealed)

♦ He failed to lean in!
Uzziah goes into the temple to burn incense (v.16), and eighty priests saw what was happening (v.17). Uzziah was told that the law forbid him to do what only a priest could do. But something has happened to Uzziah! Now, he wasn't content just to be King. Now, he wants to be priest as well and feels that he deserves more perks. Now, He wants a piece of the action in the temple. Uzziah is talking to and deceiving himself; "Why can't I do what the other 80 priests do?" "The 80 priests are no better than me." "I deserve the very same privileges." Why is Uzziah so discontent? Because Uzziah stopped leaning on God and thinks his past successes qualify him to step out of line and break the law.

♦ He failed to listen!
When Uzziah went into the temple to burn incense, he was confronted by Azariah and 80 other priests: "It is not right for you, Uzziah, to burn incense to the Lord. That is for the priests… leave the sanctuary…you will not be honored by the Lord God" (v.18). How did Uzziah respond to correction and advice? He became angry with those who loved him enough to warn him. He refused to listen to those who warned him of coming danger. His pride made him unteachable!

♦ He failed to stay low!
"His pride led to his downfall" (v.16).
Uzziah's heart was lifted up to his own destruction, all because of pride. Instead of taking the low road of humility, Uzziah thought more highly of himself than he should. He thought he could ignore the red lights, bypass the stop signs, ignore the calling voices, and that he deserved special privileges. Why? Because his heart became cold in prayer, full of pride, and resentful of correction. And the consequences?

III. Uzziah's Fall (Was a Disaster)

♦ He was **diseased** and became a leper (v.19).
♦ He was **dismissed** and thrust out of the temple (v.20).
♦ He was **demoted** and separated to an isolated place (v.21).
♦ He was **displaced** and not allowed a burial with other kings (v.23).

Why? (It's the unmistakable take-a-way)

Prayerlessness leads to pride and says to my heart: "I don't need the Lord, I can do this myself."

Nuf Sed!

"The Glory of The Cross"
Part I

"May I never boast except in the cross of our Lord Jesus Christ, through which the world has been crucified to me, and I to the world" (Galatians 6:14).

Paul is finishing his letter to the Galatians here; his audience was converted under his preaching. But now, false teachers had entered the church! What were they teaching? They were teaching two things that were tempting the church to lose its power and gospel witness to the world:

♦ That circumcision was necessary for salvation, and,
♦ To be a true Christian, you must go back under the old Jewish Law of rituals and ceremonies.

So, Paul confronts the false teachers, and exposes the three carnal motives in their hearts:

Motive # 1, was to gain **fleshly approval** instead of God's approval:
"Those who want to make a good impression outwardly are trying to compel you to be circumcised" (v.12A). The false ministers sought a good showing. They sought worldly popularity and acceptance. Their goal or motive was to have people love them more than God and the truth.

Motive #2, was to put **pleasure** before **commitment**:
"The only reason they do this is to avoid being persecuted for the cross of Christ" (v.12B).
It was very unpopular for the minister to preach that Jesus alone was the way to the Father. The preachers of law persecuted the preachers of the cross who taught the way of grace. Thus, many took the easy way out to avoid any persecution.

Motive #3, was to put on a **good show**:
"Not even those who are circumcised obey the law, yet they want you to be circumcised that they may boast about your flesh" (v.13).
The false ministers were competing and comparing and looking for validation and approval. They wanted to circumcise many so that they could boast in their numbers. Appearance and looking good before men was foremost in their thinking. In other words; image, ego and appearance all got in the way of pleasing God.

But God has a better way! He tells us what it means to boast in the Lord and glory in the cross:

1. It means the cross is the only boast of a true minister or servant of Jesus in his church.
2. It means the cross is my only approach to a Holy God.
3. It means the cross is the only thing I can ever really brag about.
4. It means the cross is the only power to change us from the inside out.

Why is the cross of Jesus the only truth we can ever boast in? Paul gives us four reasons, which we'll cover tomorrow. Today's take-a-way?
"My sin, oh, the bliss of this glorious thought! My sin, not in part but the whole, is nailed to the cross and I bear it no more, praise the Lord, praise the Lord, O my soul" (Horatio Spafford).

Nuf Sed!

"The Glory of The Cross"
Part II

"May I never boast except in the cross of our Lord Jesus Christ, through which the world has been crucified to me, and I to the world" (Galatians 6:14). Yesterday, we learned about the three carnal motives that Paul exposed in this context of Galatians 6. What did Paul confront? Leaders who minimized the cross to:

♦ Gain fleshly (man's) approval over God's approval.
♦ Seek personal pleasure before commitment to truth.
♦ Seek recognition and a good show over pleasing God.

Paul then goes, "all in", and explains how the cross has power and is our only means of boasting:

1. The Cross Has Power To "Crucify"!
"The cross of our Lord Jesus Christ, through which the world has been crucified to me" (v.14).

This liberating truth means, that the cross has the power to crucify the world's power over me. It means that the cross has the power to put to death my old carnal nature. It means the cross has the power to lasso and constrain my desires that are contrary to Jesus' desires. This means that faith in the cross of Jesus releases God's power to pour out grace and give us power to overcome sin!

2. The Cross Has Power To "Create"!
"Neither circumcision nor uncircumcision means anything; what counts is a new creation" (v.15).

The "new creation" Paul mentions here is a person who is saved by the cross alone. Paul tells us that the cross has the power to create a new heart, give a repentant sinner a brand-new spirit, change the inward nature of someone, and create new desires to please God above all else.

3. The Cross Has Power to "Calm"!
"Peace and mercy to all who follow this rule" (v.16).

This "calm" that Paul talks about is a peace and calm based on the mercy of God! It means, the cross has power to give you peace with God through the sacrifice upon it. It means, the cross has power to clear your conscience and remove all guilt. Simply, the cross (and what took place there) has power to release the peace of God within your life.

4. The Cross Has Power To "Comfort"!
"Finally, let no one cause me trouble, for I bear on my body the marks of Jesus" (v.17).

Paul isn't complaining about his scars here. Instead, he is testifying that the cross has the power to sustain and comfort him in every pain and injustice. He shows us that looking at Jesus on Calvary and remembering the price paid for our salvation, is enough to encourage and motivate us in every season.

The take-a-way?

Our focus on the cross will protect us from ever feeling cheated and thinking that we are not getting what we deserve!

Nuf Sed!

"A Timely and Encouraging Word"
Part I

"Why do you say, O Jacob, and complain, O Israel, 'My way is hidden from the Lord; my cause is disregarded by my God'?" (Isaiah 40:27)

Isaiah began his ministry around 740 B.C. and ministered for 60 years. His major thrust of preaching was the power of God, how God delivers his people in both temporal and spiritual circumstances. Isaiah's name means: "Jehovah is Salvation", and his message was delivered at a critical time in history. Moral conditions were horrible. Social conditions included the rich taking land illegally and forcing home owners out through extortion and eviction. Government conditions saw the judicial system corrupted, as bribes were taken under the table to favor the wealthy.

And, God would raise up Isaiah to give an encouraging word for God's people who were taken captive into Babylon. His message would both guide and comfort the exiles during and after their 70-year captivity. For 39 chapters Isaiah rebukes Israel for her sins. But, in chapters 40-66, Isaiah delivers a 27-chapter love letter to encourage the Jews who are about to leave captivity from Babylon. They've thought much about their past failures and future uncertainty. They are about to leave Babylon and return to a ruined Jerusalem. They'll make progress, but they need a timely word from the Lord.

What's the word from God to lift their hearts and prepare Israel for their 700 mile journey home? What does Israel need to hear before they rebuild the city and start a building program? Where will all the supplies come from to do the will of God? Notice how Isaiah invites Israel to behold the greatness of God, to build faith in their hearts as well as your heart today:

♦ In verse 4, The crooked places will be made straight.
♦ In verse 5, The glory of the Lord shall be revealed.
♦ In verse 8, The Word of God shall stand forever.
♦ In verse 11, God will feed, carry and lead His sheep.
♦ In verse 14, God doesn't need any counselors.
♦ In verse 15, Babylon is merely a drop in the bucket.
♦ In verse 22, God beholds the circle of the earth.
♦ In verse 26, God knows the number of stars in the galaxy.

But in V.27, we have a problem! Israel is being lied to by the enemy of their soul. Fiery darts must be overcome before the long journey home to Jerusalem. Notice what Israel is thinking and saying:
"My way is hidden from the Lord; my cause is disregarded by my God" (v.27).

In other words, Israel was tempted, like you are tempted, to believe two things:
1. They thought that God didn't know where they were, and,
2. They thought that God wasn't being fair in allowing the Babylonians to

retain them for 70 years.

And, in Isaiah's love letter, you will see the following take-a-ways revealed over and over again:

♦ **All things really do work together for good to those who love the Lord! (and)**
♦ **Nothing God sends is wasted and nothing he withholds is needed!**

Nuf Sed!

May 29
"A Timely and Encouraging Word"
Part II

"Do you not know? Have you not heard? The Lord is the everlasting God, the Creator of the ends of the earth. He will not grow tired or weary, and His understanding no one can fathom" (Isaiah 40:28).

Yesterday, we discovered that God raised up Isaiah to deliver a 27 chapter love letter (Isaiah 40-66) to Israel. Why? Because Israel was about to embark on a 700 mile journey back home to Jerusalem. With so much before Israel, and with so many unknowns, God wanted to bring rest to their restless hearts. His word to Israel is a word to you as well. It's a word to accept and believe today. It's a powerful faith builder that's wrapped around three undeniable realities:

I. God Has a Good "Plan" For You!

Why is Isaiah so bent on his encouraging word to Israel? Because Israel is in captivity and Isaiah sees their afflictions and temptations. He hears the people of God uttering discouraging words. He knows about the invasion of the Assyrian army. And Isaiah sees how the Hebrew exiles handle their dilemma and it isn't good. Notice what Israel says when they are being tested and tried:

♦ **"My way is hidden from the Lord"** (v.27).

Israel is saying, "The Lord has forgotten us, deserted us, left us, hid his face from us, and rejected us because of our past failures." What about you today? Maybe you've been tempted to think the same thing. Maybe you're going through deep waters or a personal crisis. Just maybe you feel that God has rejected you because of past failures. The good news is, your way is not hidden from the Lord and He is not against you, but for you! Israel also said:

♦ **"My cause is disregarded by my God"** (v.27).

Which means that Israel is saying, "God you haven't been fair, you let the Babylonians get away with something, you overlooked our pain, you waited 70 years before you intervened for us."

1. Israel thinks that God doesn't know where they are (and)
2. Israel thinks that God has missed some things that were done unjustly.

In other words, Israel became impatient while in captivity. Have you? Israel had answers to prayer delayed. Have you? Israel was detoured in their journey. Have you? Israel was focusing on her past failures. Are you? Israel was left deserted and abandoned. Have you? Israel needed to hear Isaiah's message.

Do you? The message is loud and clear and it's the take-a-way:

♦ **Your way is not hidden from the Lord** (Job 23:10).
♦ **Your times and seasons are in His hands** (Psalm 31:15).
♦ **Your steps each day are a part of a higher plan ordained by God** (Psalm 37:23).

Nuf Sed!

"A Timely and Encouraging Word"
Part III

"He gives strength to the weary and increases the power of the weak" (Isaiah 40:29).

Yesterday, we discovered that God had a good plan for Israel and that God has a good plan for you! When Israel thought that her way was hidden from the Lord and that God was being unfair, Isaiah delivered good news in perfect timing. Not only does God have a good plan for you, but:

II. God Has a Glorious "Promise" For You!
What's the promise that should bring great hope, rest and joy to your heart? Listen to Isaiah's comfort:

♦ God is never out to lunch or off duty!
"The Lord is the everlasting God, the Creator of the ends of the earth" (v.28). This means that God is constant, trustworthy and never has to take a sick day off to recoup His strength. It means that God never ceases to be at work in your life. It means that God is not moody, has no fainting spells and makes no error or mistakes. It means that you can trust Him to be at work even when you cannot see Him working!

♦God is never overwhelmed or tired!
"He will not grow tired or weary" (v.28).
This means that God never gets weary of hearing your prayers, ordering your steps, comforting your heart, forgiving your sin, receiving your praise, and giving you the wisdom that you need in the journey! God is never overwhelmed by what overwhelms you!!!

♦ God is never lacking wisdom and never needs my advice!
"His understanding no one can fathom" (v.28).
This means that God never has the nervous jitters, is never perplexed and without a plan, is never in need of plan B, is never caught off guard, is never at a loss and is worthy to be trusted!

♦ God is never unapproachable or too far away!
"He gives strength to the weary and increases the power of the weak" (v.29). What is God saying here? He is saying that He invites us to run, reach out to Him and approach Him. Why? Because he longs to share himself with you and me! Yes, God is longing to have an intimate relationship with you! The take-a-way?

God did not create us because He needed somebody to love Him; He created us because He wanted to share His love with us!   Nuf Sed!

"A Timely and Encouraging Word"
Part IV

"Those who hope in the Lord will renew their strength. They will soar on wings like eagles, they will run and not grow weary, they will walk and not be faint" (Isaiah 40:31).

In Isaiah 40, we have discovered that God has a great plan and a great promise for those who follow Him. Today, discover how God has great power to make and keep you strong. How does God do that?

"Those who hope in the Lord will renew their strength" (v.31).

The word "hope" (or wait) means: 1. To draw close to, 2. To look away from yourself and look to God, 3. To expect and not waiver. And, what happens to those who draw close to God?

"The Lord will renew their strength" (v.31).

The word "renew" means "To exchange". It means that we exchange our weakness for God's strength when we look to Him in prayer. It means that:

III. God Has Great "Power" For You to Be Strong!

So, what's the great payback for being hungry and thirsty and seeking God in prayer? It's described in Isaiah 40:31:

♦ **You Mount Up with Wings as Eagles** (your **"perception"** changes)

The eagle has incredible eyesight. And, Isaiah is saying here, that believers who draw close to God will see better. In other words, as your elevation increases, your spiritual perception increases. You mount up higher than earthly affections! You see what others don't see! You're not elite (because you're only made holy by the work of another -Jesus). You're simply rewarded for your diligence in drawing close to Jesus.

♦ **You Run and Are Not Weary** (your **"perseverance"** changes)

This means that you march forward into battle with perseverance and endurance, and refuse to quit. It means you despise the thought of dropping out, quitting, or withdrawing. It means that intimacy with God restores your heart and strength. It means that God (in prayer) renews your weakness and helps you persevere in your journey.

♦ **You Walk and Don't Faint** (your **"patience"** changes)

Walking here refers to fortitude and patience under affliction. This walking steadily means that you receive fresh grace from living close to Jesus. And, this fresh grace enables you to patiently endure without fainting in battle. It means greater is He who is in you (to make you strong) than he that is against you (to make you faint).

The take-a-way?

Living close to Jesus in prayer and communion carries its own reward!

Nuf Sed!

"Saul's Spiritual Slide"
Part I

"The Spirit of the Lord will come upon you in power and you will prophesy with them, and you will be changed…for God is with you" (I Samuel 10:6,7).

"God has turned away from me. He no longer answers me" (I Samuel 28:15).

I've heard it said, that a guardrail at the top of the cliff is better than a hospital at the bottom. And, Saul's story is definitely a guardrail. It's a picture, a warning and an illustration of how to lose the touch of God upon your heart and life. It's a story that helps us not to neglect the grace of God. Saul's story begins with Israel's cry for a king: "Appoint a king to lead us, such as all the other nations have" (I Samuel 8:5). Israel cried out for a king for three reasons:

1. There was **Division**, as Israel was a loose confederation of tribes (Judges 17:6; 21:25).

2. There was **Danger**, as the enemy Ammonites were about to attack (I Samuel 12:12).

3. There was **Defilement**, as Samuel's sons accepted bribes in leadership (I Samuel 8:1-3).

And, in the midst of this, Saul was raised up to lead and he had it all at his fingertips:

1. He was from a leading family (the tribe of Benjamin) (9:1)
2. He was physically strong and attractive (9:2)
3. He was obedient to his father Kish (9:3,4)
4. He was submitted to delegated authority (9:5)
5. He was teachable (willing to visit Samuel at the advice of his servant) (9:6-10)
6. He was promised he would find 2 lost animals (10:2)
7. He was assured that his needs would be supplied (10:3,4)
8. He was guaranteed the Spirit's enablement (10:6)
9. He was provided the laborers he needed (10:26)
10. He was the recipient of a double portion of the Spirit (11:6)
11. He was courageous to fight against the Ammonites (11:11)
12. He was a great forgiver of his critics (11:12,13)

In I Samuel 12, Samuel's great sermon is recorded. Saul is exhorted to be faithful, he is established as Israel's first King, he has a great public coronation at Gilgal and he looks so promising and victorious! Yet, soon after, God gives us insight into how Saul abused his anointing, lost his privileges and was rejected by God. It's all recorded to help us cooperate with the grace of God and overcome spiritual neglect. It's a list of subtle perils to be aware of and avoid at all cost. It's a gift from God to help us guard our hearts and glorify God's name. It's not moralism or legalism – it's wisdom to remember to protect our potential and future.

The take-a-way?

No one is exempt from temptation and none of us stay strong without continually trusting Jesus and aligning our hearts with His!

Nuf Sed!

"Saul's Spiritual Slide"
Part II

"'What have you done?' asked Samuel." (I Samuel 13:11)

Yesterday, we learned that Israel cried out for a king because there was division, danger, and defilement facing the leadership. We saw how Saul was raised up to lead and had a great coronation in Gilgal, but soon after was rejected by God. For the next three days, I want to share my discoveries from Saul's failure. They have been given to us by God to warn, guard and protect our hearts. They are simply perils to avoid at all cost!

1. Saul Was Too Proud (To Be Corrected).
"'What have you done?' asked Samuel. Saul replied…'you did not come at the set time.'" (I Samuel 13:11).

Saul was told by Samuel to wait seven days in Gilgal and then Samuel would offer burnt offerings and fellowship offerings (I Samuel 10:8). But Saul acted out of fear when he saw the Philistines gather at Michmash. He ignores Samuel's instructions, makes excuses for running ahead of God, and blames Samuel for his own impatience and disobedience. In other words, Saul's pride won't allow him to accept responsibility for his own actions, nor allow him to be corrected. Remember: We can make excuses or we can make progress, but we can't make both!

2. Saul Was Too Outward (To Be Sensitive).
"I have not sought the Lord's favor, so I felt compelled to offer the burnt offering" (I Samuel 13:12).

Saul admits something here: "I failed to make supplication unto the Lord, and so I forced myself and offered the burnt offering." In other words, Saul quit praying and as a result, his enemies on the outside became bigger than God on the inside! He became afraid (v.6), impatient (v.8,9) and anxious (v.11). Why? He went on momentum and shifted from God dependency to self-dependency. He quit seeking God for wisdom and direction. He moved from humility to pride and just didn't need the Lord anymore.

3. Saul Was Too Egotistical (To Give Glory to God)
"Cursed be any man who eats food before evening comes, before I have avenged myself on my enemies" (I Samuel 14:24).

When Jonathan spoke about the battle, God was glorified: "The Lord will act in our behalf; Nothing can hinder the Lord from saving, whether by many or by few" (v.6). But Saul's motive is vengeance and pride, not the glory of God. In other words, Jonathan gave God the credit, while Saul wanted credit for himself. And what was Jonathan's testimony about his father? "My father has made trouble for the country" (v.29). Why did Saul trouble the country? Because his ego got in the way! He wanted everybody to know that he was the big cheese! He forgot that God resists the proud and will not share His glory with any other! The take-a-way?

When the branches go out farther than the roots go down deep, the tree topples over in the storm!

Nuf Sed!

"Saul's Spiritual Slide"
Part III

"Now go, attack the Amalekites and totally destroy everything that belongs to them" (I Samuel 15:3).

Yesterday we discovered that Saul was too proud, too busy to seek the Lord, and troubled the land because of his inflated ego. Today, we'll see more perils to avoid – to be healthy and enjoy the journey.

4. Saul Was Too Shallow (To Repent of His Disobedience)
"But Saul spared Agag... these they were unwilling to destroy completely" (v.9). The Lord told Saul to destroy the Amalekites, take no spoil and burn everything burnable. Why did God command this? Because the Amalekites hated the people of God:

♦ They fought with Israel in Rephidim. (Exodus 17:8-13)
♦ They attacked Israel in Hormah. (Numbers 14:43)
♦ They joined Moab and ambushed Israel again. (Judges 3:13)
♦ They joined the Midianites and raided Israel's crops and livestock. (Judges 6,7,10)

Yet, Saul spared the king, kept the spoil and lied to Samuel. What was the result? God was angry (v.11), Samuel was grieved (v.11), and Saul was rejected (v.23). The point is, Saul refused to get rid of something that God said to get rid of. In other words, whenever we allow something to remain that God says, "get rid of", we forfeit God's favor and lose ground. So, is there anything in your life that God has been dealing with you about, to get rid of, because it's not God's will for you to entertain?

5. Saul Was Too Insecure (To Be Obedient to God)
"I violated the Lord's command and your instructions. I was afraid of the people and so I gave in to them" (15:24). Saul feared the people's opinion and disapproval more than God's! Samuel asked Saul, "Why did you not obey the Lord?" (15:19). And Saul replied, "I completely destroyed the Amalekites" (v.20). And Samuel says, "To obey is better than sacrifice" (v.22), which means; God didn't want the spoils, He wanted obedience. The lesson for us is, the fear of the Lord is what overcomes our insecurities (Proverbs 29:25). Saul proved that he could not be trusted under pressure!

6. Saul Was Too Plastic (To Be Transparent)
"Saul replied, 'I have sinned. But please honor me before the elders of my people and before Israel'" (I Samuel 15:30). Here is a revelation about Saul's great concern throughout his career. What is it? It's, "what do people think of me?" Saul even says, "Please honor me before Israel." Why? Because his

main motivation is our take-a-way today:

♦ **Image can be more important to us than our condition!**
♦ **Reputation can be more important to us than our character!**
♦ **People's approval can lead us to make excuses, cut corners and forfeit authenticity!**

Nuf Sed!

June 4
"Saul's Spiritual Slide"
Part IV

"Whatever Saul sent him to do, David did it so successfully that Saul gave him a high rank in the army" (I Samuel 18:5).

Yesterday we learned that Saul was disobedient, insecure and more concerned about his image than his condition. Today we'll conclude our study on why Saul didn't enjoy the journey, and how we can avoid the same pitfalls.

7. Saul Was Too Jealous (To be Supportive)
"They have credited David with tens of thousands," he thought, "but me with only thousands" (I Samuel 18:8). This is where David became the enemy in Saul's heart. Why? Because Saul couldn't handle David getting the praise from war that Saul wanted. Saul's jealousy viewed David as a rival and competitor. His pride and insecurities caused him to fall prey to fear, envy and anger. Saul just couldn't rejoice with those who rejoice because David had what Saul wanted -praise from the people. "Lord, protect us from envy which is that pain we feel when someone else has something that we want. Help us to be content in You."

8. Saul Was Too Angry (To Be Rational)
"Saul's plan was to have David fall by the hands of the Philistines" (I Samuel 18:25). Anger is unexpressed energy. It forms in us when our mind interprets a situation as threatening, and a biochemical reaction is triggered. This results in large amounts of energy for you to use in facing the perceived threat. And, Saul was flat out angry as, "he remained his (David's) enemy the rest of his days" (18:29). What about us today? Have we carried any unresolved anger because someone has failed to meet our needs, blocked our intended goals or offended us in some way? Have we allowed anger to poison our spirit, make us a slave to our emotions, or make us bitter in any way? Remember, "Man's anger does not bring about the righteous life that God desires" (James 1:20).

9. Saul Was Too Selfish (To Be a Servant)
"None of you is concerned about me" (I Samuel 22:8). Here we see that Saul has developed a "poor me" martyr's complex. His focus is on himself, he has become ingrown, needs attention, has a personal agenda and imprisoned himself. So much so, that when wounded in battle, he fell upon his own sword to save face in the conflict. The bottom line is, Saul's problem was Saul and no one else! In fact, it is impossible for a selfish, myopic, narcissistic person to be content and joyful. Why? Because takers can never be fulfilled, because it's all about them! The take-a-way?
Takers may eat better, but givers will sleep better!   Nuf Sed!

"Jonah's Discovery"
Part I

✔ "Those who cling to worthless idols forfeit the grace that could be theirs" (Jonah 2:8).

The book of Jonah is an amazing picture of the grace of God. The main character in the book is not Jonah, not the Ninevites, not the fish, not the sailors – but God! God is mentioned 38 times and He is the One who speaks to the heart.

Jonah was a real person and he was sent to real people. He was the son of Amittai and was called to the place of Nineveh. Nineveh was the capital of the Assyrian Empire, a city in pagan darkness, a place despised by the Jews, and the Assyrians showed no mercy to their enemies. They were cruel and deserved to be judged instead of forgiven. And then one day, God gives the call to Jonah because God desires to rescue us from ourselves. It's an incredible story that speaks specifically – wherever God finds you in your journey! Notice:

I. Jonah Is Interrupted (By a Call from God)
"The word of the Lord came to Jonah son of Amittai: 'Go to the great city of Nineveh and preach'" (Jonah 1:1,2).

Why did God call Jonah to Nineveh? Because Nineveh was filled with people who were alienated from God! Nineveh was filled with pride, splendor, and spoils from the Monarchs of Assyria! And, God called Jonah to cry against sin because God doesn't want one person to be lost for eternity. Jonah was interrupted and asked to proclaim an alarm that danger awaits those who are away from God. Jonah's call was a call to live on mission and live for what really matters – eternal things.
Question: Are you and I willing to submit to God's plan when He interrupts us for a higher plan?

II. Jonah Is Intimidated (By What Surrounds Him)
"But Jonah ran away from the Lord and headed for Tarshish" (1:3). Why did Jonah run? Because he knew that God would spare those who repented. He knew that God would save undeserving sinners. Jonah didn't want Nineveh to escape the wrath of God's judgment. He had a hard time with God being gracious to people who did not honor Him. He somehow forgot how God treated him when he didn't deserve it. He lost sight of one thing – mercy, mercy, mercy.

So, Jonah runs the other way because he is intimidated, hesitant and stubborn. And what does God do? He doesn't give up on Jonah, and He hasn't given up on you! In fact, God goes to great lengths to use Jonah, all because of His great love for people. Remember friend; Jesus didn't die by accident and He didn't die in vain. He died on purpose and He died to save those who will call upon His name (in faith and repentance).

The take-a-way?

Understanding the depth of God's mercy towards us, will translate into us being merciful toward others.

Nuf Sed!

"Jonah's Discovery"
Part II

J"Those who cling to worthless idols forfeit the grace that could be theirs" (Jonah 2:8).

Yesterday we discovered how Jonah was called by God to cry against the Ninevites, and how he responded by running away toward a place called Tarshish. Notice how much that God loved Nineveh and how much that God loves you as well:

III. Jonah Is Intercepted (By Providential Circumstances)

"But the Lord provided a great fish to swallow Jonah" (1:17). "From inside the fish Jonah prayed to the Lord his God" (2:1). While Jonah is on the run from the will of God, God sets His plan in motion with a boat, a storm, some sailors, and a fish. And from the belly of a great sized fish, "Jonah prayed to the Lord" (2:1). Did Jonah deserve to be heard in prayer? Not hardly; he was a spiritual deserter! Did the Lord hear Jonah's prayer? "I called to the Lord and He answered me" (2:22). And look how Jonah responds; notice his language:

♦ "From the depths of the grave I called for help, and you listened to my cry" (2:2).
♦ "You brought my life up from the pit" (2:5).
♦ "What I have vowed I will make good" (2:9)

And take notice of v.8:

"Those who cling to worthless idols forfeit the grace that could be theirs" (2:8). Wow!

The words, **"worthless idols"** means: an idol, pursuit, or ambition that draws us away from God and His Glory.

The words, **"Forfeit the grace that could be theirs"** means: to turn from God and His will for your life, and forfeit God's best that He has in store for you. It means, anything we pursue that God is not attached to, is self-inflicted pain and loss. It means, idols of the heart will leave us with an empty bag and have no lasting advantage in life. Simply, to place your trust in, or to treasure anything more than Jesus and the gospel, will leave us disillusioned and full of regret. Sounds like God was getting through to Jonah!

IV. Jonah Is Introduced (To the Grace of God)

"Then the word of the Lord came to Jonah a second time" (3:1). In rebellion, Jonah ran to Tarshish. In repentance, Jonah ran to God. In restoration, Jonah ran to Nineveh. In other words, Jonah was reinstated to preach and recommissioned to Nineveh. Did he deserve God's grace? Of course not; he ran from the Lord, was angry and pouted because God was merciful. Yet God teaches us one great lesson and it's our take-a-way:

♦ **We are sinful beyond belief, yet loved beyond measure!**
♦ **God is still the God of a second chance!**
♦ **The Christian life is made up of 10,000 new beginnings!**
♦ **God offers renewed opportunities to those who forfeited previous opportunities!**

Nuf Sed!

"David's Transformation"

"I acknowledged my sin to you and did not cover up my iniquity. I said, 'I will confess my transgressions to the Lord – and you forgave the guilt of my sin" (Psalm 32:5).

Psalm 32 is one of the seven penitential Psalms (6, 38, 51, 102, 130, 143). It's a record of David's pain (in conviction) and joy (in forgiveness). It's a journey of the heart, that goes from transgression to transformation. It's a true account of how God's amazing grace will change us from the inside out. The steps in the process are undeniable and unmistakable:

I. David's Conviction (v.1-4)
"When I kept silent my bones wasted away through my groaning all day long. For day and night your hand was heavy upon me; my strength was sapped as in the heat of summer" (v.3,4).

The occasion of Psalm 32 is David's experience – including his conversion, sin with Bathsheba or murder of Uriah. When David was convicted, he covered his sin, attempted to conceal it and hoped that conviction would go away. And, the results of David's cover-up are documented:

♦ There was **Decay** – as David's health began to falter (v.3)
♦ There was **Distress** – as David felt the guilt on his conscience (v.4)
♦ There was **Drought** – as David's soul dried up like a drought in the heat of summer (v.4)

Why is David suffering in his health, conscience and spirit? Because he cannot pray to God in faith and assurance: "Innumerable evils have compassed me about; my iniquities have taken hold upon me, so that **I am not able to look up**" (Psalm 40:12, KJV).

II. David's Confession (v.5)
"I will confess my transgressions to the Lord" (v.5).
After suffering the conviction, pressure and anguish long enough, David finally turns to the Lord in humility, repentance and confession. He agrees with God; he refuses to cover up; he stops trying to hide; and he takes the steps to be free from sin. He allows Godly sorrow to take him to the next step of freedom and joy. And what happens when we confess our sins to God? Notice:

III. David's Cleansing (v.1,2,5,6)
"Blessed is he whose transgressions are forgiven, whose sins are covered…whose sin the Lord does not count against him" (v.12).

Why are the forgiven so blessed? Because:

♦ **Forgiven** – means to bear all and carry away!

♦ **Covered** – means to conceal out of view!

♦ **Counted against** – means sin cannot be charged to your account nor accuse you any longer!

What happens when we truly confess and repent of our sin? "Rejoice in the Lord and be glad you righteous, sing all you who are upright in heart" (v.11). In other words, there is a song that replaces our sorrow and a shout that replaces our silence! Why? It's our take-a-way:

When Calvary covers what we uncover, there is joy unspeakable and genuine gladness of heart!

Nuf Sed!

"Paul's Radical Turnaround"
Part I

"All those who heard him were astonished and asked, 'Isn't he the man who raised havoc in Jerusalem among those who call on this name?'" (Acts 9:21).

Ever wonder how God can change someone who is angry, anti-God, and full of spiritual pride? Ever worry how God is going to save someone who seems so far from God? Ever doubt that God can change what needs to be changed in you? Then follow the story of how God changed Saul into Paul, a madman into a missionary. See the steps in his journey of transformation and triumph.

I. Saul's Persecution of Believers (Is Very Adamant)

Just take a look at how evil Saul was before his heart was changed by the grace of God:

♦ "And Saul was there, giving approval to his (Stephen's) death" (Acts 8:1).
♦ "But Saul began to destroy the church. Going from house to house, he dragged off men and women and put them in prison" (v.3).
♦ "I persecuted the followers of this Way to their death" (22:4).
♦ "I put many of the saints in prison, and when they were put to death, I cast my vote against them" (26:10).

Saul is first mentioned in Acts 7:58, seen as a supporting cast member watching Stephen being stoned to death. Saul had debated with Stephen, dragged him before the council and supported the forum of Jewish execution. Saul's one goal in life was to rid the countryside of all believers. The language of Acts 8:3 reveals that Saul kept on ravaging, fighting and doing his best to destroy the work of God. So much so, that Saul (in Acts 9:2) went to the high priests, and the Sanhedrin, to request authority to pursue the scattered believers and put them all on trial.

Can you see the evil force behind Saul's actions?
1. He consents (or willingly approves or delights) in Stephen's death.
2. He takes pleasure in arresting every believer possible.
3. He stormed the homes of believers without shame.
4. He dragged Christians through city streets.
5. He ordered Christians to blaspheme the Name of Jesus.
6. He hunted down believers in foreign cities.
7. He gave his voice for the death penalty of so many others.

And yet, God reveals to us, in Saul, that there are four things that God doesn't know:
♦ He doesn't know of any sinner that He does not love!
♦ He doesn't know of any sin that He cannot forgive!
♦ He doesn't know of any other way to be saved, then through faith is His

Son, Jesus!

♦ He doesn't know of any better time to be saved than right now!

The take-a-way?

There is nothing in your life that you have done, that is greater than the Grace of God to forgive your sin!

Nuf Sed!

"Paul's Radical Turnaround"
Part II

"As he neared Damascus on his journey, suddenly a light from heaven flashed around him. He fell to the ground and heard a voice say to him, 'Saul, Saul, why do you persecute me?'" (Acts 9:3,4).

Yesterday, we saw how Saul persecuted the Lord's church, and just how much he was angry and full of rage. Today we'll discover how the grace of God can overcome the hardest of hearts and change us from the inside out.

II. Saul's Apprehension by God (Is Very Humbling)

"'Who are you, Lord? Saul asked. 'I am Jesus, whom you are persecuting'" (9:5).

Saul had received the letters and authority that he asked for, and heads off to Damascus to hunt down believers. He journeys five or six days toward Damascus, the capital city of Syria. And, at noon on the last day of the journey, the unexpected takes place:

♦ There was an **unexpected light** from heaven (v.3). A supernatural light appeared from heaven, a light brighter than the noonday sun (Acts 26:13). This light came to Saul while he was on his mission to destroy believers. Light is the first thing experienced in salvation. It is the knowledge, awareness, quickening and understanding that Jesus is the Savior. Did Saul deserve the light? Not at all! Do we deserve the light? Not at all! The good news here is this; Saul was so steeped in sin and yet God was able to penetrate the hardest of hearts. This reveals to us, that God is able to break in and penetrate through every excuse we could ever give him. God's light can pierce any darkness and expose any hidden hardness of heart!

♦ There was an **unexpected voice** from heaven (v.4). What is the big deal about the Lord calling Saul? The voice here was a tender voice, as Jesus called Saul's name twice with love and compassion. The voice was a convicting voice, that left Saul trembling and astonished in his tracks!

♦ There was an **unexpected yet noticeable change** (v.17). "Then Ananias went to the house and entered it. Placing his hands on Saul, he said, 'Brother Saul, the Lord Jesus, who appeared to you on the road as you were coming here, has sent me so that you may see again and be filled with the Holy Spirit'" (v.17). Saul had been blind for three days and was broken in utter submission. He cries out to Jesus and surrenders to whatever God wants from him. And, what happened to Saul? He was saved by the grace of God, filled with the Spirit of God, baptized in water, strengthened, delivered from death plots, and ordained to preach the gospel to turn people, "from darkness to light, and from the power of satan to God, so that they may receive forgiveness of sins" (Acts 26:18).

The take-a-way from Saul turned into the apostle Paul?

If God could change Paul's heart and misguided affections, then there is nothing too hard for God to change in you and me!   Nuf Sed!

June 10
"The Ahimaaz Seduction"

"'Let me run and take the news to the king'... 'You are not the one to take the news today,' Joab told him. 'You may take the news another time'" (II Samuel 18:19,20).

I can remember when I felt like life was **"on hold."** **"On hold"** waiting for an open door after graduating Bible college. **"On hold"** leaving youth ministry to plant a church. **"On hold"** during pastoral transitions to a new community. Sometimes it's just uncomfortable when you hear what Ahimaaz heard; "No, not today, another time you can run with the message." I love the message that God gives us from Ahimaaz:

In II Samuel 18, Absalom has rebelled against his father, King David. A civil war breaks out, Absalom is killed and Joab needs someone to send word to David. The priest's son, Ahimaaz, begs Joab to run with the news to David. Joab tells Ahimaaz no, because Joab knows how David will process the sad news of his son being killed. Yet Ahimaaz begs and begs. There's just one problem; all that Ahimaaz wants to do is to be chosen for the big run. He yaps and yaps away to Joab, at the time when Joab needs him to just trust and be patient. In other words, Ahimaaz has trouble being "on hold"; he wants to have his own way, can't take no for an answer, and pushes himself forward. And, after outrunning the other messenger from Cush, Ahimaaz ends up in disgrace and is asked to step aside. What's the lesson when you're not chosen, tempted to resent your leadership or just plain impatient? It's practical wisdom from God to your heart and mine.

1. There's Always a Bigger Picture Than What You See!
All Ahimaaz wanted to do was run with the battle news, but Joab knew things that Ahimaaz didn't know. Joab knew how David would respond to the devastating report about Absalom. And, Ahimaaz has to make a choice; rest in God's sovereignty or shove his way forward.

2. It's Not What I Want; It's What's Best for The Team!
All Ahimaaz cares about is his running, but Joab cares about how David will process his grief of Absalom's death. This teaches me that it's team first instead of me first! This reminds me of one central truth: the freedom to do your own thing ends when you join a team!

3. It's Better to Pray Doors Open Than to Beg Doors Open!
It's obvious that Ahimaaz had difficulty in trusting God with his life and his assignment.
- "Let me run and take the news" (v.19).
- "Come what may, please let me run" (v.22).
- "Come what may, I want to run" (v.23).

Ahimaaz somehow thinks that he's the only one who can bear the message to David.

4. You Never Look Good by Making a Teammate Look Bad!
In (v.22), Ahimaaz said he would run "behind the Cushite." But in (v.23), we learn that Ahimaaz, "outran the Cushite." In other words, Ahimaaz took a short cut to beat the other runner. Yet, in the end, Ahimaaz was asked to step aside because he failed to bring the message and war report.

The take-a-way from Ahimaaz?
♦ **You can't enjoy the journey when you're in a hurry or want attention! (and)**
♦ **You can't rely on a star who wants to outshine the team!**

Nuf Sed!

June 11
"Moses' Eternal Decision"
Part I

"He chose to be mistreated along with the people of God rather than to enjoy the pleasure of sin for a short time" (Hebrews 11:25).

Someone once said, "Those who do the most for God in this life, are those who think the most about the next life." I **fully** agree!

While so much could be said about Moses' life and leadership, I want to focus on his decision that's found in Hebrews 11. God gives great detail about this decision and it speaks volumes to us today. Notice what God wants us to remember and how it will affect us day after day right now:

I. Moses Passed The "Position" Test!

"By faith Moses, when he had grown up, refused to be known as the son of Pharaoh's daughter" (Hebrews 11:24).

Moses was the adopted son of the princess, privileged with great opportunity and education, and a ruler with a government position. In fact, Stephen said, **"Moses was educated in all the wisdom of the Egyptians and was powerful in speech and action"** (Acts 7:22). It would have been so easy for Moses to stay in Egypt because:

♦ Pharaoh's daughter had saved his life.

♦ Moses was the only Jew not enslaved.

♦ Jethro's daughter thought Moses was an Egyptian (Exodus 2:19).

But Moses passed the "position" test! Why? How? Because he knew that God had a plan outside of the palace life! He knew that he was privileged to identify with God's people – Israel! He knew that his decision would seem foolish to those around him. He knew that he would be going from a **"ruler with man"** to a **"servant of God."** He knew that he was trading luxury, personal advancement, higher rank, and earthly advantages – all for the glory of God. Are we willing to do the same? Jesus did!

II. Moses Passed The "Pleasure" Test!

"He chose to be mistreated along with the people of God rather than to enjoy the pleasures of sin for a short time" (V.25).

Moses has one of two choices before him: a life of ease, pleasure and affluence in Egypt, or a life of leadership with the people of God. In other words, will Moses live for the immediate, or will Moses live for the eternal? Will we live for what is passing quickly, or will we live for that which is permanent? And, V. 25 doesn't at all mean there isn't pleasure in serving God. It means that Moses refused to participate in the pursuits that would distract his attention, crowd out God's plan, compromise his convictions, diminish his spiritual influence and forfeit his eternal reward.

The take-a-way?

If we make better decisions now, we will live with fewer regrets later!

Nuf Sed!

"Moses' Eternal Decision"
Part II

"He regarded disgrace for the sake of Christ as of greater value than the treasures of Egypt, because he was looking ahead to his reward" (Hebrews 11:26).

Yesterday, we saw how Moses passed the **"Position"** test as well as the **"Pleasure"** test. Today, discover how Moses made the right decisions and how you can too.

III. Moses Passed The "Promise" Test!
"...He was looking ahead to his reward" (V.26).

Egypt promised Moses prestige, power, pennies and position. Today, sin promises the same, and yet destroys so many through the lure of:

♦ **Greed** – which is the inordinate desire for more and the excessive hunger to possess!

♦ **Power** – which is the lust to maintain control over other people and manipulate them for personal gain.

♦ **Fame** – which is the longing to be popular and impress other people.

♦ **Pleasure** – which is the desire to fulfill sensual cravings and be satisfied at any cost. Its motto is, "If it feels good, do it!"

Why did Moses make the right decisions? Because Moses knew these four things: Life is built on **character**, character is built on **decisions**, decisions are built on **values**, and values are built on **faith** in the truth of God's Word. How did Moses make the right decisions? How can we make the right decisions as well? The key is found in V. 26: "He regarded disgrace for the sake of Christ." The word "regarded" (esteem) means 1. To Reckon and 2. To Evaluate. In other words, Moses said "no" to Egypt's offer because he evaluated correctly. He said "No" because his spiritual values were in order. And, why did Moses have no regrets for his decision? "Because he was looking ahead to his reward" (V.26). The people of God were of more value than treasures in Egypt, the reproach for Christ was of more value than Egypt's fame, and eternal promises were more valuable than temporary promises; all because he saw, "his reward" (V.26). In other words, Moses kept his eyes on the future, on the city to come, on the end, and not the immediate!

IV. Moses Passed The "Vision" Test!
"He persevered because he saw Him who is invisible" (V.27).

Israel often wanted to go back to Egypt but Moses never entertained going back. Why not? Because he, "saw him who is invisible" (V.27). In other words, he looked past Pharaoh, past Pharaoh's power, and saw the Lord! His perspective was on the long term, not the short term! And this made V.27 possible: "Not fearing the king's anger." The faith of Moses gave him such security, that he didn't live in fear, regret or worry. Why? Because he knew where he was going and he knew Who he was serving!

The take-a-way?

Faith allows you to look long term and properly evaluate from God's perspective!

Nuf Sed!

"The Power of Deflection"
Part I

"They came to John and said to him, "Rabbi, that man who was with you on the other side of the Jordan – the one you testified about -well, he is baptizing, and everyone is going to Him" (John 3:26).

The passage of John 3:22-31 answers one basic question: How can John rejoice that his popularity is declining while Jesus' popularity is increasing? How can John remain joyful while being overlooked for another? How can John deflect all praise to God, while others are envious and upset? Grasp the setting in the text:

John the Baptist's teaching on repentance and baptism has spread throughout the Asian churches (Acts 19). Jesus is now involved in a preaching and teaching ministry in Judea. Many respond to Jesus' invitations and are being baptized. And, a problem arises for some. What's the problem? **"Everyone is going to Him"** (V.26). In other words, John the Baptist's disciples became jealous because people were leaving John to follow Jesus. Jesus' popularity was growing while John's was shrinking. Controversy breaks out, a potential rivalry begins, and John responds to defuse the situation. He moves with such humility, and says five things that produce and reveal a "Gospel Centered" healthy heart:

I. Everything We Possess Is a Gift from God!
"John answered and said, "A man can receive nothing, except it be given him from heaven" (V.27, KJV).

What is John saying here? He is saying something that produces a healthy heart, a wholesome attitude and a spirit of deflection. It's unmistakable wisdom from God:
♦ Everything we have on earth has been given to us by God!
♦ Every gift and talent is on loan from above! And, because of this truth, we can never brag or boast about how great we are. Remember Paul's words:
"For who makes you different from anyone else? What do you have that you did not receive? And if you did receive it, why do you boast as though you did not?" (I Corinthians 4:7).

John says what he says in John 3 because he knows that it's not about him – it's all about Jesus! John teaches us that there's great liberty in having nothing to prove and no one to impress! John also teaches:

II. The Gifts That We Possess Have Been Given for God's Glory!
"I am not the Christ, but am sent ahead of him" (V.28).

Why is John okay with the rising popularity of Jesus? Because John's goal in life and ministry is to make Jesus famous! John's burning passion is for God's fame, not his own! John doesn't need to be exalted or remembered because it's all about God's Glory! John flat out wants people to see Jesus and not himself! The take-a-way?

Living for God's glory will protect you from envy and jealousy – so you can serve with joy and gladness and enjoy the journey!

Nuf Sed!

"The Power of Deflection"
Part II

"The friend who attends the bridegroom waits and listens for him, and is full of joy when he hears the bridegroom's voice" (John 3:29).

Yesterday, we learned how John was able to rejoice as his popularity decreased and Jesus' increased. John showed us two things as he deflected all attention to Jesus: 1. Everything we possess is a gift from above, and, 2. The gifts we possess have been given for God's glory! Today we will uncover the other three truths from John's lips that result in a healthy heart and contagious joy.

III. Living for God's Glory Brings True Joy to The Heart!
"That joy is mine, and it is now complete" (V.29).

John tells us a parable here to explain the context of his joy. In the biblical world, the friend of the bridegroom was an extremely important person. He was responsible for many of the wedding details, especially for bringing the bride to the groom. But, when he had done this, his task was over. He did not expect to take center stage! In the same way, John's joy was in uniting Jesus to the people. John's joy was found, not in wrapping people around himself, but around Jesus (the Bridegroom). So, when John received word from his disciples about Jesus, it filled his joy bucket very full! Why? Because John worked his whole life focusing on the Groom getting His Bride. John, like the bridegroom's friend, did not seek pre-eminence; it was not his day! As long as Jesus was worshipped, John could be ignored, overlooked, content and satisfied!

IV. Our Joy Is Complete According to Our Deflection!
"He must become greater; I must become less" (V.30)

Here we see the setting star (John) and the rising Son (Jesus). John knew his duty was to awaken Israel and prepare people for Christ. John does not desire that Israel follow him, but lean on Jesus. John knows that crowds need not follow the forerunner after his task is accomplished. What use is the herald after the King has arrived?

V. We Can Only Deflect Credit as We Remain Under Jesus!
"The one who comes from heaven is above all" (V.31).

The message here is, Jesus is of a heavenly origin and we are under Him as servants! So, true joy and contentment comes from possessing a servant's heart, which is: someone who advances others at the expense of themselves, cares less who gets the credit, doesn't need to be thanked for their service, and takes up their cross without complaint. This is a John the Baptist anointing, or, a heart that is not addicted to wanting to be seen, admired, esteemed or applauded.

The take-a-way?

When all you want in life is to see Christ glorified, you welcome every other person's success that points to Jesus, as a victory of your own!

Nuf Sed!

June 15
"Peter's Rescue"

"'Lord, save me!' Immediately Jesus reached out His hand and caught him" (Matthew 14:30, 31)

Matthew 14 begins the isolation season of Jesus' life and ministry. Jesus withdraws from the crowds to prepare the disciples (alone) for the impending crucifixion. In 14:13, Jesus withdraws to a desert place; in 15:21 Jesus withdraws to Tyre and Sidon; in 16:13, Jesus withdraws to Caesarea Philippi; in 17:1, Jesus withdraws into the mountain.

In the setting of today's text, Jesus commands the disciples to board a ship and cross over the lake. Jesus then goes up to the mountain alone to pray. And Jesus teaches us some marvelous lessons to enjoy the journey in an unpredictable world of joy and sorrow. I see three things that Jesus wanted His disciples and us to learn from this time on the water:

I. There Is "Divine Permission" In What Touches Your Life!"
"Jesus made the disciples get into the boat and go on ahead of Him to the other side" (Matthew 14:22).

Who was it that told the disciples to cross the lake in the dark, late at night, all alone, through contrary winds? It was Jesus! But why send them across through high winds? Because in John 6:14, 15, the crowd wanted to make Jesus King after the miracle of the loaves and fishes. The crowd believed that Jesus had come to deliver them from Herod's authority and Roman oppression. So, if the disciples stay on the shore, they will be destroyed by missing the true purpose in Jesus coming. They will be swept away and blinded by the popular excitement and frenzy of the moment. In other words, Jesus knew some things that the disciples didn't know. And Jesus wanted to spare them from greater loss in the bigger picture of life.

II. There Is "Divine Presence" In Every Storm!"
"Jesus went out to them walking on the lake" (Mathew 14:25).

Ever feel like Jesus is unaware, far away or not on time? If so, you're normal! In Mark 6:48, we learn that, "Jesus saw the disciples straining at the oars, because the wind was against them." Jesus takes the initiative, arrives at the darkest time of night, and walks on top of what threatens His disciples. What's the message? It's never so dark where His Presence can't find you! The Lord is with you right now; and always!

III. There Is "Divine Perspective" To Keep Our Attention!
"But when he (Peter) saw the wind, he was afraid, and, beginning to sink, cried out, 'Lord, save me'" (V.30).

When Peter took his eyes off Jesus, he began to sink. And Jesus rebukes Peter for allowing himself to be distracted. Jesus also stretched out His hand and caught Peter before he disappeared under water.

The take-a-way?

♦ Peter didn't deserve to be rescued, but Grace is undeserved favor from God!
♦ You and I don't deserve to be rescued, but Grace is undeserved favor from God!

Nuf Sed!

June 16
"Avoiding Rebellion"
Part I

It's no secret that satan seeks to destroy unity in relationships and the body of Christ! It's also no secret, that the primary tool satan uses is pride, which is manifested through disrespect for delegated authority. Why did Absalom split the church? Because he wanted authority that belonged to another. Absalom forgot:

"He who rebels against the authority is rebelling against what God has instituted, and those who do so will bring judgment on themselves" (Romans 13:2).

Key phrases that trigger and reveal Absalom's failure (II Samuel 15):
♦ Absalom would "stand by the side of the road leading to the city gate" (V.2).
♦ "There is no representative of the King to hear you" (V.3).
♦ "Everyone who has a complaint or case could come to me" (V.4).
♦ "Absalom would reach out his hand, take hold of him and kiss him" (V.5).
♦ "Absalom sent secret messengers throughout the tribes of Israel" (V.10).
♦ "He stole the hearts of the men of Israel" (V.6).
♦ "Say, 'Absalom is king of Hebron'" (V.10).
♦ "The conspiracy gained strength, and Absalom's following kept on increasing" (V.12).

Absalom, Lucifer, Korah, Jezebel, and Diotrephes all had the same underlining issues:
They desired authority and recognition that they did not have. Because of envy, they coveted what God had given another. They used malicious means to achieve an end, out of selfish ambition. They tried to create doors where none existed, and attracted God's anger upon themselves. They found fault with the leader and projected the image that if they were in charge, all would be much better. They convinced a following to oppose delegated authority. They hurt people and eventually brought judgement upon themselves. Why? Because rebellion is birthed in envy.

♦ **What is envy?** Envy is the feeling of displeasure when hearing about the advantages of another; it is the desire to possess something that is enjoyed by another. Envy is the pain you feel when someone else has something that you want (Absalom's problem).

♦ **What is envy's root cause?** Scripture is so clear: "If you harbor bitter envy, and selfish ambition in your hearts, do not boast about it" (James 3:14).

The root of envy is clearly outlined for us to see:
1. Envy is **"Bitter"** – it resents, instead of rejoices in the fact that God has

given something to another instead of us.

2. Envy is **"Self-seeking"** – which is strife in our hearts because of selfish ambition.

3. Envy is **"Boastful"** – which is pride that wants others to think that we are important.

♦ **What is envy's consequence?** Envy cannot be grateful for what it has, cannot be content because of internal disorder, and cannot celebrate the successes of others.

The take-a-way?

Absalom confirms the New Testament truth: "Where you have envy and selfish ambition, there you find disorder and every evil practice" (James 3:16).

Nuf Sed!

"Avoiding Rebellion"
Part II

"If only **I** were appointed judge in the land. Then everyone who has a complaint or case could come to **me** and **I** would see that he gets justice" (II Samuel 15:4).

Yesterday we learned about the root of envy in Absalom's heart. Today, we'll see the three **characteristics of an Absalom spirit**. You just can't miss these, and by all means, you'll want to avoid them like the plague.

I. A "Counterfeit Compassion" Is Displayed!

"Then everyone who has a complaint or case could come to me and I would see that he gets justice" (V.4).

Absalom stations himself on the road leading to the gate of the city, all to be seen by the people. People come to Jerusalem to meet with David, to find resolve and settlements. Absalom acts as though he really cares and feigns compassion for each petitioner! He implies that the king is too busy to care for them one-on-one. Absalom then projects that if he were in authority, he would be sure that they would come out as the winner in their grievance. Yet, it's all a show because Absalom, will soon reveal his personal agenda. While he appears to be affectionate, it's all out of selfish motivation and for personal gain. Absalom speaks, only to manipulate so he can obtain something that God hasn't given him. Never forget this truth:

♦ Gossip is saying behind a person's back what you would never say to their face (and)
♦ Flattery is saying to a person's face what you would never say behind their back!

II. A "Covert Connection" Is Deceptive!

"While Absalom was offering sacrifices, he also sent for Ahithophel the Gilonite, David's counselor, to come from Giloh, his hometown, and so the conspiracy gained strength, and Absalom's following kept on increasing" (V.12).

Absalom now enlists others to his personal cause and rebellion. He seeks out the advice of Ahithophel (the grandfather of Bathsheba). Once a wise counselor to David, he is seduced to rebel against the king and join sides with Absalom. What's the discovery here? Discontented people will enlist others and rally the troops to their cause. Rebellious people will do their best to sow seeds of discontentment to undermine the authority that God has placed in their lives. Envious people will create divisions to strengthen the vengeance in their own hearts.

III. A **"Cunning Contention"** Is Deadly!
"Strike Amnon down, then kill him" (II Samuel 13:28).

Absalom, out of anger, takes matters into his own hands. He believes that he is above the law and his father's authority. He murders Amnon who had raped his sister Tamar, and believes that he is accountable to no one. He feels that he has the license to harm whoever he wants. He's surely lost the fear of God!

The Absalom take-a-ways?

♦ **If I'm not content with what I have, I will not be content with what I want! (and)**
♦ **If ever I sow seeds of division, I have sided with lucifer and degenerative forces are at work!**

Nuf Sed!

"Your Refreshing in Prayer"
Part I

"Pray that I may be rescued from the unbelievers in Judea and that my service in Jerusalem may be acceptable to the saints there, so that by God's will I may come to you with joy and **together with you be refreshed**" (Romans 15:31,32).

Paul, in his travels, makes an incredible request of the believers in Rome. He asks for united prayer for himself; that God would do five things in answer to prayer. This is no "take it or leave it" request, but a heartfelt plea of support:

"I urge you, brothers, by our Lord Jesus Christ and by the love of the Spirit, to **join me in my struggle** by praying to God for me" (Romans 15:30).

The phrase "Join me in my struggle" comes from the Greek word *Sunagonidzomai*, which means:

♦ To agonize together with ♦ To contend as with an enemy
♦ To struggle through ♦ To battle as in a contest

In other words, Paul never reached the place of not needing others to pray for him. He knew that greater victories are won in united prayer. He needed others to stand and support him in battle! So, what does Paul ask for in prayer? And, how do we enlist prayer for ourselves? What exactly does God want to do in answer to prayer – for you, your pastor, your missionaries, your local church leaders and all those who serve the mission of your local church? I love how clear God is when it comes to prayer, and how we can cooperate with Him through your greatest ministry on earth. Oh God, teach us to make these a part of regular prayer. Remind us often that:

I. God Provides "Protection" Through Prayer!
"Pray that I may be rescued from the unbelievers in Judea" (V.31).

The word for "rescued" here means two things:
♦ It means to be delivered (and)
♦ It means to be pulled from danger.

Why did Paul ask for this protection? Because Paul knew that he was walking into a den of lions. He knew that he had previously escaped death plots on his life (Acts 9 :29, 30). He knew that he was risking his life for the gospel. He knew that there were people who wanted to stop the work of God. He knew that there were troublemakers who would attempt to disrupt, distract, discourage, and destroy the mission. Yet, Paul also knew, that God (through praying people) could stop those who satan was using to set traps and create problems. Do you see the privilege we have here? We have the privilege to restrain the evil one and further the cause of the gospel mission – through the ministry of prayer.

The take-a-way?

If we fail to pray, we will forfeit what prayer was meant to do!

Nuf Sed!

"Your Refreshing in Prayer"
Part II

"Pray... that by God's will I may come to you with joy and together with you be refreshed" (Romans 15:32).

In Romans 15:30-32, Paul asks for prayer. He asks specifically, that the believers would stand with him in prayer for five things. Yesterday, we covered the first request; Paul asked for **protection** through prayer. Today we'll look at Paul's other four requests; we'll learn how to pray for those who serve the Lord.

II. God Provides "Receptivity" Through Prayer!
"Pray... that my service in Jerusalem may be acceptable to the saints there" (V. 31).

Paul wants the believers to pray. Pray for what? Pray that his ministry will be "accepted." The word "accepted" means: pleasing, welcomed and well received. In other words, Paul knew that his mission of mercy might not be well received. He knew there were evil reports spreading around because he was receiving Gentiles into the church. Now, Paul was bringing money as a gift to these Gentiles. What's the message here? That it's biblical to pray that our ministry is warmly received wherever we go, that our motives are easily discerned and that our efforts are crowned with God's favor.

III. God Provides "Direction" Through Prayer!
"So that by God's will..." (V. 32).

The word "will" comes from the Greek word which means: Design, purpose, and plan. It means here, that Paul wants prayer so that he will always be in the center of God's will for his life. He wants wisdom to make right choices; he wants to discover the will of God; he wants to know the voice of God in his innermost being.

IV. God Provides "Joy" Through Prayer!
"Pray... that I may come to you with joy" (V.32).

The word "joy" here means gladness and rejoice. So, Paul asked for believers to pray that he be characterized with the fragrance of joy in his service for God. Paul knows that what happens in you is more important than what happens to you. He knows that a bad attitude makes a person a prisoner of their own experience. He knows that joyless leaders are not healthy or fruitful!

V. God Provides "Refreshment" Through Prayer!
"And together with you be refreshed" (V.32).

The word "refreshed" means to sooth and calm. Paul reveals here that all of us need to be refreshed from time to time, especially those in ministry. Why is being refreshed continually so important? Our take-a-way:

♦ **If we don't come apart and be refreshed, we will fall apart and be sidelined.**

♦ **A professional chef can starve to death while preparing food for other people!**

♦ **No one can do enough for others if they are always surrounded by others!**

Nuf Sed!

"Preparation for Life and Ministry"
Part I

"Come with me by yourselves to a quiet place and get some rest" (Mark 6:31).

Mark chapter 6 is one of my favorite chapters – of wisdom and preparation for healthy people! It's a message straight to the heart, if you want to be balanced, whole and prepared for the long haul.
♦ In chapter 1, Mark deals with Jesus and His message.
♦ In chapter 2, Mark reveals Jesus' impact upon sinners and theologians.
♦ In chapter 3, Mark shows us Jesus' impact on politicians, friends and family.
♦ In chapter 4, Mark gives us great parables that teach us truth.
♦ In chapter 5, Mark testifies of Jesus' power to banish demons.

But in chapter 6, we see the Son of God intentionally preparing healthy disciples to follow Him. He calls us to Himself in V. 7, and then teaches seven life lessons to help us enjoy the journey. Each one is **very important** to hear and practice:

I. Healthy Disciples Are "Optimistic" and Full of Faith" (V.1-6).
"He could not do any miracles there, except lay His hands on a few sick people and heal them" (V.5)

Jesus had just stilled a storm, cast demons out of a mad man, healed an incurable disease and raised Jairus' daughter from the dead. His fame spread like wildfire and now it was time to go home to Nazareth. Jesus comes as a rabbi (teacher) followed by His students (the disciples). And what does Jesus teach His disciples? He teaches us that He is limited – only by unbelief. In other words, the people of Nazareth see Jesus as a carpenter, the son of Mary, and a brother of family members. They are gripped with unbelief and a lack of faith in what Jesus can do. Mark says that Jesus, "Was amazed at their lack of faith" (V.6). What's the lesson? Healthy followers of Jesus believe that Jesus is still Jesus, and will accompany His Word with signs following.

II. Healthy Disciples Are "Content" (while others push and shove for possessions and status) (V.7-13). "Whenever you enter a house, stay there until you leave that town" (V.10).

What does it mean to "stay there" in V.10? Jesus is teaching His followers that healthy disciples have a spirit of contentment! And this spirit is revealed in three ways:
♦ **Contentment is rooted in absolute trust in God's provision** (V.8).
"Take nothing for the journey", means you can trust God to provide where He leads you!
♦ **Contentment is free from the love of stuff and status** (V.10).
"Stay there" whenever you enter a house, means don't think that bigger and better is around the corner. It means forget climbing the success ladder and crucify all selfish aspirations!

♦ **Contentment is secure when people reject you** (V.11).
"Shake the dust off your feet" when rejected, means refuse to be controlled by someone else's rejection of you. It means: don't allow the past to rob you of future opportunities and don't allow someone else's poor choices to determine who you become! The take-a-way?

A healthy you begins with faith in the supernatural and contentment in every season of the soul!

Nuf Sed!

"Preparation for Life and Ministry"
Part II

"Come with me by yourselves to a quiet place and get some rest" (Mark 6:31).

In Mark 6, Jesus is training those who follow Him. He teaches seven great lessons as He prepares the disciples for faithful service. He teaches us how to be healthy, and enjoy the journey on our way to heaven. Yesterday, we discovered how healthy people are full of faith and live content. Today we continue under the Master Teacher:

III. Healthy Disciples Are "Unshakable" (when things don't go as planned (V.14-29)).
"On hearing of this, John's disciples came and took his body and laid it in a tomb" (V.29).

Herod had imprisoned John the Baptist because John rebuked him for marrying Herodias, his brother's wife. Herod was in violation of Levitical Law (Leviticus 18:16,20,21) and John showed tremendous courage by publicly rebuking Herod. John's courage cost him his life as Herod played to the crowd and had John beheaded. The disciples took up John's lifeless body and processed their unfulfilled expectations. They discover what healthy believers discover in the journey:

♦ Painful things can happen to good people in the perfect will of God.
♦ Sometimes there are no answers to some of our "why Lord" questions.
♦ Jesus didn't suffer so that Christians wouldn't have to; He suffered to show us how to go through it.

So, what helps us to remain unshakable when things don't go as we had planned? We stand on Deuteronomy 29:29: **"The secret things belong to the Lord our God."** What is a secret thing? It is something that God has chosen not to reveal this side of heaven. Yet we trust Him and we love Him, because He is Sovereign, makes no mistakes, and His grace is sufficient in every season.

IV. Healthy Disciples Are "Balanced" (while the world says, "hurry up and rush ahead") (V.30-34).
"Come with me by yourselves to a quiet place and get some rest. So they went away by themselves in a boat to a solitary place" (Mark 6:31,32).

The disciples have just returned from their mission and report to Jesus. Jesus is sensitive and notices something. He is aware that ministry to people is taxing on human energy. He knows that the body needs rest after extensive labor and hard work. He knows that we will feel better and be healthier if we come apart to recharge our batteries. He knows that we can rust out, or we can burn out and both are unscriptural. Jesus knows that:
♦ If we don't take care of our own souls, no one else will!

♦ Self-care is never a selfish act!
♦ The only one that can win in a rat race is a rat!

The take-a-way?

If what we "give out" is not supported by what we "take in," then we are doomed to fail and disappoint!

Nuf Sed!

June 22
"Preparation for Life and Ministry"
Part III

"Come with me by yourselves to a quiet place and get some rest" (Mark 6:31).

The past two days we've seen Jesus training His disciples. We've learned that healthy disciples are optimistic, content, unshakable and balanced. Today, the final three discoveries as Jesus trains His own:

V. Healthy Disciples Are "Obedient" (while others hesitate because of their own limitations) (V.35-44).
"Taking the five loaves and the two fish… He gave them to His disciples to set before the people" (V.41).

Jesus, seeing the tiredness of His disciples, tries to get alone with them for rest. The crowd beats them to the spot where they are headed. When the disciples arrive, there are 5,000 men plus women and children who are hungry. Jesus then shocks the disciples by telling them, "Give them something to eat" (V.37). How do the disciples respond? They respond in two ways:

♦ On one hand, they look at themselves and acknowledge that they only have 200 Denarii, which could never buy enough food for 5,000 plus people.
♦ On the other hand, the disciples do what Jesus said to do, and pass out what Jesus hands to them. What's the lesson? The lesson is to obey the Lord at all times, even when we can't figure it all out in our natural mind! In other words, you can trust the Lord today and trust Him with all of your tomorrows.

VI. Healthy Disciples Are "Desperate" (when winds blow out of control) (V.45-52).
"They cried out, because they all saw him and were terrified" (Mark 6:49,50).

After Jesus flees the crowd of people, He sends His disciples across the lake. Why? Because the crowd wants to take Jesus and make Him king. And, after six to nine hours of rowing, contrary winds exhaust and frighten the disciples. In desperation, the disciples cry out and hear Jesus say, "Take courage, it is I. Don't be afraid" (V.50). What happens when we cry out to God in prayer? Fear is erased, strength is received and faith is accelerated! We learn here that our spirituality is revealed by the degree of peace we have in the middle of the storm!

VII. Healthy Disciples Are "Broken" (while the selfish live only for themselves) (V.53-56).
"They ran throughout the whole region and carried the sick on mats" (V. 55).

The disciples draw near to the shore line and people recognize Jesus on board. What do the people do? They, "ran throughout that whole region" (V.55) to bring their families and friends to Jesus. Why? Because they were broken to their plans and ambitions; they wanted others to experience this living Jesus! What a discovery here: That the anointing and presence of Jesus is not just to feel good- it is for you to help someone!

The take-a-way?

God doesn't work through a void; He works through human personality!

Nuf Sed!

"The Ebenezer Stone"
Part I

"Then Samuel took a stone and set it up between Mizpah and Shen. He named it Ebenezer, saying, 'Thus far has the Lord helped us'" (I Samuel 7:12).

While God is sovereign, He also responds when we seek Him in prayer! While God can do anything, He cannot answer prayers that we never pray. While God is supernatural, we can fail to see Him act because we do not prepare our hearts and align ourselves with His will. Our text today is a great illustration of how the sovereignty of God and the responsibility of man are always at work together.

The crisis and critical hour of I Samuel 7 has a remarkable setting:
In chapter 1, Hannah gives birth to Samuel.
In chapter 2, The sins of Eli's sons are documented.
In chapter 3, The Lord calls Samuel.
In chapter 4, The Ark is captured by the Philistines.
In chapter 5, The idol Dagon cannot stand against God.
In chapter 6, The Ark is too holy for Bethshemesh, and is received on a new cart (6:7). The people of God were frivolous, shouting and void of all reverence. They opened the Ark (6:19) and 50,070 men were smitten dead on the spot. Why? Because the holiness of God was ignored and taken lightly (6:20). So, the people of Beth Shemesh asked the people of Kiriath Jearim to come down and take the Ark off their hands (6:21). The Ark was brought into the house of Abinadab, and hear the sad commentary of where many people now live today:

"It was a long time, twenty years in all, that the Ark remained at Kiriath Jearim, and all the people of Israel mourned and sought after the Lord" (7:12).

In other words, the Ark of the Covenant (symbolic of the presence of God) had been carried off by the Philistines, and stalled in the house of Abinadab. For twenty years, Israel had been without the presence of God, lost many battles and been put "on hold." For twenty years, Israel had suffered oppression from the enemy, and lamented in frustration as God's Glory had departed. For twenty years Israel was thinking:
♦ How is it possible for God to bring change?
♦ How is it possible to see spiritual progress?
♦ How is it possible to go from bondage to liberty?
♦ How is it possible to experience revival where God renews what was missing for so long?

The good news is, that God raises up Samuel to lead Israel in revival and a great awakening. Why?

Because God wants us to experience His Presence each day of our journey! And, if you are hungry, thirsty, and desperate, God will respond to your desire as you align your heart with His! He will meet us as we reach out to Him in prayer.

The take-a-way?

♦ **God's part is to pour out His Spirit upon all flesh – which includes you today!**
♦ **Our part is to align ourselves and position ourselves to prepare our hearts to receive.**

I'm desperate today, how about you?

Nuf Sed!

"The Ebenezer Stone"
Part II

"He cried out to the Lord on Israel's behalf, and the Lord answered him" (I Samuel 7:9).

For twenty years Israel lamented after the Lord. Why? Because the Ark of the covenant was "stalled" in the house of Abinadab. For twenty years Israel was "on hold." But, God had not forgotten Israel, and God has not forgotten you! In fact, look how God raised up Samuel to ignite the Great Awakening in Mizpeh. Notice how Samuel prepared and aligned Israel's heart, so that the presence of God could be restored and renewed. The Holy Spirit speaks loud and clear as we prepare to cooperate with Him.

I. It All Begins with An Uncluttered Heart!

"If you are returning to the Lord with all your hearts, then rid yourselves of the foreign gods and the Ashtoreths and commit yourselves to the Lord and serve Him only" (v.3).

The message from the Lord through Samuel is quite clear: put away all the strange gods, prepare your heart, and serve Him only. Baal was the supreme male god of the Canaanite nations. Ashtaroth was the supreme female god of the Canaanite nations. What's the message to Israel? The message is clear and direct:

♦ Israel has to prepare her heart to make progress with God.
♦ Idols that interfere must be put aside.
♦ Repentance is not a dirty word – but a freeing word.
♦ A pure heart is the beginning of lasting internal change.
♦ We must narrow our interests and be serious minded, allowing nothing to compete with our deepest affections for God.

In other words, since I cannot free my own heart from sin's dominion, I can put my trust in Jesus and the gospel. Why Jesus? Because only Jesus can **satisfy** my heart and **transform** my heart! I cannot do this on my own, by myself or through my own efforts. Only Jesus makes it all possible!

How did Israel respond to Samuel's call to put away every idol and prepare her heart? Notice this:

"So the Israelites **put away** their Baals and Ashtoreths, and served the Lord only" (v.4).

Israel's response was an immediate "yes" to the call of God, the prompting of the Spirit and the preaching of Samuel. The response was without delay to allow God to capture the desires and affections of the heart. There was a willingness to be transparent that would lead to a transformation. There was God's part in speaking and Israel's part in responding. What's the message in the radical change that took place at Mizpeh? It's our undeniable take-a-way:

♦ "Go consecrate the people. Tell them, 'consecrate yourselves in preparation for tomorrow; for this is what the Lord, the God of Israel says: That which is devoted is among you, O Israel. **You cannot stand against your enemies until you remove it**'" (Joshua 7:13).

Nuf Sed!

"The Ebenezer Stone"
Part III

"When they had assembled at Mizpeh, they drew water and poured it out before the Lord. On that day they fasted and there confessed, 'We have sinned against the Lord'" (I Samuel 7:6).

The past two days we discovered how God called Israel to prepare their hearts for change and purify their hearts from lesser gods. Today, discover how God further prepares our hearts to cooperate with His plan and presence in the journey:

II. Our Hearts Are Changed According to Our Humility!
"They drew water and poured it out before the Lord" (v.6).

Pouring out the water was symbolic of pouring out the heart. It was a sign of Israel humbling themselves before God. It was Israel saying, "God, I am helpless and powerless without you; I cannot move forward unless you help me." This speaks of dependence and humility. It speaks of Isaiah's promise in Isaiah 57:15:

"I live in a high and holy place, but also with him who is contrite and lowly in spirit, to revive the spirit of the lowly and to revive the heart of the contrite."

And, what exactly is humility? It is:
♦ An inward condition of heart that gives us a proper view of God, others and ourselves, (and)
♦ Recognizing my inability to accomplish anything for God apart from His Amazing Grace! (and)
♦ Being careful not to utter a word that seeks to impress another with my own importance!

III. Humility Always Leads Us to Prayer and Confession!
"On that day they fasted and there they confessed, 'We have sinned against the Lord'" (v.6).

Israel's hunger and humility led her to fast and pray and confess her sins! The people fasted to draw closer to God in prayer. They aligned their hearts with God in preparation, all to see God's Glory return! They also confessed, "We have sinned" (v.6). This is asking God to deliver and free us from everything questionable. It is a transparency of spirit, that brings to the surface every inconsistency. It is a desperate plea, wanting nothing in my life to offend God's holiness. It is part of our personal transformation and part of preparation for revival! It is you and me allowing God's Spirit to probe and go deeper than ever before! And this prayer, confession and humility carries a great and lasting reward. And, although there was enemy resistance from the Philistines (v.7), the Philistines were beaten hands down (v.11) because of

God's intervention. What's the moral of the story? It's our take-a-way (our Ebenezer Stone reminder):

◆ God still has the power to **free us** from every sin!
◆ God still **changes hearts** that want to be changed!
◆ God still **reforms** where reform is needed!
◆ God wants to renew your heart and mine as we come to Him in **transparency, humility,** and **deep confession!**

Nuf Sed!

"Testing's Reward"
Part I

"The testing of your faith develops perseverance" (James 1:3).

James was the half brother of Jesus and the leader of the Jerusalem church. He wrote to believers who were being tested and tried for their faith. James was given supernatural insight about facing difficulty and coming out a stronger person. He reveals to us possibly the most encouraging word in all of scripture regarding those times when we are tested and tried. And remember friend, no one escapes those seasons of trial and testing.

"Consider it pure joy, my brothers, whenever you face trials of many kinds." (v.2)

So, it's not "if," but "when" we are tested. It's not "maybe," but "when." It's not "possibly," but "when." In other words, pain, loss, grief, misunderstanding, disappointment and unfulfilled expectations are common to all. And, the Greek word for "trials" in James is Peirasmos, which means: to try, to test, and to prove. So, trials are allowed by God in this broken world, and redeemed for our benefit:

♦ To try our **character!**
♦ To prove our **loyalty!**
♦ To test our **patience!**
♦ To make us **stronger!**

The question answered in James is: How is it possible to **"consider it pure joy"** (v.2) when you go through adversity? And, the answer God gives us is to understand the end result of our experience. I call it **"Testing's Reward,"** because God shows us the end result of what is produced in the life of spiritually minded people. The Lord clearly gives us five rewards of testing so that we become "victorious" and not "victims" in the journey.

Reward #1: Patience
"The testing of your faith develops **perseverance**" (patience) (v.3).

The Greek word for patience is *Hupomonen* and means to endure under adversity, to suffer long under difficulty, to bear up under pressure, to remain steadfast under stress and strain, and to hold steady for the benefit it will bring to another. The immature thing to do when tested is to run, get angry at God, or blame everybody else for your trouble. Yet the Word says, "Perseverance must finish its work" (v.4) Which means, don't run from difficulty but instead hold steady and remain faithful under the all seeing eye of God. So…

Have you been tested lately? Are you in the refiner's fire even now? Is there a swirl of discomfort you are dealing with? If so, remember this and never, ever forget it. It will keep you from running away from your problems!

It will also allow God to perfect His work in you and bring great reward. It's our take-a-way today:

If you unfix the fix that God has fixed for you to fix you, He will fix another fix to fix you!

Nuf Sed!

"Testing's Reward"

Part II

"The testing of your faith develops perseverance" (James 1:3).

Yesterday, we looked at the first reward of testing in those who cooperate with God! The first reward of submitting to God in testing, is patience. And patience is the character quality that allows you to remain steadfast under stress and strain. Today, we'll look at the other four rewards of testing:

Reward #2: Maturity

"Perseverance must finish its work so that you may be **mature**" (v.4).

The word, "perfect" (v.4) in the King James Version comes from the Greek word *Teleios*, which means: maturity of character. This reveals that God wants us to grow through our difficulties, be strengthened in our testings, and molded into His nature in every season. This also reveals that God is more concerned about our character than our convenience. It's a revelation here, that God, through our patient endurance, is growing a steadfast spirit that can be trusted. Remember:

♦ If you help a chicken out of the egg, you'll kill it.
♦ If you help a locust out of its shell, you'll kill it.
♦ If you help a caterpillar out of the cocoon, you'll kill it. Why?
Because they all must go through the patient struggle to be what God intended them to be.

Reward #3: Wholeness
"… that you may be mature and **complete**" (v.4).

The Greek word for complete is *Holokleros* which means: complete and whole. It means that the more a person is patient under trial, the more complete and whole they become. James is saying here, that the more a person is patient under trial, the more flaws and weaknesses are eliminated. This is why people who always run from difficulty when they don't get what they **want**, stay immature and fail to get what they **need**.

Reward #4: Contentment
"… not lacking anything" (v.4)

This phrase comes from the Greek words *Leipo Meden* and mean: no lack of anything; contentment. James teaches us here, that the believer who is patient in trial will want for nothing and possess a contented spirit. Why? Because instead of running, he or she draws upon the grace of God and finds that grace sufficient to satisfy their heart. Remember: if I'm not content with what I have, I will not be content with what I want!

Reward #5: Wisdom

"If any of you lacks wisdom, he should ask God, who gives generously to all" (v.5).

This wisdom here is the ability from God to know what to do in adversity. It is wisdom to handle difficulty, to see from God's perspective, and the ability to prevail over impulsiveness. It is the ability to apply God's truth when confronted with adversity. And, this wisdom will protect you from running from the very things God wants to use to perfect and promote your character.

The take-a-way?

Asking God for wisdom, instead of an easy escape in testing, will carry its own reward in your life!

Nuf Sed!

"No Right to Complain"
Part I

"Consider him who endured such opposition from sinful men, so that you will not grow weary and lose heart" (Hebrews 12:3).

Haven't we all been tempted to complain or lose heart at some time? Haven't we at least a few times, become weary in well doing? Okay, I admit it, there have been seasons when it hasn't been easy to sing, "This is the day the Lord has made, I will rejoice and be glad in it."

The book of Hebrews was written to Jewish converts in Palestine, believers who were suffering persecution. They were being tempted to abandon their new-found faith and return to the Old Testament system of Law, Ceremony, and animal sacrifices. And, God comes along with a great word to lift their hearts and protect us all – from any feelings of entitlement or feelings of being cheated. It's an incredible truth that produces a healthy heart that can enjoy the journey. It's a message that's all wrapped up in three conditions:

I. The Gospel Brings "Heartfelt Courage" (v.1-4).
"In your struggle against sin, you have not yet resisted to the point of shedding your blood" (v.4).

Believers are given two instructions in verse one:
♦ "Throw off everything that hinders and the sin that so easily entangles," and,
♦ "Run with perseverance the race marked out for us." So, what gives us the courage and motivation to follow these two instructions?

♦ We see the witnesses!
"We are surrounded by such a great cloud of witnesses" (v.1). The word witnesses means *Martyr*. It refers to the people of faith in Hebrews 11. It means the witnesses (martyrs) gone before us are witnessing to us today. They are saying two things: 1. That God's grace enabled them to stand tall and stay true until death, and, 2. That God's grace will enable you to stand tall and stay true until death as well. In other words, the God who poured out grace upon those gone before us is the same God who will pour out grace today so we can stand with courage.

♦ We see the Savior!
"Let us fix our eyes on Jesus, the author and perfecter of our faith... consider Him... so that you will not grow weary and lose heart" (v.2,3). This is pure gospel motivation that gives courage to the heart! How? Just look at Jesus on the cross! Remember how He despised the shame, disregarded His own humiliation for my benefit, and never had a pity party or cried "poor me."

And, if you are ever tempted to pout, sulk or quit, just remember verse 4:

"You have not yet resisted to the point of shedding your blood" (which means)

♦ No matter what pain, trial or disappointment you face in this life, you have never spilled your blood on a cross, and,

♦ No matter what betrayal or offense you've experienced, you have never been crucified for something that you didn't deserve!

The take-a-way?

The same grace that Jesus received to endure the cross and remain faithful, is the same grace that you will receive to do the Father's will!

Nuf Sed!

"No Right To Complain"
Part II

"And you have forgotten that word of encouragement" (Hebrews 12:5).

Yesterday, we discovered how the gospel gives us heartfelt courage in every season of life. We learned from Hebrews 12:1-4, that the God who poured out grace to the martyrs of Hebrews 11, and the Savior on the cross, is the same God who gives us grace as well. Today, notice how…

II. The Gospel Brings "Needed Correction!" (v.5-8)
"The Lord disciplines those He loves" (v.6).

Remember the context of Hebrews as you read this: Jewish converts are suffering persecution. They are being tempted to abandon their faith. They are committed to carry their cross without complaint, in doing the will of God. But, they face the danger that you and I will face when we are tested by fire. What's the danger? The danger is to forget the motive behind all correction, which is love, love, love! Notice:

"For whom the Lord **loveth** he **chasteneth**, and **scourgeth** every son whom he receiveth" (v.6, KJV).

The word "chasteneth" means to train, teach, mature and instruct. The word "scourgeth" means to correct and to squeeze to bring out something good. In other words, God will take the very things that could discourage, dishearten and deflate you – and use them to deepen His message in your life. This means that humility on our part will allow God to correct and conform us into His image. So never forget this: God is not against you; He is for you! In fact, Hebrews tells us this:

"For they verily for a few days chastened us after their own pleasure; but He **for our profit**, that we might be partakers of His holiness" (12:10, KJV).
I love those three words, "**For Our Profit!**" They mean:
♦ What you think is useless, God sees as useful!
♦ What you think detours you, God uses to direct you!
♦ What you think is loss, God will use as a ladder to higher ground!
♦ What you think is wasted, God deems as necessary!
♦ What you think has no meaning, is part of the "all things working together" for your ultimate good!

As one man said, "Nothing God sends is wasted, nothing He withholds is needed." This reminds me that God's ultimate motive in every discipline, is love on His part, and benefit on my part! It reminds me that I'm far from perfect and God isn't finished with me yet!
The take-a-way here is:
People are great works of progress that can mistakenly think they are complete!
Nuf Sed!

June 30
"No Right to Complain"
Part III

"How much more should we submit to the Father of our spirits and live" (Hebrews 12:9).

The past two days we've discovered how the gospel brings **heartfelt courage** and **needed correction** to us all. Today, discover how…

III. The Gospel Brings "Lasting Change" (v.9-13).

It's no secret that everybody changes when they go through seasons of testing and discipline. Some change for the better; some change for the worse! In fact, God gives us three dangers to avoid when He corrects us:

♦ In v.5, we can **despise** God's chastening – which means to disregard it and take it lightly.

♦ In v. 5, we can **faint** when we are chastened – which means to withdraw, slip back and fall away. (*Resist*)

♦ In v.9, we can **rebel** instead of submitting – which means to resist, become bitter and waste the opportunity to grow.

And unfortunately, these three poor responses to chastening are disastrous. They result in murmuring, complaining, self-pity, a martyr's complex and playing the blame game and victim card. Our poor response will steal our focus, render us useless and keep us from our fullest potential. *Or can we Relax*

But look at the fruit (consequences) of taking up our cross without an entitlement spirit that feels like God owes us something. Notice the lasting change inside of us when we humble ourselves before the Lord:

1. There will be **character** of heart!
"That we may share in His holiness" (v.10).
This is the nature of Jesus being formed in our hearts. It is the life of Christ being imparted to our lives.

2. There will be **peace** and **tranquility**!
"It produces a harvest of… peace" (v.11)
This fruit of peace is the opposite of strife and contention. It comes from completely yielding to the will of God for your life.

3. There will be **power over sin**!
"It produces a harvest of righteousness… for those who have been trained by it" (v.11).
This means that yielding to God will result in righteous living or power over sin and temptation. It means that the gospel message can change our behavior so that habitual sins of the present become historical sins of the past.

4. There will be **healing from within**!
"Strengthen your feeble arms and weak knees" (v.12).

"Make level paths for your feet so that the lame may not be disabled, but rather healed" (v.13).

This is a reference to heavy hands because of weariness in battle. Feeble knees refers to a heavy load that causes your knees to be weakened. And God says to, "Let it rather be healed" (v.13), which means: let God restore you with fresh optimism, new hope, and a renewed perspective. It means to let the Gospel of the cross produce a grateful spirit in the depth of your being.

The take-a-way?

We can despise, faint, or rebel when we are chastened, or we can submit to God in humility and come out better than before. Which one will you choose today?

Nuf Sed!

July 1
"The Liberating Power of The Word"
Part I

"My dear brothers, take note of this: Everyone should be quick to listen, slow to speak and slow to become angry" (James 1:19).

On the Isle of Patmos (A rocky island in the Mediterranean) John the Apostle had a vision of Jesus Christ. In the vision, John saw seven things. One of the sights was a sharp, double edged sword coming out of the mouth of Jesus (Revelation 1:16). Why the sword from the mouth? The sword of the Spirit is the Word of God. It's a two-edged sword, because the Word of God that cuts us is the same Word that heals us. It's a picture of you and me being transformed and changed by the Holy Word of God. And, in James 1:19-25, God gives us incredible wisdom about how the Word of God has power to change the human heart! It's wisdom so that you and I can cooperate with God's plan when we are exposed to the truth of the Gospel. Notice:

I. How We Can "Love" The Word (v.19,20)

James tells us that we are born again through the Word of Truth (v.18). In (v.19), he begins to describe how the Word of God produces internal change. In (v.19-25), we discover that the Word cannot change us unless we receive it in the proper way. Notice how we can love the truth in three specific ways:

♦ **"Quick to Listen"** (v.19) means there is a readiness to listen to what God has to say. It means that I am quick to hear the truth and willing for God to get in my face and speak to my heart!

♦ **"Slow to Speak"** (v.19) means we restrain our speech to talk back to God. This is a refusal to argue with God. It is refraining myself from resenting what God tells me in His Word.

♦ **"Slow to Become Angry"** (v.19) means that I will not get angry nor close my mind to what God is saying. It means that I will not rebel against the truth when the truth reveals my defects. It means that I'll quit justifying myself when God convicts me about something. It means that I will welcome (and be grateful) that the Master Vine Dresser, loves me enough to form me on the potter's wheel and trim off the branches that hinder my growth.

And, why is it foolish (unwise) to ever be angry at God?

"For man's anger does not bring about the righteous life that God desires" (v.20) which means:

♦ Carrying wrath in my heart will dam-up (prohibit) the grace of God from forming His righteous character in my life.
♦ Living with anger (instead of humility) will waste our opportunity to grow and be internally changed.

The take-a-way?
The greatest danger in reading the Word is: reading it to see what God wants to say through me, instead of reading it to see what God wants to say to me!

Nuf Sed!

"The Liberating Power of The Word"
Part II

"Therefore, get rid of all moral filth and the evil that is so prevalent and humbly accept the word planted in you, which can save you" (James 1:21).

Yesterday, we learned how to receive the word so that it can change us. James gave us three instructions – if we really love the Word: 1. Be quick to listen, 2. Be slow to speak, and 3. Be slow to become angry when God speaks to us about our defects. James then teaches us:

II. How To "Look" Into the Word with A Ready Heart (v.21).

If we really love the Word and want it to change our hearts, one thing is needed above all else. That one thing is a heart that is prepared! In (v.21), James sees the human heart as a garden with potential – for good or bad. If the garden is left alone, the soil produces weeds. If the garden is tended to, the soil produces fruit. And, James tells us how our hearts can be prepared to experience the supernatural ministry of the Word of God. It's the difference between growing fruit or weeds!

♦ Preparation 1: Is **Cleanliness**:

"Get rid of all moral filth" (v.21A).

The words, "moral filth and the evil" (v.21) mean stained or dirty. It refers to uncleaned garments or clothes. The Greek word for "filthiness" (KVJ) is *Ruparia*, which comes from the Greek word *Rupos*. *Rupos* is often used to refer to wax in the ear. A person with wax in their ear cannot hear the Word of God clearly. If we really care about hearing, we will take out the wax so that we can hear and receive the truth. So, is there anything in my life that is hindering me from receiving the Word through a clear channel? Am I willing to be honest enough to lay it aside when God puts the light on it?

♦ Preparation 2: Is **Lowliness**:

"And humbly accept the word planted in you which can save you" (v.21B)

How do we receive the Word? James says, with meekness, lowliness and humility. This means to accept and submit to the truth with an open heart and ready mind. The words "planted in you" mean engrafted or implanted to grow. It means that when we sit under the pure Word of God, what God says is actually being born within our hearts. The Word then begins to grow, live and conquer temptations that seek to destroy us.

In (v.21) the Word is compared to seed. But in (v.23) the Word is compared to a mirror. The main purpose of owning a mirror is to see ourselves and make necessary adjustments. When we see ourselves in the Word (or mirror) we can then ask God to help us make the needed adjustments!

The take-a-way?

Humility of spirit and purity of heart are the two main ingredients that allow the Word to help us reach our fullest potential! Nuf Sed!

"The Liberating Power of the Word"
Part III

"And, after looking at himself, goes away and immediately forgets what he looks like. But the man who looks intently into the perfect law that gives freedom…" (James 1:24,25).

The past two days, we discovered how to love the Word by being swift to hear, slow to speak and slow to become angry. We learned that the two main ingredients of a heart prepared for the truth are humility and purity. Today, we conclude James 1:19-25 by exploring the three possible mistakes we can make when it comes to reading and hearing the Word.

1. I Call The **"Hurried"** Mistake!

"After looking at himself, goes away" (v.24).

This is a glancing, or reading carelessly. It is reading or hearing out of duty. It is brief or quick devotions to appease my conscience. It is a mindset in a worship service that says, "Hurry up preacher, I've got things to do, places to go and people to see."

2. I Call The **"Forgetting"** Mistake!

"Goes away and immediately forgets what he looks like" (v.24).

This can happen to any of us (and does to millions every Sunday). It is hearing the truth and yet putting it aside as soon as the service is over. The truth is forgotten instead of discussed because of all the distractions in our lives. This is a looking in the mirror of the Word, but not staying there long enough to let the mirror do its job.

3. I Call The **"Deception"** Mistake!

"Do not merely listen to the Word, and so deceive yourselves. Do what it says" (v.22).

This is when we substitute hearing for doing. It's when I think that hearing alone will benefit me. It's when I shout, "Amen preacher," but then fail to remember that the blessing is in the doing of the Word, not just hearing, reading or learning it. It means our spiritual growth accelerates when we actually obey and practice what we hear from Scripture. And, what happens to us when we do (put into practice) the Word?

"But the man who looks intently into the perfect law **that gives freedom**, and continues to do this, not forgetting what he has heard, but doing it – he will be blessed in what he does" (v.25).

Why is the Bible called **"the perfect law that gives freedom?"** Because the Holy Spirit takes the law and liberates us from the servitude of sin! The Word delivers us from controlling sin, cuts away carnal tendencies, influences our thinking patterns, overcomes destructive enticements, and frees us from ourselves to serve God! The Scriptures really are the perfect **law of liberty!!!** The take-a-way?

Consistently feeding upon the Word of truth is the greatest means of God to change our sinful hearts! Nuf Sed!

July 4
"Let Freedom Reign"

"For the Word of God is quick and powerful, and sharper than any two-edged sword, piercing even to the dividing asunder of soul and spirit, and of the joints and marrow, and is a discerner of the thoughts and intents of the heart" (Hebrews 4:12, KJV).

Today we celebrate the freedom that we have in America! In our text today, we see the freedom that the Word of God brings to the hungry and seeking heart. Before we dive into Hebrews 4:12, look at a few byproducts of absorbing the Word into your heart:

1. God's Word **Brings Peace** (Psalm 119:165)
2. God's Word **Makes You Wise** (Psalm 19:7)
3. God's Word **Produces Faith** (Romans 10:17)
4. God's Word **Gives Understanding** (Psalm 119:104)
5. God's Word **Enlightens Our Eyes** (Psalm 19:8)
6. God's Word **Produces Health** (Proverbs 4:20-22)
7. God's Word **Warns Us of Sin** (Psalm 19:11)
8. God's Word **Grows Us Up** (I Peter 2:2)
9. God's Word **Renews Our Inner Man** (Psalm 119:9)
10. God's Word **Increases Our Joy** (Jeremiah 15:16)
11. God's Word **Brings Comfort** (Psalm 119:50)
12. God's Word **Cleanses Us from Sin** (John 15:3, 17:17)

Just Think of Jesus' Powerful Words:
"Whoever has my commands and obeys them, he is the one who loves me… and I will show myself to him" (John 14:21).

"You will know the truth, and the truth will set you free" (John 8:32).

And then Paul's Words:
"I am not ashamed of the Gospel because it is the power of God for the salvation of everyone who believes" (Romans 1:16).

So, the Gospel is supernatural in power, can work in anyone, will birth salvation in our hearts, and deliver us from sin and self-destruction!

Grasp the Five Take-A-Ways From Hebrews 4:12:
♦ The Word of God is **"Quick"**, which means alive, living, active and working in the human heart!
♦ The Word of God is **"Powerful"**, which means energizing and power giving to live your Christian life!
♦ The Word of God is **"Sharper than a two-edged sword"**, which means able to penetrate, convict and cut away.

♦ The Word of God is **"Piercing"**, which means able to pierce our soulish nature and separate it from the spiritual call upward and forward.

♦ The Word of God **"Discerns the thoughts and intents of the heart"**, which means to judge, sift, analyze and expose the intents (purpose) of the heart.

Oh, the Freedom of the Living Word of God! Are you allowing it to consistently (daily) change your heart to be more like Jesus?

Nuf Sed!

July 5
"The Four Soils"
Part I

"Still other seeds fell on good soil. It came up, grew and produced a crop, multiplying thirty, sixty, or even a hundred times" (Mark 4:8).

I love this parable of warning and wisdom about the four kinds of hearts that hear the Word. It's a Word from God that tells us how to get the most out of each and every opportunity we have. It speaks to you and me about the kind of heart that will grow and reach its fullest potential.

Mark (in Chapter 4) records the first formal teaching by Jesus. Up to this point, Jesus taught by His actions: driving out evil spirits, healing the sick on the sabbath, praying in solitude, confronting opposition, etc. But now, Jesus begins teaching in parables. On this occasion, Jesus got into a boat and addressed people at the water's edge. He said, "Listen" in (v.3) because this is important.

In the parable, Jesus reveals four different kinds of listeners. There is:
1. The hard hearted, closed minded religious person.
2. The shallow, emotional, non-rooted person.
3. The distracted and unfocused listener.
4. The good ground (fertile soil) listener.

The parable reveals three main ingredients:
♦ The **sower** is the one who sows seed. So that's why we place ourselves before the truth on every occasion possible.
♦ The **seed** is the Word of God, and the Word (like seed) is powerful (Hebrews 4:12) and has life in it.
♦ The **soil** is the human heart, and has the potential to fully welcome or hinder and impede the seed when it is sown.

And, Jesus says, "Listen" (v.3) because He wants to give us the "Soil Secrets" and show us four kinds of soil (hearts) to prepare us to get the most out of every opportunity.

I. The **"Hard Heart"** Soil!
"Some fell along the path, and the birds came and ate it up" (v.4).

The "path" here is the unplowed (packed down) areas around the plowed fields. These foot paths were hard ground in Palestine, and birds would come and steal the seed because it stayed on the surface. So, what's Jesus saying? He tells us in (v.15), "Some people are like seed along the path, where the Word is sown. As soon as they hear it, satan comes and takes away the Word that was sown in them." In other words, God is no respecter of persons, but He is a respecter of our preparation! And, a soft heart (of humility and meekness) allows the seed to radically change our hearts. Whereas hardness of heart allows the enemy to quickly snatch away the seed's potential, a soft heart allows the seed to penetrate and produce good fruit. A soft heart will flat out:

♦ Give birth to Godly sorrow and repentance.

♦ Never feel elite or entitled.

♦ Receive counsel and instruction.

♦ Give God access to every room in the house of our heart.

The take-a-way?

A hard heart will give satan opportunity to restrict our growth – because the seed will stay on the surface!

Nuf Sed!

July 6
"The Four Soils"
Part II

"Still other seed fell on good soil. It came up, grew and produced a crop, multiplying thirty, sixty, or even a hundred times" (Mark 4:8).

Yesterday, we looked at the first of four soils in Jesus' parable of Mark 4:3-20. We learned how a hard heart will allow the enemy to snatch away the seed's potential in any of our hearts. Today, we'll look at the other three options that Jesus said, "Listen" to:

II. The **"Shallow Heart"** Soil!
"Some fell on rocky places, where it did not have much soil. It sprang up quickly, because the soil was shallow. But when the sun came up, the plants were scorched, and they withered because they had no root." (v.5,6)

The soil in Palestine lies on a thin layer of limestone. Where the soil is thin, roots of germinating seeds cannot go far. No roots mean no water, and no water means scorching and death. So, what is a "shallow heart"?

"Since they have no roots, they last only a short time. When trouble or persecution comes because of the Word, they quickly fall away" (v.17).

A shallow heart loves great preaching but the response is purely emotional, temporary and shallow. This listener welcomes the privileges of the gospel but distains self-denial, hardship or inconvenience. They are easily offended and have no roots to endure and hold in place. This hearer is a surface hearer, and has no roots to absorb moisture. Therefore, the sun and heat expose their weakness and see the sprouting seed wither and die.

III. The **"Distracted Heart"** Soil!
"Other seed fell among thorns, which grew up and choked the plants" (v.7).

The Palestinian farmer could get lazy and cut off the tops of the weeds, above ground only. Over time, the weeds revived in strength and choked the life out of the seed nearby. What's the lesson?

"Still others, like seed sown among thorns, hear the Word, but the worries of this life, the deceitfulness of wealth and the desires for other things come in and choke the Word, making it unfruitful" (v.18,19).

Jesus said that three things hinder and distract our hearts; worry, money, and unbridled desires. This "distracted heart" is the result when we treasure anything more than Jesus. It is shopping horizontally for what only God can provide. What might be distracting you and interfering with your focus today?

IV. The **"Fruitful"** Soil!

"Still other seed fell upon good soil" (v.8).

The fruitful heart is one that will, "Hear the Word, accept it, and produce a crop" (v.20). This heart hears the Word, receives the Word, and does the Word. This text reveals to us how to make spiritual progress. The secret? By being obedient to the last thing God speaks to you about!

The take-a-way?

Preaching is wasted when our hearts are not prepared to receive it!

Nuf Sed!

July 7
"In God We Trust"
Part I

"Heal me, O Lord, and I will be healed; save me and I will be saved" (Jeremiah 17:14).

Don't you love those four words on our U.S. Currency, **"In God We Trust"**? Aren't you glad that you can trust God when all around us is being shaken? Isn't there good news for you and me, even though the Lord said that He would shake the heavens and the earth (Haggai 2:6)? I'm glad that we have a reason to be joyful and excited about the future; we really do!

The book of Jeremiah was written during the dark days of Judah's history. There was a form of godliness, but no power:

♦ The stain of sin was everywhere (2:22).
♦ There was a forsaking of the ancient paths (6:16).
♦ The harvest was being lost (8:20).
♦ There were carnal shepherds scattering the sheep (23:1).
♦ There was disrespect for the Word of God (36:21-24).

And, in the midst of all the shaking that was going on, the Lord speaks three clear messages to your heart and mine in Jeremiah 17.

I. You Can Trust God More Than You Can Trust Yourself! (v.1-4)
"Judah's sin is engraved with an iron tool inscribed with a flint point, on the table of their hearts" (v.1).

The iron stylus and diamond points were used for engraving on the hardest substances. When you inscribe something deep on a hard surface, you can only remove the inscription by destroying that surface on which it is written. Judah had tolerated sin to the extent that it had profoundly affected their hearts. Sin had such a powerful hold on Judah, that even the children had their minds polluted by the idols of their parents (v.2). In other words, the generation to follow them was affected by the generation before them. What is Jeremiah saying? He is saying that the pen of iron and the power of a diamond mean that sin always...

♦ leaves a record and a mark.
♦ creates guilt and poisons our spiritual system.
♦ robs us of our joy and enthusiasm, and,
♦ enslaves our heart to idols and lesser gods.

So, what's the answer to our dilemma? It's so clear:
1. The Lord Searches Our Hearts!
"I the Lord search the heart and examine the mind" (v.10). Which means, God turns on the light, comes by His Spirit, and convicts us out of love.

2. The Lord Delivers Us from Ourselves!
"Heal me, O Lord, and I will be healed; save me and I will be saved, for you

are the one I praise" (v.14).

Which means; we can trust God to do for us what we cannot do ourselves! In other words, the grace of God to change our hearts is greater than the pen and diamond engraving of sin upon our hearts!

The take-a-way is clear:
♦ **God is able to break the power of every controlling sin in your life! (and)**
♦ **God wants you to trust Him more than your own will-power!**

Nuf Sed!

July 8
"In God We Trust"
Part II

"This is what the Lord says: Cursed is the one who trusts in man, who depends on flesh for his strength and whose heart turns away from the Lord" (Jeremiah 17:5).

Yesterday, we looked at the first of three great truths found in Jeremiah 17. We discovered that in the midst of Judah's shaking, God was still at work – as He is today! We learned how important it is to trust God more than you trust yourself. Today, Jeremiah's second message that speaks loud and clear is:

II. You Can Trust God More Than You Can Trust Your Friends!
"Cursed is the one who trusts in man" (v.5).

This language seems a little harsh, but here's the context: Judah had put their confidence in Egypt instead of Jehovah. Judah had trusted their political allies and the Babylonian army, and were taken captive. Thus, the strong language of, "cursed is the one who trusts in man" (V.5). In other words, a million friends of yours can never do what God can do for you! So much so that God lists the consequences of those who fail to lean on the Lord. It's a clear warning to us if our, "heart turns away from the Lord" (v.5). And, God tells us exactly what happens if we drift, quit praying, stop forgiving, cease to hunger after God and trust in the arm of flesh. I'll call these the four rewards of backsliding:

♦ **"He will be like a bush in the wastelands"** (v.6).
The bush (or heath) is a dwarfed juniper tree. The wastelands refer to the desert. The tree doesn't grow much because it lives without moisture. It lives in a barren, dry and desolate climate. So, the backslider will not grow and be strong – but only exists in a spiritual desert.

♦ **"He will not see prosperity when it comes"** (v.6).
This means that the person who is a non-growing believer will not see when good comes along. It means that we can become insensitive to what God is doing in our very midst. It means that only the hungry will be satisfied when God pours out His Spirit. It means that we will forfeit the blessing of God if we are content with anything less! Wow! There really is a cost to spiritual neglect!

♦ **"He will dwell in the parched places of the desert"** (v.6).
The parched places are the gardens left unattended where weeds turn them into a wilderness. It refers to a drifting believer that allows weeds to take over their heart. It means that whatever I ignore and fail to address, will dominate and take over my life.

♦ **"He will dwell in a salt land where no one lives"** (v.6).

"Salt" means "unfit to live in". "Where no one lives" (uninhabited) means there is no life, no fruit and no one nearby. Why is no one being helped? Because you can only give out what you first take in.

The take-a-way?
Whenever our hearts "turn away from the Lord" (v.5), we never suffer alone! Those who need our help will suffer as well!

Nuf Sed!

"In God We Trust"

"But blessed is the man who trusts in the Lord, whose confidence is in him" (Jeremiah 17:7).

Yesterday, we covered Jeremiah's "four rewards (consequences) of backsliding." Today, we'll finish chapter 17 and see the four rewards of an up-to-date spirit filled believer. The past two days we learned that: 1. you can trust God to free you from every besetting sin, and, 2. you can trust God more than all the friends in the world. Jeremiah then tells us that:

III. You Can Trust God Regardless of Your Unknown Future (v.7,8).
"He will be like a tree planted by the water that sends out its roots by the stream" (v.8).

Jeremiah records the payback to those whose heart is after God, and refuse to drift and slide backwards. It's a glorious reward for those who align their hearts with God and His purpose for their life. It's a specific word to your heart and mine that dispels all fear over the future:

♦ **"It does not fear when heat comes"** (v.8).
God doesn't say that you'll escape the heat. Why? Because heat and adversity come to believers and unbelievers alike. God simply tells us that you won't fear the heat because faith sets you free from fear, worry and intimidation. And, it's truth that really frees us from ourselves to enjoy the journey. Some nails in the coffin of fear are:
1. God's way is always perfect (Psalm 18:30).
2. He will never leave us or forsake us (Hebrews 13:5).
3. Our steps are ordered by the Lord (Psalm 37:23).
4. All things work together for His ultimate good (Romans 8:28).
5. His grace is always sufficient (II Corinthians 12:9).
6. God will supply all our needs (Philippians 4:19).
7. He makes all things beautiful in His time (Ecclesiastes 3:11).

♦ **"Its leaves are always green"** (v.8).
This means that God will give you the ability to stand strong and flourish even in adverse conditions. It means that God will supply you with hidden spiritual resources to keep you stable. It means that God will supply you with a well in the desert (or refreshment in those trying seasons).

♦ **"It has no worries in a year of drought"** (v.8).
"No worries" means not anxious- but confident! It means "in a year of drought" when you're supposed to fret and pull your hair out, God will sustain you with perfect peace to keep you steady, regardless of the climate!

♦ **"And never fails to bear fruit"** (v.8).
What a promise this is to us! When you feel the drought, the heat, and the desert seasons of barrenness, God is growing fruit all the while. In other words, satan can throw things **at you** but he cannot keep God from working **in you!**

The take-a-way?
Sometimes you may think that you're buried, but God sees you as planted – all to produce a harvest of fruit that will amaze you!

Nuf Sed!

July 10
"A Spiritual Breakthrough"
Part I

"As waters break out, the Lord has broken out against my enemies before me. So that place was called Baal Perazim" (II Samuel 5:20).

Everybody has hurdles to go over! What is a hurdle? It is something that you go over on your way to the finish line. Hurdles are not to frustrate or stop you, they are to stretch you and fortify you in the journey. In our text today, David faced a hurdle.

II Samuel chapter 5 documents the tribes of Israel coming to Hebron to acknowledge David as king. There were three reasons for David's crowning:
1. David was of **their kindred**.
   "We are your own flesh and blood" (v.1).
2. David had **served them** in a time of need.
   "You were the one who led Israel on their military campaigns" (v.2).
3. David was **God's choice** to lead.
   "The Lord said to you, 'You will shepherd my people Israel, and you will become their ruler'" (v.2).
Grasp the setting before us: David makes a covenant with the elders, begins to reign at age 30, makes Jerusalem the capital of the nation, and is making progress. The tribes are unified, and in chapter six, David will gather 30,000 more men and restore the Ark as the center of worship. But in between chapter 5 and even greater progress in chapter 6, the enemy comes in like a flood to discourage David and put fear in his heart. And, God gives us three timely wisdom discoveries:

I. The "Barking Lies" of The Enemy (v.6,18)
"The Jebusites said to David, 'You will not get in here, even the blind and the lame can ward you off'" (v.6). "The Philistines had come and spread out in the Valley of Rephaim" (v.18).
    The enemy Jebusites were defiant idol worshippers. They were intent on stopping Israel's progress in Jerusalem. They barked three lies to Israel and the same three lies may come your way:
♦ **You cannot have your inheritance** (v.6)
    Or, you cannot come into Jerusalem, restore holy worship and see revival!
♦ **You cannot be strong in the Lord** (v.6)
    Or, you'll never be able to withstand the enemy in the evil day of attack!
♦ **Your victory (or loss) is determined by what you see** (v.15)
    Or, you're in the land of the giants, outnumbered, and you should be shaking in your boots!
    Has the enemy of your progress lied to you? Have you heard his whispers lately? Things like:
♦ "You'll never overcome the world, the flesh, and the devil."

♦ "You'll never see answers to your prayers."
♦ "You'll never recover God's presence in your life."
♦ "You'll never complete what God has put before you."

Why does the enemy fight you tooth and nail? Because you are making progress!

The take-a-way?
♦ **Your spiritual progress will always attract opposition (so take heart)!**
♦ **You wrestle not with flesh and blood, but against spiritual powers in the unseen world!**
♦ **Jesus, at the cross, has destroyed satan's power to intimidate you!**

Nuf Sed!

"A Spiritual Breakthrough"
Part II

"So David inquired of the Lord, 'Shall I go and attack the Philistines? Will you hand them over to me? (II Samuel 5:19).

Yesterday, we followed David to the valley of Rephaim where the Philistines spread out across the land. Why this invasion? Because the enemy was determined to intimidate and put fear in the hearts of God's people. So, how did David respond to the barking of the enemy? There was...

II. The "Bending" of The Praying Christian (v.19).
"So David inquired of the Lord, 'Shall I go and attack the Philistines? Will you hand them over to me? The Lord answered him, 'Go for I will surely hand the Philistines over to you'" (v.19).

The Philistines and Jebusites are threatened in their idol worship. As long as David ruled over a single tribe, he was of no threat to paganism. But now the enemy comes forward to remove the courageous leader. And, what does David do when he hears the barking and sees the enemy approaching? He goes down to a cave, gets alone with God in prayer and asks two things in (v.19):

♦ Lord, what do you want me to do? And, Lord, what are you going to do?

And notice God's response:

"The Lord answered him, 'Go, for I will surely hand the Philistines over to you'" (v.19).

In other words, the Lord responded when David went to prayer! And, the Lord will respond when you go to prayer! He will give you perspective, strength, and calmness. In prayer, you will experience these four things in a whole new dimension:

1. **Deeper Intimacy** in relationship! 3. **Fresh Anointing** of His presence!
2. **Clearer Direction** in your journey! 4. **Greater Faith** in every battle!

Never forget, that if you were no threat to Satan's kingdom, why would he bother you? So expect conflict, warfare, fiery darts, and hurdles to go over. And remember,

♦ When the Assyrians attacked Jerusalem, Hezekiah went to prayer.
♦ When Sanballat mocked the Jews, Nehemiah went to prayer.
♦ When the Egyptians pursued Israel, Moses went to prayer.
♦ When the enemy withstood Persia, Daniel went to prayer.
♦ When Herod arrested Peter, the church went to prayer.

And, how does God respond to "Bending Christians" in prayer?

III. The "Breakthrough" of the Lord (v.20).
"As waters break out, the Lord has broken out against my enemies before me" (v.20).

This is David's first victory as King of the new united kingdom. He calls the location of the victory Baal Perazim, which means, **"The Lord who breaks through."** What resulted when God broke through? The evil idols were burned to ashes and carried off. Why? Because God can break through anything and everything that keeps you from making spiritual progress.

The take-a-way?
"The Lord has gone out in front of you" (v.24), means: He knows where you're going, He knows what you need, and He will help you do His will to make His Name famous where you live and serve!

Nuf Sed!

July 12
"You Are Accepted"

"To the praise of the glory of his grace, wherein he hath made us **accepted** in the beloved" (Ephesians 1:6, KJV).

Paul wrote Ephesians from a Roman prison around A.D. 61. He wrote to believers in Ephesus along the coast of Asia Minor. Paul had visited Ephesus, preached Jesus for two whole years, and the church grew in a seemingly unusual place. Ephesus was a commercial city where the temple of Diana was the worship attraction. Diana was the sex goddess that promoted sensuality and prostitution. Ephesus had become pagan, and God saw fit to plant a church in the middle of sin city.

What happened in Ephesus? People started getting saved! Miracles began to happen! God worked supernaturally in a place of oriental magic and superstition! Believers even built a bonfire and set aflame all of the pagan and magical literature. And, Paul sends an incredible message to the people who had come to the Lord. He told them things that made them and us strong in the Lord. Paul's words are words of power, health and wholeness that make us strong, confident and courageous. He begins in chapter 1 with something that God wants you to know today:

1. You Are "Adopted."
"He predestined us to be adopted as his sons" (1:5, NIV).

The word "adopted" means, that by an act of God, God has given you an adult standing in His family. It means that God, by an act of Divine Grace, Love and Mercy, has adopted you because you have trusted in His Son's sinless sacrifice. In other words, we have received what we did not deserve and could not earn!

2. You Are "Accepted."
"He hath made us accepted in the beloved" (v.6, KJV).

Because of Adam's sin, we were born in sin. Because of sin, we incurred the wrath of God. Because of God's wrath, we were destined to be lost for eternity. Yet because of the work of God's Son on the cross, we are not rejected or at odds with God any longer. In other words, we have been fully accepted by God because of trusting in what Jesus has done! Once far off we have now been brought near to God! Why? Because God the Father has accepted the sacrifice of God the Son, and can now accept all who receive His Son!

3. You Are "Assured."
"Who worketh all things after the counsel of his own will" (V.11, KJV).

In (v.7) we are promised forgiveness of our sin by God's grace. But in (v.11), we see the faithfulness of God's Sovereignty in the "all things" of your life! This means that God is working and redeeming all things together for *christ*

your good and His ultimate glory. It means all things are under His control and you can trust Him fully. Yes, God is overseeing, aware and involved in all that is happening in your life right now!

The take-a-way?
While you may face rejection from people on earth, you will never face rejection from God if you are resting in the work of His Son!

Nuf Sed!

July 13
"You Are Quickened"

"Even when we were dead in sins, hath **quickened** us together with Christ" (Ephesians 2:5, KJV).

Yesterday we discovered that we are adopted, accepted, and assured of God's sovereign faithfulness. Today, we'll see what happens when we are born again because of God's great love and mercy towards us. It really is a remarkable and supernatural experience that changes the human heart!

And, if you ever take for granted what God has done in saving you, just remember what you were before salvation:

♦ We were **dead in our sins** (v.1):
Which means that we were void of spiritual life, unable to respond to spiritual things, and separated from God and the life He provides. We were dominated by our sinful nature and going in the wrong direction.

♦ We were **disobedient to God's will** (v.2):
Which means that we were slaves to the values and manners of our environment. As children of disobedience, we spent our energies living contrary to God's best for us.

♦ We were **desirous of fleshly things** (v.3):
Which means that we lived to gratify the carnal appetites of our corrupt sinful nature inherited from Adam. We lived to fulfill the lusts of our flesh that were robbing us of our God given potential.

"But because of... God who is rich in mercy" (v.4).

We have been given what we didn't deserve, and have been spared from what we did deserve. So much so, that you and I have been:

1. **"Quickened"** Together with Christ! (v.5)
We have been made alive in Jesus after being dead in our sins. This means that we are reborn in our spirit and the Holy Spirit takes up residence in us. We have been regenerated with supernatural life from God!

2. **"Raised"** Up Together with Jesus! (v.6)
This refers to being elevated to a new level of life. At conversion, we are raised up to a new power over sin, a new purpose for living, a new life in the Spirit, a new attitude, a new family of God, a new future and a new contagious joy and outlook.

3. **"Seated"** In Heavenly Places in Christ Jesus! (v.6)
Physically, our address is on earth, but spiritually our address is in heaven. It means that we live in two worlds: we live in a body down here, but fellowship with the Lord in heaven. We have the privilege of fellowship with Jesus while our feet are temporarily on earth.

The take-a-way?

When we understand what it means to be quickened, raised and seated – we understand what it means to be blessed, rich, wealthy, and honored!   Nuf Sed!

"You Are Renewed"

"And be renewed in the spirit of your mind" (Ephesians 4:24, KJV).

In Ephesians chapters 1-3, God tells us how we are accepted (1:6), quickened (2:5), and strengthened (3:16). In chapters 4-6, God shows us how to live responsibly in light of our great privileges. And, living responsibly involves two things:

1. The Mandate for Change

"You must no longer live as the Gentiles do, in the futility of their thinking" (Ephesians 4:17).

God had saved the Gentile converts in Ephesus. Paul then gives a mandate to those now saved, a mandate to make a clean break from the former life of sin. The motivation to live this new life comes from remembering what we used to be. Just think about it:

♦ We were **vain** (v.17b), which means that we were empty, aimless, futile and followed worthless things.

♦ We were **darkened** (v.18a), which means that we were blind to the good life in God and unable to see God's eternal plan for our lives.

♦ We were **alienated** (v.18), which means that we were estranged, separated and cut off from the very life we now enjoy.

♦ We were **callous** (v.19), which means that our hearts were calloused, hardened and insensible toward God. We simply did what we felt because of our unredeemed conscience! But thanks be to God for His wonderful Grace that makes a change of heart possible. Notice how we change in:

2. The Method of Change

The method of change is revealed by Paul in three clear ways:

♦ We **put off the old man** (v.22) which means that we must cooperate with God and make choices every day. We choose to obey the Holy Spirit and say "no" to the things that do not glorify God. We decide to take off everything that would lead us farther away from God. We take off every former way of life like we take off our dirty clothes at day's end.

♦ We **allow God to renew our minds** (v.23) which means that we focus our thoughts on things that result in joy and peace. It means that we fill our minds with truth (the Word) that cuts away what doesn't belong. Remember: we will become, and act out what we allow our minds to dwell upon (Proverbs 23:7).

♦ We **put on the new man** (v.24) which means that we dress up or add the spiritual disciplines to our lives. And, as we add prayer, the Word, humility, transparency and obedience – God has something to work with. The result is "the new self" created to be like God in true righteousness and holiness" (v.24, NIV).

The take-a-way?

♦ **We are what we eat every day!**

♦ **We will do what we continually think upon over time!**

♦ **We become like that which we behold!**

Nuf Sed!

July 15
"You Are Empowered"

"Be filled with the Spirit" (Ephesians 5:18).

Here's a good question: Why does God want us to be continually (daily) filled with the Holy Spirit? My guess is: so that we can do His will, His work, His way! This is why the baptism in the Holy Spirit is so important. The Pentecostal experience is to so clothe us with the Spirit of God, that we will be energized to serve in God's Kingdom. And, the anointing of the Spirit is not to make us feel good, it is for us to help somebody. Like water cannot rise above its own level, we cannot give away what we do not possess. "Lord, fill us with your Spirit continually" is my prayer today!

Paul's instructions in Ephesians 5 are really practical (and spiritual) when it comes to staying filled with the Spirit. It's a great guide to help us "keep being filled" and point people to Jesus. Before the command in (v.18) to "be filled with the Spirit," Paul reminds us of a few things:

1. "Be very careful, then, how you live" (v.15), which means to live circumspectly, carefully, pay attention, watch out and take heed.

2. "Making the most of every opportunity" (v.16), which means to redeem the time, live on purpose and take advantage of every opportunity God gives us in light of eternity.

3. "Understand what the Lord's will is" (v.17), which means to discern and discover God's plan for your life (accompanied by the peace of God, the Spirit's confirmation and alignment with Scripture).
"Do not get drunk on wine which leads to debauchery. Instead, be filled with the Spirit" (v.18).

So, instead of seeking joy, power and satisfaction in an artificial, external, temporary stimulus – how can you **"keep being filled"** with the Spirit?
♦ Through **Worship** (v.19).
"Sing and make music in your heart to the Lord." The Psalms are the Psalms of the Old Testament put to music. Hymns are songs of praise and testimony that God has given to the church. Spiritual songs are those birthed in your spirit as you walk along praising God throughout your day.
♦ Through **Gratefulness** (v.20).
"Always giving thanks to God the Father for everything." Murmuring and complaining will rob you of power and drain your emotional bucket. Gratitude and thankfulness allow God to inhabit your praises and continually fill you with joyful praise.
♦ Through **Humility** (v.21).
"Submit to one another out of reverence for Christ." The word "submit", means "to line up under", as troops would line up under their commander. It is the opposite of stubbornness and rebellion. This reveals that it is impossible

for selfish, myopic, and narcissistic people to be healthy, joyful and filled with the Spirit.

The take-a-way?
Spirit filled people will bring glory to God and be empowered to serve Him through an attitude of worship, gratitude, and humility!

Nuf Sed!

July 16
"You Are Standing"
Part I

"Put on the full armor of God so that you can take your stand against the devil's schemes" (Ephesians 6:11).

The word "stand" is a military term that means: To stand firm when assaulted in battle, and, to hold your position when under attack. Why does Paul write this section for us? Because he knows that we are in a spiritual battle and will be spiritually "assaulted" and "attacked". In fact, the enemy is described in four ways in (v.12):

♦ **"Rulers"** – which are evil powers in the unseen world.

♦ **"Authorities"** – which are demons in the lower atmosphere.

♦ **"Powers of this dark world"** – which are demon powers in control of political systems.

♦ **"Spiritual forces of evil in the heavenly realms"** – which are demonic forces organized to promote wickedness and sin of every kind.

So, what is our hope against powers like this? Our hope is in the finished work of Jesus at the cross, and the armor of God that protects us in the field of battle. Our hope is that God has provided all the protection that we need to "stand" in the days of battle. This is why we do not fear! This is why we must be prepared! This is why we "dress up" and "stand up" and live strong in the Lord and in the power of His might and provision. Oh friend, just look at what God has provided for you to "stand":

1. The Belt of Truth (v.14).

This belt, or girdle, of the Roman soldier held all the other garments in place. Its purpose was to hold the loose flowing garments tight to the body. Why? To allow freedom of movement for the soldier. If the soldier was hindered in combat, it meant trouble and death. In other words, interference in a time when agility was needed most, gave the enemy the advantage and upper hand. Without the belt secure, the soldier was sure to fall.

The application is clear: For you and me, the Belt of Truth is truthfulness or integrity in the inward parts of our heart. It is the opposite of phoniness, sham, pretense, and hypocrisy. It is transparency, sincerity and a clear conscience. Why is this so important? Because, as the tightened belt (girdle) of the Roman soldier held all the other garments in place, if we become loose with our honesty, integrity, and truthfulness, everything else begins to fall apart as well. In fact, the belt of the soldier held his sword. This means, unless we wear the belt of truthfulness, the sword of the Word will be ineffective in battle. Simply put, the effectiveness of God's Word to change my heart will only be equal to my willingness to live transparent before God. May the girdle of truth hold everything else together in your life and mine! The take-a-way?

If we have integrity, nothing else matters; If we don't have integrity, nothing else matters! Nuf Sed!

"You Are Standing"
Part II

"Put on the full armor of God so that you can take your stand against the devil's schemes" (Ephesians 6:11).

Yesterday, we saw the enemy of our souls described in four ways, compelling us to be prepared for spiritual battle. The good news from God through Paul is, we have been given the armor to stand and not fall on the day of attack. Today, we continue with the armor of God to help us enjoy the journey and be strong in the Lord.

2. The Breastplate of Righteousness (v.14).

A breastplate was worn by Roman soldiers to protect the vital organs of the body. It was a piece of armor made with metal plates and chains for flexibility. It covered the soldier's front and back, and reached from the neck to the waist. It was necessary to save the soldier from being mortally wounded in battle.

The application is clear: The **breastplate of righteousness** for you and me is:

♦ The righteousness of Jesus we receive at salvation.
♦ It is the breastplate of right standing before God.
♦ It is the armor that silences the accuser of the brethren – who says you are guilty, unworthy and not forgiven.

Why is this breastplate so important? Because it is our reminder that every believer who is trusting Jesus for forgiveness is 100% free from all condemnation. It is an awareness that God's grace has cleared you from God's wrath. And, why is this so important to you? Because this is what quenches the fiery darts of satan who wants you to keep looking back to your past. This breastplate is a reminder that you can't be accused if you are standing "in Christ". The breastplate helps us enjoy closeness to Jesus, the embrace of God and an open door for welcome.

Today, if you struggle with God the Father loving you as His son or daughter, pause for a moment and allow the following truth to free you from your self-imposed (false) accusations. Allow the Word to clothe you with the breastplate, and protect your heart from every fiery dart of accusation:

"Therefore, since we have been justified through faith, we have peace with God through our Lord Jesus Christ, through whom we have gained access by faith into this grace" (Romans 4:11).

"For if, by the trespass of the one man, death reigned through that one man, how much more will those who receive God's abundant provisions of grace and of the gift of righteousness reign in life through the one man, Jesus Christ" (Romans 5:17).

And, what does receiving the righteousness of Jesus mean to you?

It's our joyful take-a-ways:

1. Your iniquities are **cast into the depths of the sea** (Micah 7:19).
2. God remembers your sin **no more** (Hebrews 10:17).
3. You have been **cleansed from all** unrighteousness (I John 1:9).
4. Your sins are now **white as snow** (Isaiah 1:18).
5. All transgressions have been **removed from your record** (Psalm 103:12).
6. God **cannot see** your sin any longer (Isaiah 38:17).
7. God will **never** recall your sin against you (Isaiah 43:25).

Nuf Sed!

Shoes of peace

"You Are Standing"
Part III

"Put on the full armor of God so that you can take your stand against the devil's schemes" (Ephesians 6:11).

Thus far, we've looked at the first two pieces of armor. **Thank God** that He can help us maintain integrity (the belt of truthfulness) and enjoy right standing before God (the breastplate of righteousness). Today, the all important ingredient that enables us to remain calm in battle:

3. The Gospel of Peace (v.15).
"And with your feet fitted with the readiness that comes from the gospel of peace."

Today, we have dress shoes, work shoes, leisure shoes, running shoes, golf shoes, snow shoes, and many other shoes! In Paul's day, a soldier's shoes were the most important shoes in his possession. His very life could depend on his footing. Roman soldiers wore sandals with hobnails in the soles to give firm footing. These bits of metal gave the needed traction as the soldier fought in battle. The "fitted feet" enabled the soldier to walk without stumbling and fight without slipping.

What is the application today? Feet are mentioned because they represent our daily walk with God! And, in our walk with God, circumstances arise, disappointments occur and spiritual battles are encountered. One thing above all else can keep us steady in battle – the "Peace of God"! What is this "Peace of God"? The word peace comes from the word *Eirene* which means:

◆ Rest ◆ Order ◆ Harmony ◆ Security
◆ Tranquility ◆ Quietness ◆ Peace

This Gospel of Peace is:
1. Tranquility in your inner man because of God's presence in your life.
2. Security in the midst of turmoil; the eye in the middle of the storm.
3. The assurance given by God, that He is in control and over all that touches you.
4. The fruit which gives order, rest, and harmony to you on the inside.
5. That quality of God's nature imparted to a believer who is surrendered to His will.

Why is this peace so important? Two main reasons:
◆ God's Peace will **"guard"** your heart (Philippians 4:7).

The peace of God is pictured as a garrison against the enemy who seeks to invade our hearts and disrupt us. The peace we receive from God will keep constant guard and protect us from the anxieties that seek to steal our tranquility. Without this peace, our guard will be down, making us vulnerable to fiery darts of the evil one who attempts to pull our minds in many directions.

♦ God's peace will **"guide"** your heart (Colossians 3:15). ✓

God has promised us that His peace would rule, or be present, when we are in His will. The Holy Spirit will bear witness with our Spirit as we make decisions in life. If this peace is absent, we should step back and admit, "something is not right". When we are in God's perfect will, we will have His peace ruling in our hearts; His peace will assure us that we are doing what He desires.

The take-a-way?
The peace of God is that fruit and reward of a clear conscience!

Nuf Sed!

"You Are Standing"
Part IV

"Put on the full armor of God so that you can take your stand against the devil's schemes." (Ephesians 6:11).

I love the fact that God wants us to stand and not fall when tempted in battle. I'm also grateful that God has provided all that we need to be strong and "stand firm" against spiritual forces in the unseen world. Today, we'll look at the shield of faith – what it is and what it does!

4. The Shield of Faith

"Take up the **shield of faith**, with which you can extinguish all the flaming arrows of the evil one" (6:16).

In Paul's day, Roman soldiers used two common shields. The first shield was small, round, and secured to the arm by two leather straps. It was lightweight, easy to handle, and used to defend against the blow of a sword in hand to hand combat. The second shield was designed to protect the whole body. It was four and half feet high, two and a half feet wide, made of wood and covered over with metal or oiled leather. But why the shields?

Soldiers carried these shields on the front lines of battle. Archers stood behind this protection line to advance forward. They would be shielded from enemy spears and arrows. The tips of arrows were wrapped in cloth and dipped in flammable pitch. These flaming missiles would splatter on impact and spread burning bits of fire for several feet. The flames would burn whatever they could latch onto. So, what is the **shield of faith today**, and how does it extinguish "all the flaming arrows of the evil one" (v.16)?

The shield of faith Paul refers to here is not saving faith. This faith (that acts as a shield for you) is faith in the Lord when you are tested and tried. It is a confidence in God when engaged in a spiritual battle or warfare. This "shield of faith" is for daily living, and will protect your heart when fiery darts are hurled your way. This shield of faith is:

♦ Trusting in what God has said in His Word!
♦ Leaning on the Lord when you are under fire!
♦ Confidence in God in those wilderness seasons!
♦ Embracing God when your feelings break down!

And, what does this faith shield do? It quenches those fiery missiles, lies, and darts of discouragement from the evil one. It repels the lies of intimidation and fear. It sees beyond what is visible and believes in the sovereignty, integrity, and faithfulness of God! It flat out protects you and preserves you when confronted by satan's most vicious attacks!

And remember this: The body shields had latches on the side. Why? So that every single shield could be hooked together with other shields. That way the army could band together and march forward as one to defeat the enemy by the power of a united effort!

The take-a-way?
One snowflake isn't much by itself, but it takes a bulldozer to move them when they cooperate!

Nuf Sed!

"You Are Standing"
Part V

"Put on the full armor of God so that you can take your stand against the devil's schemes" (Ephesians 6:11).

The armor of God described by Paul is spiritual, practical and necessary. It has been given by God as a gift. Yet, it must be "put on" by you and me to be useful and effective. Today, we see:

5. The Helmet of Salvation!
"Take the helmet of salvation" (Ephesians 6:17).

Remember now; Paul was looking at Roman soldiers in prison. The soldiers wore helmets that were made of thick leather and brass. The helmets were worn to protect the head from blows by swords or battle axes. Cavalry men would use four-foot broad swords to split the skulls of enemy soldiers. The helmets were a must wear to win battles. So, what is the "helmet of salvation" to us?

The helmet represents something very clear to us. The head is the center of our intellect, our thought-life, and our mind. In other words, what we think about and dwell upon in our mind will determine our actions.
♦ "For as he thinketh in his heart, so is he" (Proverbs 23:7, KJV).
♦ "Wherefore gird up the loins of your mind" (I Peter 1:13, KJV).
♦ "Be ye transformed by the renewing of your mind" (Romans 12:2, KJV).

But what is the helmet of "salvation"? Paul is very clear:
"But let us, who are of the day, be sober, putting on the breastplate of faith and love; and for our **helmet, the hope of salvation**" (I Thessalonians 5:8, KJV).

So, the helmet of "salvation" is the hope and assurance from God, that your salvation is complete and takes care of your past, present and future!
1. In the **past,** you know that you have **been justified** and declared righteous before a Holy God!
2. In the **present,** you know that you are **being sanctified** and changed by a patient God.
3. In the **future,** you know that you **will be glorified** and have an assurance of seeing Jesus face to face.

And, knowing this and remembering this will quench the fiery darts (lies) of the evil one who wants to steal your hope, joy, optimism and perspective.

"Lord help us nail it down today and never forget; that our past has been covered (**justified**), our present is changing (**sanctified**), and our future is guaranteed (**glorified**)!"
The take-a-way?
Our thoughts affect our emotions; our emotions affect our wills; our wills make choices every day; and we then live with the consequences of our decisions!   Nuf Sed!

July 21
"You Are Standing"
Part VI

"Put on the full armor of God so that you can take your stand against the devil's schemes" (Ephesians 6:11).

I can't think of any greater joy or spiritual discipline than hiding the Word of God within our hearts. In fact, it's hard to comprehend what happened to me in 1974 while reading the Word on a gospel tract. It was God, through the Word, that convicted me and drew me to pray the sinner's prayer on an airplane flight from Tampa, Florida to Baltimore, Maryland. It was the Word that penetrated my heart and pointed me to Jesus! It was the Word that let me know that I needed a savior! Notice Paul's sixth piece of armor to "put on", it's called:

6. The Sword of The Spirit Which Is the Word of God (v.17).
The sword that Paul is referring to here, was the common sword carried by the Roman foot soldier (6-18 inches long). It was close at hand for ready use to defeat the enemy. But, why is the Word called the "Sword of the Spirit"? It is because, only the Holy Spirit can make the Word effectual in its working upon our hearts. In other words, the Bible is useless (a dead letter) unless we are open to the Holy Spirit's working. And, as a sword, the Word of God can change our hearts and cut away anything that doesn't reflect the nature of Jesus. It's our take-a-ways for today:

1. The Word Brings **Peace!**
"Great peace have they who love your law" (Psalm 119:165).
2. The Word Brings **Faith!**
"Faith comes from hearing the message" (Romans 10:17).
3. The Word Brings **Wisdom!**
"The statutes of the Lord are trustworthy, making wise the simple" (Psalm 19:7).
4. The Word Brings **Conviction!**
"For the Word of God... penetrates even to dividing soul and spirit" (Hebrews 4:12).
5. The Word Brings **Comfort!**
"My comfort in my suffering is this: your promise preserves my life" (Psalm 119:50).
6. The Word Brings **Direction!**
"Your Word is a lamp to my feet and a light to my path" (Psalm 119:105).
7. The Word Brings **Growth!**
"As newborn babes, desire the sincere milk of the Word, that you may grow thereby" (I Peter 2:2).
8. The Word Brings **Joy!**
"When your words came, I ate them, they were my joy" (Jeremiah 15:16).

9. The Word Brings **Obedience!**

"I have hidden your word in my heart that I might not sin against you" (Psalm 119:11).

10. The Word Brings **Steadfastness!**

"His delight is in the law of the Lord... whose leaf does not wither" (Psalm 1:3).

Nuf Sed!

July 22
"You Are Standing"
Part VII

"Put on the full armor of God so that you can take your stand against the devil's schemes" (Ephesians 6:11).

Paul, concludes his message on the soldier's armor with a final appeal. It's that one appeal that ties all the other six appeals together. I call it:

7. The Spirit of Prayer!
"And pray in the Spirit on all occasions with all kinds of prayers and requests. With this in mind, be alert and always keep on praying for all the saints" (v.18). "Pray also for me, that whenever I open my mouth, words may be given me so that I will fearlessly make known the mystery of the gospel" (v.19).

On March 11, we uncovered the pattern, power, and perseverance of prayer in this text. Today, I want to show why Paul was so emphatic about this final appeal. The seventh (and final) piece of armor is the very one that holds all the others in place. In other words, without prayer, something will be missing and the Word will not affect the way we live, the way we serve and the way we process life's ups and downs! Simply; I love to pray, because **prayer is:**

1. The greatest privilege of the Christian!
2. Conversation of my soul with God!
3. An attitude and mindset more than an act!
4. My spirit panting after God!
5. Taking hold of God's strength!
6. Connecting my need with God's spiritual storehouse!
7. Alignment of my heart with God's will!
8. What calls God's intentions into existence!
9. What releases the resources of the Almighty!
10. Relinquishing what we need not carry ourselves!
11. Our most effective weapon against the powers of darkness!
12. The road to tranquility and peace of mind!

And may we never forget:
1. If we prostrate ourselves before the Lord, we will never be prostrated before the enemy!
2. If we learn to wrestle with God in secret, we will never have to lower ourselves to wrestle with men in public!
3. The only thing that lies outside the power of prayer is that which lies outside the will of God!
4. Prayer is the breath of the soul; when I breathe, I live, when I cease to breathe, I die!
5. Failing to pray will forfeit what prayer was meant to do!

6. Prayer is the way we take our hands off and let God put His hands on!

7. God won't answer 100% of the prayers that we don't pray!

The take-a-way?

Prayer is the difference between you fighting for God, and God fighting for you!

Nuf Sed!

"The Vineyard of the Soul"

"They made me the keeper of the vineyards; but mine own vineyard have I not kept" (Song of Solomon 1:6, KJV).

If there's one thing I've learned about planting shrubs and flowers around the yard it is this: you don't have to plant weeds; they just show up and grow on their own! And, unless I weed the flowerbed, the weeds take over. I've also discovered that if I don't weed my own garden, the neighbors don't come over and weed it for me.

Our text is about a Shulamite girl who was faithfully tending the vineyards of others but neglecting her own. The pain of this revelation grieved her heart as she realized that her own garden became overgrown with weeds, fruit was being lost in the shuffle, and her personal neglect was costing her dearly. After all, what good is it, if what I <u>am</u> doesn't keep pace with what I <u>do</u>? Notice how the Lord draws all of us to Himself in this great text:

1. Jesus Is Very Attractive!
"Let him kiss me with the kisses of his mouth, for your love is more delightful than wine" (1:2).

"Let him kiss me" means: Draw me into deeper union and greater intimacy. In other words, as the Shulamite girl was attracted to Solomon, you and I are being attracted to Jesus! The phrase, "more delightful than wine" means that while wine only stirs for a temporary moment, God's presence does what wine cannot (it enriches, purifies, sustains, satisfies and changes us).

2. Jesus Is Mightily Anointed!
"Your Name is like perfume poured out" (v.3).
"My lover is to me a sachet of myrrh" (v.13).

Ointment was used for healing; so, the presence of God is a healing balm. Rubbed on, ointment penetrates! So, Jesus can get through every hang-up, excuse, and issue to heal by His power. As myrrh was used in the anointing oil for Aaron the high priest, likewise Jesus restores joy to those who need it. As myrrh was used for the incense of prayer in the tabernacle, likewise Jesus receives us in prayer with open arms. As myrrh was used for embalming the dead to prevent corruption and decay, likewise Jesus preserves us, sustains us and gives us power over sin that would defile and corrupt us.

3. Jesus Is Freely Accessible!
"Let the king bring me into his chamber" (v.4).

Here we are invited to go from the outer court into the inner court. This is Jesus inviting us to draw closer and run to Him. Even though we may feel "black" with sin (v.5) and unworthy, "do not stare at me" (v.6), we are invited into intimacy regardless of our shortcomings!

The take-a-way?

While we care for the vineyard and needs of others, may we never resist the calling voice of Jesus to come apart and commune with our Beloved!

Nuf Sed!

"Soap and Fire"

"But who can endure the day of his coming? Who can stand when he appears? For he will be like a refiner's fire or a launderer's soap" (Malachi 3:2).

Malachi was given a message to call the people back to God. What was the message? The message was that Jesus would come by His presence to do a great work in our hearts. In fact, He will come suddenly (v.1) and He will do this among us:

1. "He will be like a refiner's fire" (v.2). 2. "A launderer's soap" (v.2). 3. "A refiner of silver" (v.3).   4. "And refine them like gold" (v.4).

Why does Jesus want to do this? Two reasons:
♦ So that we can offer Him an offering (of our lives) in righteousness (v.3).
♦ So that our lives will be pleasant and acceptable to the Lord (v.4).
In other words, acceptable service can only come (flow) from a pure heart. And, here's the illustration that Malachi uses to prepare our hearts for undefiled service:

1. The Fuller's Soap!
The fuller's trade was well known in Judea. The Jews wore white garments on all festive occasions. The fuller (or launderer) cleaned the stained garments by rubbing them with a marl (or wooden mallet). The soap was a vegetable alkali taken from various plants near Joppa. The soap would extract the stains and separate them from the garments. The lesson? As the fuller would conquer every stain in the garments, so Jesus can conquer every stain in the heart. Yes, the blood of Jesus can wash, remove, clean, and extract the deepest stain we can offer Him.

2. The Refiner's Fire!
The refiner always sat so that he could watch the metal carefully. If the metal was left a minute too long or taken out a minute too soon, it was spoiled and ruined. Remember; the refiner removed the dross from the ore to make the silver shine. It's what Jesus is doing in you and me right now! And, never forget the **"silver secrets"** when God takes you through the fire:

1. Refined silver requires **care** and **skill** in the silversmith!
    ♦ The refiner measures, compensates and with utmost care he deals with the silver.
2. Refined silver requires just the right **furnace!**
    ♦ Not just any oven will do; it must be an environment to produce a good metal.
3. Refined silver requires just the right **heat.**
        ♦ All the attention of the silversmith is on the thermostat. It must be

neither too hot nor too cold. If it's too cold, the base metals and tin will not separate from pure silver. If it's too hot, the minute portions of silver will be carried off with the lead.

4. Refined silver requires just the right **timing.**

♦ The silversmith knows when to take the metal out of the heat.

The take-a-way?

"Return to me, and I will return to you, says the Lord" (3:7) means: when we draw near to God in humility and confession, God will respond and change us from the inside out!

Nuf Sed!

July 25
"Straining At The Oars"

"He saw the disciples straining at the oars, because the wind was against them" (Mark 6:48).

Two times I've been fishing when my boat motor died. Both times I had to row to shore, and neither time was fun or enjoyable. In today's text, it's not a fun time for the disciples. Yet Jesus shows up and teaches us some valuable lessons to enjoy the journey:

1. I See The "Testing" of The Disciples!

Jesus had just sent the disciples across the lake of Galilee, while sending the people away (v.45). Why? Because the multitude that was just fed by a miracle was coming to make Jesus king. The people thought Jesus had arrived to deliver them from Herod's authority and Roman oppression. So, lest the disciples remain on shore and be blinded by the frenzy and excitement of the moment, Jesus sends them across the lake to avoid the distraction. And, this would become a "testing" time:

♦ They would be **alone**, because Jesus stayed on shore.
♦ They would be in the **dark,** because it was late at night.
♦ They would be in **trouble**, as contrary winds would arise.
♦ They would be **surprised,** because Jesus never warned them about the contrary winds. *Purposely Jesus does not warn us of everything!*
    Yet, all of this is happening to get the disciples to the very place where a miracle crusade was about to take place (v.53-56).

2. I See the "Toiling" of The Disciples!

The Scripture states that Jesus, "Saw the disciples straining at the oars" (v.48). The Greek word for straining means, "baffled, tired, weary, drained and exhausted". Why were the disciples toiling and straining?
♦ Galilee was six miles across and the disciples were right in the middle. Are you in the middle of contrary winds?
♦ The disciples had been rowing against a headwind for six to nine hours. Have you been up against a headwind pressing in upon you?
♦ After 9 hours, and only half way across, the disciples discover that their strength is gone and used up. Do you find yourself weary, tired and worn?
♦ It's now the fourth watch of the night in Roman time (between 3am and 6am), which is the darkest part of the night. Do you feel like you're in the dark and can't see the end in sight?

3. I See the "Triumph" of The Disciples!

If you ever feel like Jesus is unaware of what surrounds you, isn't answering your prayers, has left you without direction, or is on a wrong time table (schedule), then remember (v.53, 56):

"When they had crossed over, they landed at Gennesaret… and all who touched him were healed"

In other words, in God's perfect timing help had arrived, a ship landed on schedule, and a miracle healing crusade took place. Why?

It's the take-a-way from our text:
♦ **No winds are wasted if they bring you closer to Jesus!**
♦ **When you can't see Jesus, He still sees you!**
♦ **What you think is wasted, God will use for His Glory!**
♦ **Contrary winds do not mean that you've missed the will of God!**

Nuf Sed!

"The True Rest of Prayer"
Part I

"When they heard this, they raised their voices together in prayer to God. 'Sovereign Lord', they said…" (Acts 4:24).

Maybe, just maybe, Acts 4:24-33 gives us the greatest rest and peace in the place of prayer. It is such a revelation of how to trust and relinquish things over to God in prayer. The three reminders from Luke bring a calm and assurance like none other. Here's the setting and context where this "rest" in prayer is born.

Two waves of persecution were initiated by the Sadducees (Acts 4:1; 5:17). They saw the apostles as agitators and heretics, went on the offensive and put Peter and John in jail overnight (4:3). After the night in jail, a court session meets to decide the fate of Peter and John. The Sanhedrin Council then asks the two apostles:

"By what power or what name did you do this?" (v.7).

Peter then speaks up in (v.8-12), the healed beggar stands before them (v.14), the court meets behind closed doors (v.15) and comes to this conclusion:

"What are we going to do with these men?... Everybody living in Jerusalem knows they have done an outstanding miracle, and we cannot deny it" (v.16).

So, the court tells the two preachers to knock it off:

"Then they called them in again and commanded them not to speak or teach at all in the name of Jesus" (v.18).

Peter and John refused to keep quiet (v.20), go back to the church (v.23), and the believers cry out to God in prayer. And, how they prayed is life changing to our spiritual man:

Do you know who you are talking to?

1. They Prayed with Faith in God's "Authority" (v.24).

"When they heard this, they raised their voices together in prayer to God. 'Sovereign Lord,' they said, 'You made the heavens and the earth and the sea, and everything in them'" (v.24).

Here's how to pray in uncertainty or in trouble! The words, "Sovereign Lord" come from the word that means: Sovereign Ruler or Sovereign Master. This word *Despotes* means:

♦ The Lord has sovereign rule and final authority.
♦ The Lord possesses all power at all times.
♦ The Lord is in charge of all things as creator and sustainer.
♦ The Lord still rules and overrules the plans of man.

The believers in the prayer meeting are acknowledging that God is sovereign (or Master) over the situation with the Sanhedrin Council. In other words, God is showing us that we can pray in faith and rest well today because God is Sovereign and has full and final authority!

The take-a-way?

♦ **Nothing happens to you without God's knowledge of it!**

♦ **God's purpose will surely be fulfilled in your life!**

♦ **God will have the final say in every matter, so you can rest and trust Him in prayer!**

Nuf Sed!

July 27
"The True Rest of Prayer"
Part II

"When they heard this, they raised their voices together in prayer to God. 'Sovereign Lord,' they said, 'You made the heavens and the earth and the sea, and everything in them'" (Acts 4:24).

Yesterday, we learned that when the Sanhedrin told Peter and John to keep quiet or else, the believers went to prayer. And, how they prayed brought a great rest, calm and peace to their spirits. The church began their praying by acknowledging that God has final authority in all matters. Why? Because He is "Sovereign Lord" (v.24) and over all! Today we'll see the next reason that the church remained confident in the midst of persecution, intimidation, and uncertainty.

2. They Prayed with Faith in God's "Providence" (v.25-28).
"Indeed Herod and Pontius Pilate met together with the Gentiles and the people of Israel in this city to conspire against your holy servant Jesus, whom you anointed" (v.27).
"They did what your power and will had decided beforehand should happen" (v.28).

"Wow" is all I can say here! The believers (in prayer) refer to David in (v.25) – how the nations revolted against the Lord. The believers see the same thing happening again with Jesus' adversaries (Herod, Pilate, the Jews and Romans, v.27). And, in prayer, the believers say:
"Lord, people did what was evil in killing your innocent Son, but you turned it around to work for your eternal good! In other words, Lord, you turned their evil deeds inside out and used them against the enemy to save and rescue every lost sinner who repents."

The believers are so confident in prayer because they have a glimpse or an understanding of God's providence and determined counsel. This simply means the following for you today – now get this:

♦ If God could overrule the worst that man has ever done, in crucifying God's best, His son, then surely God can overrule now and use anything that happens to you for an ultimate good in your life. In other words, God will bring good out of evil for those who trust Him in prayer! There is a purpose behind the pain! Nothing is wasted in His providence! There is a long-range plan unfolding! God is working all things after the counsel of His own will in your life! You can chill out today because:
♦ As the Sanhedrin tried in vain to stop the apostles, so your enemy will try in vain to stop your progress.
♦ As the enemy tried in vain to kill Jesus once and for all, so your enemy will try in vain to keep you from your destiny.
♦ As nations plotted in vain to thwart God's will in the past, so your enemy

will try in vain to hold you down.

The take-a-way?
Every attack of the enemy will prove futile as long as you stay connected to Jesus (in prayer) and trust in the Providence of God!

Nuf Sed!

July 28
"The True Rest of Prayer"
Part III

"Now, Lord, consider their threats and enable your servants to speak your Word with great boldness. Stretch out your hand to heal and perform miraculous signs and wonders through the name of your holy servant Jesus" (Acts 4:29,30).

The past two days we've looked at the response of praying believers when Peter and John were threatened. Their praying is recorded for us! Their praying brought confidence and calm! Their praying increases our faith and shows us how to have rest and a good attitude in the journey. It's just an incredible way to respond (in prayer) to the uncontrollable unknowns of life! In (v.24), the believers prayed with faith in God's **sovereign authority**. In (v.28), they prayed with faith in God's **overriding providence**. Today, we'll see that:

3. They Prayed with Faith in God's Far Reaching Compassion (v.30).
"Stretch out your hand to heal and perform miraculous signs and wonders through the name of your holy servant Jesus" (v.30).

What did the believers pray for in the midst of threats and intimidations? Two things:

♦ They prayed for boldness to speak the Word of God to point the people to Jesus! (v.29)

♦ They prayed for miracles, signs and wonders to point the people to Jesus! (v.30)

What a great revelation here: That it's okay to pray for the supernatural! It's okay to anticipate the working of the Holy Spirit! It's okay to expect God to manifest His compassion towards people! It's okay to pray that signs and wonders will attend the preaching of the Word – as visible proof that God is alive and at work today! It's okay to pray this way! Why?

"After they prayed, the place where they were meeting was shaken. And they were all filled with the Holy Spirit and spoke the Word of God boldly" (v.31). God shook the room to let those praying know that He saw their faith and heard their petitions. And, God filled the believers with the Holy Spirit to go out and speak the Word with boldness. In other words:

♦ The room shaking was God saying, "I'm alive and well, and I still answer prayer".

♦ The outpouring of the Spirit was God saying, "What happened in Acts 2 on the day of Pentecost is still happening today. I'm still pouring out My Spirit upon every available believer".

What's the lesson from the apostles leaving the courtroom for the prayer room?

It's our undeniable take-a-ways:

♦ **The strength to win our spiritual battles is won with the Lord in prayer!**

♦ **If we learn to wrestle with God in secret, we will never have to lower ourselves to wrestle with men in public.**

♦ **If we prostrate ourselves before the Lord, we will never be prostrated before the enemy!**

♦ **In prayer, we learn to fear the Lord, which overcomes every other fear and manipulation.**

Nuf Sed!

July 29
"The *Rest* of The Story"
Part I

"Come to me, all you who are weary and burdened, and I will give you rest" (Matthew 11:28).

There is not one person in the world who doesn't need to hear these words from Jesus. Why? Because all of us are tempted to work, perform, and prove our value and worthiness to God. All of our hearts are tempted to trust in what we do, in order to have favor with God. And all of us need a "rested" heart if we are really going to enjoy the journey!

Our text (Matthew 11) has an interesting context: In Chapter 10, Jesus sends out His laborers and warns them about rejection (v.14), wolves (v.16), flogging (v.17), being arrested (v.19), betrayal (v.21), being hated (v.22), fear (v.31), enemies (v.36), and losing their lives for Jesus' sake (v.39). Who wouldn't need rest in a journey with all these possibilities?

But the "rest" that Jesus refers to is captivating! It is the first of three things that Jesus promises in (v.28-30). Think slowly for a minute about what Jesus is saying to us:

♦ "Come to me, all you who are weary and burdened, and I will give you rest" (v.28).
♦ "Take my yoke upon you and learn from me, for I am gentle and humble in heart, and you will find rest for your souls" (v.29).
♦ "For my yoke is easy and my burden is light" (v.30).

Today, let's look at the first principle that Jesus said brings "rest" to your heart:

1. I Will Give You Rest" (v.28).

The Jews were laboring under the weight of ceremonial laws and the Pharisees groaned under the weight of tradition. Burdensome rights, rules, and regulations were heavy laden upon the people. Jesus' followers were getting saved out of Judaism. Many would embrace the gospel of "Justification by faith" without the deeds of the law. Yet many others were trying to mix faith and law to please God. The result was, some felt guilty because they fell short of keeping all of the law. Others felt arrogant and entitled because of their good performance in keeping the Law. In other words, people needed "rest" from a condemning conscience, a troubled mind and an anxious heart. And, Jesus comes along and tells us that we can have "rest" by understanding what Grace is all about! This "rest" for your heart simply means:

♦ You don't have to labor to gain favor with God!
♦ You don't have to work harder to make God love you!
♦ You don't have to trust in your good works to balance the scale of justice!
♦ You don't have to feel at "arm's length" because of your imperfect

performance!

The "good news" of the gospel is that God is not a hard taskmaster and you need not carry the burden that will reduce your strength, sap your joy and ruin your intimacy with Jesus. The reality is: Jesus paid it all, which means that you can't add a thing to what God has already done!

The take-a-way?
You can work harder to earn your rest or you can rest in the work that God has already done – but you can't do both!

Nuf Sed!

"The *Rest* of The Story"
Part II

"Take my yoke upon you and learn from me, for I am gentle and humble in heart, and you will find rest for your souls" (Matthew 11:29).

Yesterday, we looked at the first of three statements from Jesus in Matthew 11:28-30. We discovered that it's possible for our hearts to not be at "rest". We learned that it's possible to carry a burden that God never intended for us to carry. We saw that Jesus never desired us to be "heavy laden", but instead desires that we trust in His completed work that gives us grace, peace, joy, and "rest". Today, the second command and consequence of taking Jesus at His Word:

2. "Take My Yoke Upon You" (v.29).

Jesus used an illustration here that His hearers understood. It's the picture of a yoke of oxen where two oxen are linked together side by side. Here it refers to embracing the Savior and walking in obedience. In other words, coming to Jesus for salvation is easy. But, the next step is a deeper experience, one of surrender and Lordship. When we come to Jesus by faith (yesterday's devotion), we receive rest, peace and joy from a clear conscience. When we take His yoke upon ourselves we find a "rest" that comes from total surrender and a willingness to obey God.

To take a yoke in Jesus' day, meant to become a disciple. When Jesus says that His yoke is easy, He is saying something powerful. The Greek word for "easy" means "well fitted". This means that walking with Jesus as a surrendered, obedient disciple, results in a deep inner "rest" of heart. In other words, to be "yoked to Jesus" means:

♦ To submit to His authority as Master.
♦ To accept His rule and government for our lives.
♦ To lean upon Him in absolute dependence.
♦ To be willing to follow Him in unreserved obedience.

You might think, "Doesn't this yoke rob us of earthly joy in the journey?" Just the opposite is our reward! We actually find "rest" when we take up His yoke, because those who are yoked closely with Jesus find powerful assistance in the journey. In fact:

1. We receive a never failing supply of grace and strength!
2. We receive security throughout all of our journey!
3. We receive comfort and consolation in every duty or season!
4. We receive the aid of the Holy Spirit for every responsibility!
5. We receive all that we need to do His will on planet earth!

Why is this yoke of Jesus an easy yoke? Because Jesus is responsible to carry and bear the load that would weigh us down, weary us, and steal our enthusiasm. In other words, we never need to fear in doing the will of God. Why not? Because Jesus will never lead us where His grace will not sustain us!

The take-a-way?
The closer we stay yoked to Jesus, the more strength we receive to do His perfect will!

Nuf Sed!

July 31
"The *Rest* Of The Story"
Part III

"For my yoke is easy and my burden is light" (Matthew 11:30).

The past two days we have discovered that there is a "**rest**":
1. For our conscience when we cease to perform in order to receive God's favor.
2. In our journey when we accept the yoke of Jesus and live in absolute surrender to His will!
Today, Jesus' third statement to understand the "rest" of the story:

3. "Learn from Me… My Burden Is Light" (v.29,30).
Jesus ends this portion of Scripture with two knockout statements. So, what does it means to, **"Learn of Me"** and what does it mean that, **"His burden is light"**?

To **"Learn of Jesus"** means to grow and become more and more like Him every day. This is a process of development, stretching, expanding and learning. It is you and me cooperating with God and allowing spiritual disciplines to shape our hearts. While healings and conversions can occur immediately, learning and growing takes time – it's incremental! This means that no one can become spiritual overnight (all at once). It means that we humble ourselves before God and accept responsibility for our thoughts, attitude, motives, words and actions. It means that growing (learning) disciples are people that understand the following:

1. Nothing drifts towards excellence!
2. No one improves by accident!
3. None of us are as smart as all the rest of us!
4. Only a fool knows everything!
5. The biggest room in the world is the room for improvement!
6. The moment I stop growing is the moment I start declining!
7. Humility gives us access to wisdom through other people!

So, what happens when we "learn of Jesus"? The more we learn of Him, the more we discover that **"His burden is light"** which means: life without Jesus is a far greater burden than life with Jesus. In other words, the burden of the Lord (or living as one of His disciples) is far greater than the burden of sin and sin's dominion. Jesus is saying here that:

1. It is far easier to be a Christian than it is to be an unbeliever.
2. It is far more enjoyable to live with Jesus than to live without Him.
3. It is more pleasurable and joyful to walk the narrow way than the broad way. Why? Because Jesus is "gentle and humble in heart" (v.29). This means that the law of sin is slavery, but following Jesus is liberating. The point here is clear: On the broad way that leads to

eventual damnation, sin will chew you up and spit you out! On the narrow way that leads to life, Jesus will sustain you and strengthen you in every season of the journey.

The take-a-way?
There is a "rest" that comes from God to our hearts when we receive His grace, submit to His Lordship, and keep growing in God beyond previous boundaries!

Nuf Sed!

August 1
"Out of Distress"
Psalm 25

"The troubles of my heart have multiplied; free me from my anguish" (Psalm 25:17).
"Look upon my affliction and my distress" (v.18).

Psalm 25 is a prayer of David as he travels through some unsettling seasons. He is being plagued with many distractions and obstacles. He is being slandered by the enemy and has no way to vindicate himself. Yet, he discovers an amazing truth that still works today. What is it? Meditation is medication! In other words, David learns to pray, look to God and wait upon the Lord. He discovers and pens the truth that helps us all to live anxiety free. It's food for the soul to enjoy the journey where God has placed you:

1. Victorious People Know Where to "Look".
"To you, O Lord, I lift up my soul" (v.1).
"In you I trust, O my God" (v.2).
"No one whose hope is in you will ever be put to shame" (v.3).
"My eyes are ever on the Lord" (v.15).
While the natural, carnal man looks to natural sources, the victorious believer looks to our Supernatural God! This is David here, setting his affections and mind on the Lord. This is David's response to the enemy agitation. He is responding from his spirit, not the flesh, and refuses to contend and retaliate. He teaches us the power of perspective and the power of patient waiting.

2. Victorious People Know How to Be "Led".
"Show me your ways, O Lord, teach me your paths; guide me in your truth" (v.4,5).
David knows that his goings are of the Lord (Proverbs 20:24) and that the way of man is not in himself (Jeremiah 10:23). He knows that God will direct him (Proverbs 3:5,6) and that God will lead him through that inner voice of impression. This means, that you can trust God to lead you forward in His perfect timing. It means that you can "rest well" and not fret about your future, your plans, your journey or your unknown seasons ahead. You can rest well today my friend – you can trust your Shepherd to lead you daily!

3. Victorious People Know How to Receive "Grace".
"Remember not the sins of my youth and my rebellious ways" (v.7).
"Turn to me and be gracious to me" (V.16).
David humbles himself before God in confession and repentance and leans not upon himself, but upon the grace of God. He doesn't present his goodness or his works to God. He doesn't feel elite or entitled. He understands that he doesn't want what he really deserves. He teaches us that our distress decreases as we become more God dependent! He shows us how

to pray and have an audience with God: "Take away all my sins" (v.18). Have you prayed that prayer lately? Are you looking to God for your support? Are you trusting God to lead you today? Are you willing to humble yourself before the Lord and receive His Great Grace?

The take-a-way?
My distress decreases to the degree that my humility increases!

Nuf Sed!

August 2
"There Is a River"
Psalm 46

"There is a river whose streams make glad the city of God" (Psalm 46:4).

Psalm 46 reflects upon the invasion of Sennacherib into Jerusalem. It's a word that pours faith into the heart. Its intention is to remove all fear and worry when you encounter those troublesome seasons. It inspired Martin Luther to pen his reformation hymn, "A Mighty Fortress Is Our God". Notice what God provides so that you can enjoy the journey this side of heaven:

1. God Provides "Great Confidence" In Every Battle (v.1-3).
"God is our refuge and strength, an ever-present help in trouble. Therefore we will not fear" (v.1,2).
♦ **Our Refuge** – is a place to run to for safety and security. This is not an army, the arm of flesh, or an earthly fortress. Our refuge is God alone because all power belongs to God. Our refuge is God Himself who responds to those who put their trust in Him.
♦ **Our Strength** – is the Lord who will always be equal to our challenge. This strength from God renews us as we wait upon Him. In prayer, we receive strength from outside of ourselves. Like Isaiah said, "Those who hope in the Lord will renew their strength" (Isaiah 40:31).
♦ **Our Help** – means exactly what the psalmist is saying: "An ever-present help in trouble" (v.1). This means that God doesn't abandon you in trouble or forget you in battle! Sennacherib's army was spreading fear and terror and causing commotion among God's people. But God provided confidence in the midst of the tempest.

2. God Provides "Great Resources" In Every Battle (v.4-7).
"There is a river whose streams make glad" (v.4).
"God will help her at break of day" (v.5).
What is it that produces gladness of heart in the midst of our unsure circumstances?
♦ **Abundant Refreshment** – this "river" (v.4), is a picture or symbol of what God provides for His church. It is a river and stream that flows from God to you. It is a "thirst quencher" that fills and satisfies us in a dry and barren land. It is the water of the Spirit to refresh your inner man.
♦ **Perfect Timing** – is revealed in (v.5), because God brings help at "break of day", which means early, on time, and never late! Though you may feel that God is distant, He will deliver you in, or out of, what comes against you! God's timing is always perfect!

3. God Provides "Great Optimism" In Every Battle (v.7-11).
"The God of Jacob is our fortress" (v.7).
Why Jacob? Because the God that helped Jacob is the same God that

helps us. In other words, if God could help Jacob who was tricked, a fugitive from his brother's anger, and broken over the death of his spouse and presumed death of his son (Joseph), then God can help you in every battle as well! If God could change Jacob to Israel at Peniel, then God can change your heart and mine.

The take-a-way?
"Be still" (v.10), means that quiet prayer will bring moments of respite and calm to our spirit.

Nuf Sed!

"Peaceful and Unshaken"
Psalm 125

"Those who trust in the Lord are like Mount Zion, which cannot be shaken but endures forever" (Psalm 125:1).

Psalm 125 is a Psalm of security and peace. It was written during a time of threat and opposition. It most likely refers to the time after the captivity, when Sanballat, Geshem, and Tobiah opposed the Jews while rebuilding. The purpose of this Psalm is to encourage every believer who is facing plots, schemes, or malice from an enemy. The truth in Psalm 125 is as practical now as the day it was written. I love these "unshakable secrets":

1. What May Shake You Up, Will Not Shake You Apart! (v.1).
"Cannot be shaken but endures forever" (v.1) means:
   Trusting believers are like Mount Zion. Why? Because Zion was a mountain city built upon and surrounded by other mountains. This city of Zion (Jerusalem) had a natural fortification in the mountains surrounding it. This city was secure because of its location. What's the message? The message is, the spiritual Zion (Christ's church – you and me) is more secure than a material mountain. Our security lies in the person of Jesus. In other words, as mountains are an emblem of stability and firmness, so you are unmovable and safe as long as you're trusting in Jesus. You, my friend, are secure regardless of enemy plots, fiery darts or any circumstances you face.

2. What May Come Against You, Cannot Come Within You! (v.2).
"So the Lord surrounds his people both now and forevermore" (v.2) means:
   Jerusalem was encircled by deep ravines and an amphitheater of hills. There was a natural ring of protection for God's people. Enemies found it difficult to penetrate through the circle of defense. As mountains surround the city of Zion, so the Lord totally surrounds those who belong to Him. In other words, nothing can touch you unless it first goes through His hands! He is never caught off guard and is your "wall of defense". And, God will give you the grace to handle what touches your life.

3. What To You Is Painful, God Will Redeem As Useful! (v.3).
"The scepter of the wicked will not remain over the land allotted to the righteous" (v.3) means:
   There may be, "the rod of the wicked" (v.3, KJV), which refers to any oppressive attack of evil to dishearten or detour you. In other words, God hasn't promised us immunity from trial and battle. But He has promised us that He will never allow us to be pushed beyond extreme, He will never waste your painful seasons of testing, He will never allow evil to prevail over His will for your life, and He will never relinquish your future to anyone else!
   And, what has God promised you even in "shaking" times? "Peace be

upon Israel" (v.5), which is:
♦ The fruit of the Spirit enabling us to have quiet assurance, regardless of the circumstances.
♦ Tranquility of heart because of God's presence.
♦ The fruit of God's nature which gives us order and harmony on the inside.

Today's take-a-way?
What the enemy wants to use to shake you, God will reverse to make you into a vessel of honor!

Nuf Sed!

"From Weakness to Strength"
Psalm 6

"My Soul is in anguish. How long, O Lord, how long?" (Psalm 6:3).

Psalm 6 was written by David to the chief musician, to be sung with music. It is a prayer from David's heart when he was weak and needing to be "lifted". It is a request in the midst of some type of pain, grief or trial. Today, it shows us how we can pray, and that God is nearby to hear our cry. David's prayer put to music shows us how we can be transparent and honest with what's on our heart. Notice how it's okay to tell God how we feel. In fact, praying with sincerity will allow God to pour in His grace and change our perspective.

1. David Prays When He Is "Weak"!
"Be merciful to me, Lord, for I am faint; O Lord heal me, for my bones are in agony" (v.2).

The Hebrew word for "faint" in (v.2) means: to languish, wither, or droop as a flower. David is weak because his bones are vexed, which means that David is harassed in his thinking, consumed with anxious thoughts and pulled apart in his mind. What results when we worry and are anxious?
♦ David's strength and enthusiasm was sapped; he became exhausted.
♦ David became drained of all vitality, uptight and weak.

2. David Prays When He Is "Weary"!
"How long, O Lord, how long?" (v.3).
"I am worn out from groaning" (v.6).
"My eyes grow weak with sorrow" (v.7).

The words, "worn out from groaning" mean: David's grief was constant and his strength was failing. It means that David became disheartened from extreme disappointment and unfulfilled expectations. David's eyes growing weaker means that his ability to see was obscured and his vision was blurred. It other words, the enemy was distracting David from God's long-range plan for his life. David was being swallowed up by his immediate pressures. Have you been losing sight of the "bigger picture" in recent days? Have you lost the long-range view for your life? Is immediate weariness pushing you to lean upon Jesus more and more?

3. David Prays When He Is "Weeping"!
"I flood my bed with weeping" (v.6).
"The Lord has heard my weeping" (v.8).
"The Lord has heard my cry for mercy" (v.9).

Tears, tears, and more tears ran down David's cheeks. Yet in them all, David learned where to plant his tears – with God! David confesses something that God wants you to remember: "The Lord has heard my weeping" (v.8).

In other words, his prayers with tears didn't fall to the ground unattended. In fact, it was in prayer where David was given courage and stamina to press on.

What's the take-a-way?

Prayer gives God the tool He needs to lift us from where we are to where He intends for us to be!

Nuf Sed!

August 5
"When Sea Billows Roll"
Psalm 107

"He stilled the storm to a whisper; the waves of the sea were hushed" (Psalm 107:29).

Psalm 107 is the song of the redeemed. It was composed to record the marvelous acts of the Lord towards His people. It was used to celebrate God's goodness and sung at the dedication of the temple. The psalmist tells us about God's intervention because:

♦ We were lost travelers, but now we are found (v.1-9)
♦ We were chained prisoners, but now are free (v.10-16).
♦ We were suffering patients, but now are healed (v.17-22).
♦ We were sinking sailors, but now are safe (v.23-32).
♦ We were dry deserts, but now are watered well (v.33-38).

Our focus today is the fourth illustration God gives us. It's a revelation and message to your heart and mine. It's a clear picture of God's sovereignty; how God speaks and commands the wind and the waves. We discover that believers do travel through deep waters at times. Yet, we are reminded that God is sovereign and still in charge! Notice three things today:

1. The "Confusion" Of the Waves
"In their peril their courage melted away" (v.26). "They were at their wit's end" (v.27).

What can unexpected waves and tempests do to your heart? "Courage melted away" and "at their wit's end" means: To become disheartened, to be exhausted, to be confused, to feel that you've done all that you can do. I love how God doesn't cover up or ignore our feelings. He is telling you here that "you are normal" and "it's okay". Unfulfilled expectations deeply affect the heart!

2. The "Crying" Of the Waves
"Then they cried out to the Lord in their trouble" (v.28).

What's the answer when you don't know what to do in the storm? You do what experienced spiritual sailors do; you cry out to God in prayer and relinquish what is outside of your control! Why pray? Because prayer will bring God into focus, anchor you until the waves subside, lift you above your natural inclinations, and alleviate your panic and fear. True heartfelt prayer will align your heart with God's and leave you with a rest and trust beyond description. Real prayer, intimacy and communion will allow God to bring new meaning to your heart. You will learn that God is worthy to be trusted in every season of the soul.

3. The "Calming" Of the Waves

"He stilled the storm to a whisper; the waves of the sea were hushed" (v.29).

The enemy whispers to all of us when we are in the middle of the storm. He says, "you will never get through these great waters". But the scripture declares that God, "guided them to their desired haven" (v.30). In other words, our "Great Captain" will complete what He has started in you! He always has your end in view! He will finish and fulfill His perfect will in your life!

The take-a-way?
When sea billows roll, that's the very time to "stand still", "hold steady", "patiently wait", and trust your Heavenly Captain!

Nuf Sed!

August 6
"Joy Is Restored"
Psalm 51

"Cleanse me with hyssop, and I will be clean; wash me and I will be whiter than snow" (Psalm 51:7).

Psalm 51 is David's response to the conviction of sin. David had sinned with Bathsheba (II Samuel 11:4) and covered up his sin. God sent Nathan along to confront David about his cover up (II Samuel 12:7). David then prays and cries out to God for mercy, and his prayer speaks volumes to our hearts today. It's God's way to enjoy the journey and live with a transparent heart.

1. David Prays for A "Transparent" Heart!
"Blot out my transgressions" (v.1).
"Wash away all my iniquity and cleanse me" (v.2).
"Against you, you only, have I sinned" (v.4).
"Cleanse me with hyssop and I will be clean" (v.7).
"Blot out all my iniquity" (v.9).
"Create in me a pure heart, O God" (v.10).

David feels the guilt of his own sin and finally yields to the Spirit's convicting power. He agrees with God, that God desires, "truth in the inner parts" (v.6). So David prays and asks God for a clean, pure, and transparent heart. A "pure" heart is one "without mixture". It means that God is calling you and me today, to pray like David prayed: "Cleanse me with hyssop" (v.7). Hyssop was a bright green vine that grew in the Sinai Valley. It was a plant used by the Jews in their purification and sprinkling ceremonies. Hyssop alone could, by Levitical Law, cleanse from the defilement of leprosy (Leviticus 14:4), and contact with a corpse (Numbers 19:18). Hyssop was a shadow, or type, of the New Testament sprinkling of the blood of Jesus (Hebrews 9:19-26). So, David is praying because he knows that nothing but the blood of Jesus can purge his sinful heart! O friend; Christ's blood is the only way that our sin, debris, and defiled heart can be cleansed and made as white as snow (v.7).

2. David Prays for A "Steadfast" Heart!
"Renew a steadfast spirit within me" (v.10).

The word "renew" means: to increase my watchfulness Lord, so that I'll be strong and able to stand when tempted. It means to pray that our hearts will be resolute, single-minded, and undivided. It means to ask the Lord in prayer, that He will help us to be vigilant, constant and steadfast in guarding our hearts.

3. David Prays for A "Conscious" Heart!
"Do not cast me from your presence or take your Holy Spirit from me" (v.11).

Here we are taught to pray that God's Spirit will prick our conscience when necessary. We are taught to give God permission to convict us when we stray off course. We are instructed to ask God for a sensitive spirit that is yielding to His presence. Will you pray this with me today, that our hearts will yield to the initial promptings of the Holy Spirit?

The take-a-way?
The "joy" of our salvation (v.12) is increased, to the degree of our transparency before God!

Nuf Sed!

"Bird Language Overcome"
Psalm 102

"I am like a pelican of the wilderness; I am like an owl of the desert. I watch, and am as a sparrow alone upon the house top" (Psalm 102:6,7, KJV).

Psalm 102 is called, "A prayer of the afflicted". It is the diary of a man pouring out his lament before the Lord. He is lamenting over the Babylonian captivity, the ruins of Jerusalem, and the opposition to the restoration. He is so disheartened that two things occur:

♦ **The loss of appetite** (he can't even eat).
"My heart is blighted and withered like grass; I forget to eat my food" (v.4).

♦ **The loss of joy** (He is reduced to tears).
"For I eat ashes as my food and mingle my drink with tears (v.9). Notice what happens:

1. The Lot of His Heart (3 Fiery darts and lies).

♦ **"My days vanish like smoke"** (v.3), which means: My days are vanishing away as nothing and accomplishing no good thing. The enemy is insisting that his wilderness is a wasted season. But the truth is, God will use your weaknesses for His Glory, redeem what you feel is wasted, and use your pain to distribute His grace to other people.

♦ **"My heart is blighted and withered like grass"** (v.4), means: I'm in a drought and drooping like a parched flower. But the truth is, your faltering strength can be made strong once again!

♦ **"My days are like the evening shadow"** (v.11), means: I've lost sight of the bigger picture and cannot see what good can come from all of this. But the truth is, nothing God sends is wasted and nothing He withholds is needed. Your present season is preparing you for the next season!

2. The Language of His Heart (Bird Language).

Here's what happens when we feed on our feelings:

♦ "I am like a **pelican** of the wilderness" (v.6, KJV).
The pelican can sit alone for hours in solitude with its beak on its breast. It is a symbol of **loneliness**!

♦ "I am like an **owl** of the desert" (v.6), KJV.
The owl will sit and constantly twist its neck, nervously looking around. It is a symbol of **anxiety**!

♦ "I watch and am as a **sparrow** alone upon the house top" (v.7, KJV).
The word "watch" means "to stay awake". It's a picture of the sparrow afraid to sleep. It is a symbol of **sleeplessness**!

3. The Lord of His Heart (Lifts Us All Out of Despair).

After the lamenting in v.1-11, the psalmist is lifted out of despair when he remembers what God wants you to remember. Don't ever forget what lifted his heart: The Lord sits "enthroned forever" (v.12), has "compassion" (v.13), "will rebuild Zion" (v.16), "respond to the prayer of the destitute" (v.17), and "remain the same" (v.27). Wow! How can we not trust a God like this?

The take-a-way?
Whatever season you are in today, God wants to be the glory and the lifter of your head!

Nuf Sed!

August 8
"Strength From Above"
Psalm 138

"Though I walk through the midst of trouble, you preserve my life" (Psalm 138:7).

Psalm 138 is a turn-a-round Psalm! Why? Because in Psalm 137:
♦ David is weeping while in Babylon (v.1).
♦ David has hung his harp on the willow tree (v.2)
♦ David is being mocked by his persecutors (v.3).

    The problem is documented for us to see: The people of God were in exile in a strange land, they could not sing because of heavy hearts, they remembered the former days of joy in Zion, and they were in need of a lifting word from God! So, what is it that can take our hearts from weeping to singing? What is it that God can use to make us vibrant, hopeful, and strong in the journey?

1. Strong Believers Know How to Worship (v.1,2).
"I will praise you, O Lord, with all my heart" (v.1).
"I will bow down toward your holy temple and will praise your name" (v.2).
♦ Worship was **fervent in devotion**: "All my heart" (v.1) means to praise without reservation, regardless of my circumstance and based upon worthiness of the one who is worshiped.
♦ Worship was **fearless in disposition**: "Before the gods I will sing" (v.1), means that David refused to allow the false gods of neighboring nations to silence his praise.
♦ Worship was **free from pollution**: "Toward your holy temple" (v.2) means that I must approach the Lord with a pure heart and no pretending. It means that any hypocrisy will spoil my praise!

2. Strong Believers Know How to Pray (v.3-7).
"When I called you answered me; you made me bold and stouthearted" (v.3).
    David, when overwhelmed, made earnest prayer to the Lord. He cast his cares upon the Lord and God made him "bold and stouthearted" (v.3), or strengthened him from the inside out! This means that real prayer:
♦ Increases our intimacy, union, and imparts courage and strength.
♦ Renews us inwardly like nothing else can do.
♦ Changes our fainting hearts to face whatever lies ahead.
    In fact, God revives us in trouble (v.7), which means that you can experience renewal regardless of your less than perfect circumstances and environment!

3. Strong Believers Know How to Trust (v.8).
"The Lord will fulfill his purpose for me" (v.8), means that David can quit fretting about the captivity in Babylon, and quit worrying about his plans being

deferred. Why? Because God has promised to "fulfill His purpose" (v.8) or perfect His intentions. In other words, your interests are in safe keeping with God! God's will cannot be circumvented in your life! His plans for you will be completed! Your times are in His hand! You can trust Him to make all things beautiful in His time (Ecclesiastes 3:11).

The take-a-way?
Trusting God will protect you from birthing too soon what is not God's best for your life!

Nuf Sed!

August 9
"Cause For Rejoicing"
Psalm 126

"The Lord has done great things for us, and we are filled with joy" (Psalm 126:3).

Psalm 126 is titled, "A Song of Degrees". It is a fervent song of joy and gladness. Why are the Jews in Psalm 126 rejoicing? They are rejoicing with singing and gladness because of three things that God did for them. And, God has provided and promised the same three things for you today.

1. There Was (And Is) Deliverance from Captivity (v.1-3).
"When the Lord brought back the captives to Zion, we were like men who dreamed" (v.1).

The deliverance here was when the Lord delivered Jerusalem from the enemy Assyrian Army (II Kings 18, 19; II Chronicles 32: Isaiah 36, 37). Hezekiah (a godly king) refused to pay tribute to Assyria. Sennacherib then sent his army to subdue Jerusalem. Hezekiah went to prayer with Isaiah, and God slew 185,000 Assyrian soldiers in one night by an angel of the Lord. The psalmist said it was like a dream come true, because God's people were delivered and freed out of bondage. This is why there was singing (v.2), gladness (v.3), and joy (v.5). So, what has God delivered you from that brings joy and a grateful heart? What gives you reason to pause and rejoice for the freeing power of the gospel today?

2. There Was (And Is) Distribution of Living Water (v.4).
"Restore our fortunes, O Lord, like streams in the Negev" (v.4).

The psalmist leaves the city of Zion (Jerusalem), and takes us to the country. The word *Negev* means "dry", because it was the land south of Israel near the desert. During the summer seasons, the riverbeds would be empty and dry. When the rains came, the riverbeds would be filled to overflowing. This is why Israel prays, "Restore our fortunes, O Lord, like steams in the Negev" (v.4). And, like Israel needed water for the crops to grow, so you and I need to be filled, full and replenished with water from above. The good news is: God has promised to pour the water of the Spirit on all who are thirsty (Isaiah 44:3).

3. There Was (And Is) Doubtless Fruit That's Coming (v.5,6).
"Those who sow in tears will reap with songs of joy" (v.5).

The Assyrians had ravaged the land and caused destruction. So, what will the people eat in order to live? Should they turn their seed into food for today, or plant the seed for a harvest down the road? No wonder the sowers were weeping as they scattered their seed. Yet, God promises us in (v.6), that seeds we sow in faith will surely be returned at harvest. Friend, you will be more than compensated for every seed and every tear you planted on earth! The take-a-way?

"Weeping may remain for a night, but rejoicing comes in the morning" (Psalm 30:5). Nuf Sed!

"God's Keeping Power"
Psalm 116

"The Lord protects the simple hearted; when I was in great need, he saved me" (Psalm 116:6).

Psalm 116 is a great song of gratitude and praise. It was written when Israel was delivered from bondage, or when the psalmist was helped during a specific ordeal in his life. Notice the cause and effect:

♦ In (v.16), **he remembers!**

"I am your servant, the son of your maidservant; you have freed me from my chains."

♦ In (v.17), **he rejoices!**

"I will sacrifice a thank offering to you and call on the name of the Lord" The psalmist is ecstatic as he holds the cup and pours it out in the drink offering (v.13). He magnifies God because he was kept and preserved during a season of affliction. Notice how you and I have been preserved as well; notice our cause for rejoicing:

1. God Keeps Us in Times of Trouble!
"I was overcome by trouble and sorrow. Then I called on the name of the Lord, 'O Lord, save me'" (v.3,4).

What did the psalmist discover about God in his trouble? He learned that, "God is full of compassion" (v.5), and "protects the simple hearted" (v.6). The word simplehearted doesn't mean simpleton or stupid. It refers to the believer who has a simple trust in God. It means the Lord preserved and kept the psalmist even in his trouble. What should have swept him away, was met with sufficient grace to sustain him.

2. God Keeps Us in Time of Sorrow!
"For you, O Lord, have delivered my soul from death, my eyes from tears" (v.8).

Do we experience pain, grief, loss, sorrow, and tears on earth? Yes; no one is exempt! The good news is, there is a healing balm where the heart is healed and given supernatural grace in every season! Instead of the psalmist becoming a victim of his circumstances, his heart was kept from bitterness, anger, skepticism, pessimism and destruction. In other words, God's grace is equal to what causes our tears!

3. God Keeps Us in Times of Temptation!
"For you, O Lord, have delivered... my feet from stumbling" (v.8). "You have freed me from my chains" (v.16).

The psalmist testifies here of being preserved in the face of temptation. He is a witness that God can keep us from falling. He proclaims that God's grace is greater than sin and satan. He wants us to know that God has made it possible to crucify and mortify the deeds of the flesh! The good news is, backsliding is not the norm and God has made a way to be free from sin's dominion (in Jesus)!

The take-a-way?
"Be at rest once more, O my soul, for the Lord has been good to you" (v.7).

Nuf Sed!

"Love Lifted Me"
Psalm 30

"I will exalt you, O Lord, for you lifted me out of the depths and did not let my enemies gloat over me" (Psalm 30:1).

Psalm 30 is a great Psalm of praise expressing thanks to God. David writes this Psalm at the dedication of the altar on the threshing floor of Araunah the Jebusite (II Samuel 24:1-25). David had numbered the people (v.1-9), his heart smote him (v.10), he was chastised with a plague (v.11-17), and was instructed by God to build an altar (v.18). David obeyed God, the plague was stayed and it was at the dedication of the altar that Psalm 30 was sung.

David's journey in Psalm 30 is your journey and mine. It is a record of how the gospel alone can change our human hearts. It's a revelation of where we would be without the cross, the sacrifice, and the amazing grace of God! It's a story that will never grow old.

David was grief stricken when he saw Israel suffering from the plague. He was filled with remorse over his sin in numbering the people. He was consumed with grief over the consequences of his choices and sin. And what does David do? He tells us in (v.2): "O Lord my God, I called to you for help and you healed me". And what did God do? "O Lord, you brought me up from the grave; you spared me from going down into the pit" (v.3).

In other words, David was rescued (and lifted) from sin to salvation! And notice his response:

1. David's Restoration Is Documented!
Notice what God did for David in (v.1): David was rescued from the "depths" and his "enemies". He had been so distraught because God hid his face from David (v.7). In other words, David was out of communion with God and was missing intimacy with his Lord. Sin had caused David to weaken and wither. But when David repented, he was restored to the joy of his salvation. Friend, the Lord wants to restore you as well! He wants to give you **deeper intimacy, clear direction** and **fresh anointing** in prayer!

2. David's Rejoicing Is Documented!
"Weeping may remain for a night, but rejoicing comes in the morning" (v.5). "You turned my wailing into dancing; you removed my sackcloth and clothed me with joy" (v.11).
"That my heart may sing to you and not be silent. O Lord my God, I will give you thanks forever" (v.12).

Sackcloth was a coarse garment made of goat's hair. It was used to illustrate sorrow, grief, and affliction. In other words, God was angry over David's sin (for a moment) and David was troubled and weeping. But, when David repented in true humility, God replaced a heart of sackcloth with a heart of gladness, joy, and singing! How do we experience the same? It's found in (v.8): "I cried for mercy", and (v.10): "Be merciful to me".

The take-a-way?
Until I feel bad enough about my sin, I cannot be delivered from that sin!

Nuf Sed!

"Divine Memory"
Psalm 111

"He provides food for those who fear him; he remembers his covenant forever" (Psalm 111:5).

Psalm 111 was sung at Pentecost, the Passover and at the Feast of Tabernacles. It is a hymn of praise that magnifies God's faithful care. It was written to reveal the "behind the scenes" activity of God, written from a heart ablaze for God. It contains truth that makes it easy to celebrate, rejoice and be grateful to God. I think you'll agree why the psalmist just had to say, "I will extol the Lord with all my heart" (v.1). His motivation just might be yours as well. Notice:

1. God's Road Map for Your Life Is Perfect (v.1-8).
"Great are the works of the Lord" (v.2).
"The Lord is gracious and compassionate" (v.4).
"Glorious and majestic are his deeds" (v.3).
"The works of his hands are faithful and just" (v.7).

Why did the psalmist pen this truth – that the works of God are perfect, glorious, and just? Probably because all of us have questioned God at some time, or asked "why this" or "why that". And, the enemy of our souls wants us to get angry at God and believe that God has let us down, made a mistake or forgotten us. The accuser of the brethren whispers to you when trouble comes. He insinuates lies like, "you must have sin in your life, you must not have enough faith, you must be out of the will of God". Yet the psalmist destroys the lies with truth when he declares:

♦ **God is Gracious** (v.4), which means that God is full of favor toward you because of Jesus' finished work at Calvary.
♦ **God is Compassionate** (v.4), which means that He is full of feeling and care towards imperfect human beings (you and me).
♦ **God is Faithful** (v.5), which means He provides food for those who honor Him (just as He did for 40 years in the wilderness).
♦ **God is Mindful** (v.5,9), which means, "He remembers His covenant forever" (v.5) and, "He ordained his covenant forever" (v.9).

When God made a covenant with His people, He promised to arrange His providence for the welfare of those who would follow Him. And, God has promised this to you: **"I will not violate my covenant or alter what my lips have uttered"** (Psalm 89:34). And, **"For He who promised is faithful"** (Hebrews 10:23).

2. God's Power Is Mighty on Your Behalf (v.6).
"He has shown his people the power of his works, giving them the lands of other nations" (v.6).

This power refers to God when he enabled Israel to overcome every nation, and bring the land into total possession. Today it means, that God (through Jesus) has overcome and broken satan's power to dominate you with sin, carnality and every controlling habit! It means that the Jesus in you is greater than every temptation against you!

The take-a-way?
"I will never break my covenant with you" (Judges 2:1).

Nuf Sed!

"Prayer in A Cave"
Psalm 142

"I cry to you, O Lord; I say, 'You are my refuge, my portion in the land of the living'" (Psalm 142:5).

Psalm 142 was written by David when he was alone in a cave. Why the cave? Because David was hiding from Saul who wanted to kill him. There were two times we find David in a cave:

♦ At Engedi – when he snuck up on Saul and cut off part of his robe (I Samuel 24:3).
♦ At Adullam – when he was anxious and feeling abandoned (I Samuel 22). At Engedi, David's mighty men were with him. At Adullam, David is alone (and he writes Psalm 142). Grasp the context of this prayer:

David flees to Samuel at Ramah. He flees to Nob for food. He flees to Achish for protection. But now he is 16 miles southwest of Jerusalem in a cave. Under the mountains of Judah, in a valley between Philistia and Hebron, David prays this prayer while hiding in a limestone cave. And, here's what we learn in the cave of Adullam:

1. In the Cave, God Hears Your Praying!
"I cry aloud… I lift up my voice… I pour out my complaint… before Him I tell my trouble" (v.1,2).

What's the discovery here? That caves make great closets of prayer, and caves cannot separate you from the love of God. I also learn, that it's okay to get down emotionally but it's not okay to stay down! David cried out to God, got God into focus, poured out his complaints and presented his case to God. He felt all alone (v.4), had no earthly support (v.4), and was unsure of his next step (v.3). But David also discovered:

2. In the Cave, God Knows Your Whereabouts!
"When my spirit grows faint within me, it is **you who know my way**" (v.3).

The light comes on when David prays. What does he discover? He discovers that just because he cannot see – doesn't mean that God is blind! "**Know my way**" (v.3) means that God is aware of every step you take, is not surprised by your journey, and is still in ultimate control of your delays, detours and disappointments. Oh friend, your steps and seasons are ordered of the Lord!

3. In the Cave, God Restores Your Soul!
"Set me free from my prison, that I may praise your name" (v.7).

Saul was a monarch; David was a fugitive. Saul had an army; David was alone. Saul was strong; David was weak. And, in desperation David prayed, "**Rescue me… for they are too strong for me**" (v.6). The good news is that

David opens the psalm with crying and despair – but ends with singing and rejoicing. Why? Because God restored David's inner man with hope, confidence and joy! So much so that he came out of the cave without bitterness or resentment. Yes, God restored David and God will restore you as well.

The take-a-way?
Life might sometimes put you in a cave, but life cannot keep God's presence out of the cave. He is as close as the mention of His Name!
Nuf Sed!

"From Guilt to Gladness"
Psalm 130

"If you, O Lord, kept a record of sins, O Lord who could stand? But with you there is forgiveness; therefore you are feared" (v.3,4).

Psalm 130 is listed as a song of degrees, a rapid progression from despair to delight. It is a psalm of answered prayer in extreme distress. It is the sixth of the seven penitential psalms.

This psalm reveals the terror of the writer and why he feels such deep distress. He reveals that self-help cannot bring the answer that his heart longs for. His trouble is not like many of the other psalms (laments); this one is different. His pain is not from an illness, or an enemy, or a fear, or homesickness, or an unfulfilled expectation. His pain is from guilt! The good news is, God reveals how you and I can live free from guilt and a condemning conscience. I love what God teaches us in this psalm. Notice the guilt to gladness story:

1. The Expression of Guilt Is Comforting!
"Out of the depths I cry to you, O Lord; O Lord, hear my voice! Let your ears be attentive to my cry for mercy" (v.1,2).

The psalmist turns to the Lord in prayer. Why? Because he feels "the depths" (v.1) of his sin. He understands that he is a sinner and it's too deep to climb out of on his own. The good news is, he understands that you are never so deep that you are separated from the love of God. That's why he prays and reaches out to God for mercy. What a comfort to know that there is no sin that God cannot forgive you of.

2. The Reason for Guilt Is Universal!
"If you, O Lord, kept a record of sins, O Lord, who could stand?" (v.3)

This is a picture of the greatest trial in all of eternity. We are all seen standing in a courthouse before the Judge. We've been made aware of our own sins. We are without a defense (or any excuse) for crimes committed against God. So much so, that if God tells the truth about us, none could stand in His presence (v.3). And, what will the Judge do when He sees our failures and sin? How will the Judge respond when we cry out for mercy in light of our sin and guilt? Notice:

3. The Remedy for Guilt Is Grace!
"But with you there is forgiveness" (v.4).

What is forgiveness? It is the cancellation of a debt as if it never existed! How can we be forgiven? By asking God to forgive us by His grace – purchased on the cross by Christ Jesus. Will God forgive us of every sin? Absolutely, without question! Not because we are good, but because He is good! But remember, Calvary only covers what we uncover! And, the good news is, if God forgives at all — He must forgive of all!

The take-a-way?
"The Lord has laid on Him the iniquity of us all" (Isaiah 53:6), which means: your good is not good enough to make God love you; and your bad is not bad enough to make God reject you!

Nuf Sed!

"Taming Your Emotions"
Psalm 42 & 43

"My soul is downcast within me; therefore, I will remember you" (v.6).

Psalm 42 was written to the chief musician, Maskil, for the sons of Korah. Korah's sons were in charge of arranging the music for the sanctuary. They were a family of Levitical singers. It was from these sons that David selected a number to preside over the sanctuary music. Psalms 42 and 43 were written for one reason – to point us to the Lord. They were written to show us the God who gave the Psalms. They reveal that God knows what's in your heart and God knows how to move you forward. These two psalms teach us how to stop feeding on our feelings, and how to find new meaning when our questions go unanswered. Notice David's journey:

1. David's Feelings Are Exposed!
"My tears have been my food day and night" (42:3).
 "Why are you downcast, O my soul?" (v.5).
"Why have you forgotten me?" (v.9)
"Why so disturbed within me?" (v.11).
"Why must I go about mourning?" (43:2).

Why are David's raw feelings exposed for all to see? Because David's son Absalom was in rebellion, David was driven from his throne and normal place of worship, he was in exile beyond the Jordan River, and he needs to remind himself of some things while he processes his feelings. He needs a word from the Lord for the cloud of heaviness over his heart. He needs to practice better "self-talk" and move from his feelings to truth, from himself to the Lord.

2. David's Future Comes Alive!
While David struggles with his memories of past joy: "I used to go with the multitude, leading the procession to the house of God, with shouts of joy" (42:4), he finds hope in God for his future!
♦ **God puts hope in his heart!**
"Put your hope in God, for I will yet praise him" (v.5). Hope is a word that means to trust and believe that your future is secure with God.
♦ **God gives him a song in the night!**
"At night his song is with me" (v.8). This means that happiness is not a place but a state of mind. It means that God's presence is with you in every season of the soul.
♦ **God is the strength of his heart!**
"You are God, my stronghold" (43:2). Never forget this; that when you are weak (and leaning on God), you are really strong.
♦ **God will direct his path!**
"Send forth your light and your truth, let them guide me" (43:3). The Lord will lead you as well.

♦ God will finish what he started!
"Then will I go to the altar of God, to God, my joy and my delight. I will praise you" (43:4).

The take-a-way?
Where you are is just a season, it is not your final destination, and it will give way to a new season if you patiently wait on the Lord!

Nuf Sed!

"The Servant Leader's Reward"
Part I

"When the chief Shepherd appears, you will receive the crown of glory that will never fade away" (I Peter 5:4).

First Peter was written by the apostle Peter around 64 A.D. He wrote to the believers who were in Jerusalem on the day of Pentecost now living in Pontus, Galatia, Cappadocia, Asia, and Bithynia (now modern Turkey). He wrote to these believers to encourage them in their suffering, affliction, and disappointments. And, in the midst of Peter's epistles, the Lord speaks to those who lead and serve. Why? Because servant leaders have a sobering responsibility:

"No one knows about that day or hour, not even the angels in heaven, nor the Son, but only the Father. Be on guard! Be alert! You do not know when that time will come. It's like a man going away: He leaves his house and puts his servants in charge, each with his assigned task, and tells the one at the door to keep watch" (Mark 13:32-34).

In Mark's parable, Jesus identifies Himself as the "man going away" (v.34). The "house" (v.34) is His church. You and I are the "servants in charge" (v.34) with our "assigned tasks" (v.43) to lead, feed, and protect the flock of God! In other words, it's the Holy Spirit that empowers the church to do His will. On the other hand, what happens in the Lord's church is largely left up to us (as servant leaders). Bad leadership with a lack of vision, passion, and mission means that the house falls into disrepair. Good leadership means that the house moves forward and gains new ground continually. The lesson is, we dare not just settle down and decorate the house! Our task is to be intentional and forward-moving, so that when Jesus returns, He will be delighted in the condition He finds His house in. So, what does Peter tell us that a healthy servant leader looks like in I Peter 5:1-4? These characteristics (to remember) relate to all of our hearts:

1. You Remember God's Grace!
"I appeal as a fellow elder, a witness of Christ's sufferings" (v.1).
Peter says that he remembers Christ's sufferings, or he is reminded of his part in those sufferings. Peter remembers how he followed Jesus into the courtyard of the High Priest's house, and in the time of weakness denied that he even knew the Lord (Matthew 26:69-75). Peter is now recalling how he messed up and grieved the Lord. Why does Peter recall this with those he writes to? To remind you and me of God's grace in his own life. To remind us how Christ forgave him and changed him. To remind us that Jesus uses imperfect people to get the job done. To show us that it's okay to admit it when we are wrong. To tell us that humility will attract God's favor. To let you know today, that God doesn't use you because you are great, or smart, or cool, or perfect. He uses you because He is great, and wise, and powerful, and full of grace!

The take-a-way?
That God would use us as imperfect people, should continually soften our hearts and make us grateful beyond human words.

Nuf Sed!

"The Servant Leader's Reward"
Part II

"Be shepherds of God's flock that is under your care" (I Peter 5:2).

Yesterday we looked at the first characteristic that Peter reminded us of to never forget as we serve people. What is it? It is to remember how gracious God has been to us as imperfect people! Peter was humbled when he remembered how God used him, even after he had denied the Lord. Today, we'll uncover the four other reminders that help form a healthy heart in all who serve:

2. You Think Like a Shepherd!
"Be shepherds of God's flock" (v.2).

Peter reminds us that we exist for the flock. Whose flock is it? It's the flock of God. What do we do? We feed the flock. The word "feed" is the Greek word *Poimante*. It doesn't mean to just preach or teach. It means to tend and care for people. It means to guide, protect, feed, restore and go after those who stray. It means to sacrifice your own self for the sake of those you serve. This means that we don't use people for our goals, instead we resource them for their potential. In other words, it's all about the sheep and not about us! We don't have to do this, we are privileged to do this!

3. You Serve with Privilege!
"Not because you must, but because you are willing, as God wants you to be" (v.2).
♦ "Not because you must" means not out of pressure and obligation.
♦ "Willing" means an emotional desire that's eager to serve.
♦ "Not greedy for money" means not for personal profit.
In other words, it is an honor and privilege that God has called us to His eternal work! God honors us by allowing us to participate in something eternal.

4. You Lead by Example!
"Not lording it over those entrusted to you, but being examples to the flock" (v.3).

Peter reminds us that healthy servants are not arrogant, intimidating or dictatorial. Instead, they lead by example and model the gospel. "Not lording it over" means humility defers credit to others, leaves my ego at the door and needs no attention to be joyful or motivated. It means that you live to make "His" Name famous and not your own!

5. You Maintain Long-Term Perspective!
"You will receive the crown of glory that will never fade away" (v.4).

This is God (through Peter) telling us that healthy servants are not temporal driven! In other words, our reward is when the Lord returns. This keeps us sowing with joy and optimism because we know that pay day is coming!

The take-a-way?
If you ever feel cheated in serving God, you have served Him for the wrong reason!

Nuf Sed!

August 18
"Renewed In Affliction"
Part I

"Therefore we do not lose heart. Though outwardly we are wasting away, yet inwardly we are being renewed day by day" (II Corinthians 4:16).

The Apostle Paul wrote II Corinthians to: 1. Encourage the church to forgive a member who caused some trouble, 2. Give to the needs of the saints in Judea, 3. Explain the authority he had from the Lord, and 4. Help the believers not to lose heart or faint in difficult times. In chapter 4, the Lord inspires Paul to instruct all of us in how to be positive when we're going through the negative. In (v.8-18), God gives us three revelations that defeat a fainting spirit

1. Expect some afflictions along Life's Journey!
Was Paul tempted to faint, become sour and angry as he faced afflictions in the will of God? Notice:
♦ **"We are hard pressed on every side, but not crushed"** (v.8). The word "pressed" means to be troubled, squeezed, opposed or pressured.
♦ **"Perplexed, but not in despair"** (v.8). The word "perplexed" means to be at loss, to doubt, to question, or to wonder which way to go.
♦ **"Persecuted, but not abandoned"** (v.9). The word "persecuted" means ridiculed, threatened, slandered or abused.
♦ **"Struck down, but not destroyed"** (v.9). The words "struck down" mean to be smitten or knocked down.
And, in the midst of Paul's afflictions, he discovered what God wants you to discover. What is it? That God's grace more than matched his afflictions: He was not crushed, not despairing, not abandoned, not destroyed! In fact, Paul didn't faint or crash in affliction because of these three discoveries:
  1. In (v.10), the more we die to ourselves and to self-justification, the more the life of Jesus lives through us.
  2. In (v.11), the more we are willing to die to what we want, the more that our afflictions affect us in a positive way.
  3. In (v.12), the more we serve the Lord and embrace the cross, the freer we become from the carnal, fleshly, and sinful man.
In other words, what satan wants to use to discourage you, God will use to reveal Himself to you! And, isn't that your goal in life, to know Him better and make Him known? The key here is to humble ourselves before God and get more grace to grow. Otherwise, pride will cause us to become offended at our cross and cause us to faint and quit. The take-a-way here?
The only way that our afflictions can work for us, is if we humble ourselves before God, and be protected from a spirit of entitlement!
Nuf Sed!

August 19
"Renewed In Affliction"
Part II

"Therefore we do not lose heart. Though outwardly we are wasting away, yet inwardly we are being renewed day by day" (II Corinthians 4:16).

Yesterday we saw how God's grace enabled Paul to turn a negative into a positive. We learned how the cross actually works for us and not against us – revealing Jesus to the world:

♦ "We always carry around in our body the death of Jesus, so that **the life of Jesus** may also be revealed in our body" (v.10).

♦ "For we who are alive are always being given over to death for Jesus' sake so **that His life may be revealed** in our mortal body" (v.11).

♦ "So then, death is at work in us, **but life is at work in you**" (v.12).

Paul not only taught us to expect some afflictions in this journey called life; he also taught us to:

2. Evaluate afflictions in light of their fruitfulness!
"All this is for your benefit" (v.15).

How did Paul overcome satan's temptation to live angry, sour, bitter, entitled and play the victim card? Paul knew this one thing and kept it always before him: He understood that everything he went through, God was going to use to benefit someone else! In other words, sufferings are not wasted. Why not? Because God promises to use them to minister life through you to someone else. What's the discovery? Why do you go through what you go through? How can God use it for good? Two ways:

♦ God has you in mind – to draw you to Himself and sanctify your inner man!

♦ God has someone else in mind – that you will help one day in the future!

And what makes all of this possible?

3. Endure affliction by receiving God's grace!
"The grace that is reaching more and more people" (v.15).
"We are being renewed day by day" (v.16).

This grace is the impartation of life from God! It is God's grace and strength that renews our inner man day after day. Even though our physical man is weakening, we faint not because God adds strength as we look to Him continually. In fact, God gives us so much grace that we live with a long-term perspective in every affliction; we remind ourselves:

♦ Every affliction is temporary and not eternal (v.17).

♦ Every affliction can work for you instead of against you (v.17).

♦ Every affliction is light compared to eternity (v.17).

♦ Every affliction pales in light of the world to come (v.18).

The take-a-way?

In every affliction, connecting your life to the world to come will lighten your load, comfort your sorrow and give meaning to your difficult days.

Nuf Sed!

August 20
"The Anchor Holds"
Part I

"We have this hope as an anchor for the soul, firm and secure" (Hebrews 6:19).

Hebrews was written to Jewish believers who were being tested and tried. Some were thinking about leaving grace to go back under the Law, while others were tempted to spiritually drift and slip backwards. Many needed a fresh word to remind them Who their Anchor was! Does God want us to be lifted, strengthened and encouraged by this word? It's undeniable:

"God did this so that, by two unchangeable things in which it is impossible for God to lie, we who have fled to take hold of the hope offered to us **may be greatly encouraged**" (v.18).

In other words, God gives us three absolute truths (guarantees) that will build, edify, and make strong your heart and mine. And, it's truth that frees us from ourselves to enjoy the journey with God. Don't forget these three things:

1. We are "greatly encouraged" because of God's Word to Abraham.
"God made his promise to Abraham… saying, 'I will surely bless you and give you many descendants'. And so, after waiting patiently, Abraham received what was promised" (v.13-15).

What was God's promise to Abraham? It was "descendants as numerous as the stars in the sky" (Genesis 22:17). God had promised Abraham a son. God then kept His promise and Isaac was born. So how does this encourage your heart today? Abraham was 75 years old when God promised him a son. But Abraham didn't see the answer of a son until he was 99 years old. In other words, Abraham had to patiently wait for 24 years to obtain his promise! He had to endure many obstacles, his circumstances were less than ideal, he made mistakes along the way, and saw no visible signs for 24 years. But he had a promise from God!

Maybe you are "waiting" for answered prayer like Abraham. Maybe you feel "on hold" like Joseph was. Maybe you feel "fenced in" like Job did. Maybe you're a little "anxious" like Elijah was. Maybe the enemy is hurling fiery darts your way and insinuating that God won't keep His Word to you. But God does have a word for you today; it's a word to **"mightily encourage"** your heart. What is it?

"If I promised and came through for Abraham, then be encouraged, because I'll come through for you." In other words, your answer is not based upon what you see, how you feel, where you are, how difficult it seems or how long it's been. Your answer is based upon who God is and what He has said to you.

The take-a-way?

Just as God could not lie to Abraham, God cannot lie to you!

Nuf Sed!

"The Anchor Holds"
Part II

"We have this hope as an anchor for the soul, firm and secure" (Hebrews 6:19).

Yesterday we learned the first reason to be **"greatly encouraged"** in God. It was because of God's Word to Abraham. In other words, even though Abraham had to wait 24 years for God's promise to be fulfilled, God was faithful as He had promised! Today, the other two reasons to be strong in faith:

2. We are "greatly encouraged" because of God's Word to Himself!
"Men swear by someone greater than themselves, and the oath confirms what is said and puts an end to all argument. Because God wanted to make the unchanging nature of his purpose very clear to the heirs of what was promised, he confirmed it with an oath" (v.16,17).

When a witness takes an oath in court, he is asked to repeat the words, "so help me God". He is calling upon the great one (God) to witness for the lesser one (himself). There is none greater than God, so God says, He is answering (or making an oath) to Himself. In other words, God pledged Himself to Abraham, God heard the oath He made, and guess what? "It is impossible for God to lie" (v.18).

Why is this so important? It's important today because of (v.17); "The heirs of what was promised". Who are the heirs of promise? They are you and me: "Those who have faith are blessed along with Abraham" (Galatians 3:9). This means that we are Abraham's spiritual seed as people of faith in Christ. And, God could not lie to Abraham or He would be lying to Himself. Neither can God lie to you as well.

3. We are "greatly encouraged" because of God's Word to us! What is God's Word to us today?
♦ We have a **refuge:**
"We who have fled to take hold of the hope" (v.18). This refers to the Old Testament cities of refuge. God appointed six cities where a man could flee if he accidently killed someone. Nothing and no one could harm the person as long as he remained in the refuge. Today, Jesus is our refuge (v.20), our high priest, and nothing can touch us without His approval.
♦ We have an **anchor:**
"We have this hope as an anchor for the soul, firm and secure" (v.19).
The hope we have in Jesus is the anchor of our souls. In other words, hope does for the soul what our anchor does for a ship! An anchor preserves the ship when the waves pound against it! An anchor brings security in the midst of agitation. An anchor enables the ship to endure so it can stay on course. Who is our Anchor? It is the One who has entered "behind the curtain" (v.19)

in heaven. And Jesus is "firm and secure" (v.19), which means: sure and steadfast, who cannot slip and cannot break!

The take-a-way?
If you need forgiveness today, you can run to the Refuge (Jesus). If you need calm for a troubled heart, you can hold on to the Anchor (Jesus) and He will sustain you!

Nuf Sed!

"The Sacred Invitation"
Part I

"I slept but my heart was awake. Listen! My lover is knocking: 'Open to me, my sister, my darling, my dove, my flawless one'" (Song of Solomon 5:2).

The Song of Solomon was written by Solomon in the tenth century B.C. It is both poetical and practical. It describes both the love of King Solomon for a peasant girl and the love of Christ for His church. It reveals the sacredness of married love, but most of all, it's the picture of communion between Christ and every believer. The purpose of the book is to deepen the union between Jesus and His people. The intention is to unite our hearts with Jesus more than ever before. God's drawing power is all over the eight chapters:

♦ "Take me away with you" (1:8)
♦ "Arise my darling... and come with me" (2:10).
♦ "I will search for the one my heart loves" (3:2).
♦ "Let my lover come into his garden" (4:16).
♦ "Open to me, my sister" (5:2).
♦ "Come back, come back, O Shulamite" (6:13).
♦ "Many waters cannot quench love" (8:7).

I pray that you feel God's drawing power in your own heart today. I pray that all of us will draw closer and respond to "the Sacred Invitation".

1. The desire of the Bridegroom

"I slept but my heart was awake. Listen! My lover is knocking: 'Open to me, my sister, my darling, my dove, my flawless one'" (5:12).

Why was the bride awakened? Because Jesus cried out, "Open to me, my sister" (v.2). This is a picture of the desire of Jesus (the Bridegroom) towards you and me (His Bride). It is Jesus desiring to be admitted, welcomed and received. In chapter 4:16, the Lord was invited to come close. In chapter 5:1, He came close as requested but in chapter 5:2, the believer has fallen asleep and locked the door, What's the meaning of the bride falling asleep in (v.2)? It's two-fold:

♦ It's possible to close the door to Jesus by slipping into an inattentive state.
♦ Jesus is resolved to come close, even to those who are unaware and undeserving.

How do we know that Jesus wants to reveal Himself to us? Because of what it cost Him:

"My head is drenched with dew, my hair with the dampness of the night" (5:2).

This refers to the heart of Jesus, busy in the night seasons, even while the bride is in bed asleep. It's a picture of Jesus searching in the dark to find the one who has wandered away. It's the Lord taking painstaking effort to restore anyone who is in need of being forgiven or brought close once again.

The take-a-way?
When busy becomes too busy, that's the time to stop, recalibrate, and draw close to the Only One who can satisfy and transform your heart.
Nuf Sed!

"The Sacred Invitation"
Part II

"Open to me my sister" (Song of Solomon 5:2).

Yesterday, we saw the desire of the Bridegroom to be close to His bride. We learned that it's possible for us to slip into a spiritually careless state. We saw just how much that Jesus wants to be close to us. Today, the story continues and speaks clearly to a choice we all can make.

2. The disappointment of the Bridegroom (v.3).
"I have taken off my robe, must I put it on again? I have washed my feet; must I soil them again?" (v.3).

Solomon's bride (the church) makes excuses. She heard the knock and the voice, saw his hand on the door, but didn't yield to the call of her bridegroom. Why was the Lord so disappointed? Because the bride didn't quickly respond to the King's call! She forgot what Christ did for her, she wasn't willing to deny herself and get up, she became careless in the journey and she thought for a moment that she could make it without Jesus. Does Jesus ever quit on us?

"My lover thrust his hand through the latch-opening; my heart began to pound for him" (v.4).

This refers to the custom of the day. When a man was in love with a woman, he would go to her home and leave, not a card, but a fragrance. When there was no response at the door, the man placed myrrh on the inside handle of the door. When she came to the door the fragrance was transmitted to her fingers (v.5). In other words, she knew he had been there, but she grieved him by her hesitation to open the door. What a lesson this is to us! We don't just want the myrrh; we want the myrrh giver – Jesus Himself!

3. The delight of the bridegroom (v.8).
"If you find my lover… tell him I am faint with love" (v.8).

In (v.6), the bride finally opened the door but her beloved had withdrawn Himself. Fellowship had been broken because of personal neglect. The result? She was smitten, wounded and in pain. But wait; notice what she did and how she responded? "If you find my lover… tell him I am faint with love" (v.8). In other words, tell Him how much I miss Him and long for His presence! Tell Him I can't be satisfied without intimate communion! Tell Him I'm sorry for my foolish delay!

And, how did the Lord (her Bridegroom) respond? She discovered that God is the God of a second chance! She returned with all of her heart and found the God of forgiveness. She testifies to you and me today that "sacred invitations" are given to respond to! She reminds us that your Heavenly Bridegroom is calling your name to come close to Him today!

The take-a-way?

There's no time like the present to respond to the drawing power of the Holy Spirit – to draw close to Jesus!

Nuf Sed!

"Power in the Cross"

"When you were dead in your sins and in the uncircumcision of your sinful nature, God made you alive with Christ" (Colossians 2:13).

Paul writes to the church in Colosse, a church founded by one of his converts named Epaphras. Paul writes from prison to warn the church about a heresy that threatened the doctrinal purity of the believers. The heresy was called Gnosticism (a combination of oriental mysticism and Jewish legalism). Gnostics believed that someone could reach "spiritual perfection" out of a close union with God. They believed that angelic beings ruled heavenly bodies (a form of astrology). They believed that the rite of circumcision would increase spiritual development (legalism). They promoted asceticism, which is isolating yourself from the world and good provisions. They claimed to lift Christianity to a higher level through legalism, philosophy, astrology, mysticism and asceticism. And, Paul confronts the false teaching head on. How? He makes it clear that we are complete in Jesus (2:10, 14-17), and that Jesus has settled the sin question once and for all.

"And through him to reconcile to himself all things, whether things on earth or things in heaven, by making peace through his blood, shed on the cross" (1:20).

And, what the cross means to you and me today is revealing, freeing, and life changing:

1. Cancellation!
"Having cancelled the written code, with its regulations that was against us and that stood opposed to us; He took it away, nailing it to the cross" (2:14). This means that the Law that pronounced us guilty (because none of us could meet all of its demands) has been cancelled. How? Jesus Himself cancelled the debt against us when He Himself was nailed to the cross. Jesus alone has satisfied God's just demand for a sin payment, and in doing so has washed away the debt we could not pay. We are now forgiven, justified in Christ, and every voice of accusation has been silenced.

2. Demonstration!
"And having disarmed the powers and authorities" (2:15). The word "disarmed" means spoiled, subdued and conquered. It means that every evil spirit and power that once enslaved us has been broken. It means that every satanic and destructive influence in your life has no legal authority to control you any longer. It means that you are free (in Christ) to demonstrate a Christian life that glorifies God!

3. Celebration!
"He made a public spectacle of them, triumphing over them by the cross"

(2:15). The word "triumph" refers to a Roman General in Paul's day. When a general won a great victory, he was honored by an official parade and would show off his prisoners captured in battle. It was a celebration of the victory won. And, this is what Jesus did for you! He defeated satan and his power to rule you any longer! And, it all took place at the cross of Jesus!

The take-a-way?
The cross represents the demonstration of God's power, allowing you to live free from sin's control, and respond with joy unspeakable and full of glorious praise!

Nuf Sed!

"Your Heart Can Be Rekindled"
Part I

"So the Lord stirred up the spirit of Zerubbabel… and the spirit of the whole remnant of the people" (Haggai 1:14).

The text above is a great declaration and word of encouragement. Why did Haggai give it? Because the Lord saw the hearts of the workers and knew they needed "lifting" in their spirits.

♦ (v.6) "You have planted much, but have harvested little".

♦ (v.9) "You expected much, but see, it turned out to be little".

Here's the context in a nut shell: Seventy years of Babylonian captivity are over for God's people. The people return home to Jerusalem to rebuild the city and restore the temple. The workers encounter rejections, opposition, and frustration. It was the perfect storm to be distracted and discouraged. And, God raised up Haggai and Zechariah to prophesy and speak a lifting word to every worker. Why was this timely word so important? Because the rebuilding of Jerusalem and the Temple meant two things: 1. The restoring of pure worship back in Jerusalem, and 2. The witness to the unbelieving nations who were observing nearby.

And, that's why God has put you where you are! First, to make His name famous in the church and get all the glory, and secondly, to make His name famous to the world who is watching and needing a gospel witness. So, how does God take us from Ezra 4 which says, "The work on the house of God in Jerusalem came to a standstill" (v.24). To Ezra 6:14, 16, which says, "They finished building the temple according to the command of the God of Israel, and… celebrated the dedication of the house of God with joy."

I have one word for your heart, before we see the stoppage and completion of the work. What is it? It is the word **process**! That's right, **process**! You and I are always in **process**. Remember:

In 605 B.C, the first Jewish exiles were deported to Babylon.

In 597 B.C, the second deportation to Babylon took place.

In 586 B.C, Nebuchadnezzar destroyed Jerusalem and the third deportation to Babylon occurred.

In 539 B.C, Cyrus (King of Persia) conquers Babylon and issues a decree in 538 B.C.

In 537 B.C, 50,000 Jews return home to Jerusalem.

In 536 B.C, the temple foundation is laid.

In 536 B.C, the progress is interrupted because of opposition (a 16-year delay).

In 520 B.C, the work resumes again under the ministry of Haggai and Zechariah.

In 515 B.C, the temple restoration is completed.

In 458 B.C, Ezra arrivers in Jerusalem.

In 444 B.C, Nehemiah arrives, rebuilds the walls, and a great Bible conference soon follows.

Why all the details just listed? To show you that you can't rush time, don't need to live in a hurry, and God has perfect timing for your life and future! To remind you that you can rest well today, be patient, and trust God with what's outside of your control!

The take-a-way?

When you get bogged down with all of the details, detours, and delays in life, just remember that God is still sovereign over your "process".

Nuf Sed!

"Your Heart Can Be Rekindled"
Part II

"Then the peoples around them set out to discourage the people of Judah and make them afraid to go on building" (Ezra 4:4).

Y ou really didn't think that your life and mission was going to be a bed of roses, did you? Surely you weren't planning to just waltz upon earth and slide into heaven with ease, were you?

Yesterday, we learned that God's plan involves a **"process"** in your life. We saw how God raised up Haggai and Zechariah to rekindle the spirit of the workers in Jerusalem. Today, notice the three challenges that God's people had to overcome to make progress. You will face these three as well as you move forward in your journey, so get ready:

1. There was temptation to compromise (Ezra 4:1-3).
"When the enemies of Judah and Benjamin heard that the exiles were building a temple for the Lord, the God of Israel, they said, 'Let us help you build'" (v.2).

The invitation was very pleasurable; "Let us help you build" (v.2). The response to the offer was quick and direct; "You have no part with us in building a temple to our God. We alone will build it for the Lord" (v.3). The first attack of the enemy was very subtle. The Samaritans (the former Northern Kingdom) offered to work with the Jews. These Samaritans were a mixture of many races and didn't worship the one true God. Their sole purpose in offering help was to co-mingle, corrupt, and defeat God's people by having them inter-marry with the heathen. In other words, the enemy's plan was an inside job to tempt the people inwardly and weaken them gradually. Has the enemy of your heart been trying to pollute your conscience and sow toxic ideas to compromise your convictions?

2. There was intimidation to fear (v.4-6).
"Then the people around them set out to discourage the people of Judah and make them afraid" (v.4).
"They hired counselors to work against them" (v.5).
"They lodged an accusation against the people" (v.6).

The enemy strategy was to demotivate God's people by criticism, slander, accusation, manipulation, intimidation, and fear. They did all they could to frustrate the workers who were building for God! Are you facing critics or doubters that want to distract you today?

3. There was legislation to suppress the vision (v.21).
"Issue an order to these men to stop work, so that this city will not be rebuilt" (v.21).

Shimshai sent a letter to the king, and the king ordered the building project to be stopped. And for 16 years, (536 B.C to 520 B.C.) the work of God was put "on hold". A 16 year delay forced the people of God to be still, wait and pray. Has the enemy tried to steal your dream and vision because of a delay of some kind? You're normal, and tomorrow you will see the word from the Lord in moving forward.

The take-a-way?
When the enemy comes in like a flood, it must mean that God has great victories planned for you!

Nuf Sed!

"Your Heart Can Be Rekindled"
Part III

"'Be strong, all you people of the land', declares the Lord, 'and work. For I am with you,' declares the Lord Almighty'" (Haggai 2:4).

The past two days we've discovered two things: 1. Life is contextual and involves a process beyond our own visibility, and 2. You will always have challenges to overcome as you move forward in God's will. Today; the final piece of the puzzle as the Jews completed the work.

When the going got tough in the rebuilding process, the workers needed an encouraging word. How do we know this? It's obvious:
"Who of you is left who saw this house in its former glory? How does it look to you now? Does it not seem to you **like nothing**?" (Haggai 2:3)

In other words, the temple was in ruins, recovery was slow, people were remembering the way it used to be, times were hard, and the leaders were discouraged. Some were thinking, "Is it really worth it? Can we rebuild and see a turnaround? Will the Lord fulfill His promise to us?" And, just at the perfect time, the Lord had something to say:

"On the twenty-first day of the seventh month, the Word of the Lord came through the prophet Haggai" (2:1).

What was God's message? It was a promise from God that brought dramatic change. It was a message that prompted the completion of the rebuilding project. It was a message for then, and it's a message for now to your heart today! Receive this relevant promise from the Lord:

1. God promises you **Himself!**
"'I am with you,' declares the Lord... 'my Spirit remains among you. Do not fear'" (2:4,5). Haggai didn't deny that times were hard or that the people were delayed for 16 years. He simply let the people know that the Lord was with them (as He is with you today).
2. God promises to **answer prayer!**
"I will fill this house with glory" (v.7). God was saying that He would keep His word, fulfill His promise, and answer prayer. His desire was that every servant leader and worker be filled with faith and optimism.
3. God promises to **provide for his work!**
"'The silver is mine and the gold is mine,' declares the Lord Almighty'" (v.8). The economy was bad and the resources were low. Yet God caused the Persian Empire to pay the expenses for rearing the massive walls. In other words, God provided from unseen sources.
4. God promises to **deliver from the powers of darkness!**
"I will overturn royal thrones and shatter the power of the foreign kingdoms. I will overthrow chariots" (v.22). God promises here to free His people from

the things that defile, pollute, and contaminate His nature in them!

The take-a-way?
If you are on God's side and God is on your side, it doesn't matter who's on the other side!

Nuf Sed!

"The Scapegoat Blessing"
Part I

"On this day, atonement will be made for you, to cleanse you. Then, before the Lord, you will be clean from all your sins" (Leviticus 16:30).

Leviticus 16 is all about one thing: the day that sin died to accuse you any longer. And, the whole book of Leviticus is a manual of worship. It's a book that shows us how to live so that our worship will be acceptable to God. Leviticus impresses three basic principles upon the heart:

♦ There can be no fellowship with God except on the basis of atonement for sin.
♦ Man is unable to atone (or cover) his own sin.
♦ The covering of sin must be according to a divine plan with a mediator.

The word "holy" is used 91 times in Leviticus. Words connected with "cleansing" and "uncleanness" are found 199 times. Why is there such an emphasis on holy and unholy? Because what health is to your physical man, holiness is to your spiritual man. In other words, many people are in pursuit of happiness (not holiness). And the wrong pursuit produces an unhealthy person. Here's the dilemma: If I want Jesus to fix all of my problems and give me what I want, but I don't want Jesus to change me inwardly, then I miss the whole purpose of God's grace, sins forgiven, and my own existence. So, grasp the setting of our text:

Chapter 16 is the high point in the book of Leviticus. It describes the most important day of the year for an Old Testament Jew. It was Israel's most high and holy day: **"The Great Day of Atonement"** (Yom Kippur). It was the day when God atoned for (or covered) all the sins of all the people and gave the nation a brand-new beginning. This day of atonement took place on the tenth day of the seventh month. On the first day of the seventh month, the trumpets were blown to announce the beginning of a new year (Rosh Hashanah) (Leviticus 23:23-25). The tenth day was the Day of Atonement (Leviticus 23:26-32). And the fifteenth day began the Feast of Tabernacles (or booths) and lasted for one week (Leviticus 23:33-44). What's the big deal about Leviticus 16? The trumpets blowing could announce the New Year, but only the shedding of blood could forgive sin and give the people a brand new beginning! And, **thank God**, we serve a God of new beginnings!

Your "new beginning" is revealed in Leviticus 16. It's in this chapter where forgiveness is offered, grace is revealed, and sin is covered. It's in this chapter where God shows us how He forgave all of Israel's uncleanness, iniquities, transgressions, guilt, sin, and past errors.

The good news is, Leviticus 16 reveals how God rescues us. How? By showing us how Jesus does for us now what the Old Testament Priests did for Israel then. Since God is holy and cannot overlook sin, and since man is sinful and cannot approach God in his sin, we have a dilemma.

The good news is, Jesus became our Savior, and the "Scapegoat" of Leviticus 16 shows us how. Get ready to learn how the slain goat and the live goat are a beautiful picture of Jesus.

The take-a-way?
The scapegoat blessing reveals that we cannot save ourselves – but we can fully trust in what Jesus has fully done!

Nuf Sed!

August 29
"The Scapegoat Blessing"
Part II

"The goat will carry on itself all their sins to a solitary place; and the man shall release it in the desert" (Leviticus 16:22).

Yesterday, we looked at the principle of the Scapegoat Blessing. Today, discover the Person of the Scapegoat Blessing and what it means to your life this very moment. In fact, notice the setting and context of the Scapegoat: "The Lord spoke to Moses after the death of the two sons of Aaron, who died when they approached the Lord" (v.1).

The Great Day of Atonement was established on the heels of the death of Nadab and Abihu. These two men had offered strange (profane) fire before the Lord. The word profane means, "To show disrespect for sacred things". It means that Nadab and Abihu were careless, loose, and unqualified to approach a Holy God. And, God answers our dilemma in two ways:

1. The "Purpose" of the Scapegoat!
"Atonement is to be made once a year for all the sins of the Israelites" (v.3,4).

The purpose of the Scapegoat was atonement. The word "atonement" means to cover or remove by paying a price. It means that Divine favor is secured through the price (blood) of another. It was only blood that could cleanse the high priest, his family, the tabernacle, and the people of Israel (16:16,17). And, this blood was to be sprinkled on the mercy seat (the golden lid on the Ark of the Covenant) to allow sinful man to have access to a Holy God.

2. The "Person" of the Scapegoat!
"Aaron shall bring the goat whose lot falls to the Lord and sacrifice it for a sin offering" (v.9).

Two goats were chosen for one sin offering. The priest cast lots over the goats and one was chosen to die. One goat was slain and its blood sprinkled on the mercy seat. The other live goat was called "the scapegoat" (v.8). Aaron placed his bloody hands on the head of the live goat, confessed the sins of Israel, and then sent the goat to disappear in the wilderness (v.20-22). Aaron's hands laid upon the live scapegoat signaled it as the sin carrier of Israel! And, oh what good news this is! The scapegoat was a picture, type or shadow of Jesus to you and me! The releasing of the live goat symbolized the sins of the people being carried away, never to be held against them again. This is the Calvary of the Old Testament:
♦ The slain goat symbolized **payment** for sin by blood!
♦ The live (scapegoat) symbolized **removal** of sin forever.

The scapegoat lead away in the desert (wilderness) was sent beyond the camp to carry all the sin, be completely out of view, and never to return again. And it's all a picture of our Wonderful Jesus! Our New Testament scapegoat

has promised:
"Their sins and lawless acts I will remember no more" (Hebrews 10:17).

The take-a-way?
Our Scapegoat Blessing (Jesus) means that you can be free from the guilt of sin – not by trying harder, but by trusting fully in Jesus!

Nuf Sed!

August 30
"Overcoming The Silent Killer of Envy"
Part I

"But if you harbor bitter envy and selfish ambition in your hearts, do not boast about it" (James 3:14).

If godliness with contentment is great gain, then ungodliness without contentment is great loss. In fact, if our joy is our strength, then we must live free from envy because envy will steal our strength. So, what is envy anyway? Envy is the displeasure we feel when we hear about the advantage of another. It is a resentful awareness when someone else has something that we want. Envy is the pain you feel over someone else's success! The danger of envy is:

♦ It cannot be grateful and content for what it already has!
♦ It cannot rest in who it is in Christ Jesus!
♦ It cannot celebrate the victories of others!

Unfortunately, envy is destructive and not new at all:

1. Lucifer envied God and wanted His glory.
2. Cain envied Abel because Abel's sacrifice was acceptable to God.
3. Rachel envied her sister when Leah bore children.
4. Sarah envied Hagar when Ishmael was born.
5. Miriam envied Zipporah because of the position she enjoyed as Moses' wife.
6. Hannah envied Peninnah because she had children.
7. Peninnah envied Hannah because she was Elkanah's favorite wife.
8. Korah envied Aaron because he had authority to be the High Priest.
9. Lot's herdsmen envied Abram's herdsmen.
10. Ishmael envied his brother Isaac.
11. Isaac's son Esau envied his brother Jacob.
12. The sons of Jacob envied their brother Joseph.
13. Saul envied David and perceived David as a competitor.
14. Absalom envied David because he had the affection of the people.
15. Adonijah envied David because God chose his brother (Solomon) for the throne.

What is the root cause of envy? It's unmistakable:

1. Envy is **"Bitter"** (v.14).
♦ James reveals that envy is empowered by an embittered heart.

2. Envy is **"Self-Seeking"** (v.14).
♦ The words "selfish ambition" mean that envy is fueled by a self-seeking heart that always produces friction and strife.

3. Envy is **"Boastful"** (v.14).

♦ The word "Boastful" means that envy is rooted in pride, wants others to think we are special, and has to advertise its own importance.

The take-a-way?

When you see outward continued strife and contention among relationships with people, that is a sign of an inward flawed relationship with God.

Nuf Sed!

"Overcoming The Silent Killer Of Envy"
Part II

"For where you have envy and selfish ambition, there you find disorder and every evil practice. But the wisdom that comes from heaven is… " (James 3:16,17).

Yesterday, we learned that envy is the pain you feel when someone else has something that you want. We also learned that envy is fueled (or caused) by three things:

♦ Envy is **bitter**, or empowered by an embittered and resentful heart.
♦ Envy is **self-seeking**, or fueled by a self-seeking heart that results in strife and friction.
♦ Envy is **boastful**, or rooted in pride that wants to advertise its own importance.

Today, we'll see the cure of envy, how to live to advance others instead of ourselves, and what kind of wisdom produces a healthy heart that is envy free. It's found in seven words that James says is, "the wisdom that comes from heaven" (James 3:17). This wisdom that defeats envy is:

1. **"Pure"**
The word "pure" means: free from defilement, without mixture, and integrity of heart. It is the quality of heart that provides the foundation for all others.
2. **"Peace-loving"**
This means: to bind or weave together. It means that a healthy person reconciles people, doesn't defile with evil reports and never sows discord.
3. **"Gentle"**
The word "gentle" means: courteous, considerate and patient. It is the opposite of critical, censorship, and harshness. It speaks of a person who interacts with respect, not out of anger.
4. **"Submissive"**
This word means: teachable, willing to listen, and someone who welcomes input and advice. It is the opposite of stubborn and rigid. It is open to suggestions and is easy to be entreated.
5. **"Merciful"**
This word means: to offer compassion with the feelings of affection and kindness. This is a person who understands how merciful God has been to them.
6. **"Impartial"**
The words "without partiality" mean: to show no favoritism or prejudice. It means to offer help to others without being influenced by their dress, position, title, or rank.
7. **"Sincere"**
This word means: To be transparent, without hypocrisy, and free from

playacting or wearing a mask." This wisdom from above never tries to fake people out!

This wisdom is what protects us from envy, insincerity, and hype.

The take-a-way?
Envy that produces strife and tension never needs to be, because the Jesus that lives in you, will never fight with the Jesus that lives in me!

Nuf Sed!

September 1
"The Ahava Awakening"
Part I
"The gracious hand of our God is on everyone who looks to Him" (Ezra 8:22).

As a pastor, I always loved September. Most vacations were over, people returned from summer camps, kids were back in school and church life seems to "pick up" a step. Each September we would begin a new mid-week series and Sundays carried an emphasis on renewal, revival, and spiritual awakening! For that reason, the next few devotionals will be the messages we saw the Lord use in drawing people to Himself. Since the Word of God is timeless, we pray that the Holy Spirit uses His truth to gain new ground in your heart and mine. We begin in Ahava:

Ezra 8 has a remarkable setting and message for us. Ezra, a priest, comes along at a critical time in history. In 606 B.C., the Babylonians conquered Jerusalem and deported many Jews. They destroyed the city, then the temple in 587 B.C. In 538 B.C., King Cyrus of Persia granted permission for the Jews to return to their land. Nearly 50,000 Jews returned under the leadership of Zerubbabel (Ezra 1-6) to rebuild their temple. There was opposition and the project was stopped in Ezra 4 (an interruption for a brief season). In Ezra 5 and 6, the rebuilding resumed under the preaching of Haggai and Zechariah (prophets of encouragement). In Ezra 7 and 8, Ezra will go to Jerusalem in 458 B.C with about 2,000 Jews to serve in the temple ministry. He will lead this second group of exiles back to Jerusalem. But there's just one problem. In Ezra 8:15, Ezra gathers the people on the banks of the Ahava River. He wonders, thinks, and contemplates how he will make the long journey from Babylon to Jerusalem. How will he get the wives, children, and sacred vessels back to the temple? How will he ever see the return, the revision, and the restoration of God's glory? And, the river actively speaks three things loud and clear to us today:

1. The Ahava River Reveals "Coldness and Neglect"!
"When I checked among the people and the priests, I found no Levites there" (Ezra 8:15).

After gathering at the river and resting for three days, Ezra discovers a deficiency; there were no Levites except those who were priests. In other words, the very ones who should have been the most eager to return to Jerusalem were missing. Why? Because they found a more comfortable way of life in Babylon while "on hold" in captivity. Many of the Jews had become wealthy in captivity. Archaeologists have discovered that the Jews (formerly a nation of farmers) had become a nation of shopkeepers and business people while in Babylon. These Levites would trade the comfort and riches in Babylon for the rebuilding process back in the Promised Land. Why such a failure?

    1.   The Jews had received permission to return home to the priesthood,

altar, temple, and manifest presence of God, but were found among the missing!

2.   These same Levites who refused to make the pilgrim journey sent treasures instead. In other words, "You can have my money, God, but not my heart".

The sadness is, the Levites missed their opportunity to be a part of a spiritual awakening. Coldness of heart and avoidance of sacrifice kept them behind in Babylon.

The take-a-way?
God has so much more for all of us, yet it's possible to be deceived into remaining snug where we are!

Nuf Sed!

"The Ahava Awakening"
Part II

"So we fasted and petitioned our God about this, and he answered our prayer" (Ezra 8:23).

Yesterday, we discovered the spiritual neglect of the Levites who stayed in Babylon when they had permission to travel back to Jerusalem. Today, we'll see a remarkable answer to prayer, revealing again how prayer aligns us with what God is wanting to do! Notice the intervention of God in prayer:

2. The Ahava River Reveals "Faith and Prayer"!

"I was ashamed to ask the king for soldiers and horsemen to protect us from enemies on the road" (v.22).

Why was Ezra ashamed to ask the king for an escort of soldiers through enemy territory? Because he had gone out on a limb and said that God would take care of his own children. Ezra told the king what God wants you to hear today as well in (v.22):

♦ God is interested in what touches your life!
♦ God is gracious in his dealing with you!
♦ God is faithful to those who look to him!

So what did Ezra do that speaks to you and me?

"There, by the Ahava Canal, I proclaimed a fast so that we might humble ourselves before our God and ask him for a safe journey" (v.21).

"So we fasted and petitioned our God about this, and he answered our prayer" (v.23).

Ezra was about to return to Jerusalem and embark on a dangerous trip. He was ashamed to rely on the earthly king. Yet, he believed in the power of fasting and prayer to deliver him from enemy traps. Ezra flat out teaches us how to pray:

♦ We pray and fast with **humility**!

"We might humble ourselves before our God" (v.21). This means to acknowledge our total dependence upon God in prayer.

♦ We pray and fast with **confidence**!

"And ask him for a safe journey" (v.21)

Ezra prayed for a prosperous journey, one of protection from the schemes of the enemy. He was confident that God would hear and answer his petition.

♦ We pray and fast with **earnestness**!

"So we fasted and petitioned our God about this, and he answered our prayer" (v.23). Ezra was earnest in doing battle God's way! He won the battle in private before he went out in public. He teaches us, that if we prostrate ourselves before the Lord we won't be prostrated before the enemy.

The take-a-way?

Ezra teaches us that prayer is cooperating with God to see God's will done on earth!   Nuf Sed!

September 3
"The Ahava Awakening"
Part III

"On the twelfth day of the first month we set out from the Ahava Canal to go to Jerusalem. The hand of our God was on us, and he protected us from enemies and bandits along the way" (Ezra 8:31).

Thus far, we've seen two major pieces to this Ahava activity. We've documented the neglect and the prayers of God's people. Today, notice God's favor and forgiveness He offers you and me.

3. The Ahava River Reveals God's "Favor and Forgiveness".

"So we arrived in Jerusalem, where we rested three days" (v.32).

Here we discover that confidence in God is vindicated. Why did the Jews make it safely home? Because God's favor was upon them! Why was God's favor upon them? Because God is gracious and responds when we align our hearts with Him. What's the lesson today? Our battles are not fought and won with fleshly means; they are won in the secret place of devotion, intercession and faith in God's ability to intervene. Remember friend, it's not the level of your faith, it's the object of your faith – Jesus! And if you're feeling that you don't deserve answers to prayer, take heart and remember this:

"Then the exiles who had returned from captivity, sacrificed burnt offerings to the God of Israel: twelve bulls for all Israel, ninety-six rams, seventy-seven male lambs, and as a sin offering, twelve male goats. All this was a burnt offering to the Lord" (v.35).

Why did the Jews worship this way? Because in the sacrifices, Israel was confessing and acknowledging their sin before God. They were acknowledging that only a blood covering could atone (cover) their sin. They were agreeing with God, that the only way to find forgiveness was through the sacrifice of another. And, every animal sacrifice was a type or a foreshadow of the Lamb of God to come. It means that Jesus has become your sin offering and forgiveness flows from His heart today. So if you entertain the thought of, "I don't deserve for God to hear me in prayer", then join the rest of us in obtaining God's favor and forgiveness:

♦ No one can earn God's favor and pardon!
♦ No one can stand in prayer on their own merits!
♦ No one can trust in their own works and goodness!
♦ No one can depend on their own behavior to have an audience with God!

Our only hope to obtain God's favor and forgiveness is to look away from ourselves and trust in the good news of the gospel! Only Jesus and His sacrifice can give us access and entrance to our wonderful God!

The take-a-way?

Ahava's message to you is this: trust in the sacrifice of Jesus, and you will stop trusting in your own performance – which can never be good enough to obtain the favor of God!   Nuf Sed!

"The Awakening Under Hezekiah"
Part I

"So, the service of the temple of the Lord was reestablished. Hezekiah and all the people rejoiced at what God had brought about for his people, because it was done so quickly" (II Chronicles 29:35,36).

Second Chronicles records five Great Awakenings for us to learn from:
♦ Under King Asa, chapter 15.
♦ Under King Jehoshaphat, chapter 17.
♦ Under King Joash, chapter 23.
♦ Under King Hezekiah, chapters 29-32.
♦ Under King Josiah, chapter 34 and 35.

The setting of our text today is convicting as well as faith producing. It shows us how God can prepare our hearts for spiritual renewal. Second Chronicles is addressed to the Jewish people who returned from the 70 years of captivity. Ezra records the revival 430 years before Christ. It's a detailed account of Judah's spiritual journey, how negligence and apostasy turned into a spiritual reformation. It shows us what God can do when we are hungry and open to the Holy Spirit. Notice the process and progress that God gives us:

1. The "Signal" of Revival (v.1-11).
"They also shut the doors of the portico and put out the lamps. They did not burn incense or present any burnt offerings at the sanctuary to the God of Israel" (v.7).

Look at the signals that God was about to do something:
♦ **The doors were closed** (v.7) means: There was no access to God in the Temple and there was no service by the people for God. Tons of potential was simply put "on hold".
♦ **The lamps were out (**v.7) means: There was no oil burning, so you could not see the showbread on the table (which speaks of Jesus).
♦ **The altar was cold** (v.7) means: the incense that was symbolic of prayer rising to God was vacant and absent.
♦ **The sacrifice was missing** (v.7) means: The burnt offering which was the consuming of the entire animal sacrifice had ended. This sacrifice symbolizes the entire consecration of the people unto the Lord. It was a picture of total surrender. How does all of this relate to you and me?
1. Like closed doors, maybe you feel like you're disconnected from God and access to Him has been lost.
2. Like lamps out, maybe the oil and flame in your heart needs to be rekindled.
3. Like the cold altar, maybe your life of prayer (incense) rising from your heart has been neglected.
4. Like the sacrifice, maybe you're holding back and afraid to totally surrender to the Lord.

The take-a-way?
Like God wanted to reestablish spiritual life for Hezekiah, so God wants to reestablish the passion and fire in YOUR heart once again!

Nuf Sed!

September 5
"The Awakening Under Hezekiah"
Part II
"When they had assembled their brothers and consecrated themselves, they went in to purify the temple of the Lord, as the King had ordered, following the Word of the Lord" (II Chronicles 29:15).

Yesterday, we discovered the situation that Hezekiah found himself in. It was a context that desperately needed a spiritual awakening. The temple doors were closed, the lamps were out, the altar was cold, and the sacrifice was missing. God was simply waiting for His people to get serious, draw close to Him, and prepare their hearts for restoration and reformation. I love how God records the people's response to Hezekiah's preaching. Notice:

2. The "Sifting" of Revival (v.12-19)
What was the command of Hezekiah? It was as clear as the noon-day sun: "Listen to me Levites! Consecrate yourselves now and consecrate the temple of the Lord, the God of your fathers. Remove all defilement from the sanctuary" (v.5). Hezekiah responded with deep conviction and a call for repentance. He didn't look for a shallow response or verbal promises. All that he wanted was to see the people's hearts prepared for the manifest presence of God to return. And how did the people respond?

"When they had assembled their brothers and consecrated themselves, they went in to purify the temple of the Lord, as the King had ordered, following the Word of the Lord" (v.15).
What happened next in (v.16)? I love this:
♦ The priests went into the **inner part** of the sanctuary.
♦ The priests went out to **carry out** all of the rubbish.
In other words, there had to be a holy place for God to dwell in and be comfortable. And, I must let God go into the inner parts of my heart as well. I must then take action and get rid of everything that pollutes and defiles His presence in me. Is it worth the effort? The rubbish was dumped in the Kidron Valley, never to come back in again. It was forgiven by God because:

"We have purified the entire temple of the Lord" (v.18).
What happens when we cleanse ourselves from everything questionable? A victorious celebration takes place. It's...

3. The "Song" of Revival (v.20-36)
"Singing to the Lord began also" (v.27). "The whole assembly bowed in worship, while the singers sang and the trumpets played" (v.28). "They sang praises with gladness" (v.30). Why was there so much joy? Because:
♦ The **sin offering** was celebrating the receiving of total forgiveness from God.
♦ The **burnt offering** was celebrating the people being totally consumed by God.

♦ The **thank offering** was the people's response to God because deep repentance brings holy joy.
"All the people rejoiced at what God had brought about for His people" (v.36).

The take-a-way?
When your sins are forgiven by the blood of Jesus, your heart will be filled with gladness beyond measure!

Nuf Sed!

September 6
"Awakening Prayer"
Part I

"For though we walk in the flesh, we do not war after the flesh: For the weapons of our warfare are not carnal, but mighty through God to the pulling down of strong holds" (II Corinthians 10:3,4, KJV).

In 1974, I prayed a sinner's prayer while reading a gospel tract on an airplane. How could God get through to me when my parents never took me to church once and never told me how to be born again? My Pentecostal grandmother was praying for me in Leesburg, Virginia. Plain and simple, I had a spiritual awakening because someone stood in the gap and did battle in the unseen world!

Paul the apostle explains how the "weapon of prayer" is effective in praying for the awakening of lost people. And, why is this text (and subject) so important? Three reasons:

1. There is the "Warfare" of Prayer!
"For though we walk in the flesh, we do not war after the flesh" (v.3, KJV).

This means that we are not in conflict with natural forces (people). We are in a conflict against spiritual forces. Remember; satan was once the chief angel, the anointed cherub, and the star of the morning – all until he rebelled against his Creator and tried to usurp God's power and glory (Isaiah 14:12-17, Ezekiel 28:1-10, Revelation 12:7-9). This evil one is identified as the ruler of demons, ruler of this world, prince of power of the air, dragon, roaring lion, vile one, tempter, accuser of the brethren, and the spirit working in the sons of disobedience. He is called "satan", which means adversary, 52 times in scripture. He is called "the devil", which means slanderer, 35 times. This fallen archangel and his fallen angels (called demons) are the enemy. We see this enemy clearly in scripture:
♦ Opposing God's work (Zechariah 3:1)
♦ Perverting God's word (Matthew 4:6).
♦ Hindering God's servant (I Thess. 2:18).
♦ Snaring the wicked (I Timothy 3:7).
♦ Appearing as an angel of light (II Cor. 11:14).
♦ Fighting with the archangel Michael (Jude 9).
♦ Hindering the Gospel (II Cor. 4:4).

The enemy in this warfare is exposed in Scripture:
"For we wrestle not against flesh and blood, but against principalities, against powers, against the rulers of the darkness of this world, against spiritual wickedness in high places" (Ephesians 6:12, KJV).

1. Principalities (Archas) means: "rulers" or a high order of demons.
2. Powers (Exousias) means: "authorities" of another rank.
3. Rulers of darkness (Kosmokratoras) means: rulers in the dark world, possibly demons who have infiltrated various political systems of the world.

4. Spiritual wickedness in high places (Pneumatika) means: highly organized and structured armies of demons which promote the most vile and wretched immoralities.

What's the take-a-way from exposing the real enemy?
We are wasting our time battling against people; the real enemy who controls and uses people to oppose God's work is in the unseen world!

Nuf Sed!

September 7
"Awakening Prayer"
Part II

"For the weapons of our warfare are not carnal, but mighty through God to the pulling down of strong holds" (II Corinthians 10:4, KJV).

Yesterday, we looked at the "warfare" of prayer. We learned that our real enemy is in the unseen world! The next step Paul the Apostle gives us, is to show us what our spiritual praying is really up against. Thank God that:

2. The "Weapon" of Prayer Is Good News to All!
Paul used the words, "strong holds", or *Ochuroma* in (v.4) which means three things:
♦ To have or to hold
♦ A fort, castle, or prison
♦ The place from which to hold something strongly
Strong holds are not demons or evil spirits, they are simply the places from which they work from. Paul lists three **"strong holds"** that the enemy uses to enslave the unsaved person:

♦ **Imaginations** (*Logismos*), which means: The sum total of information learned over time. This is accumulated wisdom, reasoning, logic, and the beliefs of someone. This means that the mind that hears the gospel must filter the gospel through years of processed information. The mind that hears your witness, hears the gospel plus whatever else they've learned up to that point.

♦ **Pride** (*Hupsoma*) means: "Every high thing" (v.5, KJV) which refers to any elevated place or thing. It is the boastful desire to be your own boss in life. And, only prayer can pull down this strong hold so that the unsaved will humble themselves and cry out to God for mercy.

♦ **Temptations** (*Noema*) means: those thought patterns and temptations that satan uses to lead people further into sin and darkness. It's in prayer that we ask God to shield our loved ones from satan's schemes, plans, and devices to devour them. And, what are the weapons we use in prayer to win the war?
1. The Name of Jesus – which gives you the **authority** to announce His presence and all the He stands for!
2. The Blood of the cross – which gives us **access** to the throne of God in prayer. The cross represents the death of Jesus, which broke satan's power to rule your life.
3. The Word of God – which is our source of faith and promised **assurance** of ultimate victory!

The take-a-way?
It is in prayer where we use our weapons to enforce what Jesus has already purchased!

Nuf Sed!

September 8
"Awakening Prayer"
Part III

"Casting down imaginations and every high thing that exalteth itself against the knowledge of God, and bringing into captivity every thought to the obedience of Christ" (II Corinthians 10:5, KJV).

In the past two devotionals, we've looked at the "warfare" and "weapons" of prayer. Today, we'll see...

3. The "Winning" of Prayer!

Is prayer really that effective against the powers of darkness that hold unsaved people captive? Notice Paul's declaration:
"For the weapons of our warfare are not carnal, but mighty through God to the pulling down of strong holds" (v.4, KJV).

The word for "mighty" is *Dunatos*, which means: Divinely powerful, miracle, and possible now. The words "pull down" and "cast down" mean: to demolish and to destroy. In other words, in prayer we can demolish, destroy, and pull down the fortress and strong holds that ensnare our loved ones. This clearly means, that you have power with God in fervent prayer! You have the weapon that wins in secret! You have the privilege of capturing rebels for God!

In fact, it's **only in prayer** that:
1. We **enforce** what Jesus has already purchased.
2. We **represent** Jesus and what He completed.
3. We **drive back** the forces of evil.
4. We **disappoint satan's efforts** against God.
5. We **obtain God's objective** by releasing His Spirit to go to work.
   Putting God's Word into practice in prayer:
1. Pray that God will **"pull down"** or demolish the stronghold of pride over your loved ones.
2. Pray that God will **"pull down"** the thought patterns formed in their minds that are against God.
3. Pray that God will **protect** your loved ones from evil thoughts and temptations.
4. Pray that God will **hover over** them by His Spirit to protect them until they humble themselves before God.
5. Pray that God will **send godly people** into the pathway of your unsaved loved ones to sow the seed of life.

And never, ever forget the fact that satan exists against you as a believer, to encourage you to quit and give up in the place of prayer. I pray that we never give up until the answer comes!

The take-a-way?
The greatest way that we can cooperate with God in His mission to save people, is to align ourselves in believing prayer! Nuf Sed!

"The Jerusalem Outpouring"
Part I

"All of them were filled with the Holy Spirit and began to speak in other tongues as the Spirit enabled them" (Acts 2:4).

In Acts 2, I see five significant events taking place:
♦ There is the outpouring of the Holy Spirit.
♦ There is the birth of the Lord's Church.
♦ There is the great sermon by Peter.
♦ There is the Lord adding people to the church.
♦ There is the unity, fellowship, praying, and sacrifice of believers.
    But how did the Lord prepare the 120 to be baptized in the Holy Spirit in Jerusalem?

1. There Was "Expectation"! "For John baptized with water, but in a few days you will be baptized with the Holy Spirit" (1:5). Jesus wanted people to hear about the Holy Spirit so that we could expect to experience the Holy Spirit.

2. There Was "Obedience"! "Do not leave Jerusalem, but wait for the gift my Father promised" (v.4). "Then they returned to Jerusalem... they went upstairs to the room" (v.12,13). The people did exactly what Jesus said.

3. There Was "Unity"! "They all joined together" (v.14). Everyone was of the same mind and heart to receive the baptism in the Holy Spirit!

4. There Was "Praying"! "They all joined together constantly in prayer" (v.14). The word for "prayer" means: "to continue, to persist, and to pray until" all were baptized in the Holy Spirit. All of this preparation leads us to Acts 2, which says, "When the day of Pentecost came, they were all together in one place" (2:1).
    The Day of Pentecost was the feast day held 50 days after the Feast of First Fruits (Leviticus 23:15-22). Every Jewish male was to visit the temple on the three major feast days: 1. The Feast of Passover, 2. The Feast of Pentecost, and 3. The Feast of Tabernacles. All three Jewish feasts outline the work of Jesus.
♦ Passover pictures His death as the Lamb of God (I Corinthians 5:7).
♦ The Feast of Firstfruits pictures His resurrection from the dead (I Corinthians 15:20-23).
♦ The Feast of Pentecost pictures the gathering and formation of the church. Pentecost was a great day of celebration, a one day festival of joy. It commemorated the end of the harvest, and the priest would wave two loaves of bread before the Lord. Why? To acknowledge the goodness of God for His bountiful supply. It was on this Feast Day of Pentecost that God poured out

His Spirit as He said He would. It was on this day that God kept His word and ushered in the Holy Spirit to give you power and strength to be a witness!

The take-a-way?
Pentecost, or the Baptism in the Holy Spirit, is to be expected as part of God's outpouring to reach this generation with the gospel!

Nuf Sed!

"The Jerusalem Outpouring"
Part II

"All of them were filled with the Holy Spirit and began to speak in other tongues as the Spirit enabled them" (Acts 2:4).

Yesterday, we discovered how Jesus prepared the 120 to be baptized in the Holy Spirit. There was expectation, obedience, unity, and prayerfulness. We also learned that Jesus kept His promise and poured out His Spirit upon hungry, praying believers who took Him at His word. Today, discover how Pentecost is a powerful and personal experience.

Remember, Pentecost was even prophesied by:
♦ Solomon (Proverbs 1:23)
♦ Joel (Joel 2:28)
♦ Ezekiel (Ezekiel 36:26)
♦ Isaiah (Isaiah 44:33).

And also by John the Baptist: "I baptize you with water for repentance. But after me will come one who is more powerful than I, whose sandals I am not fit to carry. He will **baptize you with the Holy Spirit and with fire**" (Matthew 3:11).

1. Pentecost Is A "Powerful" Experience!
"You will receive power when the Holy Spirit comes on you" (Acts 1:8). "Stay in the city until you have been clothed with power from on high" (Luke 24:49).

So, what makes the baptism in the Holy Spirit a powerful experience in your life? Acts 2 spells it out for us:
♦ There was a **Sound** from heaven (Acts 2:2). This was the sound of a strong wind – to get the attention of all who were gathered in prayer. This sound was from heaven, it was supernatural, and gave evidence that the power was from heaven, not from natural means.
♦ There was an **Appearance** from heaven (v.3). Believers saw many tongues (looking like fire) resting upon each believer. God illuminated the tongues to symbolize the presence of the Holy Spirit. Why? To show us that God was anointing believers to share the gospel with their own tongue and be an effective witness.

2. Pentecost Is A "Personal" Experience!
"All of them were filled with the Holy Spirit and began to speak in other tongues as the Spirit enabled them" (v.4).

The **sound** from heaven was to get the attention of everyone present. The **fire** from heaven was to anoint our tongue as we witness. The tongues, or **new language** from heaven, is to help us pray apart from our weaknesses and limitations in prayer.

The disciples were aware that they were speaking, but equally aware that the Holy Spirit was the Holy fire in their speech. The disciples would now no longer dwell on their own inadequacies, but instead be filled with assurance and boldness.

The take-a-way from the Jerusalem outpouring?
The Baptism in the Spirit will quicken your mind (John 14:26), your body (Romans 8:11), your Spirit (I Corinthians 14:4), your praying (Romans 8:26), and your worship (I Corinthians 14:15).

Nuf Sed!

"The Samaria Outpouring"
Part I

"When they arrived, they prayed for them that they might receive the Holy Spirit" (Acts 8:15).

Acts 8 records the great revival in Samaria. It's a detailed account of how the Holy Spirit brings change to people's hearts. Who was the preacher? It was Philip, one of the first deacons (Acts 6:5). How was his preaching received?

"When the crowds heard Philip and saw the miraculous signs he did, they all paid **close attention** to what he said" (8:6).

There was a willingness to hear the Word, to give heed to the message and to cooperate with what God was saying. And, what was the evidence and proof that God was alive and well?

1. **Lives were changed** – as people were being healed, evil spirits were cast out, and miracles occurred (v.6,7).
2. **Joy was very present** – as people rejoiced that God was at work (v.8).
3. **Sin's power was being broken** – as Simon the sorcerer was exposed and freed by God's power (v.9-13).
4. **The Holy Spirit was being poured out** – as water baptized believers received the baptism in the Holy Spirit (v.14-17).
5. **Evangelism was quickly increasing** – as the apostles took the good news to "many Samaritan villages" (v.25).

Why was there such an awakening in Samaria? Because lost people are all around us, they matter to God, and they need to be found. Lost people are why we exist! Notice God's wisdom in Samaria:

1. God Turns Our Pain Into His Gain!
How did Samaria have the gospel brought to them? It was the result of pain and persecution. Stephen was stoned for his witness (Acts 7:58) and the church was persecuted by Saul (Acts 8:1-3). Saul was brutal towards Christians:
♦ He gave his approval for Stephen's death (Acts 8:1).
♦ He attempted to destroy the church (v.3).
♦ He "dragged off men and women and put them in prison" (v.3).
♦ He voted to have believers killed (26:10), and severely punished Christians (26:11).

And what was the result of Saul's abuse? "Those who had been scattered preached the Word wherever they went" (Acts 8:4). In other words, Saul's plan backfired! Instead of scaring believers into silence, it scattered them throughout Judea and Samaria.

What's the take-a-way for you today?

♦ **What Satan means for evil, God can reverse and turn to good!**

♦ **What for you is painful, God can redeem and make beneficial!**

♦ **What might hurt or humble you, God can use to advance His grace in you!**

♦ **What to you seems wasteful, God can sovereignly use to promote you!**

Nuf Sed!

"The Samaria Outpouring"
Part II

"When they arrived, they prayed for them, that they might receive the Holy Spirit" (Acts 8:15).
"Then Peter and John placed their hands on them, and they received the Holy Spirit" (v.17).

Yesterday, we saw how satan's plan to crush the church was overruled by God. What did Saul's persecution end up producing? It led to a spiritual awakening in Samaria! Notice how God reverses the enemy's attempt to stop the progress that God wants to give:

2. God Turns Our Heart Through the Gospel!
Philip, a layman, was scattered down to Samaria because of the persecution by Saul. Philip then leads the first evangelistic thrust outside of Jerusalem. What does Philip preach?

♦ He preached **"Christ"**! "Philip went down to a city in Samaria and proclaimed the Christ there" (Acts 8:15). This means that Philip preached the forgiveness of sin through Jesus alone!

♦ He preached **"The Kingdom of God"**! "He preached the good news of the Kingdom of God" (v.12). This means that Philip preached God's rule and reign in every area of your life! It means that God wants to establish His Lordship through the surrender of our wills each day.

♦ He preached **"The Name of Jesus"**! "He preached... the name of Jesus Christ" (v.12). This means that Philip's message was one with liberating power – to free the Samaritans from every bondage of magic, sorcery, evil, and sin. There is authority in Jesus' Name!

How did (and does) the Word penetrate and change our human hearts? Philip preaching the gospel had great results because of the content he delivered:

♦ The **Christ** – means conversion and forgiveness **by** His Name.
♦ The **Kingdom of God** – means surrender **to** His Lordship.
♦ The **Name of Jesus** – means authority **in** His Name over sin's control.

And, what did the apostles in Jerusalem do when they heard about the awakening in Samaria? They sent Peter and John down to visit. Why? "They prayed for them that they might receive the Holy Spirit" (v.15). And what happened?

"Peter and John placed their hands on them, and they received the Holy Spirit" (v.17).

In other words, Peter and John travel north to Samaria to visit the people converted under Philip's preaching. They were compelled to bring the message of Pentecost to these believers. Why? Because God wanted to empower the

Samaritans to live out the gospel and bring many to salvation. And the same God wants to fill you with the same Spirit to make His Name famous where you live and serve!

The take-a-way?
The outpouring in Samaria is a beautiful picture of **conversion** through forgiveness of sin, **surrender** to the Lordship of Jesus, **authority** over sinful behavior, and **power** to be a spirit-filled witness.

Nuf Sed!

September 13
"The Caesarea Outpouring"
Part I

"While Peter was still speaking these words, the Holy Spirit came on all who heard the message. The circumcised believers who had come with Peter were astonished that the gift of the Holy Spirit had been poured out even on the Gentiles. For they heard them speaking in tongues and praising God" (Acts 10:44-46).

"As I began to speak, the Holy Spirit came on them as he had come on us at the beginning" (11:15).

"Then I remembered what the Lord had said: John baptized with water, but you will be baptized with the Holy Spirit" (v.16).

Acts 10 is a pivotal point in the life of the church. Salvation traveled from the Jews in Acts 2, to the Samaritans in Acts 8, and now to the Gentiles in Acts 10. It's an amazing account of how God is at work behind the scenes of your life! It reveals the heart of God to accept, forgive, lead and empower you to enjoy the journey. In Acts 10, we see God at work as He has a message for Cornelius, Peter, the Gentiles, and you and me. The message produces spiritual health, spiritual hunger, and spiritual power to live on mission and serve our generation!

1. There Is the Word of The Lord to "Cornelius" (v.1-8).
"Cornelius… send men to Joppa to bring back a man named Simon who is called Peter" (v.3,5).
 Cornelius was a Roman soldier in charge of 100 men. His job was highly honored for special service to Caesar. This Roman soldier was described by Luke in Acts 10:2,3:
♦ He was **devout** and had reverence for God.
♦ He was **generous** and loved to help people.
♦ He was **God fearing** and took God very seriously.
♦ He was **praying** and spending much time in prayer.
 And, notice what happens to Cornelius one ordinary day: In (v.3), God gives him a vision of an angel. In (v.4), the angel tells Cornelius that God has noticed his praying and giving. In (v.5), Cornelius is told to send some men down to Joppa to find a man named Simon Peter. In (v.6), Cornelius is informed that Simon is staying with another man named Simon who works with leather for a living.
 What does Cornelius do with this Word from the Lord? He immediately obeys God and sends his servants to Joppa to find Simon Peter. Without hesitation, Cornelius sends his men to Joppa (30 miles away).

What's the take-a-way as this story unfolds?

♦ **We are responsible to do what God tells us to do. And, God is responsible to do what He promised to do!**

♦ **God is always working ahead of us in ways that we cannot see today!**

♦ **Cornelius teaches you and me that we can rest well with the unknown details of tomorrow for the Lord has gone before us!**

Nuf Sed!

"The Caesarea Outpouring"

"While Peter was still thinking about the vision, the Spirit said to him, 'Simon, three men are looking for you. So get up and go downstairs. Do not hesitate to go with them, for I have sent them'" (Acts 10:19,20).

Yesterday, we discovered that God took notice of Cornelius' devotion and spoke to him at three in the afternoon one day (v.1-8). We learned that if we obey God in the present, He will orchestrate the details of our future. Today, we'll see that:

2. There Is the Word of The Lord To Peter (v.9-23).

What happened in Joppa while Cornelius' men traveled from Caesarea? God was preparing Peter for things that he had no idea about. I call this the timing, wisdom and sovereignty of God. And, what was God's word to Peter?

♦ In (v.9), Peter goes to prayer at noon.

♦ In (v.10-16), Peter has a vision of clean and unclean animals to eat.

♦ In (v.17), the men that Cornelius had sent discover the house where Peter is staying.

And, what was the invitation to Peter? The visiting men said:
"We have come from Cornelius the centurion. He is a righteous and God-fearing man, who is respected by all the Jewish people. A holy angel told him to have you come to his house so that he could hear what you have to say" (10:22).

Why did God give this vision to Peter? Because Peter was a strict Orthodox Jew. He considered the Gentiles in Caesarea as unclean, aliens, strangers, and outsiders of God's redemptive plan. So what is God saying to Peter, and to you and me? He is saying that He loves both the Jew and the Gentile and wants them both to be saved. God has broken down the wall between Jew and Gentile through the cross of Jesus. God has purposed that His church has no higher, middle, or lower class of people. In other words, the vision from the Lord to Peter was to prepare Peter (the Jew) to take the Gospel to Cornelius (the Gentile) and expand the borders of the Lord's church. And, what happens at the exact time that the Lord gives the vision to Peter? While Peter is praying, the three men that traveled from 30 miles away knock at the door where Peter is staying (Acts 10:17). And, what does Peter do? He invites the men into his house (v.23):
"The next day, Peter started out with them, and some of the brothers from Joppa went along. The following day he arrived in Caesarea. Cornelius was expecting them and had called together his relatives and close friends... Peter went inside and found a large gathering of people" (v.23, 24, 27).

Why was Peter called to go to back to Caesarea? It's unmistakable and clearly defined for us to see. "Send to Joppa for Simon, who is called Peter. He will bring you a message through which you and all your household will be saved" (11:13,14). God sends an angel to tell Cornelius to call for Simon Peter to his house. Why? To explain to everyone how they can be saved. Wow!

The take-a-way?
♦ **If we spend time in prayer listening to God, God will send people who will listen to us.**

Nuf Sed!

"The Caesarea Outpouring"
Part III

"While Peter was still speaking these words, the Holy Spirit came on all who heard the message. The circumcised believers who had come with Peter were astonished that the gift of the Holy Spirit had been poured out even on the Gentiles. For they heard them speaking in tongues and praising God" (Acts 10:44-46).

In the past two days, we've discovered the word of the Lord to Cornelius and Peter. We've seen how God's timing is perfect and His purpose is all-consuming to rescue people. Today, we will see the exact message from Peter to Cornelius and all those gathered together. It was a message to the Gentile world then, and it's a message to your heart and mine now. It's one of the most "gospel centered" messages in all of scripture. Notice:

3. The Word of the Lord to the Gentiles (v.24-28).
"When Peter arrived at Cornelius' house in Caesarea, he heard Cornelius say these words, 'We are all here in the presence of God to listen to everything the Lord has commanded you to tell us'" (10:33). And Peter's message focused on these realities:

♦ **The Impartiality of God!** "God does not show favoritism" (v.34) means: If God could save Peter and baptize him in the Holy Spirit, then God can save and baptize the non-Jewish people in Caesarea as well. In other words, Jesus died for everyone and there is no discrimination because of race, nationality, position, background, or past sins.

♦ **The Peace of God!** "Telling the good news of peace through Jesus Christ" (v.36). This means that the gospel satisfies and transforms the heart, and the result is an abiding peace that can only come from God.

♦ **The Power of God!** "Jesus of Nazareth... how he went around doing good and healing all who were under the power of the devil" (v.36). This is clear, that Jesus has been anointed to liberate and free anyone who is oppressed or bound by sin's power. God's power is greater than every other power that seeks to rob you of your fullest potential.

♦ **The Forgiveness of God!** "Everyone who believes in him receives forgiveness of sins through his name" (v.43). Forgiveness is the cancellation of a debt as if it never existed. It means that Jesus paid our sin debt in full, and we can have right standing before God because of his grace and mercy.

♦ **The Strength of God!** "The circumcised believers who had come with Peter were astonished that the gift of the Holy Spirit had been poured out even on the Gentiles" (v.45).

Ten years after the initial outpouring on the Day of Pentecost, God poured His Spirit out upon the Gentiles. Why? To strengthen them to live on mission and rescue those far from God. And, God is doing the same work today!

The take-a-way?

The "full gospel message" is revealed in Caesarea; that God will forgive your sin, bring great peace in your heart, deliver you from besetting and harmful sin, and strengthen you with the power of the Holy Spirit!

Nuf Sed!

September 16
"The Ephesus Outpouring"

"While Apollos was at Corinth, Paul took the road through the interior and arrived at Ephesus. There he found some disciples and asked them, 'Did you receive the Holy Spirit when you believed?' They answered, 'No, we have not even heard that there is a Holy Spirit'" (Acts 19:1,2).

The Ephesus outpouring is the fifth recorded time that the Spirit is poured out on a group of people. There was:
♦ The Jews in Jerusalem (Acts 2)
♦ The group gathered in a prayer meeting (Acts 4)
♦ The people in Samaria (Acts 8)
♦ The Gentiles in Caesarea (Acts 10)
♦ And now the disciples in Ephesus are baptized in the Holy Spirit (Acts 19)

Why did God send Paul to this group of John's disciples in Ephesus? God sent Paul to ask something and to do something:
1. "Did you receive the Holy Spirit when you believed?" (v.2)
2. "When Paul placed his hands on them, the Holy Spirit came on them, and they spoke in tongues and prophesied" (v.6).

In other words, Apollos could only teach as much as he knew. So God leads Paul to Ephesus, where he makes a discovery. There was a lack of spiritual gifts and there was a lack of spiritual power. So, Paul teaches the believers gathered together on the baptism in the Holy Spirit. After Paul teaches, three distinct things are seen taking place:
1. Paul lays his hands on them in prayer to aid them in their faith.
2. The disciples received the infilling of the Holy Spirit.
3. Each one gathered together began to speak in other tongues as the Spirit was poured out.

The discovery in the text is clear and direct. In (v.2-4), John's baptism of repentance was not enough. This baptism of repentance means to turn from sin and turn to God with all of your heart. It means that these believers asked God for mercy, grace, and forgiveness of sin; and were willing to forsake all sin.

Secondly, these believers were water baptized to show the world that they were willing to obey God and do what God was asking (v.5). In other words, in repentance we stop and turn from our sinful behavior. In water baptism, we come out of the water to live in obedience to God.

But thirdly, we ask God to fill us with His Spirit so that we can serve Him in power to reach the lost for Jesus. This baptism in the Spirit is always tied to the mission of the church – reaching the one who is far from God! So, if you are hungry and thirsty for more, understand that the baptism in the Holy Spirit is a gift from God. Open your heart in faith and prayer to God, and get ready for God to saturate you with His Spirit and presence.

The take-a-way?

The baptism of repentance means that I turn from sin; water baptism means that I've risen with Christ to live for Him; and the Spirit baptism means that I am energized and strengthened to be all that God wants me to be!

Nuf Sed!

"The Damascus Outpouring"

"Brother Saul, the Lord Jesus who appeared to you on the road as you were coming here – has sent me so that you may see again and be filled with the Holy Spirit" (Acts 9:17).

Saul's persecution of the believers and apprehension by God is covered in the June 8th and 9th devotionals. Today, I want you to see the effects and contents of a great gospel centered message in Acts 9. The outpouring of grace upon Saul on the road to Damascus is clearly documented:

♦ Saul was freed from **"sin"** through the gift of conversion.
♦ Saul was freed from **"sickness"** through the gift of healing.
♦ Saul was freed from **"self-dependency"** through the gift of the Holy Spirit.

Why was the baptism in the Holy Spirit so important for Saul? I can see two main reasons in our text:

1. There would be lots of **"responsibility"** for Saul:
"This man is my chosen instrument to carry my name before the Gentiles and their kings and before the people of Israel" (Acts 9:15).

2. There would be lots of **"rejection"** for Saul:
"I will show him how much he must suffer for my name" (v.16).

So, why did Saul need to be filled, baptized, and saturated with the Holy Spirit? Because the task was so big and his resources were too small. Why do you and I need to be filled with the Spirit day after day in the journey? Because our task is so big and our resources are too small. This is why God sent Ananias with a specific message for Saul, and records it in Scripture for us all: "Brother Saul, the Lord Jesus, who appeared to you on the road as you were coming here, has sent me so that you may see again and **be filled with the Holy Spirit**" (v.17).

Saul of Tarsus was turned into Paul the apostle because of his radical conversion and Pentecostal baptism! Paul would go on to say:

"I thank God that I speak in tongues more than all of you" (I Corinthians 14:18). He would also say: "He who speaks in a tongue edifies himself" (v.4).

The bottom line for you and me is this: God poured out His Spirit in Jerusalem, Samaria, Caesarea, Ephesus, and Damascus. And, God wants to pour out His Spirit in your life today. Will you let Him? Are you hungry and thirsty? Don't you need resources outside of yourself? I know I do!

The take-a-way?
If Jesus said that I need to be filled with the Spirit, then I need to be filled with the Spirit!

Nuf Sed!

September 18
"Gospel Motivation"
Part I

"For Christ's love compels us, because we are convinced that one died for all, and therefore all died. And he died for all, that those who live should no longer live for themselves but for him who died for them and was raised again" (II Corinthians 5:14,15).

One Saturday on a leader's retreat, a person made this statement: "I work my fingers to the bone in this church, and what thanks do I get?" I thought to myself, "You serve for thanks?" In other words, why we do what we do is just as important as what we do. And Gospel motivation is the only healthy and sustainable motivation that leaves the heart with joy and peace.

In fact, hasn't the church world seen enough of carnal and fleshly motivation? Isn't it easy to discern the subtlety of bribery, status, fear, guilt, manipulation, intimidation, pride, etc.? Haven't the consequences of frustration, exhaustion, burn-out, anger, and feeling used left a multitude of people disillusioned? That's why I love the phrase Paul used in (v.14):

"For Christ's love **compels us**". Which means:

♦ This is not the love that we have for Christ.

♦ This is the love that He has for us which was displayed on the cross.

God is saying through Paul that our greatest source of motivation in service to God and people is what took place at Calvary! This means three things:

1. If Calvary is not enough to motivate me where I am, then nothing else will ever be enough where I might go.

2. If Jesus is not enough to satisfy me where I am, then nothing else will satisfy me where I might go!

3. If ever I feel cheated in serving God, I am serving for the wrong reason!

How does this truth affect us when it sinks deep within our hearts? It helps us put into practice what follows (v.14): "Those who live should **no longer live for themselves**, but for Him who died for them and was raised again" (v.15).

When we truly grasp the gospel (or the love that Christ displayed for us at Calvary) it affects our motivation, attitude and service in every way. How?

♦ The cross keeps you going if you ever feel underappreciated!

♦ The cross keeps you serving when people don't say "Thank you"!

♦ The cross keeps you humble if you ever feel like boasting!

♦ The cross keeps you grateful when you are offended or ignored!

♦ The cross keeps you sensible when you're tempted to feel entitled or elite!

♦ The cross keeps you healthy if you ever forget that you are a steward and not an owner of anything on earth!

The take-a-way?

We do not honor God by serving Him; He honors us by allowing us to participate in His eternal work!

Nuf Sed!

September 19
"Gospel Motivation"
Part II

"For Christ's love compels us, because we are convinced that one died for all" (II Corinthians 5:14).

"God made him who had no sin to be sin for us" (v.21).

Yesterday, we looked at the greatest and healthiest motivation to serve God in all the world. What is it? It is the love that Christ has for us that He displayed on the cross! The gospel of Jesus (on the cross) is by far the overruling and purest motivation for service on planet earth. Paul also lists some other values or reasons that motivated him to spend his life for eternal things. Each one speaks to us and draws us to give our lives away for the right reasons:

1. How God "Views People" Motivates us!
"So from now on we regard no one from a worldly point of view" (v.16).

Paul talks about his change of heart here. At one-time Paul evaluated Jesus from a worldly "after the flesh" point of view. As an educated Jew, Paul was looking forward to the Messiah. But on the Damascus Road, Paul encountered Jesus and was radically changed. Paul's encounter with Jesus convinced him of two things:

♦ Jesus died to provide salvation for Jews and Gentiles alike.
♦ Everyone must receive this Jesus or be eternally lost and separated from God.

In other words, Paul's total perspective in life was changed. He now sees Jesus as the only One who can forgive sin and change the human heart. He sees people "not after the flesh", as merely fleshly human beings, but as spiritual beings who will live forever in one of two places. He views people not as Jew or Gentile, rich or poor, man or woman, black or white. Instead, he sees every person as an immortal soul that must be reached with the good news of the gospel.

2. How We've Been "Privileged" Motivates Us!
"All this is from God, who reconciled us to himself through Christ and gave us the ministry of reconciliation" (v.18).

Since believers have been reconciled to God, we now have the priority, privilege, and responsibility to tell others about God's gift of eternal life. Paul is emphatic here, that our number one goal in life is to glorify God by connecting people to Jesus – not ourselves. Our responsibility is to find every way possible to reach and rescue and see unbelievers reconciled to God! Why is this reconciliation ministry so important? Because this is eternal work: "Since, then, we know what it is to fear the Lord, we try to persuade men" (v.11).

The word for *fear* means, "To stand in awe of God". It means to hold the Lord in the highest regard, convinced that everyone will stand before Him one day. Beloved, your life and service in reconciling people to God is simply the most important work throughout your lifetime.

The take-a-way?
A hundred years from now only one thing will matter – who is in heaven, and who is not!

Nuf Sed!

"Gospel Motivation"
Part III

"For Christ's love compels us, because we are convinced that one died for all" (II Corinthians 5:14).

The past two days we've discovered three ways that God motivates healthy believers:

♦ How Jesus "died on the cross" motivates us!
♦ How God "views people" motivates us!
♦ How we've been "privileged" motivates us!

Today, we'll complete Paul's address to the Corinthians about the ministry of reconciliation. Notice the other three reasons that Paul considered, in feeling motivated in his service to God:

1. The Ambassador Label Provokes Us!

"We are therefore Christ's ambassadors, as though God were making his appeal through us" (v.20). The word *ambassador* means: Someone who is sent forth to represent the sender and announce the message of the sender. The four characteristics of an ambassador are:

♦ They belong to the one who sent them out.
♦ They are commissioned to be sent out and exist only for the purpose for which they are sent.
♦ They possess the authority and power of the one who sent them.
♦ They are sent forth with the message of the sender.

Is this a passive responsibility? Not hardly! In fact, notice Paul's intense words: "We implore you on Christ's behalf" (v.20). This word *implore* means: To beg, plead, intreat, and cry out for people to be reconciled to God! It is a passionate appeal asking people to respond to the gospel. This is such a critical message (because of the consequences) that we are to passionately plead with people to turn from sin and turn to God!

2. The Glory of God Provokes Us!

"If it seems that we are crazy, it is to bring glory to God. And if we are in our right minds, it is for your benefit" (v.13, NLT). Paul was charged with being a mad man because of his extreme zeal. Paul accepts the charge as true, but he says it was all for one reason – God's glory! Paul was a fool for the sake of God's glory, all to rescue people from the fires of hell. Paul paid the price of criticism for the glory of God in seeing lives forever changed!

3. The Needs of People Provoke Us!

"If we are in our right mind, it is for you" (v.13).

Paul was acting with extreme passion out of a pure heart. He had no interest in position or titles. He testifies that he did everything for the glory of God and the welfare of the Corinthians. His sole motivation was the gospel – to reach (evangelize) and grow (disciple) people through the local church. He was a servant leader at the expense of himself, and cared less who got the credit.

The take-a-way today?
Gospel motivation is never stagnant, static, or passive- it is energized by the Spirit and is always outward in focus!

Nuf Sed!

September 21
"Lydia Lessons to Live By"
Part I

"One of these listening was a woman named Lydia, a dealer in purple cloth from the city of Thyatira, who was a worshiper of God. The Lord opened her heart to respond to Paul's message" (Acts 16:14).

Paul's second missionary journey is recorded in Acts 15:36-18:22. It's a great background story that leads us to a woman named Lydia. God would lead Paul from Antioch through Syria, Asia Minor, and into Europe. It was an eventful missionary journey, but notice how it begins:

1. There was "Contention" (Acts 15:36-41).
"They had such a sharp disagreement that they parted company" (v.39).
　　Paul and Barnabas agreed on the mission, but disagreed on the personnel. Paul felt that Mark wasn't ready to go to Europe, yet Barnabas felt that Mark was ready. A Christian conflict arose and the contention caused Paul to take Silas and Barnabas to take Mark. And, how did God redeem the conflict for His glory?
♦ A former deserter (Mark) was reclaimed for ministry by Barnabas.
♦ Silas, a new disciple, was born as Paul's companion in mission.
♦ A new missions team was founded as Barnabas took Mark and went to Cyprus, while Paul took Silas and went into Syria and Alicia. In other words, two cities would now be reached instead of one as the gospel would spread a little further. God ruled and overruled to accomplish His purpose!

2. There was "Strengthening" (Acts 16:1-5).
"He came to Derbe and then to Lystra, where a disciple named Timothy lived... they traveled from town to town... so the churches were strengthened in the faith and grew daily in numbers" (v.1,4,5).
　　Paul took young Timothy as his helper, placed him as the pastor in Ephesus, and the churches were strengthened and increased.

3. There was "Disappointment" (Acts 16:6-11).
"They tried to enter Bithynia, but the Spirit of Jesus would not allow them to" (v.7).
　　Paul was stopped from going where he intended to go, westward into Asia Minor (v.6). He was forbidden to go Northward into Bithynia (v.7). He ends up in Troas where he receives a vision and a call to go to Macedonia. Why this change of plans from God? Because God wanted to save Lydia, a slave girl, and a jailor! What are the take-a-ways here that speak to your heart today?
♦ **God can use what disappoints us to increase His work in us!**
♦ **God will close doors that are not in our best interest!**
♦ **God's timing is wiser than our timing – be patient!**
♦ **God can redeem our pain and tension for His ultimate glory!**

♦ God knows how to get you where you need to be, to reach the Lydias who are waiting for the gospel!

Nuf Sed!

"Lydia Lessons to Live By"
Part II

"Lydia, a dealer in purple cloth… the Lord opened her heart" (Acts 16:14).

Yesterday, we discovered how God went to great lengths to get Paul headed towards Philippi of Macedonia. Today, we'll see why God changed Lydia's heart! It's a diary of how Lydia cooperated with God in the process. Notice the specifics here:

Paul had a vision one night. The vision was of a man in Macedonia, who was saying, "Come over to Macedonia and help us" (v.9). Paul then leaves Troas for Philippi of Macedonia, and on the Sabbath, went down by a river and met a group of women (v.13). Among the women was Lydia, who was in the very place where God would give entrance of the Gospel into Europe. I love what God reveals about Lydia that provokes us to healthy spirituality:

1. God Honors A "Praying" Spirit (v.13)
Paul and his friends were resting a few days to prepare for ministry. Paul then goes out by the Gangites River and meets Lydia. What is Lydia doing? She is gathered together with friends to pray. What precedes the gospel coming to these women? Hearts that are being prepared in the place of prayer down by the river. What is prayer? Prayer is communication of my soul with God. It is aligning my heart with what God wants to do. It is the very place where we discover:
♦ **Deeper intimacy** with God!
♦ **Fresh Anointing** and strength from above!
♦ **Clear Direction** for the journey ahead!
Lydia was a woman of prayer! And Lydia also discovered that…

2. God Honors a "Worshiping" spirit (v.14)
Scripture reveals that this professional business woman from Thyatira was a worshiper of God! In other words, this seller of purple fabric was on the road. She had a business in Thyatira, but was selling her product in Philippi. Her fabrics were in great demand in Rome and yet she makes time in her schedule to worship God. The Jews believed that God was alive, holy, pure, and actively involved in the lives of people. So, Lydia takes time out to ascribe worthiness to God for who He is. What is worship? It is:
♦ My response to the goodness of God.
♦ My expression of gratitude for His greatness.
♦ My life poured out in surrender to God.
♦ My willingness to bow down.
♦ My humble acknowledgment that everything I am and have is because of the grace of God!
♦ My life of service offered to God without restraint or a price tag.

How ironic that Paul showed up to hungry hearts who were praying and worshipping God.

The take-a-way?
You can pray to God anywhere, you can worship Him anywhere, and He is aware of your seeking heart this day!

Nuf Sed!

September 23
"Lydia Lessons to Live By"
Part III

"She attended unto the things which were spoken of Paul" (Acts 16:14, KJV).

Yesterday we saw how God honored Lydia's praying and worshipping spirit down by the Gangites River. Today, notice what else God reveals about Lydia that speaks to our hearts:

3. God Honors A "Receptive" Spirit (v.14)

The word "attended" means "heard or listened". The Greek word means: to perk up and pay attention to the gospel! It means to keep on listening to the gospel that's being taught. This is a hearing of the gospel with the intent to do what it says. It's a receptivity with the desire to learn, grow, and change. Doesn't this provoke you to read and hear the word with an eager and hungry heart?

4. God Honors An "Obedient" Spirit (v.14)

"The Lord opened her heart to respond to Paul's message... she and the members of her household were baptized" (v.14,15).

This infers that Lydia led her whole household to the Lord. She obeyed the Lord in water baptism, influenced those related to her, and became a witness of the gospel. Without hesitation or reservation, she obeyed the Lord and the gospel through Paul. Have you obeyed the Lord in your own life? Is there any area of your life that God is speaking to you about? Remember: Our progress in God will go no further than our obedience takes us!

5. God Honors A "Servant's" Spirit (v.15,40).

"Come and stay at my house" (v.15)
"After Paul and Silas came out of prison, they went to Lydia's house, where they met with the brothers and encouraged them" (v.40).

Who is this woman named Lydia? She is a "servant", which means:
♦ One who advances others at the expense of themself.
♦ One who cares less who gets the credit.
♦ One who doesn't need to be thanked for their service.
♦ One who takes up their cross without complaint.

Why did Lydia respond with such gratitude to the gospel? **"The Lord opened her heart"** (v.14). In other words, unless the Lord opens our own hearts and those that we speak to, the gospel will have no effect!

The take-a-way?
God will gain new ground in our hearts to the degree that we are receptive, open, and obedient to what He has to say!

Nuf Sed!

September 24
"The Spirit of Courage"
Part I

"Be strong and courageous. Do not be terrified; do not be discouraged, for the Lord your God will be with you wherever you go" (Joshua 1:9).

My heart is overwhelmed today with God's word to Joshua! It's a timely word that reveals God's grace, God's presence, and God's plan to move us forward. It's a word that God has given to gain "new ground" in your heart and mine. In the days ahead, discover the gospel through Joshua, Rahab, Jordan, Gilgal and Jericho. Blessed reading!

The book of Joshua is a book of new beginnings for God's people. It illustrates how the gospel makes it possible to say, "good bye" to the old life and embrace the new life. Remember, Joshua was commissioned to do three things:
1. Lead the people into the promised land.
2. Defeat the enemies that stood in the way.
3. Claim the inheritance that was promised by God.

Joshua's name means, "Jehovah Saves". His main purpose was to cross over the Jordan and take back what really belonged to God (Jesus did this at Calvary). His message to us is this: we have a race to run, a crown to gain, and the Lord to lead us from the wilderness to the place of rest.

For 40 years, Moses had been Israel's leader in religious, domestic, judicial, military, and civic matters. Moses' leadership comes to an end and Joshua will now fulfill what Moses had begun. Moses was not allowed to lead Israel into the Promised Land because of disobedience (Numbers 27:12-14). Moses asked God to give the people a leader and God appointed Joshua and told the people that God would use him to defeat their enemies. Moses encouraged Joshua not to be afraid (Deuteronomy 3:22), then laid his hands on Joshua and God imparted the spirit of wisdom for the task at hand (34:9).

What's the lesson for you and me in all of this? When Israel was in Egypt, the enemy was making life miserable. Israel crosses the Red Sea and the enemy is behind them. But when Israel crosses the Jordan River, enemies are in front of them – to be conquered by faith! The lesson is, God knew what Israel would need and knew where they were going! And, God knows where you are, where you are going, and exactly what you need. That's why God's word to Joshua from Moses is recorded in scripture. It's a timely word that overcomes worry and anxiety over your unseen tomorrows. It's a word from God that you can trust in:

"The Lord your God **will be with you** wherever you go" (Joshua 1:9).

The take-a-way?
If the Lord is on your side, and you are on His side, it doesn't matter who is on the other side!

Nuf Sed!

September 25
"The Spirit of Courage"
Part II

"So Joshua fought the Amalekites as Moses had ordered... so Joshua overcame the Amalekite army with the sword" (Exodus 17:10, 13).

Yesterday we saw how God encouraged Joshua when he was handed the reins of leadership from Moses. Today and tomorrow, I want you to have a closer inside look at Joshua. Why? Because God doesn't do His work through a void or vacuum, He works through human personality. Notice the characteristics of Joshua that God records; character traits that God wants to grow and perfect in your life and mine:

1. The Spirit of Prayer (Exodus 17:8-13).
Joshua comes into focus for the first time in this passage. Amalek (Esau's grandson) was the ruthless enemy of Israel. Joshua goes to war and makes a discovery. When Moses' hands are up in prayer – Joshua prevails. When Moses' hands are down in prayer – Joshua loses. What did Joshua learn? He learned that our battles are fought in the physical but won or lost in the spiritual. He learned that a courageous spirit is born and maintained in a spirit of prayer. He discovered that there really is spiritual warfare and an unseen conflict behind the scenes. He teaches us that in prayer we align ourselves with God's purposes and cooperate with His plan.

2. A Patient Spirit (Exodus 24:13-16).
The second time Joshua is mentioned was when Moses was called up to the top of Mount Sinai to receive the Law and the Tabernacle blueprints. Moses and Joshua left Aaron and Hur and approached the cloud covered summit. On the seventh day, God called Moses to come up to His presence. Joshua was not allowed to enter the cloud of Glory, but was told to just wait. And, for 40 days Joshua was alone, patient, and faithful. He refused to run ahead of God!

3. An Eternal Perspective (Exodus 33:11).
In Exodus 32, Moses cleaned house, ground the golden calf idol into powder and took the tabernacle and set it up outside the camp. Moses put the people to a test to see who really wanted to worship the One True God. Who is really willing to separate themselves and live for what really matters? Following a season of worship, Moses returned to the camp. And what did Joshua do? "But his young aide Joshua, the son of Nun, **did not leave the tent**" (Exodus 33:11).

Why did Joshua refuse to leave the tabernacle with Moses and go back to camp? Because he wanted to continue to fellowship, intercede, and spend time in God's presence. Joshua was willing to give up something temporal for something eternal. His perspective was long term. He traded his time back at camp for eternal good, deeper intimacy, and strength in God's presence.

The take-a-way?

When I narrow <u>my interests</u>, I can focus more on the "long term" and enjoy what "really satisfies"!

Nuf Sed!

September 26
"The Spirit of Courage"
Part III

"Do not rebel against the Lord. And do not be afraid of the people of the land, because we will swallow them up" (Numbers 14:9).

Yesterday we followed Joshua as God gave him a praying spirit, a patient spirit, and a long term perspective. Today, notice the other qualities that God records before Joshua takes over the reins of leadership from Moses. Let's pray as we read, that God by His Spirit will work these in us:

4. Unwavering Faith to Go Forward (Numbers 14:6-9).

In Numbers 13, God sent 12 spies to scope out the land. When the spies returned, ten of the 12 said, "No way, they are stronger than us, and we are like grasshoppers in our own sight". And what did Joshua say? He said, "The Lord will lead us into that land… and will give it to us" (v.8). Ten spies said, "God can't". Joshua and Caleb said, "God can". In other words, the ten who doubted did three things:
♦ They looked at the size of their problem.
♦ They looked at the little that they had.
♦ They left the Lord out of the picture.

Yet, Joshua and Caleb would be the only adults to cross over Jordan into the Promise Land of Canaan. A whole generation of doubters would spend 40 years in the wilderness!

5. A Spirit Filled Vessel (Numbers 27:15-23).

The next recorded event in Joshua's life is his appointment as Moses' successor. Moses had prayed that God would raise up someone to follow him (27:15). And, what kind of person does God choose to lead? "So the Lord said to Moses, 'Take Joshua son of Nun, a man in whom is the spirit, and lay your hands on him'" (v.18). What is it that will give you courage to face every mountain in life? The Holy Spirit filling you to obey the promptings that He places upon your heart!

6. A Servanthood Mindset (Numbers 34:16,17)

Joshua is mentioned next as one of the men to divide the land for the various tribes. This was a behind the scene, detailed, administrative, non-glorious job that needed to be done. Yet, this appointment by God would encourage and prepare Joshua for greater responsibility. Joshua was willing to advance God's kingdom at the expense of himself. He cared less who got the credit and served without complaint.

7. A heart Full of Assurance and Trust (Deuteronomy 31:7,8).

This is the final charge before Joshua takes over for Moses. And what is it that God wants Joshua to hear? It's a word for your heart, and mine as well:

"Be strong and courageous. Do not be afraid or terrified… for the Lord your God goes with you; He will never leave you nor forsake you" (v.6). The good news is this: The one who has begun a good work in you will complete it! He will go with you, before you, and He will not fail you.

The take-a-way?
The Promises of God are for you to believe in, and this will result in a rested and peaceful heart!

Nuf Sed!

September 27
"The Legacy of Rahab"
Part I

"Then Joshua, son of nun, secretly sent two spies from Shittim. 'Go, look over the land' he said, 'especially Jericho'. So they went and entered the house of a prostitute named Rahab and stayed there" (Joshua 2:1).

"By faith the harlot Rahab perished not with them that believed not, when she had received the spies with peace" (Hebrews 11:31, KJV).

Have you ever heard this statement: "Every saint has a past and every sinner has a future?" The truth of this is revealed in Joshua 2:1-24, through the life of Rahab. Here's the setting of the text:

Joshua sends out two spies to view the city of Jericho. The spies lodge in the house of Rahab the harlot. The king of Jericho is told about the spies and he sends someone to apprehend them. So, how do the spies find Rahab's house in the midst of a totally pagan city? Only by the providence of God! Her house was the only safe place in Jericho. Her house was the only provision of lodging for the two spies that Joshua had sent ahead. The word "providence" comes from two Latin words, which mean "pro" (before) and "video" (to see). In other words, the providence of God means that God is going before you, and can see ahead to accomplish His will in your life. The two spies in Rahab's house teach us that, if we do the known will of God today, God will reveal His unknown will tomorrow. God's "providence" means that we are responsible to obey Him; He is responsible to work out the details unknown to us right now. Notice three things about this woman that God used:

1. Rahab Had "Faith" (v.4-8).
How do we know that Rahab had faith in God? Because she revealed her faith in saving the spies. How can God use the worst of sinners? Because faith in God can change any human heart! Remember:
♦ In Matthew 1:5, Rahab is identified as the great grandmother of David (the family line which Jesus came from).
♦ In Hebrews 11:31, Rahab is identified with Sarah as the only two women listed in the Hall of Fame of Faith!
♦ In James 2:25, Rahab is identified with Abraham because of her faith.

How can this be? Because faith in what Jesus did on the cross alone gives us access to God! Rahab is called, "Rahab the harlot" in the Old and New Testament. This is not to bring up her past life again. It is to emphasize the marvelous grace of God that saved her because she believed! It's a message to you and me, that there is not one sin that God is not able to forgive. There is not one person that God does not love. There is not one heart that God cannot change. And, the record of all your sin is removed from the sight of God forever! How? By faith in what Jesus has done to pay the debt that you could not pay!

The take-a-way?
Grace is still greater than any (and every) sin that you and I have ever committed!

Nuf Sed!

"The Legacy of Rahab"
Part II

"Before the spies lay down for the night, she went up on the roof and said to them, 'I know that the Lord has given this land to you'" (Joshua 2:9).

"We have heard how the Lord dried up the water of the Red Sea for you" (v.10).

"The Lord your God is God in heaven above and on the earth below" (v.11).

Yesterday, we saw how Rahab's faith in God was revealed by her works. Remember:
♦ She took in the two spies that Joshua had sent (v.4).
♦ She hid the spies under stacks of flax on her roof (v.6).
♦ She risked her very life so that the spies could get back to Joshua.
♦ She was willing to stand alone in Canaan, a culture of pagan gods.

What else enabled this woman of faith to be used by God in His redemptive plan? Two things stand out to me:

2. Rahab Had "Focus" (v.9-13).

In (v.9) she said, **"The Lord"**. In (v.10) she said, **"The Lord"**. In (v.11), she said, **"The Lord"**. In other words, in this emergency crisis with the spies and arresting officers at her door in Jericho, she declares her faith in God by saying, "**The Lord** your God is in heaven above and on the earth below" (v.11). And it's this faith and focus on God that will carry us through every season of life on earth. Also notice:

3. Rahab Had "Favor" (v.14-24).

Rahab pleaded with the spies to show favor to her entire family when they returned to conquer the city (v.13). The spies then promised Rahab, "We will treat you kindly and faithfully when the Lord gives us the land" (v.14). Rahab was then instructed to hang a "scarlet cord in the window" (v.21), and promised that her entire family would be saved from death. Scarlet (or crimson) is the color of blood. As blood on the doorposts saved the Israelites in Egypt, so the scarlet rope would save the house of Rahab.

Did Rahab deserve to be rescued? She was a citizen of Canaan and under condemnation. She was a Gentile outside of the covenant of God. She was destined to die without God's favor and mercy. But, as the scarlet on the doorposts spared Israel, and as the scarlet in the window spared Rahab, so the scarlet (blood) of the cross spares you and me! Did Rahab deserve to be saved? No! Did her family deserve to be saved? No! Do you and I deserve to be saved? Not a chance! But the undeserved favor and grace of God makes it possible to be forgiven of all sin and fully accepted in His Beloved Son.

The take-a-way?

Rahab's one concern was that her family know this one thing: Judgement is coming to those unsaved, and salvation is available to all who believe!

Nuf Sed!

"The Jordan River"
Part I

"When you see the ark of the covenant of the Lord your God... move out from your positions and follow it" (Joshua 3:4).

In Joshua chapter 1, we saw how God wants us to have a spirit of courage as we love and serve Him. In chapter 2, we discovered Rahab's faith, focus, and favor because of God's grace. Today in chapter 3, notice how God's Presence makes all the difference in your journey.

In Joshua chapters one and two, the Israelites were moving toward the Jordan River. But in chapter three, they must go through the river to get to the Promised Land. Why was it so important for Israel to follow the Lord's instructions? Because God said this:

"You have never been this way before" (v.4). In other words, there were unknown paths ahead and unpredictable obstacles before the Israelites. Today, maybe you are traveling through unchartered territory or unfamiliar surroundings. Maybe you are facing pressure, sorrow, or uncertainty. Maybe God is taking you on a journey where you've never been before. The good news is, that God will lead you and His presence will go with you. Notice what preceded and prepared Israel to go to the next level in their journey:

1. There Was A **"Necessary Patience"!**
The Israelites were waiting by the Jordan River and a million people were anxious to march forward. Joshua orders the people to travel 10 miles from Shittim to Jordan, where they, "camped before crossing over" (v.1). How long did they camp? "After three days... "(v.2). There was a three-day delay before crossing over. Why? Because God wanted the people to be still, get quiet, hear the final instructions and not run ahead of God's plan. Remember friend, waiting seasons are not wasted seasons when you are in the will of God!

2. There Was A **"Genuine Transparency"!**
Joshua said, "Consecrate yourselves, for tomorrow the Lord will do amazing things among you" (v.5). On one hand, God was telling the Israelites to sanctify, cleanse, and prepare their hearts. On the other hand, God promised to work wonders for those whose hearts were ready. The message is: repentance prepares us for renewal and transparency prepares us for transformation!

3. There Was An **"Unwavering Obedience"!**
What was the directive to Israel? "When you see the ark of the covenant... move out from your positions and follow it" (v.3). The Ark of the Covenant was the presence chamber of God in Israel's journey. Obeying and following the Ark were God's conditions for victory in battle. The Ark was a reminder

of God's covenant – that He would go with them wherever He led them. Wow! God was saying here, that in His presence, miracles will happen to make His Name famous on the earth!

The take-a-way?
We are responsible to follow "His" instructions; God is responsible to show Himself strong on our behalf!

Nuf Sed!

September 30
"The Jordan River"
Part II

"The priest who carried the Ark of the Covenant of the Lord stood firm on dry ground in the middle of the Jordan" (Joshua 3:17).

In Joshua 3:1-5, God promised to do amazing things if Israel would cross the Jordan and march forward. In fact, God said, "Set foot in the Jordan; its waters flowing downstream will be cut off and stand up in a heap" (v.13). And what would be the purpose of this miracle for the Israelites? The purpose is clearly stated:

"This is how you will know that the living God is among you and that he will certainly drive out before you the Canaanites" (v.10).

In other words, when the miracle of the Jordan waters takes place, you will know two things:
1. You will know that the Lord **is present** with you.
2. You will know that the Lord will **drive out** every enemy in the battles ahead of you.

This means that God's presence is to increase our faith, which will reduce our fear, worry, and nervousness over the future. In other words, if God does what He promises to do at the Jordan, then you can trust Him for all of your future obstacles and hurdles. In other words, you can rest well and chill out in the journey ahead. So, what happened and why?

What happened was this: the priests carried the Ark ahead of the troops, and when they stepped into the water, the water stood up on edge and the people passed through on dry ground. Why does this happen? Because the presence of God was producing faith in God! And, the Ark of presence was a type of Jesus our Captain. In Joshua 6 when the Ark was carried around Jericho, the walls came down. In I Samuel 5, when the Philistines put the Ark next to their false idol Dagon, it fell into pieces. The Lords says:
"The hills melted like wax at the presence of the Lord" (Psalm 97:5, KJV).

♦ **"Hills"** represents anything in your life that is not God's will for you.
♦ **"Melt"** means: To clear a pathway and dissolve.

The lesson in this "Jordan River miracle" is this: In the presence of God – something happens!

1. God builds our Faith! Israel was edified at the presence of the Ark
2. God Motivates to Action! Israel walked into the middle of the Jordan.
3. God Overcomes Every Obstacle! The Lord held back the water until everyone passed over.

The take-a-way?
In the presence of the Lord, we are comforted in the face of our Jordans. We are convicted and changed for the better. And we are challenged to go forward and pursue God's will as never before!

Nuf Sed!

October 1
"Voices from Gilgal"

"What do these stones mean?" (Joshua 4:6).
"What do these stones mean?" (v.21).

In Joshua chapter one, we see the importance of a courageous spirit. In chapter two, we have the legacy of Rahab. In chapter three, there is the crossing of the Jordan River. But in chapter four, God gives us a memorial that speaks loud and clear today. Here's the context and the gospel message: The whole nation crosses the Jordan, and the Lord speaks to Joshua. He instructs Joshua to choose 12 men to each take a stone from the Jordan. The stones are to be a sign, or a memorial, to the people forever; a message of the faithfulness of God. The Lord also instructed Joshua to have the priests carry the Ark of the Testimony out of the Jordan. When the priests touched dry ground, the waters returned to the flood stage as before. The people, then went up from Jordan to camp at Gilgal some eight miles away. But what happened between Jordan and Gilgal?

"About forty thousand armed for battle crossed over before the Lord to the plains of Jericho for war. That day the Lord exalted Joshua in the sight of all Israel" (v.13, 14). The Lord gives a great victory in battle on the heels of crossing Jordan. And what does Joshua do?

"And Joshua set up at Gilgal the twelve stones they had taken out of the Jordan" (v.20).

Why did Joshua do this? To be a message (or memorial) of the great work of God as He made a way for Israel to cross the Red Sea, the Jordan River, and gain new ground in battle. "He did this so that all the peoples of the earth might know that the hand of the Lord is powerful so that you might always fear the Lord your God" (v.20).
♦ The monument in the Jordan reminded the Jews of God's power to deliver them from the past.
♦ The monument at Gilgal reminded the Jews that God's presence was with them in all of their battles ahead.
This is the Gospel message now:
♦ Jesus, at the cross, has broken sins power and delivered us from the slavery of sin!
♦ Jesus, by his spirit, has promised to be with us in every step of our journey forward.
The monuments at Jordan and Gilgal are speaking loud and clear today. They are not good advice – they are good news:
1. The stones remind us of God's great love for His people.
2. The stones remind us that God's presence is always with us.
3. The stones remind us that Jesus never fails.

4. The stones remind us that you can trust Jesus and His plan for your life.
5. The stones remind us that Jesus is not nervous about the Jordans you must pass through.

The "Memorial Stones" take-a-way?
To remember what God says to remember, is to refresh and renew your faith each and every day.

Nuf Sed!

"Final Preparation For Victory"

"Now when Joshua was near Jericho, he looked up and saw a man standing in front of him with a drawn sword in his hand. Joshua went up to him and asked, 'Are you for us or for our enemies?' 'Neither', he replied, 'but as commander of the army of the Lord I have now come'" (Joshua 5:13,14).

The Israelites have safely crossed over the Jordan on dry land. The Canaanites (Israel's enemy) are afraid and panic is setting in. It now seems like the perfect time for Israel to launch an all out attack. And what does the Lord say? "Not yet, hold on, wait a moment, let's prepare for battle." How does God prepare Israel to march forward toward the Jericho walls?

1. There Was Circumcision (v.1-9).
"The Lord said to Joshua, 'Make flint knives and circumcise the Israelites again'" (v.2). This was a painful surgery and ritual that made the Jews a marked people. God had given circumcision as the sign of His covenant to Abraham and his descendants (Genesis 17:9-14, 23-27). For 40 years this sign of separation had been neglected in the wilderness. But now, before Israel can inherit the Promised Land, they must be circumcised to signify three things: It would restore their covenant relationship with God, it reminded them who they belonged to, and it reiterated to the Jews that they were a chosen people. Today, Jesus separates unto God through His work on the cross (Galatians 6:14-16).

2. There Was Passover (v.10-12).
"While camped at Gilgal on the plains of Jericho, the Israelites celebrated the Passover" (v.10). Only twice before had Israel held the Passover:
♦ In Egypt, blood was sprinkled on the doorposts (Exodus 12).
♦ At Mount Sinai (Numbers 9:5).

The Passover was a celebration of emancipation from Egypt and slavery. It was a recognition of protection and provision through the blood. Right under the noses of the enemy Canaanites, God was declaring His watchful care of His people. Today, we celebrate victory as well because our Passover Lamb has been slain for us!

3. There Was Visitation (v.13-15).
"Now when Joshua was near Jericho, he looked up and saw a man standing in front of him with a drawn sword in his hand" (v.13). Joshua was out viewing the military situation. Standing in the way was Jericho, a great fortress of Canaan. Joshua was wondering how the walls would ever come down, and the pre-incarnate Jesus visits Joshua before the battle. What does Joshua hear from his Commander in Chief?
♦ "It's my battle Joshua, not yours."
♦ "I am the Captain, not you."

♦ "It's holy ground because I am with you."

The take-a-way?
If God calls you to do something for Him, He will equip you, prepare you, and go with you!

Nuf Sed!

October 3
"Jericho Walls Come Down"
Part I

Joshua is a book of conflict, victories, and new beginnings. It is a record of how we can rest in the Lord with His peace, while at the same time moving forward to gain new ground. In Joshua 6, the siege of Jericho was ready to begin. Jericho was one of the "city states" of Canaan. It was a stronghold, hurdle and obstacle to impede Israel's progress. It guarded the passes to the interior of Canaan, and it stood in the way of Israel moving forward. And, don't we all have some "Jerichos" that God wants to capture and conquer? Isn't there some Jericho "walls" in all of us that the gospel wants to bring down? We discover in Joshua 6, that it's not about trying harder; it's more about trusting our Captain as He leads us forward. Notice what God has recorded that brings rest, even in battle:

Unwavering Faith in the Promise of God (6:1-6).
As long as Jericho stood, the land of milk and honey (Canaan) could not be possessed by God's people. As long as we allow "Jerichos" in our own hearts, Jesus cannot fully do what He's wanting to do! But is it our efforts that win the spiritual battle? Not hardly:

"By faith the walls of Jericho fell, after the people had marched around them for seven days" (Hebrews 11:30).

In other words, Joshua believed that God could pull the walls down! The people believed that God could pull the walls down! It's all in the Word so that you and I can believe that God is able to do what we cannot do. Remember friend:
♦ Israel was weak and powerless.
♦ Israel was not trained in warfare strategy.
♦ Israel had no weapons to overcome the enemy.
♦ Israel knew that only God could pull down the walls.
♦ But Israel had faith to believe in the power and ability of God!
And, even though the plan to march around the walls and shout seemed foolish, the walls fell down flat so that the city could be taken. Even though the battle plan was to march while carrying the Ark of The Covenant, blow trumpets and shout, God was committed to keep His Word. In other words, in the weakness of the people, God made His Name famous in Jericho. It wasn't the savvy and slick wisdom of Israel; it was the greatness of God to magnify His Name!
Isn't this what Jesus has done? Isn't this how our salvation has been secured? Isn't this a picture of God saving the world though the crucifixion of His Son? Isn't this an illustration of how God took what seemed foolish to man (at the cross) and yet used it to make a way so that we could enter the eternal Canaan of Heaven? Hasn't God always been able to use what we feel

is wasted, small, unfair, or insignificant to bring glory to His Name on the earth?

The take-a-way?
When God works a miracle, it is never to draw attention to us, it is always to draw attention to Himself!

Nuf Sed!

"Jericho Walls Come Down"
Part II

"Do not give a war cry, do not raise your voices, do not say a word until the day I tell you to shout" (Joshua 6:10).

Yesterday, we learned how "by faith the walls of Jericho fell" (Hebrews 11:30). It wasn't by the power of Israel; it was by the power of God! It wasn't by the people's greatness; it was by God's greatness! It wasn't the wisdom of Israel; it was the wisdom of God! And yet, the people cooperated with God in following His instructions. In other words, the sovereignty of God was at work with the training of Israel to move forward. I notice three ways that Israel cooperated in the miracle of the fallen walls. Just maybe, the Lord is working these three in your heart today:

1. I See A "Restful Patience"
"Do not give a war cry, do not raise your voices, do not say a word until... (Joshua 6:10). Have you ever heard this: "Hurry is not of the devil, it is the devil"? Have you ever had to be patient and wait "until"? Ever feel like time is wasting while you are put "on hold"? The people following Joshua were tempted to be impatient, impetuous, and wanting to rush ahead. To some, the seven-day wait seemed like a waste of time. For others, two hours a day traveling from camp, walking around the city, and returning to camp was useless. Maybe a few followers were hoping that God would hurry up just a bit. But, instead of murmuring, Israel practiced a "restful patience". And what Israel learned was this:
♦ God's delays are certainly not His denials.
♦ If we knew what God knew, we wouldn't resent what God does.

2. I See a Recognition of "God's Grace"
"But Joshua spared Rahab the Prostitute" (v.25). There was one exception to the judgment upon Jericho; it was Rahab and her family. Why was she spared? Because of her faith revealed by her obedience. The scarlet (blood red) rope in Rahab's window allowed her to be accepted by God. Did she deserve to be saved? No! Could she ever be good enough to be saved? No! Could you or I ever merit God's favor and be saved by our works? No, not a chance! So how can Rahab and the rest of us be spared the judgment our sins deserved? Only by Amazing Grace that saved a wretch like me!

3. I See "Absolute Surrender" to God!
"Keep away from the devoted things, so that you will not bring about your own destruction" (6:18).

God told Joshua to demolish everything in Jericho and not take anything for himself. In other words, allow nothing in Jericho to defile or pollute your spirit. God was saying:

♦ Live surrendered and holy for the purposes of God.
♦ Live free from contamination and compromise.

Why serve only One Master? Because it cost the death of God's Son to free us from both sin's power now, and sin's penalty later!

The take-a-way?
If we follow God's leading today, He will take care of every obstacle that would rob us of His blessing tomorrow!

Nuf Sed!

October 5
"Inside the Tent of Achan"
Part I

"Consecrate yourselves in preparation for tomorrow... you cannot stand against your enemies until you remove it" (Joshua 7:13).

Joshua 6 ends with a glorious note of victory: "So the Lord was with Joshua and his fame spread throughout the land" (6:27). Yet, Joshua 7 opens with that little word "but", and signals that things are about to change. Remember, only three opposing enemies withstood Israel in the Promise Land: Jericho, Ai, and the Gibeonites. Isn't it interesting that the only battle that Israel lost in possessing the land was at Ai. And, this only defeat didn't come from without, but from within. The Ai account in chapter 7 reveals the following truth loud and clear: **An enemy in the heart is worse than 10,000 in the field!** In other words, God was teaching Israel, you, and me a valuable lesson. What is it?

♦ What goes on inside of us, is far more important than what goes on outside of us!

♦ It is possible to do good things for God without allowing the gospel to shape and conquer our hearts.

Notice the message that God communicates to us in the Ai battle:

1. The Defeat of Israel is Documented (v.1-5).
"About three thousand men went up; but they were routed by the men of Ai" (v.4).

In (v.2), Joshua sent men from Jericho to spy out the city of Ai. The men returned with a confident report (v.3) that defeating Ai would be a piece of cake. In fact, only a small band of soldiers will be needed to take the city. What happened instead was that, 36 Jewish soldiers were slain and Israel ended up fleeing from Ai in defeat (v.4,5). Why the defeat? The Israelites made some poor choices:

♦ They trusted in the past victory at Jericho.
♦ They didn't ask God for His help and enablement.
♦ They never recognized their own weaknesses.
♦ They allowed sin to destroy them from within.

In this first battle at Ai, I notice two things:

1. Israel never went back to Gilgal which was their camp of refreshment. Instead, they went up on the momentum of Jericho's win.
2. Israel never took the Ark (the presence chamber of God) along as they had in Jordan and Jericho. They failed to ask the Lord for help.

The take-a-way from Israel's defeat?
Momentum is deceptive whenever it causes us to trust in ourselves, trust in our past, or trust in our own strength!   Nuf Sed!

"Inside the Tent of Achan"
Part II

"I will not be with you anymore unless you destroy whatever among you is devoted to destruction" (Joshua 7:12).

Yesterday, we saw how Israel was defeated at Ai because their character didn't keep pace with their gifting and reputation. At the battle of Ai, Israel simply trusted in the momentum of the victory at Jericho, and neglected to trust in God's presence (they left the Ark of Presence at home). Notice the consequences and lessons that flow out of the Ai defeat. They speak to us all about integrity and transparency:

After the defeat at Ai, Joshua went from being magnified in (6:27), to mortified in (7:6). He falls on his face (7:6), moans and groans (v.7), expresses fear (v.9), and God tells him to get up off his face (v.10), and deal with the "disgraceful thing in Israel" (v.15). God then instructs Joshua to single out the tribe of Judah, the family of the Zerahites, the household of Zabdi and a man named Achan (v.18). Joshua says to Achan, "Tell me what you have done, do not hide it from me" (v.19). Achan replies by saying, "I have sinned against the Lord" (v.20). How did Achan sin? He confessed, "I saw... I coveted...and took. They are hidden in the ground inside my tent, with the silver underneath" (v.20,21). Achan's "steps to default" are a lesson and warning to our hearts:

1. There was "Curiosity"
♦ Achan's first mistake was to look and look again at the spoils he would take.
♦ Maybe he couldn't help the first look, but his eyes wandered back into forbidden territory.
♦ Achan forgot that what enters the eye sinks into the heart.

2. There was "Compromise"
♦ Achan called the treasures he stole the "spoils".
♦ They were not the spoils; they were the Lord's portion dedicated to Him.
♦ But Achan compromised in calling it what it was to justify his disobedience.

3. There was "Covetousness"
♦ Achan failed to thank God for the victory in Jericho.
♦ Instead, he entertained thoughts of keeping what belonged to God.
♦ Achan's insecurity caused him to sin with excessive greed.

4. There was a "Cover Up"
♦ Achan forgot that God sees and knows everything.
♦ He covered up what God wanted to dig up so that progress could be made.

◆ He ignored the warning signals.

The take-a-ways?
◆ **The second look is the devil's hook!**
◆ **When Jesus is just useful and not beautiful to us, lesser gods will crowd our hearts and lead us in the wrong direction!**

Nuf Sed!

October 7
"Inside the Tent of Achan"
Part III

"Why have you brought this trouble on us? The Lord will bring trouble on you today" (Joshua 7:25).

The past two days we've seen how Israel was defeated at Ai, and how Achan was deceived by sin. I can't imagine what Achan went through after the Lord said, "In the morning present yourselves tribe by tribe...He who is caught with the devoted things shall be destroyed by fire" (7:14,15). Do you think Achan got any sleep that night? I hardly think so.

In looking deeper into Joshua 7, some things come to the surface that alert us to spiritual danger. They awaken us to the deception and power of sin. They impact our choices and caution us to live "on guard" against idols of the heart. The following truths remind us that there is much to gain – and so much to lose!

Tent Secrets from Achan's Decisions:

1. **Concealing sin does not erase it!**
   ♦ Achan hid the stuff but could not hide his sin.

2. **Sin never allows you to suffer alone!**
   ♦ Achan's whole family (and Israel) suffered because of his sin.

3. **The consequences of sin may be delayed, but cannot be ignored!**
   ♦ There was a season of time that seemed to tell Achan he got away with his thievery.

4. **What is committed in secret will be broadcast in public!**
   ♦ Achan sinned alone, but the whole assembly would eventually find out.

5. **The sting of sin is sharper than its pleasure!**
   ♦ Achan's grief far outweighed his pleasure in sinning.

6. **To delay in repenting is to hasten God's Displeasure!**
   ♦ While Achan delayed and covered up, the anger of the Lord was kindled.

7. **To conceal sin is to forfeit God's help in battle!**
   ♦ God promised Joshua that he would not favor Israel until the sin was removed from among them.

But thank God for His grace and good news today: "He who conceals his sins does not prosper, but whoever confesses and renounces them finds mercy" (Proverbs 28:13).

The good news is, when I agree with God about my sin, He gets to the root of it and leads me forward in a glorious path!

The take-a-way?

Transparency with God is the first step to overcome what could ultimately destroy us!

Nuf Sed!

"An Excellent Spirit"

"Then this Daniel was preferred above the presidents and princes, because an **excellent spirit** was in him; and the king thought to set him over the whole realm" (Daniel 6:3, KJV).

Over the next seven days, I want you to see why Daniel was referred to twice as a man with an **excellent spirit**. He was born around 620 B.C., and was four years old at the time of the great revival in Judah, under King Josiah (II Chron. 34). Daniel was ten years old when Josiah died and 13 years old when Nebuchadnezzar deported a number of Jews to Babylon (including Daniel and his friends). He comes on the scene as a teenager (with his three companions) and finds himself 1,500 miles from home serving under four different rulers. Why was this book of Daniel written? Three reasons:

1. To reveal the sovereign will of God in the nations and in your life.
2. To reveal how God can even use pagan rulers to accomplish His purposes.
3. To reveal how man proposes, but God disposes, and always has the last say.

The book of Daniel is the key to all biblical prophecy. The book of Revelation cannot be unlocked without the prophecies of Daniel. The "Man of Sin" in II Thessalonians 2:3 needs Daniel to be clarified. Only the book of Daniel can unlock the prophetic in Matthew 24, 25; Mark 13; Luke 21; and all of Revelation. Remember:

♦ The first six chapters of Daniel are **historical**, and reveal Daniel's **excellent spirit** of integrity.

♦ The last six chapters of Daniel are **prophetic** and reveal end times events.

Since Daniel 1-6 reveal David's choices and consequences (that resulted in an excellent spirit), let's prepare our hearts today for the next six days. Let's ask God to soften and open our hearts to cooperate with truth that frees us from ourselves. Let's get specific and pray for what unfolds in Daniel chapters 1-6. Notice what God records about young Daniel:

1. A Spirit of **Integrity** - In Daniel 1, a willingness to do right when the environment is all wrong!

2. A **Grateful** Spirit – In Daniel 2, a willingness to thank God when blessings come your way.

3. A **Courageous** Spirit – In Daniel 3, a willingness to choose companions who fear God above every other opinion.

4. A **Secure** spirit – In Daniel 4, a willingness to speak the truth in love, even when it hurts.

5. A **Servant's** spirit – In Daniel 5, a willingness not to use God for personal gain.

6. A **Praying** spirit – In Daniel 6, a willingness to seek God in the midst of calm or crisis.

The take-a-way from Daniel's life?
We can have a mediocre life, or a life with an excellent spirit; it is our own choices to cooperate with God that will determine the outcome!
Nuf Sed!

"The Reward of Integrity"
Daniel I

"But Daniel resolved not to defile himself with the royal food and wine, and he asked the chief official for permission not to defile himself this way" (Daniel 1:8).

Yesterday, we learned that Daniel was noticed, preferred, and used by God because of his "excellent spirit". His excellent spirit was the result of six choices that he made, all outlined in Daniel 1-6. Today, we'll see choice number one, which is a willingness to do what's right, even when the environment is all wrong.

1. Daniel's "Temptation" (v.1-7)
In Daniel chapter 1, we see that Nebuchadnezzar besieges Jerusalem and heads for Babylon with his treasures and hostages. The king chooses gifted servants to train for leadership. And, Daniel finds himself facing two battles, temptations, and predicaments. One is the food test, and the other is the name test:

♦ The king's meat (v.5), refers to the food of the pagans; the wine was forbidden for Nazarites as well (Numbers 6:3).

♦ The second test for Daniel and his three teenage friends was this: the chief official (v.7) gave new names to the four teens in deference to the pagan gods. Daniel is renamed Belteshazzar, which means, "worshipper of Baal". Hananiah is renamed Shadrach, which means, "inspiration of the sun". Mishael is renamed Meshach, which means, "one who belongs to the goddess Sheshach". Azariah is renamed Abednego, which means, "servant of Nego, the morning star".

So, what do you do when you find yourself tempted with a choice to make?

2. Daniel's "Purpose" (v.8-16).
What did Daniel do? He, "resolved not to defile himself with the royal food and wine" (v.8). In other words, Daniel and his friends refused to yield to the Babylonian culture, diet, food, and name change. Why? Because Daniel knew that he wanted to please God above every other lesser god and idol put before him. He knew that sin would defile his conscience, ruin his testimony, steal his joy, and disappoint his God! He knew that every temptation is a lie, promising you something that it cannot deliver. Notice Daniel's reward:

3. Daniel's "Reward" (v.17-21).
What happened when Daniel dared to take a stand against the majority in a pagan context? Two things are documented:

♦ God increased his **health**! "At the end of the ten days they looked healthier and better nourished than any of the young men who ate the royal food" (v.15).

◆ God increased his **wisdom**! "To these four young men, God gave knowledge and understanding… and… the king found none equal" (v.17,19). In fact, the king, "found them **ten times better** than all the magicians and enchanters in his whole Kingdom" (v.20).

The take-a-way?
Like Daniel, the Lord will vindicate your integrity with less stress in this life, and great reward in the next life!

Nuf Sed!

October 10
"The Power of A Grateful Spirit"
Daniel 2

"I thank and praise you, oh God of my fathers: you have given me wisdom and power, you have made known to me what we asked of you, you have made known to us the dream of the king" (Daniel 2:23).

In Daniel chapter 2, King Nebuchadnezzar dreams a dream and cannot sleep. He says to all of his helpers nearby, "I have had a dream that troubles me, and I want to know what it means" (2:3). He then angrily declares that all of his wise men surrounding him will be executed. Daniel then steps up and asks the king for a little time (v.16), and then he goes to prayer with his friends (v.17). What happens after Daniel and his three companions pray? "During the night the mystery was revealed to Daniel in a vision" (v.19). How did Daniel respond to God's intervention? "Then Daniel praised the God of heaven and said: 'Praise be to the name of God for ever and ever; wisdom and power are His'" (v.19, 20). Notice Daniel's praying and gratitude:

1. Daniel "Prays" Immediately!
"He urged them to plead for mercy from the God of heaven concerning this mystery" (v.18).

Daniel spoke with, "wisdom and tact" to the king's guard commander (v.14), but then speaks to his three close friends and appeals to God (v.18). I love how these four believers opened in prayer:

♦ They prayed in **agreement** and aligned their hearts as one.
♦ They prayed in **faith** and believed that God would answer them.
♦ They prayed in **humility**, leaning on God's mercies (v.18), and not on their own righteousness.

And what happened through prayer? "The mystery was revealed to Daniel in a vision" (v.19). What does the King do when Daniel interprets his dream? He responds with, "Surely your God is the God of gods and the Lord of kings" (v.47). "Then the king placed Daniel in a high position… and made him ruler over the entire province of Babylon" (v.48). What does Daniel do after he retreats to prayer and receives his answer?

2. Daniel Expresses "Gratitude" to God Immediately!
"You have made known to me what we asked of you" (v.23). Before Daniel is promoted, he deflects all praise to God in a spirit of humility, adoration, and thankfulness! He thanks God specifically for His Wisdom, His Power, and His Omniscience (V. 20-22). Daniel's gratitude was prompt, full, and expressed without reservation. What's the lesson in all of this?

♦ Prayer connects our weaknesses to the Omniscience of God!
♦ Prayer overcomes fear when we get God into focus.
♦ Prayer is to get God's will done, not our own will done!
♦ Prayer is to bring glory to God, not attention to ourselves!

♦ Prayer, true prayer, results in a grateful spirit that leaves the heart restful and at peace.

The take-a-way?
It's amazing what God will do through our praying when we refuse to take credit for Divine intervention!

Nuf Sed!

October 11
"The Fiery Furnace"
Daniel 3

"If we are thrown into the blazing furnace, the God we serve is able to save us from it… but even if he does not… we will not serve your gods" (Daniel 3:17,18).

In Daniel 1, we saw Daniel's integrity. In chapter 2, we saw his gratefulness. Today we'll see the courage of three Hebrews under pressure.
"King Nebuchadnezzar made an image of gold, ninety feet high and nine feet wide" (v.1) is a telling statement. The king has just had a dream about being the head of gold (2:38). Instead of humbling himself, the king exalted himself and became intoxicated with his own importance. He then built an image of gold to represent the kingdom he had built. After the pride of the king is revealed, three events occur:

1. The Faith of the Hebrews Is Displayed (v.8-18).
After the king built his ninety-foot image to himself, he commanded everyone to worship it (3:5). He then intimidates and says, "Whoever does not fall down and worship will immediately be thrown into a blazing furnace" (v.6). And what do Shadrach, Meshach, and Abednego do? They refuse to compromise their convictions! Why? Because God's approval is more important than anyone else's approval.

2. The Fury of The King Is Exposed (v.19-23).
"Then Nebuchadnezzar was furious" (v.19). He ordered the furnace heated seven times hotter" (v.19). "Throw them into the blazing furnace" (v.20). Here is where we learn that there is a cost and a price to be a true disciple. Here is where God prepares our hearts to be rejected at times. Here is where God strengthens us to bring glory to His name. Here is where we show the world that Jesus is beautiful to us – and not just useful to us!

3. The Faithfulness of Jesus Is Experienced (v.24-30).
"Then King Nebuchadnezzar leaped to his feet in amazement and asked his advisors, "Weren't there three men that we tied up and threw into the fire?" (v.24)

"Look, I see four men walking around in the fire… praise be to the God of Shadrach, Meshach, and Abednego, who has sent his angel and rescued his servants" (v.25, 28).

How was faith and courage rewarded? The three Hebrews experienced the presence of Jesus and were given a promotion from the king. What's the message to your heart and mine in Daniel, chapter three?

The take-a-way message is:
- ◆ God's presence will be with you in every season of your life!
- ◆ God's grace will be sufficient in every step to uphold you!
- ◆ God's favor will sustain you when you have to stand alone!
- ◆ The Lord is with you today (and everyday), so take heart as you march forward!

Nuf Sed!

"Mercy Triumphs Over Judgement"
Daniel 4

"Now I, Nebuchadnezzar, praise and exalt and glorify the King of Heaven, because everything He does is right and all His ways are just. And those who walk in pride He is able to humble" (Daniel 4:37).

In this chapter (4), Daniel speaks the truth in love even when it hurts. His message to the king was risky, and the context speaks volumes to your heart and mine today:

The setting takes place 10 years after the building of the golden image in chapter three. Nebuchadnezzar has swept the world with his conquests. He has succeeded in designing and building Babylon. Yet in the midst of his flourishing, he is discontent. He's self-made and thinks that he can make it without God:

♦ He has money on the outside (but is empty on the inside).
♦ He is boastful on the outside (and prideful on the inside).
♦ He is busy making buildings (but too busy to make a life).

1. We See The "Message" of the Dream (v.4-25).
"I had a dream that made me afraid... the images and visions that passed through my mind terrified me" (v.5).
In the vision, Nebuchadnezzar sees a tree (v.10), the tree reaches heaven (v.11), the tree has food and shade (v.12), a messenger from heaven comes down (v.13), and a voice says to cut down the tree and strip off the branches (v.14). The king calls Daniel in to interpret the dream, and Daniel tells the king that he will be humbled and chastened but, "will be restored... when you acknowledge that Heaven rules" (v.26). So why the dream? To show the king two things:

♦ God is holy and has to judge the pride (sin) of Nebuchadnezzar.
♦ God loves the king and wants to extend mercy and kindness.

2. We See The "Mercy" of the Dream (v.26-29).
♦ In (v.26), the **"stump"** reveals God's **mercy**. Though the tree was cut down, the stump was left to revive, be restored, and grow again!
♦ In (v.27), the **"appeal"** reveals God's **mercy** as Daniel implores the king; "O king, be pleased to accept my advice: renounce your sins by doing what is right". It's a cry from Daniel's broken heart to rescue the king.
♦ In (v.29), the **"delay"** reveals God's **mercy**. "Twelve months later" (v.29) means that Nebuchadnezzar rejected the appeal for one year, yet God was longsuffering all the while.

3. We See the "Ministry" of The Dream (v.31-37).
What happens when pride comes between us and God? God spoke these words: "Your royal authority has been taken from you" (v.31). The king was

humiliated and driven to the fields to eat with the animals. His pride collapsed him until he came to his senses and acknowledged the God of heaven!

So what's the clear take-a-way for our own hearts in Daniel 4?
♦ **The purpose of God's chastening is not vengeance but salvation!**
♦ **God's mercy is always greater than our sin when we turn to Jesus!**

Nuf Sed!

October 13
"The Party Is Over"
Daniel 5 - Part I

"But you his son, O Belshazzar, have not humbled yourself, though you knew all this. Instead, you have set yourself up against the Lord of heaven… you did not honor the God who holds in his hand your life and all your ways" (Daniel 5:22, 23).

Daniel 5 is the account of a keg party like no other. Belshazzar's father is in the field with the Chaldean army, fending off the attacks by the Medes and the Persians. The armies of Cyrus have surrounded the capital as their final prize. The time when Belshazzar is needed the most, we find him at his least. Notice what happens while the enemy is preparing to attack the city people:

1. I See the "Carnality" of Belshazzar (v.1-4).
"King Belshazzar gave a great banquet… as they drank the wine, they praised the gods of gold and silver, of bronze, iron, wood, and stone" (v.1-4).

Belshazzar ignores the Persian threat just outside the city walls and throws a party. It's an orgy of food, wine, women, and song. One thousand lords with beautiful women, golden lamps hanging from ivory and pearl ceilings, the richest rugs from India, couches cushioned with velvet, bands of music playing, dazzling costumes, and satan lets loose the lie of fermentation and intoxication. But why was this a party like none other? Because this party was the ultimate mocking of Jehovah God! Notice that Belshazzar, "gave orders to bring in the gold and silver goblets that Nebuchadnezzar, his father, had taken from the temple in Jerusalem, so that… his wives and his concubines might drink from them" (v.2).

While Belshazzar was intoxicated, he ordered his servant to bring in the vessels taken out of the house of God. For anyone to use the vessels of the temple without being an appointed priest meant certain death. The party thrower knows full well that those vessels are consecrated to the service of God alone. But why does Belshazzar mock the Lord in his drunken pride? Because he thinks he is so cool, that he wants everyone to see that he can even dare God at this party. His intoxication gave evil a free access to his heart. So, Belshazzar lifts his toast to the lusts of his flesh and teaches us some valuable lessons to live by. His carnality reveals to us some unforgettable truth:

♦ **Sin has the power to lead us to "party on" and push God far from our thoughts!**
♦ **When reverence for God is lost, the door opens wide for the fleshly nature to take over!**
♦ **It is foolish to presume that rebellion doesn't carry negative consequences!**
♦ **Pride is our greatest enemy, humility is our greatest friend!**

And remember: since only Jesus and the Gospel can satisfy and transform our hearts, why would we waste time looking in any other direction?

Nuf Sed!

October 14
"The Party Is Over"
Daniel 5 – Part II

"Suddenly the fingers of a human hand appeared and wrote on the plaster of the wall" (Daniel 5:5).

"So, King Belshazzar became even more terrified and his face grew more pale. His nobles were baffled" (v.9).

Yesterday, we documented the carnality of Belshazzar. Today, we'll see the consequences of poor choices. What happens when Belshazzar flaunts his excess and allows his intoxication to take over? His party comes to a crashing end!

2. I See the "Confrontation" of the Lord" (v.5-24).
"You have set yourself up against the Lord of heaven" (v.23).
Without warning, the Lord crashed Belshazzar's party. God supernaturally writes a message on the wall and the party goers are stunned. Someone who is omniscient is present and knows what's going on! The attendees watch the writing, as a hand with fingers leaves a message. The king becomes troubled, and looks for the interpretation. Daniel acts with boldness and tells the king why his party was interrupted:
♦ "But you his son, O Belshazzar, have not humbled yourself" (v.22).
♦ "You have set yourself up against the Lord" (v.23).
The king's attention is arrested so that Daniel can explain the interpretation.

3. I See the "Consequences" and The Message to Us All (v.25-31).
"Mene, Mene Tekel, Parsin" (v.25).
Four cryptic words (written in Chaldean) glowed on the plaster wall. But what do they mean?
♦ **"Mene, Mene"** means, "God has **numbered** you". It means that our days are numbered, life has its limits, and none of us can waste the opportunity in serving God.
♦ **"Tekel"** means, "God is **weighing** you". It means that all of us will give an account to God for our life on earth. While we trust in the work of Jesus alone for salvation, reward will be given for our labors in His Name!
♦ **"Parsin"** means, "**Divided**". For Belshazzar, the Babylonian kingdom was divided and given over to Media and Persia. For you and me, there must be a dividing, sifting, and separation of what is holy and what is sinful. The message from the party is in three words:
  1. Numbered: Your life and mine has its limit of days.
  2. Weighed: You and I will give an account to God one day.
  3. Divided: You and I will live in eternity with our choices made on earth.

The take-a-way?

The party goers could keep the Persians outside with walls (for a season), but they couldn't keep God outside the party. The Holy Spirit can break through and interrupt when we least expect it.

Nuf Sed!

October 15
"When Lions Roar"
Daniel 6 – Part I

"Now when Daniel learned that the decree had been published, he went home to his upstairs room where the windows opened toward Jerusalem. Three times a day he got down on his knees and prayed, giving thanks to his God, just as he had done before. Then these men went as a group and found Daniel praying and asking God for help." (Daniel 6:10, 11)

If you've ever wondered what to do when you don't know what to do, Daniel 6 gives us wisdom from above. It's the account of how Daniel processed his betrayal in the place of disciplined prayer. He teaches you and me how to take a stand for God, regardless of the cost. Here is the context of the "lions' den" chapter.

From Daniel chapter 5 to 6, a new government has been introduced. Although Cyrus was the conqueror, Darius the Mede is introduced as the ruling monarch in Babylon. Whereas Nebuchadnezzar's reign was autocratic and absolute (he shared authority with no one), Darius had 120 princes who shared responsibility and leadership. Over the 120 princes, there were three presidents of whom Daniel was preferred.

What did the 120 princes do? They were in place to:
♦ Assure the orderly levying of taxes and maintain a system of collection and accounting.
♦ Prevent anyone from stealing from (or undermining) the king.

So, what happened to Daniel because he was preferred above the other presidents and princes? What happened when his good job reflected on those around him? What happened when Daniel's virtue exposed the vice in those nearby? What happened in the hearts of those filled with jealousy and envy who worked along side of Daniel?

"The administrators and the satraps tried to find grounds for charges against Daniel in his conduct of government affairs, but they were unable to do so. They could find no corruption in him, **because he was trustworthy and neither corrupt nor negligent**." (v.4)

The rivals lied to the king, saying that everyone was united in a new decree. The decree stated that no one could pray to anyone except King Darius (v.7). King Darius put the decree in writing (v.9), and Daniel had a choice to make: will he bow to the pressure, or will he stay true to the Lord? Notice Daniel's response:

"When Daniel learned that the decree had been published, he went home… got down on his knees and prayed, giving thanks to his God, **just as he had done before**" (v.10).

Wow! Even after being threatened with the den of lions, Daniel refused to bow down to intimidation. Why? Because Daniel feared the Lord and wanted to stay true to God. Daniel flat out counted the cost and refused to get even with his betrayers. Daniel teaches us valuable truths to enjoy the journey with a healthy heart: The take-a-ways?

♦ **The fear of God conquers every other fear!**

♦ **A consistent prayer life prepares you for the unexpected!**

♦ **True, inward security is found in our walk with God, not our work for God!**

Nuf Sed!

October 16
"When Lions Roar"
Daniel 6 – Part II

"I issue a decree that in every part of my kingdom people must fear and reverence the God of Daniel" (Daniel 6:26).

Yesterday, we learned that Daniel feared God, which conquered every lesser fear. We saw Daniel's response to the lies of his co-workers and the decree of the king. We discovered Daniel's spiritual response when in between a rock and a hard place.

Today, notice the overruling principle of God revealed in Daniel 6. Notice the clear practical take-a-ways in the midst of Daniel's betrayal. Remember now:

♦ The schemers had a fail proof plan to eliminate the godly man they envied.
♦ They dug a pit that Daniel could not escape.
♦ They had the highest authority in the land on their side.
♦ They thought for sure that the lions would rid them of the one they considered a rival.

But God had another plan for Daniel, and God has another plan for you. Look at what the Holy Spirit is saying as you enjoy the journey and walk with the Lord:

1. There Is the Principle of "Prayer"!
"Now when Daniel learned that the decree had been published, he went home to his upstairs room… got down on his knees and prayed" (v.10).

In the face of death, Daniel put his focus on God and allowed God to calm his heart and steady him. He prayed to the One who is over all and determines all. Daniel focused on the solution more than the problem! His consistent walk with God had prepared him for the unexpected!

2. There Is the Principle of "Presence"!
"O King, live forever! My God sent his angel, and he shut the mouths of the lions" (v.21, 22).

What's the discovery in the lion's den? It is this: God doesn't shield us from every pain, threat, and loss in life – but His presence goes with us every step of the journey! In other words, as you do the will of God from the heart, the Lord will never leave you, nor forsake you! You really do have a **Blessed Assurance!**

3. There Is the Principle of "Promotion"!
"So Daniel prospered during the reign of Darius and the reign of Cyrus the Persian" (v.28).

What happened to Daniel's accusers? They ended up in the pit prepared for Daniel. What happened to Daniel? He was promoted and favored because God is God, and man is just man. Daniel teaches us to trust God with the things and people outside of our control. He teaches us to "rest" in God's sovereignty! He teaches us to focus on the Lord and not our enemies whenever we are betrayed.

The take-a-way?
♦ **Man proposes, but God disposes!**
♦ **Man cannot curse or stop what God has blessed and favored!**

Nuf Sed!

October 17
"Suffering With Joy"
I Peter I

"Though you have not seen him, you love him; and even though you do not see him now, you believe in him and are filled with an inexpressible and glorious joy" (I Peter 1:8).

Peter wrote this letter to encourage believers who were going through afflictions and disappointments. He mentions suffering 16 times, by using eight different Greek terms. He gives us incredible wisdom and insight – how God gives us joy in the midst of the vicissitudes of life.

1. Your Joy Is Founded Upon "Right Standing"
"Who have been chosen according to the foreknowledge of God the Father, through the sanctifying work of the Spirit for obedience to Jesus Christ and sprinkling by his blood: Grace and peace be yours in abundance" (v.2).

Peter begins with the basis of all joy, which is knowing that we've all rebelled and broken the Law of God, and we've all stood guilty before a Holy God! Yet, God in His mercy has sprinkled Christ's blood at Calvary and made us guiltless in God's sight. In other words, the "work of the Spirit" (v.2) draws us to Jesus, and leads to obedient living. The end result is **"grace"** (v.2), which is undeserved favor, and **"peace"** (v.2), which is security in God's acceptance of us.

2. Your Joy Is Founded Upon A "Future Hope"
"Praise be to the God and Father of our Lord Jesus Christ! In His great mercy he has given us new birth into a living hope through the resurrection of Jesus Christ from the dead" (v.3). The "living hope" Peter writes about is something functioning inside of every believer:

♦ You know that as Jesus was raised from the dead, so you will be raised from the dead.

♦ You know that as Jesus ascended to heaven, so you will spend eternity in heaven.

♦ You know that as Jesus was kept by His Father, so you will be kept by your Father.

In fact, our future inheritance "can never perish, spoil, or fade- kept in heaven for you" (v.4).

3. Your Joy Is Founded Upon a "Deep Assurance"
"Who through faith are shielded by God's power" (v.5).

The word "shielded" means to be kept, protected, guarded, and garrisoned about. Peter used a military term here that refers to soldiers who guard someone for safekeeping. It refers to the continual nature of God's keeping power. It means that God will keep you and sustain you in every season of your life. This takes the worry out of living.

4. Your Joy Is Founded Upon "Life Change"

"These have come so that your faith – of greater worth than gold, which perishes even though refined by fire – may be proved genuine and may result in praise, glory, and honor when Jesus Christ is revealed" (v.7).

What gives us joy when we go through the fire or suffering? Like gold, you know that you'll come out better than you went in. In other words, fire can refine us, grow us, and make us more like Jesus. And this results in "inexpressible and glorious joy" (v.8).

The take-a-way?
Humility will allow trials to produce something good; pride will leave us worse off than before!

Nuf Sed!

October 18
"Suffering with Patience"
I Peter 2

"If you suffer for doing good and you endure it, this is commendable before God." (v.20)

You are not exempt! That's right; you are not exempt from criticism, mistreatment, betrayal, misunderstanding, pain, or being offended. The issue is not the event; the issue is how you process the event. Certain events and people we cannot change. But, our attitude towards people and events – we can change! And Peter shows us how to be patient when facing injury. We learn the reward and blessing of refusing to retaliate or get even. Notice the two absolutes that surround this text:

1. We All Will Have Injustices to Endure!
"For it is commendable if a man bears up under the pain of unjust suffering because he is conscious of God" (v.19).

Peter is addressing Christian slaves or workmen under someone's authority. Many were getting saved and found themselves facing injury and unfair treatment. But, how do you endure grief and take it patiently when you are injured? Only one way:

"Because he is **conscious of God**" (v.19), which means: the natural tendency is to spit back when spat upon. But when we are "**conscious of God**" (v.19), we allow our born again conscience to dictate our behavior and not our injury. In other words, when we are "**conscious of God**" (v.19), we are aware that God is aware of what happens to us. We are conscious that God will render justice and will right all wrongs. We are conscious that God will be our strength in the meantime. And this allows us to "endure it" (v.20) and remain patient under fire.

2. We All Have an Example to Follow!
"Christ suffered for you, leaving you an example, that you should follow in his steps" (v.21).

How could Jesus "not retaliate" (v.23) and, "when he suffered, he made no threats" (v.23)? Because: "He entrusted himself to him who judges justly" (v.23).

The word "**entrusted**" means, "to deposit for safe keeping." It means to "entrust" or to "hand over" to our Heavenly Father. The words, "judges justly," means that Jesus knew that His Father would vindicate what needed to be vindicated. It means that we don't have to waste time defending, plotting, scheming, or fretting. It means that if you've been insulted, injured, slandered, mistreated, or betrayed, you can turn it over to God by looking at Jesus. And as you look at Jesus, God will give you grace to endure with patience!

The take-a-way?

The more that we look at Jesus, who suffered on our behalf, the more we can be patient when tempted to retaliate!

Nuf Sed!

October 19
"Suffering with Forgiveness"
I Peter 3

"Do not repay evil with evil or insult with insult, but with blessing, because to this you were called so that you may inherit a blessing." (I Peter 3:9)

Peter's audience was experiencing pain, hurt, and injury. Yet Peter tells the recipients of his letter, here is how you can enjoy the journey and be spiritually healthy. He says in I Peter 3: "Whoever would love life and see good days" (v.10). In other words, if you want to "inherit a blessing" (v.9) and "love life" (v.10), you will have to be a good forgiver in your journey. Without a forgiving spirit, we will default and "repay evil with evil" and, "insult with insult" (v.9). And none of us are exempt from the temptation that Peter is addressing: All of us will be tempted to retaliate (v.9). All of us will be tempted to lash out (v.10). All of us will be tempted to do evil (v.11). All of us will be tempted to quit praying and take matters into our own hands (v.12). But if we, "would love life and see good days" (v.10), God tells us how through Peter's instructions. We are invited to cooperate with God in three ways:

1. We Enjoy Life Through a "Forgiving Spirit"
"But even if you should suffer for what is right, you are blessed" (v.14).

What makes it possible to still enjoy life when you suffer wrongfully at the hands of another? A forgiving spirit that doesn't keep score of wrong doing! A willingness to cancel a debt as if it never existed. A decision to relinquish over to God what someone else has done to you. Why is forgiveness so important to live life with joy and health? Because an enemy in the heart is worse than 10,000 in the field! So, if you're suffering pain at the hands of another, why not pray this way today: "Lord callous my knees and not my heart."

2. We Enjoy Life Through An "Undivided Heart"
"But in your heart set apart Christ as Lord" (v.15).

The words "set apart" mean to sanctify, honor, and give the primary place of. It means to commit and surrender every area of my life to the Lordship of Jesus. It means to live transparent, refuse to cover up, and abhor the thought of living life with a divided heart.

3. We Enjoy Life Through A "Clear Conscience"
"Keeping a clear conscience, so that those who speak maliciously against your good behavior in Christ may be ashamed of their slander" (v.16).

A clear conscience is one that doesn't accuse you of sin and disobedience. A clear conscience provides you with tranquility and power amidst every lie and accusation. A clear conscience is your greatest defense in every disappointment, detour, and delay in your journey.

So, what's the Gospel motivation to forgive, live undivided and transparent? "For Christ died for sins once and for all, the righteous for the unrighteous, to bring you to God" (v.18).

The take-a-way is easy to discern today:
♦ **It's easy to forgive when we comprehend how much God has forgiven us!**

Nuf Sed!

October 20
"Suffering with Obedience"
I Peter 4

"Therefore, since Christ suffered in his body, arm yourselves also with the same attitude, because he who has suffered in his body is done with sin. As a result, he does not live the rest of his earthly life for evil human desires, but rather for the will of God" (I Peter 4:1,2).

It's no secret at all, that everyone will experience unfulfilled expectations, spiritual warfare, and criticism while faithfully serving God. It's also no secret, that we will be better off or worse off after suffering in the flesh. How can suffering be a friend in disguise? Only by responding God's way so that sin loses its power within our hearts. Remember this: suffering in and of itself never produces spiritual growth. Growth and fruit only come as we obey God and do His will in the midst of our pain. Grasp the following two realities:
♦ When we submit to God, humble ourselves, and deny our flesh, we will grow beyond previous boundaries. But...
♦ When we justify our unresolved anger, stew in our own juice, and sour inwardly, we fall prey to satan's scheme and our pain works against us.
This is why (I Peter 4:1, 2) is powerful and speaks so clearly about a healthy heart in the journey:

1. We Have An "Example" to Follow!
"Therefore, since Christ suffered in his body" (v.1).
This means that Jesus suffered the ultimate degree for his obedience. It means that Jesus denied himself and refused to retaliate or attack. It means that Jesus was hurt and suffered to bear reproach for our sin. Jesus remained steadfast and would not be detoured from his Father's will which was the cross on our behalf.

2. We Have An "Exhortation" to Obey!
"Arm yourselves also with the same attitude" (v.1).
Which means, that we must be willing to embrace the same mind of Jesus as He refused to be detoured. It means that we must be wise and alert to not retaliate when our flesh is wounded. It means that we can be "armed" to defend against enemy attacks to sour and sideline us. It means that beholding Jesus will allow us to become like Jesus!

3. We Have An "Encouragement" to Receive!
"He who has suffered in his body is done with sin. As a result, he does not live the rest of his earthly life for evil, human desires, but rather for the will of God" (v.1, 2).
This is you and me cooperating with God by obeying the initial promptings of the Holy Spirit. As we do this, to that same degree the decisions of the flesh will lose their appeal and power in our hearts. As we

obey God in our suffering, we receive grace from above. As we draw closer to Jesus in our pain, we will be able to forgive our offenders and make progress in God.

The take-a-way?
♦ **Healthy people build with the bricks that others throw at them!**
♦ **Healthy people allow their sufferings to purge them instead of poison them!**
♦ **Healthy people allow their crosses to crucify their flesh instead of ruin their spirit!**

Nuf Sed!

"Suffering with Reward"
I Peter 5

"And the God of all grace, who called you to his eternal glory in Christ, after you have suffered a little while, will himself restore you and make you strong, firm, and steadfast" (v.10).

Peter concludes his letter on some very victorious notes, and the truth revealed is "Good News" to your heart. We are left with a great reminder, and it revolves around three realities.

1. There Is A "Calling" Upon Your Life!
"Who called you to his eternal glory in Christ" (v.10).

This calling refers to the divine summons and royal invitation for all believers. It is a calling to the eternal glory awaiting every Christian. This eternal glory is the ultimate consummation of what we all live for. It is the ultimate expectation and eternal prize that will never fade or be touched by sin. What is it? It is the privilege, joy and honor of living with Jesus forever in our glorified bodies in a real place called heaven. In other words, God wants you to enjoy Him now and forever! He wants you to live on earth with great expectation – both now and for what is coming.

2. There Is A "Contradiction" We All Have to Face!
"After you have suffered a little while" (v.10).

The contradiction is clear here: On one hand, God gives us grace to sustain us in every season of life. On the other hand, we have an eternal future with Jesus in a place called heaven. But in between we have to live with the tension of: "After you have suffered a little while" (v.10). Peter's audience was suffering great pain, severe trial, and being tried by fire. So, God speaks the truth that helps us all through our wilderness seasons. What's the truth? The truth is:
Suffering is a part of the Christian life, but it's only for a season, or a "little while" (v.10).
♦ Every season is just a season; it is temporary and will pass!
♦ Every season is orchestrated by the same faithful God!
♦ Every season is preparing you for the next season!

Remember friend; wishing you were somewhere else will waste the season you are in!

3. There Is "Character" Reward for The Faithful!
"God… will himself restore you and make you strong, firm, and steadfast" (v.10).
♦ The word **"restore"** means: to take broken limbs and mend back together. And when others see God do this, they will glorify God in you!
♦ The word **"strong"** means: to establish and make firm and solid. This is

God making you reliable and faithful in your character.

♦ The word **"firm"** means: to strengthen and empower to withstand every attack. It is God making you strong in your inner man.

♦ The word **"steadfast"** means: to settle, secure, or ground. It is God changing our character so that we can be trusted in every season.

The take-a-way?

Pain can have a refining influence on the soul, and point people to God when they see God in us!

Nuf Sed!

October 22
"Jesus In the Church"

"Do not be afraid, I am the First and the Last. I am the Living One; I was dead, and behold I am alive for ever and ever" (Revelation 1:17,18).

O ver the next ten days, I want you to see Jesus in the church. I want you to see what John saw when the Lord pulled back the curtain of Heaven to reveal Himself. What John saw speaks volumes to you and me; it's a message that is relevant and life changing! Remember:

John had refused to worship the Roman Emperor and was banished to a 50 square mile island called Patmos. Patmos was a Roman Colony for prisoners. It was here that Jesus revealed Himself to John, and John was told to write down the revelation and send it to the seven churches in Asia Minor. But who is this Jesus that revealed Himself to John? Jesus is called:

♦ **"The Faithful Witness"** (v.5), which means, Jesus is the One Person who can be depended on in every season of life!

♦ **"The Firstborn from the dead"** (v.5), which means Jesus is the "first" in a long line of believers who will be resurrected as well.

♦ **"The Ruler of The Kings of The Earth"** (v.5), which means, Jesus has been exalted and remains Sovereign of the earth.

♦ **"Freed Us From Our Sins By His Blood"** (v.5), which means Jesus is our redeemer and has released us from our debt of sin.

♦ **"Made Us To Be A Kingdom And Priests To Serve"** (v.6), which means that you and I have been given access into the very presence of God.

But what is Jesus doing now and what did John see in his vision of Jesus? It reveals His ministry in your life this moment:

1. **John saw the Flowing Garment** (v.13) which is a picture of the priestly robe and Jesus ministering as our high priest on behalf of His children.

2. **John saw the White Hair** (v.14), which refers to the purity, holiness, wisdom and perfection of Jesus.

3. **John saw the Eyes as a Flame of Fire** (v.14), which symbolizes Jesus' ability to see and penetrate the innermost recesses of the heart.

4. **John saw the Feet of Brass** (v.15), which speaks of sin being judged and consumed, and that Jesus can eradicate sin that wants to control us.

5. **John Heard the Voice** (v.15) revealing that Jesus still speaks to His sheep and communicates His will to us.

6. **John saw the Right Hand** (v.16) holding the seven messengers. This is a picture of Jesus keeping and protecting those who serve Him.

7. **John saw the Sword** (v.16), which reveals the ability of the Word to pierce through and change any human heart.

How do we respond when we really see Jesus as He is? "When I saw Him I fell at His feet as though dead" (1:17)

The take-a-way?

Those who really see Jesus never strut – but are reduced to awe, reverence, and deep humility!

Nuf Sed!

October 23
"Restored To Your First Love"
(The Church In Ephesus)

"You have forsaken your first love" (Revelation 2:4).

Jesus told John to write to the "angel" (v.1) or pastor of seven local churches. Jesus is seen (or revealed) walking in the midst of His church. While all the churches are imperfect, Jesus is still present because it's His local church – not ours.

The first church addressed was the church in Ephesus. Ephesus was a busy metropolis where Paul had planted a church. God had wrought spectacular miracles to get the attention of the people. Lives were transformed, and Jesus reveals three things about this local church:

1. There Was a Commendation from Jesus!
"I know your deeds, your hard work and your perseverance. I know that you cannot tolerate wicked men... and have endured hardships for my name" (v.2,3).
♦ Jesus commends **servanthood**, because the believers suffered personal loss to advance the local church.
♦ Jesus commends **patience**, because the believers endured under trial and test, and refused to quit when fatigued.
♦ Jesus commends **convictions**, because the church stood firmly while many worshipped the god of sex and sensuality.
♦ Jesus commends **discernment**, as the believers stood up against false teaching to maintain doctrine purity.

2. There Was a Correction from Jesus!
What was the one thing that Jesus said was missing in Ephesus? Believers had "forsaken" their first love. The one danger that had crept in was this: believers were going through the motions, but intimacy with Jesus was fading away. The second generation of believers were losing their fire and fervor for Jesus. Labor, service, and busyness was replacing intimacy with the Savior. There was a "cooling off" and loss of joy, fervency, and sweetness. Prayer was neglected, priorities were misplaced, and Jesus gave us a call for action:

3. There was a Call to Return!
"Remember that height from which you have fallen! Repent and do the things you did at first" (v.5).
Stop! Hear what Jesus is saying! His message reveals that it's never too late to start over again!
♦ **Remember** where you used to be and where you can be again!
♦ **Repent** and turn from what has distracted you from Jesus!
♦ **Repeat** your first works, and place yourself before the Lord for His rest, renewal, and refreshing!

The take-a-way?

Jesus, out of love, interrupted church life in Ephesus. And Jesus, out of love, is calling you and me aside to intimacy, union, and oneness this day!

Nuf Sed!

October 24
"You Are Rich"
(The Church in Smyrna)

"I know your afflictions and your poverty – yet you are rich" (Revelation 2:9).

The Lord had a great word for the believers in Smyrna, and the Lord speaks the same word to you and me. It's a word that lifts the heart and tells us what Jesus wants you to always remember.

Smyrna was a city located 35 miles north of Ephesus. It was a commercial center filled with pagan temples, and still exists today. Today, it is called Izmir. The name Smyrna means, "bitter". It received the name from one of its chief commercial products called Myrrh. Myrrh was a bitter gum like substance taken from a shrub. It was used primarily in five ways:
♦ For making perfume (Psalm 45:8).
♦ For the holy anointing oil (Exodus 30:23).
♦ For embalming the dead (John 19:39).
♦ For purification of women (Esther 2:12).
♦ For relieving pain (Mark 15:23).

Myrrh had to be crushed to become useful, and Smyrna was experiencing crushing affliction and persecution. Many new believers were being persecuted because they would not worship the gods and goddesses of the day. Jewish leaders were influencing the city officials to stamp out the Lord's church. And in the midst of this personal attack, Jesus looks out of heaven and sends an encouraging word. What does Jesus say?

1. "I know your afflictions and your poverty – yet you are rich" (v.9). The affliction refers to the most severe persecution. The believers were suffering at the hands of the Roman government. Christians were being imprisoned, abused, scorned, robbed, and martyred. The poverty refers to being destitute, all because of refusing to proclaim that "Caesar is Lord". And Jesus says, **"I know"** (v.9) what you are going through, both then and now!

2. "I know the slander of those who say they are Jews and are not, but are a synagogue of satan" (v.9). To "slander" (or blaspheme) means to speak evil of someone. It means: to ridicule, discredit, and lie. The enemy of the believers was using their tongues to stir up trouble and turn people against one another. And Jesus says, **"I know"**. And how does Jesus want you to respond when you are criticized unjustly?

3. "Do not be afraid of what you are about to suffer… be faithful even to the point of death, and I will give you a crown of life" (v.10). What protects us from fear, wrong, and intimidation? Knowing that Jesus is, **"The First and The Last"** (v.8), which means He is in charge and over everything that touches your life! What else protects us from fear in the face of persecution? Knowing that, **"The Crown of Life"** awaits the faithful! The

"Crown of Life" is the reward of eternal life and living with Jesus when this earthly life is over. Oh friend, the only way to really enjoy the journey, is to live in light of the life to come!

The take-a-way?
Since Jesus knows all about your afflictions, your accusers, and your fears – you can rest well and trust in His amazing grace and divine support!

Nuf Sed!

October 25
"Manna, Stones, and A New Name"
(The Church In Pergamos)

"To Him who overcomes, I will give some of the hidden manna. I will also give him a white stone with a new name written on it, known only to him who receives it" (Revelation 2:17).

The third letter from Jesus to the seven churches was to the believers in Pergamos. Pergamos was a city north of Smyrna in the western part of Asia Minor; and it was filled with temples devoted to idol worship. Jesus described it as a city, "where Satan has his throne" (v.13). Yet Jesus had a message as a "sharp, double edged sword" (v.12). This means that His word can cut through the hardest heart and separate the sinner from their sin. It means His word is law (to expose our hearts) and grace (to heal our hearts). The heart of Jesus is revealed to us in three ways in Pergamos:

1. I see the "Joy" of Jesus:
"I know where you live... yet you remain true to my name. You did not renounce your faith in me" (v.13).

Jesus observes, delights, and commends the believers in Pergamos. Why? Because of their loyalty, purity, and tenacity. The church was faithful to Jesus despite the culture and cesspool of temptation. Believers remained pure in their doctrine, teaching, and testimony. Jesus reveals to us, that His grace is sufficient to keep you steadfast regardless of your environment, setting, workplace, or surroundings.

2. I See The "Correction" of Jesus:
"Nevertheless, I have a few things against you: you have people there who hold to the teaching of Balaam... likewise you also have those who hold to the teaching of the Nicolaitans" (v.14,15).
♦ The doctrine of Balaam came from Balac, the Moabite king near Palestine. He hired Balaam to curse Israel, with no results. He then conceived a plan (Numbers 22-25) to corrupt Israel from the inside out. He advised the Moabite girls to seduce Israel's men to intermingle and intermarry. The result was idol worship, immorality, and church members tolerating what God hated.
♦ The doctrine of the Nicolaitans was believing that the sins of the body did not affect your spiritual man. This gave license to be a playboy in the temple while being a choir boy in the church. The result was sexual immorality being practiced, condoned, and accepted by a group within the Pergamos church.

3. I See The "Provision" of Jesus:
"To him who overcomes, I will give... hidden manna... a white stone... a new name" (v.17).

What is your reward in choosing to live for God with an undivided heart?
What's the payback for resting in and trusting in Jesus for your salvation?

♦ The Hidden Manna – means that Jesus will provide all the spiritual food (grace) you need to be sustained in your journey.

♦ A White Stone – refers to divine acquittal, full acceptance, and total innocence because of the work of Jesus on your behalf.

♦ A New Name – represents our enrollment into the New Jerusalem for all eternity. And, it is "known only to him who receives it" (v.17).

The take-a-way?

The name "Pergamos" means, "married", which reminds us that a husband or wife that is 99 percent faithful is really not faithful at all!

Nuf Sed!

October 26
"A Holy Inspection"
(The Church In Thyatira)

"You tolerate that woman Jezebel, who calls herself a prophetess. By her teaching she misleads my servants into sexual immorality and the eating of food sacrificed to idols" (Revelation 2:20).

I'm calling this devotion, "A Holy Inspection" because Jesus said, "I am he who searches hearts and minds" (v.23). He is searching us inwardly, not to destroy us, but to change us where change is needed. So, what needed changing in Thyatira?

Thyatira was a city between Pergamos and Sardis. It was known for its trade guilds and unions. The two major industries were wood and a purple dye. Jesus wrote to the believers in Thyatira for one major reason; they were being deceived and corrupted by the doctrine of Jezebel. Notice the message from Jesus to our hearts:

1. The Church Was "Busy" and Active!
"I know your deeds, your love and faith, your service and perseverance, and that you are now doing more than you did at first" (v.19)

Jesus commends our works, care for the needy, service offered, faithfulness under adversity, patience under trial and commitment to growth, expansion and progress. But something was happening in the Thyatira church that couldn't be ignored.

2. The Church was "Deceived" and Beguiled!
"Nevertheless… you tolerate that woman Jezebel" (v.20).

Jezebel was an actual woman teaching in the church, who was deceiving people by promoting her teaching:
♦ That believers could still worship pagan idols after their salvation.
♦ That believers could be sexually active outside of marriage to guarantee social acceptance.
♦ That believers didn't need to separate from sin or offend any compromising heart.

The result of this seduction was that believers were backsliding, church leadership were losing their convictions, and hearts were being destroyed from within. The subtlety of sin was weakening the testimony and witness of the Lord. Believers were willing to compromise their morality to be accepted by the majority. In fact, Jesus called Jezebel's teaching, "Satan's so-called deep secrets" (v.24). But notice God's mercy and grace for us all:

3. The Church Was "Invited" To Stand Tall!
"Only hold on to what you have until I come" (v.25).

How can we "hold on" and be spiritually strong? By grasping what Jesus says; "I am he who searches hearts" (v.23). In other words, Jesus searches our hearts by the spirit and brings to the surface what I need to change. Why? So that you and I can be healthy in the Lord! It's so important that Jesus cries out, "Unless they repent of her ways" (v.22). Jesus calls us to repent for one reason – so that He can offer his mercy and grace that brings life change. And, God will restore, forgive, and empower us to live strong in the midst of a world full of the Jezebel spirit!

The take-a-way?
When Jesus captures our hearts completely, every lesser idol and god will lose its captivating power to control us!

Nuf Sed!

October 27
"Restored Back to Life"
(The Church In Sardis)

"Wake up! Strengthen what remains and is about to die, for I have not found your deeds complete in the sight of my God" (Revelation 3:2).

The tendency of fire is to go out! And, unless we do our part in the process, it's possible for any of us to dry up, cool off, or flame out. There's just no such thing as an anointed (full of fire) couch potato (lazy person). Sardis believers were in trouble! The city of Sardis was the capital of Lydia and located on a commercial trade route. Two times Sardis has been overcome and conquered by the enemy: once by Cyrus of Persia, and once by Alexander the Great. Both times the city neglected to watch the city walls. Thus, we have language from Jesus, "Wake up" (v.2), "Remember" (v.3), and, "I will come like a thief" (v.3).

Before Jesus gets specific with us, He tells about the "seven spirits and the seven stars" (v.1). The sevenfold spirits are a picture of the burning lamp (4:5). It refers to life, fullness, and power of the Holy Spirit which gives us life, vitality, renewal, and revival. The seven stars refers to the local pastors in the church who are responsible for the spiritual condition where they serve. In other words, the church leadership is accountable for what goes on, the spiritual climate, and what is being taught. Notice the two things that Jesus speaks to your heart and mine:

1. The "Condition" Of the Sardis Believers!
"You have a reputation of being alive, but you are dead" (v.1).

In other words, Sardis churchgoers had an appearance of life, a good reputation, and lots of good works. But one thing was missing – the fullness and presence of God's spirit. There was a form of worship, ritual and ceremony, activity and labor, and preaching and teaching. Yet, the indictment against Sardis, was people who were attending meetings, but not meeting God in the meetings. Jesus said there was deadness in the Sardis church. Deadness may mean that there was worship of the past, more concern with form than life, love of tradition over love of Christ, or loss of fervor to reach the lost. "Lord renew the deadness in every area of my life", is a good prayer for us all!

2. The "Calling" of the Sardis Believers!
What does Jesus call us to?
♦ **"Wake up"** (v.2), which means to stir up your desire to be up-to-date in your spiritual life!
♦ **"Strengthen"** (v.2), which means that God intends to renew, revive, and restore your vitality.
♦ **"Remember"** (v.3), which means to remind yourself of God's peace, forgiveness, freedom and future resurrection.
♦ **"Repent"** (v.3), which means to turn back to God who will restore and

baptize you in the Spirit over and over again!

What happens when we turn our hearts toward God? We will walk with Jesus, **"dressed in white"** (v.4) because we trust and rest in the righteousness of Jesus – and not ourselves!

The take-a-way?
"If you do not wake up" (v.3), means that all of us can be spiritually awakened, renewed, and restored, and we can experience divine life and power in our inner man!

Nuf Sed!

October 28
"An Open Door"
(The Church In Philadelphia)

"I have placed before you an open door that no one can shut" (Revelation 3:8).

This letter from Jesus was given to the believers in Philadelphia and to us! Philadelphia was located on the borders of Lydia, Mysia, and Phrygia. It was a city where God planted a church, a church that was alive and faithful. Jesus had no rebukes or complaints against this church. Why? Because the believers were committed to one purpose – to carry out the great commission and reach the unreached! The one goal of the congregation was to make insiders out of outsiders. They flat out lived on mission! And, Jesus had a message for all of us to hear and believe. The words of Jesus are believable and guaranteed because of three reasons:

1. Jesus is **Holy** – which means, pure and without mixture.
2. Jesus is **True** – which means, genuine, worthy and reliable.
3. Jesus **Holds the Key of David** – which means Jesus alone has the authority to give us entrance into the very presence of God for communion and right standing.

And what does the Holy, True, and Reliable Jesus say to you and me? "I have placed before you an open door that no one can shut" (v.8). The church was alive and missional. The church also encountered resistance, rejection, and opposition. And, in the face of those who were serving the purpose of Satan (v.9), Jesus promised this to the faithful:

♦ No one can stop the church that is missional and outward!
♦ No one can close the door that Jesus has opened!
♦ No one can prevent Jesus from building His church!
♦ No one can withstand the congregation that lives to make Jesus' Name famous in their town!

In other words, it is impossible to shut down the church that has its mind off of itself. In fact, Jesus will even cause those with evil intentions to acknowledge that He is Lord:

"I will make them come and fall down at your feet and acknowledge that I have loved you" (v.9).

Jesus not only promises to build His church, but He also promises to remember and take notice of some things:

1. Jesus praises "little strength" (v.8), as the people were serving faithfully to see his work move forward.
2. Jesus praises those who "have kept My word" (v.8), or obeyed Him with joy and enthusiasm.
3. Jesus praises believers who, "have not denied My Name" (v.8), or refused to compromise under pressure and live for the god of approval.
4. Jesus praises believers who, "kept my command to endure patiently" (v.10) or remain faithful in spite of sorrow, pain, trial, and disappointment.

What is the take-a-way for those who "hold on" (v.11) and let no one "take your crown" (v.11)?

Nothing and no one has the power to keep you from doing what is right – because Jesus hasn't relinquished His authority over to anyone!

Nuf Sed!

October 29
"Let's Go Shopping"
(The Church In Laodicea)

"I counsel you to buy from me gold refined in the fire" (Revelation 3:18).

Many people love to shop. Have you ever picked up something in a store, viewed the price tag, and said to yourself, "It would be nice to have, but it cost too much."? The sticker shock surprised you and turned you off because it was just too expensive. Even Christians like to "window shop". In fact, Laodicea was filled with window shoppers. Laodicea was a wealthy banking center 40 miles East of Ephesus. It was known for its banking industry, a glossy black wool cloth, and a famous medical school. People in the church were settling for less than God's best because it cost too much. A whole group of people were not willing to pay the price. Some were unwilling to part with something valuable, to make room for something more valuable. Jesus pointed out two things in Laodicea that speak to our hearts:

1. There Was An "Offense" To Address!
"Because you are lukewarm, neither hot nor cold – I am about to spit you out of my mouth" (v.16)

Why were church goers an offense to the gospel?

♦ Believers had lost their **fervency**! "You are lukewarm" (v.16), means that some had become on-again-off-again with the Lord.

♦ Believers had lost their **humility**! "You say, 'I am rich; I have acquired wealth and do not need a thing'" (v.17), means that pride kept people from crying out to God. Their prosperity made them feel self-made and in need of nothing.

♦ Believers had lost their **sight**! "You do not realize that you are… blind" (v.17), means to be short-sighted with loss of vision for what is eternal.

♦ Believers had lost their **clothes**! "You are… naked" (v.17) means, to be unclothed in the righteousness of Jesus – believing that good works, religious duties, and material prosperity gives you right standing with God.

This provoked Jesus to say the following: "You are neither cold nor hot. I wish you were either one or the other" (v.15). The spiritually cold make no claim to be Christian. The spiritually hot are on fire for Jesus and make a difference for the kingdom. But the lukewarm appears to be something useful, yet in reality cannot be depended on. So, Jesus invites us:

2. There Was An "Offer" To Go Shopping!
"I counsel you to buy from me gold refined in the fire… white clothes to wear… and salve to put on your eyes" (v.18).

♦ **Gold** – refers to the things that really make your life rich (joy, peace, security, and hope).

♦ **White Clothes** – refers to being clothed in the righteousness of Jesus – innocent before God!

♦ **Anointed Eyes** – refers to seeing and sensing God's presence in your life and in His church.

Jesus invites us to buy (and go all in) and He stands at our heart's door and knocks! "Be earnest and repent" (v.19), means, "to boil and burn with zeal in turning around".

The take-a-way?
We will never enjoy this life unless we go all in and live for the world to come!

Nuf Sed!

October 30
"For Thy Pleasure"
Revelation 4:1-11

"For you created all things, and by your will they were created and have their being" (Rev. 4:11).

The setting in Revelation 4:1-11 is clear: John sees the throne of God! Sitting upon the throne is God's son, Jesus. John is overwhelmed with this vision and here's the reason why:

1. John sees a door open in heaven (the rapture has occurred).

2. John hears a commanding voice and is called to come up to Heaven to see something.

3. John has a deep spiritual experience (he sees the One sitting upon the throne of God).

Why is the Lord pictured as sitting upon the throne? To remind us that the Lord is still the Supreme Authority in all the world, that He reigns over everything that touches your life, and that He is the only One authorized to orchestrate end-time events. Notice what John sees in heaven:

♦ **A Jasper Stone** (v.3). The jasper is a diamond like stone and looked like a transparent crystal. John's vision was one of a flawless diamond of perfection in Jesus. The truth communicated to us here is, Jesus is flawless, perfect, makes no mistakes, and can be trusted at all times in your life. He is wise, always right and you can rest in His control and character.

♦ **A Carnelian (Sardine) Stone** (v.3). While the jasper stone is crystal clear, the sardine stone is a deep red. It is a beautiful cut ruby that gives off a fiery red glow. How can we look upon God like a jasper stone (so perfect and holy)? Only because the sardine red ruby reveals the price Jesus paid to declare us not guilty. John sees Jesus as a jasper stone, and John sees Jesus as a sardine stone, redeeming and paying the price to cover our sin.

♦ **The Rainbow** (v.3). The rainbow (Genesis 9:11-17) was a reminder to Noah and us, of God's faithfulness towards His own. It is a sign from God, that as God remembered Noah, so God will never forget you. It speaks clearly today; God knows who you are, where you are, what you need, and what He is doing! What else does John see around the throne? He sees 24 elders clothed in white with crowns upon their heads. The elders represent all of the redeemed (12 Patriarchs) from the tribes of Israel in the Old Testament and 12 apostles from the New Testament. They reveal:

1. **Accessibility to God** in the presence of Jesus (v.4).

2. **Acceptance by God** because we are clothed "in white" (v.4)

3. **Rest** like a "sea of glass" which is a picture of perfect peace (v.6).

John also saw the four living beings (cherubim/angels) which are a clear picture of Jesus (v.7):

♦ The **Lion** pictures Christ as King of the Jews -Matthew.

♦ The **Calf** pictures Christ as the obedient Servant – Mark.

♦ The **Man** pictures Christ as the Son of man – Luke.

♦ The **Eagle** pictures Christ's Divinity – John.

And, what are the angels doing in heaven? "Day and night, they never stop saying: 'Holy, Holy, Holy is the Lord God Almighty, who was, and is, and is to come'" (v.8). There is thanksgiving, and worship! No polishing of our halos, and no boasting of our crowns takes place! Just an acknowledgement that we were created for His pleasure!

The take-a-way?
God formed you in your mother's womb for His pleasure on earth; what an honor that is!

Nuf Sed!

October 31
"Worthy Is the Lamb"
Revelation 5:1-14

"You are worthy to take the scroll and to open its seals" (v.9). "Worthy is the Lamb, who was slain, to receive power and wealth and wisdom and strength and honor and glory and praise" (v.12).

On October 31, 1517, Martin Luther took his stand in Germany. Why? Because he knew that we are justified by faith alone; he knew that there is only One worthy who gives us entrance to a Holy God! What Luther saw in Scripture changed him forever! What John saw on the Isle of Patmos changed him forever as well! The scene in Revelation 5 reveals true worship! It's a scene where a problem and a solution collide. The following truth produces a worshipful heart like none other:

1. There Is a Problem Revealed By Tears (v.1-4)
"I wept and wept because no one was found who was worthy to open the scroll or look inside" (v.4).

The scroll (or book and document of events) represents man's original inheritance forfeited over to satan by sin. None of Adam's descendants are qualified to pay the redemption price of the world. Someone worthy (without sin) must be found to make restitution for us all. John began to weep (v.4) because no man or angel was worthy to approach God, open the book, and carry out the events of human history. If no redeemer can be found, then the curse is not removed, and creation forever remains in the hands of satan. But notice...

2. There Is a Person with The Answer (v.5-8)
"Then one of the elders said to me, 'Do not weep! See the Lion of the tribe of Judah, the Root of David, has triumphed. He is able to open the scroll and it's seven seals'" (v.5). Then I saw a Lamb, looking as if it had been slain" (v.6). "They sang a new song: 'You are worthy to take the scroll and to open its seals, because you were slain, and with your blood you purchased… from every tribe and language and people and nation'" (v.9).

The Lamb slain (Jesus) was symbolized in the Passover. The Lamb (in Egypt) was sacrificed so that the judgment of God could pass over the people. John sees Jesus as the center of attention in heaven because:
♦ Jesus has prevailed over satan in taking the book (v.7).
♦ Jesus has prevailed over sadness (v.8).
♦ Jesus has prevailed over sin and redeemed us (v.9).
♦ Jesus has prevailed over the second death as we "will reign" (v.10).

And, what is heaven's response to the Only One worthy of all our praise? "In a loud voice they sang: worthy is the Lamb" (v.13). "And the elders fell down and worshipped (v.14). Wow! All of heaven responds because Jesus has "purchased men for God" (v.9). So why do we sing and praise and worship?

Because worship is my response to the goodness of God. It is ascribing worthiness to God because of what He has done in opening the Book (scroll) to purchase and secure our ultimate destiny.

The take-a-way?
When I truly see what God has already done, my heart cannot help but respond in gratitude!

Nuf Sed!

"He Has Done Everything Well"

"People were overwhelmed with amazement. 'He has done everything well'; they said" (Mark 7:37).

For the next several days, I want you to see the healing ministry of Jesus. Before we do, I want to be very clear: Nobody knows why some people are miraculously healed while others are not! Nobody knows why God heals some and doesn't heal others the way we think He should. But this one thing we do know; we are taught in scripture to lay hands on the sick and pray for their recovery! We are taught that Jesus still heals the sick and performs miracles today!

In Mark 7, Jesus teaches us practical lessons and builds our faith. Mark is the only one of the evangelists to record this account of Jesus. Jesus has retired to a house to get some rest (v.24), but is now seen traveling through the region of Decapolis. Decapolis consisted of 10 cities which had been granted special privileges by the Roman conquerors in 65 B.C. . Notice:

"Some people brought to Him a man that was deaf and could hardly talk" (v.32). Notice what Jesus does:

1. Jesus separates and He spits!
"He took him aside… then He spit and touched the man's tongue" (v.33).

Jesus drew the man apart to remove his distractions and focus his attention. Jesus wanted to "narrow his interests" and there's a message in this text: Jesus knows that all of us must come apart or fall apart! He longs for intimacy in His presence. Jesus then touched the man's ears to awaken his faith and excite his expectations. When Jesus spit and touched the man's tongue, He was telling the man that healing virtue flows out from Jesus alone! The message is, Jesus wants to be merciful and exercise His healing power.

2. Jesus sighs and He speaks!
"He looked up to heaven and with a deep sigh said to him, 'EPHPHATHA'" (v.34).

Jesus looked up to heaven to let us know two things:
♦   Only the Father above has the power to answer prayer! and,
♦   He wanted us to know where our help comes from in time of need!

So why did Jesus sigh? The word "sigh" (v.34) means to groan – and to be touched with the feeling of our infirmities. It means that Jesus is moved with compassion towards the sick, infirmed and those enslaved by sin. And, why did Jesus speak the word "EPHPHATHA" (v.34)? This is an Aramaic word that means "Be released." Jesus releases the man from his bondage and Jesus still releases people today who call upon His Name! He breaks the power of canceled sin and sets the prisoner free!

The take-a-way?
  Sickness and sin are still subject to Divine authority – not because we are good, but because God is good!

Nuf Sed!

"When All Else Fails"

"Take heart, daughter, he said, your faith has healed you. And the woman was healed from that moment" (Matthew 9:22).

In Matthew 9:18, Jesus was approached by a devout Jew named Jarius. Jarius' daughter had died, and Jesus was asked to come quickly and pray for her. While Jesus was on His way to pray for the daughter, He was interrupted by a desperate woman in need of healing.

"Just then a woman who had been subject to bleeding for twelve years, came up behind him and touched the edge of his cloak. She said to herself, 'If I only touch his cloak, I will be healed' "(v. 21).

This woman had an incurable hemorrhage, living in misery for 12 long years. For 12 years she lived with "hopes deferred", waiting for the answer to arrive. On this particular day, she came up behind Jesus to touch Him. Why behind Him? Because according to Levitical law she was ceremonially unclean (Leviticus 15:19). In fact, she was considered defiled, an outcast, not good enough, and kept at a distance from Jesus.

♦ Jarius was a Jewish leader, (The woman had no prestige).
♦ Jarius was a church goer, (The woman was not allowed to worship).
♦ Jarius' need was public and known, (The woman's need was private and personal).

But take heart friend! No one in the world may know where you are, what you need and how long you've been praying. Yet, Jesus knows exactly the disappointment you carry upon your Heart! He knows where you live and He cares more than you can imagine. Notice the woman's actions:

1. She Was "Determined"!
"She said to herself, if I only touch his cloak, I will be healed" (v.21).
The woman was so determined that she let nothing and no one stand in her way. She didn't care who saw her pressing in to touch Jesus. She ditched every possible excuse you could use. She did her part to draw nigh to Jesus!

2. She Was "Delivered"!
"She told why she had touched him and how she had been instantly healed" (Luke 8:47).
Jewish men wore tassels of blue twisted cords on the corners of their outer garments. The woman chose to touch this part of Jesus' garment (the hem). When she did, she was immediately healed. Why healed? "Your faith has healed you. Go in peace" (v.48).

3. She Was "Distinguished"!
"Jesus turned and saw her. 'Take heart, daughter, he said' " (Matthew 9:22).

The woman planned to slip away unnoticed, but Jesus dealt with her publicly for all to see. Why? Because Jesus wanted all of us to understand the word **"Daughter"**. In other words, though people thought she was unclean and unworthy to receive a miracle, grace gives us right standing before God! Grace gives us the privilege of coming into the presence of Jesus! Grace makes us worthy because of Jesus' death, burial and resurrection!

The take-a-way?
It's not about trusting in what we have done; it's all about trusting in what "He" has done!

Nuf Sed!

"Peter's Mother-In-Law"

"Simon's mother-in-law was suffering from a high fever, and they asked Jesus to help her. So he bent over her and rebuked the fever, and it left her" (Luke 4:38, 29).

Jesus had just left Nazareth to set up His headquarters in Capernaum. Capernaum was the home of Peter, Andrew, James and John (on the northern edge of the Sea of Galilee). It was here where Jesus would live during His Galilean ministry. Why live here?
♦ To teach regularly in the synagogues.
♦ To have a home base to branch out and touch people with His compassion.
♦ To exercise power over demons and devils.
On this occasion, Jesus was in the synagogue (v.33) and encounters a man with an unclean spirit. Jesus rebukes the devil, delivers the man and then leaves the crowd and increasing fame (v.35-38). He then travels to Simon's house and teaches us some valuable (and practical) lessons:

1. Jesus May Not Be Early, But for Sure He's Never Late!
"Jesus left the synagogue and went to the home of Simon" (v.38).

In perfect timing, Jesus visited Simon as Simon's mother-in-law was suffering from a great fever. Fevers were common in the spring time near the marshy lands of Tabiga. And, this unscheduled illness and interruption doesn't throw Jesus off balance. Why not? Because Jesus knows more about your tomorrows than you know about your yesterdays! Your times and seasons really are orchestrated by the same faithful God!

2. Jesus Knows That Everybody Will Need Somebody Sometime!
"And they asked Jesus to help her" (v.38).

Peter and his comrades stood in the gap and petitioned Jesus to do something for Peter's wife's mother. They sought the Lord on behalf of another! In fact, Jesus was in Peter's house because Peter asked Jesus to be there. I discover right here, that all of us will encounter seasons when we are not strong! None of us are an island to ourselves! No one gets where they are alone! We really are a "body" and a "building" of lively stones connected together by Jesus.

3. Jesus Has Absolute Rule and Authority Over Sin and Sickness
"And laying his hands on each one, he healed them" (v. 40).
"Moreover, demons came out of many people, shouting, 'You are the Son of God' " (v. 41).

Jesus stood over the feverish woman, rebuked the fever, and she arose at once and began to serve those in the house (v. 39). And, not only was Peter's mother-in-law healed, but people brought many others to Jesus for prayer.

Jesus, then, healed the sick and cast demons out of hurting people. Wow! What's the moral of this story? It's simple:

♦ Jesus has authority over sickness (and)
♦ Jesus has authority over every sin of the heart!

The take-a-way?
Pride could have kept Jesus with the big crowds alone, but humility leaves you content with ministry to the one!

Nuf Sed!

November 4
"Down Through The Roof"

"He got up, took his mat and walked out in full view of them all. This amazed everyone and they praised God, saying, 'We have never seen anything like this' " (Mark 2:12).

Today you will see this one truth: Jesus has the power to deal with your sin and your sickness! In our text of Mark 2, Jesus was rejected by the Gadarenes and ended up back in Galilee one day. He is now in a house in Capernaum, where peasants and religious leaders are pressing in to investigate as He teaches. As Jesus teaches, we are told that, **"The power of the Lord was present for him to heal the sick" (Luke 5:17).**

While Jesus is teaching, four men take their sick friend to the house meeting. They can't get in because of the crowd, so they take the infirmed friend to the roof. They remove the tiles off the thatched roof and lower the man with ropes in the middle of the service. The teaching stops! People are stunned! The religious leaders are suspicious! But, Jesus is not indignant with the interruption. Why not? Because Jesus knows two things:

1. Jesus Can Handle Our Sin!
"When Jesus saw their faith, he said to the paralytic, 'Son, your sins are forgiven' " (Mark 2:5).

The religious scribes were furious when they heard this:
"Why does this fellow talk like that? He's blaspheming! **Who can forgive sins but God alone?" (v.7).**

The scribes were filled with indignation because Jesus claimed to be equal to God in forgiving sins. How does Jesus respond? He shows them that He has the power on earth to forgive sin (a miracle that you can't see) by performing a miracle that you can see (in healing the paralyzed man). As Jesus knew that He could forgive every sin of the man; today Jesus can forgive every sin of you and me! In fact, He has already paid the price to forgive us – all we need to do is trust in His grace! We serve a forgiving God – a God of new beginnings!

2. Jesus Can Handle Our Sickness!
"He got up, took his mat and walked out in full view of them all. This amazed everyone and they praised God" (v.12).

"Jesus saw their faith" (v.5) and was moved by the four friends who believed that Jesus could heal their friend. Jesus also knew what the religious leaders, "were thinking in their hearts" (v.8). And, in between the tension of the faith of friends and the doubt of religious leaders – Jesus heals the sick. Why? Because Jesus wanted to reveal:
♦ How much He loves people!
♦ How deep He can see into our hearts!

- How faith still pleases Him today!
- How a changed life can make "His Name" famous where we live and serve!

The take-a-way?
Jesus is a friend to both the sinner and the sick!

Nuf Sed!

"The Widow's Son at Nain"

"The dead man sat up and began to talk, and Jesus gave him back to his mother" (Luke 7:15).

If you've ever wondered or doubted about the timing of God in your life, this message is for you! I know your first name, it is you! God has truth to communicate to your heart today! And, it's truth that frees us from ourselves.

Luke 7 is all about the heart of Jesus being revealed. Jesus is confronted with four opportunities of ministry:

♦ The centurion's servant about to die (v.1-10).
♦ The grieving widow whose son had died (v.11-18).
♦ The bewildered prophet, John the Baptist (v.19-35).
♦ The repentant woman who broke the box (v.36-50).

On this particular occasion (in v.11-18), Jesus had just healed the centurion's servant. Jesus then began walking from Capernaum to Nain. Nain was a town 25 miles from Capernaum, and Jesus goes there without an invitation. And lest you believe in luck, or fate, or chance – grasp the set-up in the sovereignty of God. I call it the "cemetery confrontation".

The first group of people mentioned were Jesus "**disciples and a large crowd**" (v.11). The second group of people was, **"a large crowd from the town"** (v.12). In other words, Jesus is walking toward Nain and runs into a funeral procession. The funeral crowd is surrounding a grieving mother whose son had died. The son is in a coffin and: "When the Lord saw her, his heart went out to her and he said, **'Don't cry'**" (v.13). Think it was accidental or incidental that these two companies of people met on this day? Neither do I! So, what's the lesson?

♦ Had Jesus been too early, He would have missed the funeral procession!
♦ Had Jesus been a little late, He would have missed the meeting as well!

My discovery here is evident; Jesus has a perfect time-table so you can chill, rest easy and depend on His timing! He may not be early, but He is never late! And, if Jesus doesn't prevent your sorrow, He will pour out His grace to sustain you in every moment of every day. Why am I certain of this? Because;

1. **Jesus said, "Don't cry"** (v.13) which means Jesus has the power to get our focus on Him and His ability to comfort us in every sorrow and in every season!

2. **Jesus revealed His grace** when He "touched the coffin, and those carrying it stood still" (v.14). Anyone who touched the dead was considered ceremonially unclean according to Levitical law. Jewish rulers would never allow this defilement. But Jesus revealed His grace in touching the dead. In other words, no one is too soiled, defiled, dirty or out of reach of His grace.

3. **Jesus conveyed the mission** when He raised the dead man back to life and gave him back to his mother. "They were all filled with awe and praised God", and said, "God has come to help his people" (v.16). And this is exactly why Jesus died and rose again – so that God would get the glory in rescuing us in (and from) our sin!

The take-a-way?
Jesus has the desire and the power to restore and redeem every dead area of your life and mine!

Nuf Sed!

"The Pool of Bethesda"

" 'Get up! Pick up your mat and walk'. At once the man was cured; he picked up his mat and walked" (John 5:8).

In our text, Jesus has just traveled to Jerusalem to attend an unnamed feast. It could have been the feast of Purim in March, the feast of Trumpets in September, or the Passover Feast. Jesus moves in and out among the people and is about to stir up His enemies for healing on the Sabbath. He makes His way to the Pool of Bethesda, located on the East Side of Jerusalem. The word Bethesda means "House of Mercy"; it's a place where mineral springs still exist today. The pool had five porches to accommodate the invalids who came to use the waters. The pool was fed by a spring, it was a place where God chose to heal people, and it was a place surrounded by people who expected to be healed. Notice what Jesus experienced as he visited the pool:

1. Bethesda Was a Place of "Waiting"!
"In these lay a great multitude of impotent folk, of blind, halt, withered, waiting for the moving of the water" (v.3, KJV).

Who was at the pool? People who were blind, lame, and withered. The curse of Adam's sin results in all three:
♦ Sin blinds our eyes to truth and the glory of God.
♦ Sin makes us lame so that we cannot walk and follow after God.
♦ Sin withers up our strength and leaves us weak and vulnerable.

What were the people doing at the pool? They were **"waiting"** (v.3), one of the toughest things we have to do! At times the spring was quiet. Other times it bubbled up and whoever stepped in was made well. People were waiting on all five porches, thinking, "This could be my day". Maybe you've been waiting – for healing, a spouse, a job, an open door, a prodigal, an answered prayer of some kind. Waiting may not be fun, but patience pays great dividends!

2. Bethesda Was a Place of Complaint!
When Jesus asked, "Do you want to get well?" (v.6, NIV), the man replied, "I have no one to help me into the pool when the water is stirred. While I am trying to get in, someone else goes down ahead of me" (v.7). Instead of just saying "Yes Lord, I want to be healed", the man blames his 38 year condition on what others have not done for him. Because of his "hopes deferred", the man's heart was withered as well. His spirit and attitude were as withered as his body. While he may have been normal, the lesson is clear: As long as we blame other people for what's inside of us, it's difficult to change!

3. Bethesda Was a Place of Power!

"At once the man was cured" (v.9).

Jesus in His mercy and compassion healed the man's body! His power was manifested and the man was found in the temple (v.14). He then testified, "that it was Jesus who had made him well" (v.15).

The take-a-way?

How I respond to what happens to me, will determine what happens in me over time!

Nuf Sed!

November 7
"Crumbs From The Table"

"She said, but even the dogs eat the crumbs that fall from their master's table" (Matthew 15:27).

The year of opposition has now begun for Jesus! Herod is suspicious of Him, the Pharisees can no longer conceal their hostility and hatred, and people are taking deep offense at His words. Jesus feels the need for solitude and rest, so He travels to a friend's house for privacy. While at the house, a desperate mother disturbs Jesus because her daughter is in trouble:

"My daughter is suffering terribly from demon possession" (v.22). What follows reveals a great truth to grasp – to really enjoy the journey with God:

1. The Desperate Mother Teaches Us!
"Lord, Son of David, have mercy on me!" (v.22)

The mom interrupts the privacy of Jesus because she has a child possessed by the devil. The mom is a Canaanite woman (a Gentile of the Gentiles). She's from a heathen land, is non-Jewish, and knows that she doesn't deserve God's mercy. Yet the healing needed is far beyond the scope of ordinary physicians.

♦ Her nationality was against her because she was a Gentile and Jesus was a Jew.
♦ Her gender was against her because Jewish rabbis paid little attention to women.
♦ Her enemy was against her because one of satan's demons had taken control of her daughter.

But the lesson here is; we must never construe that a delay is refusal! We must never forget: **Just because God is silent doesn't mean that He is absent!** Mom has a dilemma that is normal, and maybe you face the same today:

♦ She has an intense burden for someone she loves.
♦ She has questions and feels inferior as she approaches Jesus.
♦ She has a delay to pray through and overcome.

2. The Discouraging Disciples Teach Us!
"His disciples came to him and urged him, 'Send her away.'" (v.23).

The disciples of Jesus believed that the woman had no right to God's mercy. Why? Because she was not a part of, "the lost sheep of Israel" (v.24). She was outside of the family circle! She was a Gentile! She was (in the mind of the disciples) not worthy of God's grace and mercy!

3. The Delivering Savior Teaches Us!
"It is not right to take the children's bread and toss it to their dogs" (v.26).

The word "children" refers to the Jews. The word "dogs" refers to the Gentiles (those sunken in impurity). Jesus wasn't calling the woman a dog; He simply knew that the woman was a dog in the mind of the disciples and the Jews. The woman responded by saying" Even the dogs eat the crumbs that fall from their masters' table" (v.27). In other words, she agrees with Jesus that she isn't worthy, her people are heathen Canaanites, and she's an outsider (not from Israel). And Jesus honors her faith and heals her daughter – because she believes that Jesus is the One who can save, deliver, and heal whoever He desires to!

The Take-A-Way?
It's not the "level" of your faith, it's the "object" of your faith, and Jesus has crumbs of mercy and grace for the undeserving!

Nuf Sed!

"A Hand Out Stretched"

'Stretch out your hand'. He did so, and his hand was completely restored"
(Luke 6:10).

The context of this healing by Jesus is important. Why? Because we can
sometimes forget, that Jesus cares more about people than outward form,
ritual, ceremony and appearance.

♦ **In v.1-5, Jesus takes us to a grain field:** The disciples pluck the heads
of wheat, rub them in their hands, and eat because of hunger. The
Pharisees then criticize Jesus for allowing this on the Sabbath Day. Jesus
responds by telling about David and his men eating 12 loaves of
showbread when they were hungry (bread that only the priest was to eat).
Jesus was teaching that God is more concerned about David and his men
receiving strength, than allowing them to perish for the sake of keeping
a temporary law.

♦ **In v.6-10, Jesus takes us to a synagogue:** The Pharisees knew that Jesus
would be teaching on the Sabbath Day. Their desire was to gather more
evidence to build a case against Him. It was on this occasion that Jesus
would heal a man with a withered (diseased) hand. Notice:

1. The Man Was "Fervent" In This Meeting!
" 'Get up and stand in front of everyone'. So he got up and stood there" (v.8).
Why did the man have to be bold and fervent in this gathering? Because he
knew that something evil was going on in the meeting. The man needing
healing would have to make a choice:
♦ On one hand, the Pharisees are waiting to trap Jesus for healing on the
Sabbath.
♦ On the other hand, the sick man believes that Jesus has compassion for
hurting people.
So, the man has a choice to make: He can stay in his seat so the Pharisees
don't get upset. Or, he can stand up when Jesus says, "stand up".

2. The Pharisees Were "Furious" In Their Response!
"They were furious and began to discuss with one another what they might do
to Jesus" (v.11)

The religious leaders became indignant that Jesus would heal on the
Sabbath! Out of pride, they used their laws and traditions to justify their
prejudice. A true Pharisee used their religion to judge people and elevate their
own spirituality. The Pharisees were so jealous of Jesus' popularity that they
actually missed who He was. Jesus exposed their hearts and became their
enemy.

3. The Lord Was "Faithful" To His Mission!

"His hand was completely restored" (v.10)

The withered hand was from an accident, disease or atrophy (possibly from bricklaying). Jesus responded to the man's faith, standing up, and his courage in front of people. The man in need, simply gave Jesus the opportunity to prove His Lordship over sickness and disease.

The Take-A-Way?

There will always be doubters (it's expected), but there will always be Jesus (who has the power to address sin on the inside and sickness on the outside)!

Nuf Sed!

November 9
"An 18 Year Infirmity Is Healed"

"When Jesus saw her, he called her forward and said to her, 'Woman, you are free from your infirmity' " (Luke 13:12).
"When he said this, all his opponents were humiliated, but the people were delighted with all the wonderful things he was doing" (v.17).

This miracle takes place under two noticeable conditions, and Luke is the only one who records the event:

♦ It takes place in the synagogue – where people are gathered together to receive instructions.

♦ It takes place on the Sabbath – when certain work was forbidden. Jesus was watched more on this day of the week than any other day. Why? Because legalists wanted to trap Him in some breach of the law. The legal formalists valued sacred ceremonies and religious rites more than the needs of hurting people. Notice the message from our healing Jesus:

1. The Glorious Healer Exercised His Power!
"He put His hands on her, and immediately she straightened up and praised God" (v.13).

This woman (for 18 years) had some kind of nervous disorder, dislocation of the vertebrae, or spinal trouble. She was "bent over and could not straighten up at all" (v.11). I notice here, that even after 18 years of delay, she never became bitter against God. She is still present to hear the Word! She is gathered with other people the very day that Jesus attends the service! And, when Jesus saw her, "He called her forward and said ….. " 'You are set free from your infirmity' " (v.12). Oh friend; Jesus saw her – and Jesus sees you! He knows all about your worries, hopes deferred, illness and expectations. While we do not serve a "useful" Jesus (but a "beautiful" Jesus), He is aware of everything that touches your life today! He really is The Great Physician!

2. The Grumbling Ruler Revealed His Anger!
"Indignant because Jesus had healed on the Sabbath, the synagogue ruler said to the people, 'There are six days for work. So come and be healed on those days' " (v.14).

The ruler had tunnel vision, and was more about appearance than ministry. So much so that Jesus answered him, "You hypocrites!" (v.15). The word "hypocrite" is the Greek word for "actor" and means "second face". Jesus declared that the ruler was wearing a religious mask and was a spiritual fake. The woman was called a "daughter of Abraham" (v.16) because she believed in God, obeyed Jesus' command, and didn't pretend to be something she was not! The genuine gifts of the spirit in operation – do have a way of revealing those hungry for God verses those who only care about form and appearance!

3.   The Grateful Congregation Expressed Their Gratitude!
"The people were delighted with all the wonderful things he was doing" (v.17).

This gift of healing testified of the reality and existence of God! The congregation gave praise to God when Jesus freed the woman. In other words, Jesus has the power to free us from ourselves, and when He does, pain can turn to praise!

The Take-A-Way?
In our pain we can become bitter or better, and staying close to Jesus is what protects us from self-destruction!

Nuf Sed!

November 10
"Healing Authority"

"Lord, I do not deserve to have you come under my roof. But just say the word, and my servant will be healed. For I myself am a man under authority" (Matthew 8:8, 9).

Authority is defined as the power to enforce an order, make decisions, give commands, give approval or grant permission. Our text reveals what can happen when we believe what the centurion believed about authority. Notice the reason why Jesus was "astonished" (v.10), and why Jesus said, "I have not found anyone in Israel with such great faith" (v.10).

1. There Was An Anxious Request!
"When Jesus had entered Capernaum, a centurion came to him, asking for help. 'Lord, he said, 'my servant lies at home paralyzed and in terrible suffering' " (v.5, 6).

A centurion was an officer in the Roman Army, in charge of 100 men. This centurion had a servant that was suffering great pain. When Jesus offered to come and heal him, the centurion said, "I do not deserve to have you come under my roof" (v.8). I wonder if you ever entertain the same, **"I'm not worthy"** thoughts? I wonder if you ever slip in the area of condemnation? Remember friend; If you are a Christian and live with condemnation, you are actually saying this to yourself:
- The blood of Jesus was not sufficient to cover your sin.
- You must work harder to earn God's favor and grace.
- God's justice has not been satisfied by the death of His son.
- You are a lesser Christian in comparison to others.

2. There Was Authority That Was Recognized!
"Just say the word, and my servant will be healed. For I myself am a man under authority, with soldiers under me" (v.8, 9)

How did this centurion have such great faith and believe that Jesus could answer prayer from long distance? Because the centurion understood authority! In other words, if the centurion could give commands and see them obeyed – then surely Jesus could do even more! If a human officer in the Roman Army could speak and see his wishes carried out, we must believe that Jesus can speak and see His wishes carried out as well! Why did Jesus call the centurion's faith **"great faith"** (v.10)? Because the centurion didn't ask for a sign, he only believed in Christ's authority! He was confident in Jesus' power, ability and authority!

3. There Was An Answer Received Through Faith!
" 'It will be done just as you believed it would'. And his servant was healed at

that very hour" (v.13).

This is a record of an instantaneous healing from long distance! It was an answer to prayer by remote control! We see that grace triumphs in an unlikely place, because the centurion believed that Jesus had all authority!

The take-a-way?
There is power in the name of Jesus – over sin, satan and sickness!

Nuf Sed!

"Bruised But Not Broken"

"A bruised reed he will not break, and a smoldering wick he will not snuff out" (Isaiah 42:3).

Isaiah 42 (like 40 and 41) is addressed to the exiled Jews in Babylon. The 70 year captivity is almost over and the Jews are about to return to Jerusalem to rebuild the temple. They still remember their past failures, sin and disobedience. They flat out need confidence in the Lord to go forward! And, God gives a specific word to Isaiah, to Israel and to us. What is it?
1.   God can make **something beautiful** out of the ashes of your past! (and)
2.   Your past **does not** have to dictate your future!

God is so wanting Isaiah to convey this message of hope to your heart! The message of hope will result in such an inward change, that it cannot be kept silent:
◆   "Sing to the Lord a new song" (v.10).
◆   "Shout from the mountaintops" (v.11).
◆   "Proclaim his praise in the islands" (v.12).

So, what is it that produces great hope in your heart? Why is Jesus upheld by the Father and anointed by the Spirit (v.1)? What does God tell Israel that will help them face the journey from Babylon to Jerusalem? Notice the compassion of Jesus:

1.   "A Bruised Reed He Will Not Break" (v.3)
A "reed" refers to a cane or calamus plant that grows in swamps and marshy lands. The word "bruised" means fragile, weak, feeble or crushed. The promise here is, anyone who is under pressure, feeling weak, crushed by their own sin, or strained by some adversity – shall not break! This means that Jesus will embrace you, lift you, restore you and uphold you in your journey – in every season! It means that God will never allow more than you are able to bear!

2.   "A Smoldering Wick He Will Not Snuff Out" (v.3)
The flax or wick can get dim, weak, feeble and be almost out. This refers to the believer whose fire of spiritual devotion is low because the oil is almost fully consumed. The promise here is, that Jesus wants to tend to our hearts and trim, feed, rekindle and supply fresh oil. In other words, while you might be low on hope, faith, and optimism – Jesus sees you restored to a brilliant shine.

3.   "He Will Not Falter or Be Discouraged" (v.4)
This means four things that you must never forget:
◆   The Lord will not fail to accomplish His purpose in you.

- The Lord is not taken "off guard" by what happens to you.
- The Lord will not quit what He has started in you.
- The Lord, "will turn the darkness into light…..and make the rough places smooth" (v.16), which means you can rest well and chill out! Why? Because God will take your dark and dismal events and use them to promote His work in you!!!

The Take-A-Way?

What you feel is wasted – God sees as useful because He can redeem the worst to bring out the best!

Nuf Sed!

November 12
"The Year of Jubilee"

"The Spirit of the Sovereign Lord is on me, because the Lord has anointed me to preach good news to the poor ….. bind up the brokenhearted, to proclaim freedom for the captives and release from darkness ….. to proclaim the year of the Lord's favor" (Isaiah 61:1,2).

Jesus opened His public ministry in Nazareth by quoting from this chapter (Luke 4:16-19). It's in this chapter (Isaiah 61), where God reveals to us the glorious results of the ministry of Jesus today. We clearly see the purpose for which the Messiah has been appointed (v.1-3), as well as the effects of this redemption upon those who receive it (v.4-11). Notice Jesus' words:

"The Spirit of the Sovereign Lord is on me" (v.1). In other words:
Jesus was publicly consecrated to His work when the Holy Spirit descended upon Him at His water baptism (Matthew 3:16). Jesus has also been imparted with the Spirit of God without measure (John 3:34). This means that no devil or demon from hell can prevent Jesus from touching people today. It means that the wind of the Holy Spirit blows where He wills and no one can stop Him (John 3:8). But what is Jesus doing today for those who trust in Him?

1. **"Preach Good News To The Poor"** (Isaiah 61:1).
The word "poor" refers to someone who has been injured or distressed. Israel has been afflicted by captivity in Babylon, and God promises them (and us) that He will pour out grace to go on.

2. **"Bind Up The Brokenhearted"** (v.1).
The brokenhearted refers to anyone who is hurting from something. It could be the pain we feel from our sin, a loss, a disappointment, or any unfulfilled expectation. This means that Jesus is our healing balm of comfort and consolation in times of sorrow.

3. **"Proclaim Freedom For The Captives"** (v.1).
As the exiles in Babylon were set free after 70 years of captivity, so Jesus ministers the same to you and me today. He sets at liberty those who are held captive to sin's dominion.

4. **"Release From Darkness For The Prisoners"** (v.1)
While this is a reference to the release of those confined in Babylon, today it is a clear picture of deliverance for you and me. It is the promise of a fresh new beginning for all who trust Jesus.

5. "Proclaim The Year Of The Lord's Favor" (v.2)

This is reference to the "Year of Jubilee" in (Leviticus 25:1-17). Every seven years the Jews were to observe a sabbatical year to allow the land to rest. After seven sabbaticals, Israel was to proclaim the fiftieth year as the "Year of Jubilee". Why? To prevent the oppression of the poor, retain equity in society, and preserve a balance among the tribes. Three things took place: All debts were canceled and forgiven. All slaves that had sold themselves to liquidate their debts were freed. All property and possessions that had been taken as collateral were returned to their original owner.

The Take-A-Way?

Jesus has done the same for you; He paid your sin debt in full, He freed you from the present slavery of sin, and offers you a brand new beginning!

Nuf Sed!

"Beauty For Ashes"

"To bestow on them a crown of beauty instead of ashes, the oil of gladness instead of mourning, and a garment of praise instead of a spirit of despair" (Isaiah 61:3).

Yesterday in Isaiah 61:1, 2, we discovered how Jesus has been anointed with the Holy Spirit and has the power to **redeem us**. Today we will discover how Jesus has the power to **restore us** in light of our redemption.

Since Jesus is anointed and has the authority to pay for our sins and rescue us from sin's power, what are the consequences of His work in our hearts? Since Jesus has accomplished His task, mission and purpose, how do we respond in light of our redemption? I love how Isaiah puts it in words:

1. Jesus Restores With Beauty For Ashes! (v.3)
It was common for oriental people to cast dust upon their heads as an expression of grief. It was also easy for Israel to grieve over their past sin while in captivity. But now in Jesus, things have surely changed for you and me! We no longer live with grief over our shortcomings. We no longer gravel in condemnation because our guilt has been replaced with the righteousness of Jesus.

2. Jesus Restores With The Oil Of Joy For Mourning! (V.3)
Oil was used as a symbol (or expression) of joy and gladness. Whereas "Beauty For Ashes" refers to our right standing before God, the oil of joy refers to a deep seated confidence in our hearts. The confidence comes as a result of God's presence in our lives. It is the fruit of being God centered (in focus) and this fruit gives us strength and lifts the spirit of those around us.

3. Jesus Restores With A Garment Of Praise Instead Of Despair! (v.3)
The word "despair" means heaviness, fainthearted and feeble. It's a word that is used to describe a weak and flickering lamp about to go out. This means that Jesus actually overcomes the lie of the evil one to discourage you and bring heaviness upon you. Remember friend; discouragement is a lie of satan to blind you in the present of what God is going to do in the future!

So, what is the result or consequence of allowing God to restore your heart, spirit, joy and praise?
You, **"will be called oaks of righteousness, a planting of the Lord for the display of his splendor"** (v.3).
In other words, you will be inwardly strong (planted) and God will be glorified in your life ("The display of his splendor") (v.3). So much so, that people will be drawn to the God you serve because they observe your peace, joy, confidence and rest in Jesus!

The Take-A-Way?

When we allow God to redeem our past and restore our present joy, we too will say, "I delight greatly in the Lord; my soul rejoices in my God" (v.10).

Nuf Sed!

November 14
"Renewed For The Journey"
Part I

"Forget the former things; do not dwell on the past. See, I am doing a new thing …..I am making a way in the desert and streams in the wasteland" (Isaiah 43:18, 19).

The language in this text is so gospel centered and powerful that it literally stops us in our tracks. In Isaiah 43, God is asking us three undeniable questions:

♦ Do you need to be forgiven of sin to enjoy the power of a clear conscience?

♦ Do you need the Holy Spirit to fill your cup, strengthen you, and pour faith into your heart?

♦ Do you need to adjust your priorities so that you can live your life for God's glory alone?

Remember the context of Israel as you approach the scripture today: The Jews are about to leave captivity in Babylon after 70 years "on hold". They will return to rebuild Jerusalem. Their tomorrows are uncertain and questions circle in their minds. Assyria was giving them an ulcer, Sennacherib was planning their failure, and Israel's soldiers were found weeping. But, God! Yes, God had a word for then and God has a word for now. What is it?

♦ He is not intimidated by your circumstances!

♦ He is not late, but right on schedule!

♦ He is not unaware of your feelings, desires, plans and prayers!

So, let's allow the Lord to speak for Himself – straight from the text. It's truth that renews your heart today:

1. Renewed People Know The Unchangeable Love Of God!
"This is what the Lord says – he who created you, O Jacob, he who formed you, O Israel; 'Fear not, for I have redeemed you; I have summoned you by name, you **are mine**'" (v.1).

"When you pass through the waters, I will be **with you**" (v.2).

"I am the Lord, your God, the Holy One of Israel, **your Savior**" (v.3).

"You are precious and honored in my sight …..because **I love you**" (v.4).

"Do not be afraid, for I am **with you**" (v.5).

The undeniable message in (v.1-5) is, that God loved Israel on their worst days as much as he did on their best days. While their disobedience brought self-inflicted pain, the love of God never changed. God's love wasn't based upon Israel's performance, it was based upon his unchangeable love (that for us is undeserved). In other words, we cannot **achieve His love** – we can only **receive His love**! Because Jesus alone satisfied the law that we could not satisfy, we can now walk with our Heavenly Father's smile because of the work of another – Jesus! Remember friend; because of the unchangeable love of God, the gospel makes the following truth real and life changing:

♦ We can never feel **entitled** (because we deserve death, yet God's grace has given us what we don't deserve). This produces a **grateful** spirit!

♦ We can never feel **elite** (because we are sinners and are only made holy by the work of another – Jesus). This produces a **humble** spirit!

♦ We can never feel **exempt** or cheated (because the cross proves there is nothing that God cannot ask of us). This produces a **contented** spirit!

The Take-A-Way?
We can stop pretending (and embrace our flaws) and we can stop proving ourselves (by resting in "His" resume and not our own!)

Nuf Sed!

"Renewed For The Journey"
Part II

"I, even I, am he who blots out your transgressions for my own sake, and remembers your sins no more" (Isaiah 43:25).

Yesterday we began looking at Isaiah 43, learning what God said to Israel to renew them for their journey back to Jerusalem. While it would be difficult for Israel to travel and rebuild their temple back at home, the Lord had a word that renewed Israel and renews us as well. In v.1-13, we discovered that "renewed" people know the unchangeable love of God! Notice what else God has to say to us in Isaiah 43:

2. Renewed People Know God's Power Over Sin!
How do we know this? Because the Lord tells us that:
♦   He brought down the Babylonians in their pride (v.14).
♦   He made a path through the Red Sea (v.16).
♦   He "snuffed out" the chariots and horses (v.17).

And, as great as that deliverance was, God said He would do a "new thing" (v.19) under the coming Messiah! While Israel's redemption was liberating (in the Old Testament), a greater redemption will occur when Jesus appears (in the New Testament). In other words, like Israel was delivered from Pharaoh's rule, the Jordan River and the Babylonians – so Jesus now delivers us from the rule and reign of sin's power in Christ Jesus (Romans 8:2, 3). This means that you and I can now walk after the Spirit and not be controlled by the sinful nature of our flesh!

3. Renewed People Know God's Provision Throughout Their Journey!
"I am making a way in the desert and streams in the wasteland" (v.19) means; the Lord will supply all that is necessary for your journey – in every season of life! It means that God will pour out His Spirit on the thirsty and sustain you, which takes the worry out of living. In fact, God wants to prove Himself sufficient in your life so much, that people will see you and magnify His Name:

"The people I formed for myself …..may proclaim my praise" (Isaiah 43:21). This means that God has formed us for Himself and delivered us from sin – all for the purpose of pointing people to Jesus! And, this is our purpose for existence!

4. Renewed People Know God's Promise Of Forgiveness!
"And remember your sins are no more" (v.25) means: That even though Israel didn't call upon God (v.22), didn't give proper offerings (v.23), and wearied God with their sin (v.24), God in His mercy "blots out your transgressions" (v.25). And, this is the Gospel all over again; that forgiveness is not

something we achieve – but something we receive! The result is that you can live with freedom from guilt, condemnation, and fear of rejection by God! Why? Because Jesus canceled your sins and took them upon Himself!

The Take-A-Way?
There is no good reason for you to carry your sin any longer – since Jesus has already paid your debt in full!

Nuf Sed!

"Doors That Never Close"
Part I

"Your gates will always stand open, they will never be shut, day or night"
(Isaiah 60:11).

Isaiah chapter 60 is a glowing report of life in the church under the Messiah.
It details specific ministry of the Lord to your heart and mine.

God gives us the picture of a shining light that affects everyone within its'
influence. It's a revelation of how Jesus ministers to your heart today! While
Isaiah records how the Lord will restore the city of Zion for Israel, he also
records how the Lord restores the life of every believer. Get a little glimpse
of the good news from the chapter:

♦ "Arise, shine, for your light has come" (v.1).
♦ "Your heart will throb and swell with joy" (v.5).
♦ "In favor I will show you compassion" (v.10).
♦ "Your gates will always stand open" (v.11).
♦ "The Lord will be your everlasting light" (v.19).
♦ "I have planted the work of my hands, for the display of my splendor"
(v.21).

Today and tomorrow I want you to see the great provision under the
gospel. The good news is, "Your gates will always stand open" (v.11) which
means that gates can be open or closed. When Isaiah says that the Lords'
gates will be open continually, he's telling us two things:

1. There will be so many new converts coming to Jesus, that heaven's gates
must stay open to receive them all, (and)

2. The gospel under the dispensation of grace will be constantly available to
minister to those who trust Jesus. This reveals two powerful truths:

♦ The doors of Christ's church are never closed! (and,)
♦ No one will ever be excluded who repents and turns to Jesus! So what
happens to those who walk through the door of the grace of God because
of Jesus? Four things:

1. The Lord Will "Enlighten" You! (v.1-3)

"Arise, shine, for your light has come" (v.1) Why is Israel told to arise?
Because Israel has been in a long season of affliction and disappointment.
There were the 70 years of captivity in Babylon and worship in the temple in
Jerusalem was vacant. But now, "Light has come" (v.1) which means:

♦ For Israel, God sees the restored city of Zion (in a dark age).
♦ For you and me, God sees the gospel of grace poured out (in a dark age).

In other words, even though Isaiah sees, "darkness and thick darkness" (v.2)
over the people of the earth, he also sees the Lord rising upon us and His
"glory" (v.2) appear! This refers to Jesus illuminating us with the gospel of
light like the Shekinah glory was a light to Israel! What an incredible gospel
promise is given here: God has promised to enlighten our path, guide us

continually, and expose any darkness within us to bring internal change! Light will expose and conquer our hearts under the gospel! The gospel really does have the power to capture our affections and bring lasting change.

The take-a-way?
Like a light overcomes darkness in a room at night time, so the gospel is effective in removing the darkness from our affections and innermost being!

Nuf Sed!

November 17
"Doors That Never Close"
Part II

"Your gates will always stand open, they will never be shut, day or night" (Isaiah 60:11).

Yesterday we learned that Isaiah was writing about two realities in Isaiah chapter 60:
1. The Lord was going to restore the city of Zion for Israel after the 70 year captivity in Babylon and,
2. The Messiah (Jesus) was going to restore the heart of people under the dispensation of grace. When we walk through the gates of grace, the Lord records four things that happen to us. Yesterday we discovered that the Lord "Enlightens" us, or exposes and removes the darkness from our hearts! Today, notice the other three things that occur because of the gospel:

2. The Lord Will "Enlarge" Your Influence! (v.4-9)
"All assemble and come to you" (v.4).

This is what happens when we allow the light of the gospel to change our hearts: the Lord attracts people from all walks of life! He draws people to Himself when the church reflects His nature and character. For Israel, the people were coming back to the heart of holy worship in a restored Jerusalem. In fact, they would be "carried on the arm" (v.4), which means to be nursed, sustained, supported and satisfied. The people would also be drawn to "the honor of the Lord your God, the Holy One of Israel" (v.10). In other words, when our hearts "throb and swell with joy" (v.5), this healthy fear of God, awe, and reverence will draw people to Jesus. The presence of God in you will actually be an instrument of God to draw people to Himself!

3. The Lord Will "Encourage" You! (v.10-16)
"Although you have been forsaken and hated, with no one traveling through, I will make you the everlasting pride and joy of all generations" (v.15).
"And your days of sorrow will end" (v.20).
Why will the fortunes and disappointments change? Because:
♦ The Lord will send people to rebuild the ruined city walls (v.10)
♦ No one will be able to close the gates and stop God's work (v.11)
♦ Those opposing God's work will be dry and barren (v.12)
♦ Glorious things will take place in "His" presence (v.13)
Isaiah is telling us, that the presence of Jesus in your life is greater than the facts surrounding your life. This means, that as long as we treasure and trust Jesus above every other lesser thing, we will live in a joyful and safe place.

4. The Lord Will "Exchange" You! (v.17-22)

"Instead of bronze I will bring you gold, and silver in place of iron. Instead of wood, I will bring you bronze, and iron in place of stones" (v.17).

The meaning of v.17 is: Isaiah sees the period of grace that we now live in. It's a picture of Gentile unbelievers embracing the gospel and being changed. It's a picture of Jesus changing whatever needs to be changed in our lives. And, this is why there is an open door and open gate (v.11) - so that we can receive God's Grace and be forever changed and free from sin's dominion.

The take-a-way?

When God enlightens us, enlarges us, and encourages us, we will be changed and never stay the same!

Nuf Sed!

"When East Winds Blow"
Part I

"With his fierce blast he drives her out, as on a day the east winds blow" (Isaiah 27:8).

In the Bible, the "east wind" is never used in a positive way:
♦ Jonah's gourd was shattered by **the east wind!**
♦ The locusts that plagued Egypt were driven by **the east wind!**
♦ The ships of Tarshish were broken up by **the east wind!**
♦ Job's friend declared that Job was driven by **the east wind!**
♦ God told deserting Ephraim that they would perish by **the east wind!**

And, there will come a time when the east wind will blow across and test all of us. The good news is, God gives you a promise in the day of your east wind. In Isaiah 26, Israel is singing to the Lord. She sings about salvation v.1, faith v.2, perfect peace v.3, our eternal rock v.4, enemies brought down v.5-6, grace shown to the wicked v.10, and this great truth: "Lord, you establish peace for us; all that we have accomplished you have done for us" (v.12). Then in Isaiah 27, the Lord sings about Israel. He sings how He is faithful to His vineyard (His church), and how He stays the rough wind in the day of the east wind. He tells us how He cares for those who trust in Him and not themselves. He gives you great hope today, regardless of the battle or season that you are in. Take heart and discover today and tomorrow, how much that God truly cares for your wellbeing! Notice God's care in the east winds of life:

1. The Lord "Preserves" You In The East Wind!
"In that day – sing about a fruitful vineyard. I, the Lord, watch over it; I water it continually. I guard it day and night so that no one may harm it. If only there were briers and thorns confronting me! I would march against them in battle; I would set them all on fire" (v. 2-4).
In v.2-3, God's people are described as a vineyard, and God records how He cares for us:
♦ God **Watches** Over Us!
The word "watch" in v.3 means that God will keep you and preserve you in your east wind. It means that God will never allow more than you are able to bear!
♦ God **Waters** Us Continually!
"I water it continually" (v.3). This means that God waters His vineyard, or provides living water to sustain you in every season of the soul. There is a well of living water for all who believe.
♦ God **Wins** Your Battle Over Sin's Temptation!
"I would march... and set them all on fire" (v.4) is God's part against our "briers and thorns" (v.4). "Briers and thorns" are the enemy of a vineyard. God is emphatic here, telling us that He will burn, consume, and conquer the

things that keep us from growing strong in the Lord! He will conquer the sins and distractions that keep us from our fullest potential! Yes; God will capture our hearts fully as we treasure and trust in Jesus above every other idol and lesser god to satisfy our hearts! His presence will melt away what interferes with our intimacy, fellowship and union with Jesus.

The take-a-way?
Jesus the Vinedresser will complete what He's begun in you, and always sustain you as you lean in and lean on His amazing grace!

Nuf Sed!

November 19
"When East Winds Blow"
Part II

"With his fierce blast he drives her out, as on a day the east wind blows" (Isaiah 27:8).

Yesterday we learned how we are God's vineyard. We learned that God Himself is committed to keep us, sustain us, and overcome sin's temptation when the enemy comes in like a flood. We discovered that the Lord "preserves" His beloved in every season of the soul! Notice the other two promises from God that we can depend upon in our journey of life:

2. The Lord Gives Us His "Peace" In The East Wind (v.5) "'Let them come to me for refuge; let them make peace with me, yes, let them make peace with me' " (v.5). The New Testament word for peace means rest, order, harmony, security, quietness and tranquility. God's peace is:
♦ Tranquility in your inner man because of God's presence in your life.
♦ Security in the midst of turmoil; the eye in the middle of the storm.
♦ That quality of God's nature imparted to those who are yielded to the Holy Spirit.
♦ The fruit of the Spirit that gives order, harmony and inward rest.
Don't you love these words from God through Isaiah:

"You will keep in perfect peace him whose mind is steadfast, because he trusts in you" (26:3).

3. The Lord Gives Us "Progress" In The East Wind (27:6-10)
"Israel will bud and blossom and fill all the world with fruit" (v.6).
    The Lord promised that His people would flourish greatly after returning from the Babylonian captivity. After being captured and put on hold for 70 years, many of the people became discouraged and fatigued. Many could see no further than their present detours, delays and disappointments: But God saw their future and recovery beyond their present discomfort. In other words, there is a message that God desires to communicate to your heart today:
♦ "I see your tomorrows so you can rest at ease"
♦ "I have a plan in place when your east wind is over"
♦ "I know what I am doing in your life, so you can chill"
    In fact, God is so great and yet so personal, that He declares: "No Asherah poles or incense altars will be left standing. The fortified city stands desolate, an abandoned settlement, forsaken like the desert" (v.9-10).
    This is reference to Babylon, now desolate. It's a picture of God's people, once held against their will in captivity. The place that once held Judah and stole their joy has now been destroyed. It's a clear picture of how Jesus can free anyone from sin's dominion and slavery. It teaches us that Jesus can give

us spiritual progress in every season, as well as penetrate and break through the things that hold us back! Like God tore down the groves and images (v.9) and burned up the briers and thorns (v.4) – so God today can free us from self-destructive thinking and behavior!

The take-a-way?
Israel learned in the East Wind, that God can redeem your hard seasons, and God can use them to crowd us closer to Jesus!

Nuf Sed!

November 20
"No Rain"
Part I

"Now I will tell you what I am going to do to my vineyard ….. I will command the clouds not to rain on it: (Isaiah 5:5, 6).

While everything we receive from God is by His grace, we also have the responsibility to prepare our hearts to receive. We can align our hearts with God or we can be out of alignment. In other words, there is God's part to pour out His grace upon us and there is our part to prepare the soil of our hearts. Isaiah paints a clear picture for us, how the sovereignty of God works together with the responsibility of man!

In chapters 1-4, Isaiah addresses the need for repentance (1:18), how pride brings us down (2:11), how we can grieve God's presence (3:8), and how God will usher in a revival and great awakening (4:2). Then in chapter 5, we have the Parable of the Vineyard. It's a song about God's care as well as His disappointment. We see why rain is so necessary, and we see how it is possible to cause the Lord to hold back the rain. And, rain is essential for seed and fruit to grow! "No rain" is a terrible condition in a dry climate. Spiritual rain withheld is a terrible condition for the soul. Today and tomorrow I want you to see how:

- ♦ God holds the key to the rain of the Spirit's outpouring.
- ♦ God alone can send the shower of rain to our souls.
- ♦ God is the answer to every hungry, dry and barren heart.
- ♦ God opens the heavens in response to our willingness to prepare our hearts.

Discover with me the Hope, Hindrances and Healing of the vineyard:

1. The Hope Of The Vineyard (v.1-4)
"I will sing for the one I love a song about his vineyard: My loved one had a vineyard on a fertile hillside ….. he looked for a crop of good grapes but it yielded only bad fruit" (5:1, 2). God is singing here – about His church! He expresses how He feels and hopes that we will understand that:

♦ **God Is Loving!**
The words "loved one" (v.1) mean beloved, friend, and greatly loved. It refers to God's affection for people, for you! It reveals that you are the constant object of God's attention and great care!

♦ **God Is Longing!**
The words "fertile hillside" (v.1) refers to God planting His vineyard in a place where He expects fruit. For Israel, this was the land of Canaan. For you and me, this is the place wherever God has placed you. It means that God has rescued you to use you – to bring glory to His Name!

♦ **God Is Looking!**
"He looked for a crop of good grapes, but it yielded only bad fruit" (v.2).
The words "bad fruit" here mean "wild grapes" or "corrupted". It reveals
that God was looking for healthy fruit from Israel, but Israel had become
offensive and polluted from compromise. Wild grapes are not what God
is looking for!!!

The Take-A-Way?
**If we prepare the clean soil of our hearts, God will grow every fruit that
He has planned to grow in us!**

Nuf Sed!

"No Rain"
Part II

"Now I will tell you what I am going to do to my vineyard ….. I will command the clouds not to rain on it" (Isaiah 5:5, 6).

Yesterday we began to discover the importance of this Parable of the Vineyard. It is a song about God's loving care and desire for His people, His church. It is a picture of how it is possible for us to stop the rain from growing fruit in our hearts. It's a revelation of how wild grapes can overtake good grapes, how you and I can shut up the rain clouds! Yesterday we learned the "Hope" of the vineyard; today we'll see the "Hindrances" and "Healing" of the vineyard, Christ's Church, your heart and mine:

2. The "Hindrances" Of The Vineyard (v.5-30)
In Isaiah 5, the Lord shows us how the wild grapes overtake the good grapes in the vineyard. I call them "cloud stoppers" – that will keep the rain of God's Spirit from flowing in our lives. Lord protect us from these so that Your Name will not be shamed:

♦ A heart "**unpruned**"
"Neither pruned" (v.6).
A heart unpruned is someone who resists the voice of conviction, rejects the hand of purging and resents the hand of correction. It allows the dead leaves to hang on and the weeds to keep growing. The unpruned heart is harsh with others but justifies its own carnality.

♦ A heart "**unbroken**"
"Nor cultivated" (v.6)
A heart unbroken is unplowed, uncultivated and hard. It fails to see its poverty of soul and doesn't mourn over its depraved condition. It doesn't see its need of God, doesn't cry out to God for mercy and fails to allow God to break up its fallow ground.

♦ A heart "**unbridled**"
"Woe to those who rise early in the morning to run after their drinks ….. till they are inflamed with wine ….. they have no regard for the deeds of the Lord, no respect for the work of his hands" (v.11, 12).
Israel became intoxicated and yielded to the passions of their flesh. They became unashamed to serve two masters and played their sacred instruments while forgetting God in the process.

♦ A heart "**undiscerning**"
"Woe to those who call evil good and good evil, who put darkness for light and light for darkness" (v.20).
God tells us here, that Israel added one little sin to another little sin until the thin cord turned into a thick rope (v.18). This teaches us that, little sins unrepented of will lead us deeper into sin that makes it harder to escape.

3. The "Healing" Of The Vineyard

What's the answer to our barrenness of soul and clouds that refuse to give rain? The healing comes from Jesus in response to our humility, repentance, obedience and prayer! While we cannot earn God's favor nor force His hand, we can align and position ourselves to allow God to work and go deeper. When we cooperate with God's sovereignty, transformation of our hearts will take place.

The Take-A-Way?

"Who may ascend the hill of the Lord? Who may stand in his holy place? He who has clean hands and a pure heart, who does not lift up his soul to an idol" (Psalm 24:3, 4).

Nuf Sed!

November 22
"Power In Transparency"
Part I

"Why have we humbled ourselves, and you have not noticed?" (Isaiah 58:3).

The above question begs another question: What exactly is it that can cause the Lord not to hear and notice our prayer and fasting? Have you ever wondered how it's possible to be religious and yet not have an audience with God in prayer? Isaiah 58 gets to the root of the problem, and leads us into deeper intimacy and transparency with God. While God appointed Isaiah to comfort His people (40:1), God also appointed Isaiah to convince us of some things that need to change:

"Shout it aloud, do not hold back. Raise your voice like a trumpet. Declare to my people their rebellion and to the house of Jacob their sins" (58:1). Why was the Lord so concerned about His people who were seeking God and keeping religious ceremonies? Because outward service was not reflective of inward reality. In other words, God's people were fasting but God was looking for more. He was looking for inward hearts that were void of all pretense and transparent before God. Notice: **1. The "Deception" Of Fasting:**

♦ **There Was A "Carnal Spirit"**
"On the day of your fasting, you do as you please" (v.3).
Israel, while fasting, was indulging in the lusts and appetites of the flesh. They were fasting outwardly, yet entertaining certain idols and ignoring things that God wanted to address.

♦ **There Was An "Unforgiving Spirit"**
"And exploit all your workers" (v.3).
On one hand Israel was expecting God to be gracious and forgiving towards them, but on the other hand, they were unwilling to forgive those who needed their mercy. God was oppressed because people who were fasting were unwilling to relinquish their debtors.

♦ **There Was A "Competitive Spirit"**
"Your fasting ends in quarreling and strife" (v.4).
Many Jews were divided into factions and parties. Sides were drawn as each side was striving to get their own way. People were disgracing God's name by putting their personal agendas ahead of God's agenda. Pride was feeding the cancer of strife and competition.

♦ **There Was An "Angry Spirit"**
"Your fasting ends in quarreling and strife, and in striking each other with wicked fists" (v.4).
People were actually worshipping and fasting unto God while stuffing

their unresolved feelings of anger inside their hearts. God was wanting to heal the heart, so that prayers were being offered out of a healthy and whole heart.

♦ **There Was A "Legalistic Spirit"**
"Is this the kind of fast I have chosen…..for bowing one's head like a reed and for lying on sackcloth and ashes?" (v.5).
People were thinking that their fasting was meritorious in nature. They believed that their hunger pains and self-denial gained them more favor with God. They actually bent their heads over and spread ashes on themselves to appear more spiritual. The Take-A-Way?

God is not impressed with me looking spiritual; He desires that my heart be changed!

Nuf Sed!

November 23
"Power In Transparency"
Part II

"Why have we humbled ourselves, and you have not noticed?" (Isaiah 58:3).

Yesterday, we discovered the deception of fasting and prayer, how it's possible to approach God with a heart that is full of unhealthy attitudes. The reality is: God has designed fasting to accomplish His will on earth. And, He documents what He's looking for in Isaiah 58. The only kind of worship and devotion that God accepts, is that which flows from a heart full of love, unselfishness, and transparency. The motive in our fasting that sees God intervene, is a motive that is revealed by our willingness to do the following:

♦ loose the bands of wickedness (injustice).
♦ undo heavy burdens.
♦ let the oppressed go free.
♦ break every yoke.
♦ share food with the hungry.
♦ offer shelter to the poor.
♦ provide for your family that is dependent upon your care.

As we allow God to purify our hearts (while we fast and pray), God has promised to respond. I call this: **2. The "Deliverance" of Fasting.** Notice what God promises:

♦ **Plan To Be Restored!**
"Light will break forth like the dawn, and your healing will quickly appear" (v.8).
Israel was told to expect to be restored following the calamities that were inflicted upon them. God wants us as well, to expect the gospel to free us from sin and heal our broken hearts!

♦ **Plan To See Answered Prayer!**
"Then you will call, and the Lord will answer; you will cry for help, and he will say: Here am I" (v.9).
God tells us here, that if we renounce our sin and selfishness, pray from a pure heart that's full of faith, then communion and intimacy will be restored with God.

♦ **Plan To Be Joyful Instead of Discouraged!**
"Your night will become like the noonday" (v.10).
The darkness of night refers to Israel's season of trial and pain. God is clearly telling us something here: Life is seasonal and every season is followed by a new season! In other words, where you are is not where you are staying. "Noonday" in v. 10, is a picture of brightness and joy returning to the heart!

♦ **Plan To Be Led And Guided Along In Life!**
"The Lord will guide you always; he will satisfy your needs in a sun-scorched land" (v.11).
This means that the Lord will direct your path and provide refreshing streams of water from above. It means that God will be your relief in the weariness seasons of life! His grace simply cannot be exhausted by your asking and receiving!

The Take-A-Way?
Isaiah 58 clearly teaches us that God can never answer prayers that we have never prayed!

Nuf Sed!

November 24
"Divine Resources"
Part I

"You have been a refuge for the poor, a refuge for the needy in his distress, a shelter from the storm and a shade from the heat" (Isaiah 25:4).

Isaiah chapter 25 has an important context: In Isaiah 1-6, Isaiah denounces personal sin in the lives of the people. In chapters 7-12, Isaiah deals with the national sins in the leadership. In chapters 13-23, Isaiah addresses the sin of the Gentiles surrounding Judah and Israel. But in chapters 24-27, Isaiah pens a song of hope and praise. Chapter 25 is a song of praise to God that gives us great assurance in an unpredictable world. Notice this:

♦ In 25:8, the emphasis is on the tears of our faces.
♦ In 25:9, the emphasis is on the gladness of our faces.

So, how does a person go from tears to gladness in the journey of highs and lows? What is it that lifts your spirit and protects you from a toxic "poor me" attitude? What strengthens us in the "night seasons" and "dark nights" of the soul? What Divine Resources are available to those who are gospel centered and walk with Jesus? God records three that you can trust in:

1. You Have The "Promises Of God" To Trust In!
"I will exalt you and praise your name, for in perfect faithfulness you have done marvelous things, things planned long ago" (v.1).

Isaiah tells us here that God's counsels (or promises) are faithful and true! The writer is speaking about God delivering His people from the 70 year Babylonian captivity. Isaiah prophesies the event before it occurs. He has faith (or trust) that God's plan will be fulfilled. How can Isaiah be so confident and sure that God's plan will be completed in our lives? Because God's counsels and promises are done, "in perfect faithfulness" (v.1). This means that, what God has promised, planned, purposed and proposed for you will be accomplished! Why is this so meaningful? Because Israel would experience a detour in Babylon and be put "on hold" for a season. They would seem to be forgotten by God during a period of testing (70 years). Yet, what Israel thought was a bump in the road, God was using to fulfill His long range plan! Captivity in Babylon was bumpy and King Cyrus was doing his own thing. But even ungodly Cyrus would be used by the Lord in God's bigger picture!

Maybe you have an unfulfilled expectation in your own life. Maybe you have to deal with an ungodly Cyrus, someone attempting to bring harm to you. Maybe you feel "on hold", detoured or delayed. If so, remember God's Word so that you can rest and relax in your spirit: His promises and counsels are faithful and always true (without fault). He really is working all things together for your good and His glory!

The Take-A-Way?

When the road seems bumpy and things don't go as you have planned, remember, the bumps are what you climb on!

Nuf Sed!

"Divine Resources"
Part II

"You have made the city a heap of rubble, the fortified town a ruin, the foreigners stronghold a city no more" (Isaiah 25:2).

Isaiah chapter 25 reveals God's great care for His people. Even though Israel was put "on hold" in Babylon for 70 years, God showed Himself strong in three ways. Yesterday, we saw how God keeps His promises; today see the other two Divine Resources we have to enjoy the journey:

2. You Have The "Power Of God" To Withstand Temptation!
"You have made the city a heap of rubble" (v.2).
Isaiah is speaking of the Jews who would return from Babylon. King Cyrus would invade Babylon, take it over, and God's people were set free from their captivity. In other words, as great as Babylon was, God made the city a heap of ruin. Babylon became "no more" (v.2) because God's power was displayed. God's power broke the evil power that held Israel in bondage, freed those confined behind walls, and raised up a chosen generation for Himself. And, this is what Jesus has done for you! Like God freed the Jewish people to be a witness to the onlookers nearby, so Jesus has broken sin's power to rule and control your life. Jesus (at the cross and resurrection) destroyed satan's power to dominate your life and force you to sin. Sin will lure, tempt and entice you, but sin has no authority to control you because of Jesus!

3. You Have The "Provision Of God" To Rejoice In!
God doesn't promise that we will escape the distress and storms of life. He does promise however, that He will sustain us in every season. Notice how specific the Lord is in caring for you and me. Notice how, "the song of the ruthless is stilled" (v.5):
♦ **God is a refuge for the poor and needy** (v.4):
This means that God will sustain you in distress, and in your weakness impart to you His strength.

♦ **God is a shelter in the storm** (v.4):
This means that God will be your place of retreat and safety. His presence will be your security which protects your heart from anxiety and fear.

♦ **God is your shade from the heat** (v.4):
This means that as Israel found relief in the shadows from the intense sun, so Jesus will keep you from withering up under trial.
So much so will be God's help to you, that Moab (Israel's enemy) will be trampled down, brought down in pride, laid low, and be like dust (v.10-12). In other words, you have no need to fear as you walk out your journey on earth! The Lord will be enough to steady you at every turn!!

The Take-A-Way?
If God could bring down Babylon in dust to free His people, then God can surely clear your pathway to get His will done in your life!

Nuf Sed!

"Appetite Is Everything"
Part I

"Come, all you who are thirsty, come to the waters; and you who have no money, come, buy and eat! Come, buy wine and milk without money and without cost" (Isaiah 55:1).

Isaiah 55 is called by many the **"Invitation Chapter"** from the Lord. It is a picture of Jesus calling out to you and me to respond to Him. It is a plea to align ourselves with God so that He can satisfy the innermost longings of our hearts. Why is this so important? Because if we fail to find our complete joy in the Lord, our hearts will default to lesser gods, created things and unfulfilling idols. Notice how this works in your heart and mine:

"Why spend money on what is not bread, and your labor on what does not satisfy? Listen, listen to me, and eat what is good, and your soul will delight in the richest of fare" (v.2).
The Lord is clearly telling us two things here:

1. Earthly objects (created things) can never fill the void created by God – for God! and,
2. Eternal aspirations are the only things that can satisfy and transform our hearts.

Isaiah gives Israel and us clear instruction and an invitation for spiritual health and contentment:

"Come to the waters.....buy wine and milk without money" (v.1).

♦ **Water** is symbolic of the Holy Spirit:
It's the Holy Spirit that refreshes, cleanses and renews us.
♦ **Wine** is symbolic of gladness of heart:
It was used in the feasts on occasions of great joy.
♦ **Milk** is symbolic of nourishment:
It refers to the Word which nourishes and feeds our spiritual man.
It's obvious that some Israelites were feeding on spiritual junk food. They were attempting to be fed and satisfied by external (temporal) things. That's why God reminds us to:

"Eat what is good and your soul will delight in the richest of fare" (v.2). While the gospel is not about **achieving** but about **receiving**, we do have a part to play in spiritual discipline. It's our responsibility to respond to God's great grace. It's our privilege to:

♦ Partake of the things that nourish our souls!
♦ Pursue what has value for all eternity!

- Possess an appetite that moves us closer to Jesus!
- Practice daily habits that allow God to make us stronger! *Prayer model*
- Present ourselves to God and narrow our interests to overcome distractions!

The Take-A-Way?

Lest we ever seek God to draw attention to ourselves, may we never forget Isaiah's great reminder: "This will be for the Lord's renown" (v.13).

Nuf Sed!

November 27
"Appetite Is Everything"
Part II

"Seek the Lord while he may be found; call on him while he is near" (Isaiah 55:6).

Isaiah chapter 55 is one incredible invitation from the Lord! We are invited to the Lord's table to drink, to pray and to sing. Yesterday we learned the reason to "come, all you who are thirsty" (v.1).
We discovered the reason to drink from the fountain of the Lord. The reason? Because God offers us:

♦ Wine – that produces a gladness within our hearts.
♦ Water – that refreshes, renews and cleanses us.
♦ Milk – that nourishes and feeds us from the Word.

Today, notice the other two reasons that we've been invited to respond to the Lord's invitation:

2. We Have A Reason to Pray!
"Seek the Lord while he may be found; call on him while he is near. Let the wicked forsake his way and the evil man his thoughts. Let him turn to the Lord, and he will have mercy on him, and to our God, for he will freely pardon" (v.6, 7).

To, **"Seek the Lord while he may be found"** (v.6) means to:

♦ Take advantage of those times when God is drawing you to Himself.
♦ Take God seriously when He speaks to your heart.
♦ Refuse to resist, when the Lord deals with you about something.
♦ Don't put off till tomorrow, what God is asking of you today.
♦ Be sensitive to those seasons when the Spirit is drawing you closer.

Why are we invited to draw near to God continually and in humility? How and why is it possible to draw near to God when all of us are imperfect sinners? How can we approach God (for intimacy) when there is wicked and evil tendencies in our hearts? Because when we " turn to the Lord" (v.7), we will discover two things:

1. First, we discover that **God is merciful!**
"Let him turn to the Lord, and he will have mercy on him" (v.7).
This means (because of Jesus) that you will receive what is needed instead of what is deserved! It means that God is ready to respond to you because Jesus has overcome the distance between you and God!

2. Secondly, we discover that **God will abundantly pardon!**
"For he will freely pardon" (v.7).

This means that God abounds in his capacity to forgive, and, willingly wants to cover our transgressions! It means that (because of Jesus' sacrifice) God rejects no one who turns from their sin and turns to Jesus. It means that God is anxious and longing to forgive us, and cleanse us, and restore us to intimacy and fellowship.

The Take-A-Way?
When we seek the Lord and respond to His drawing of our hearts, God will have mercy and pardon every sin – because Jesus paid it all!

Nuf Sed!

November 28
"Appetite Is Everything"
Part 3

"You will go out in joy and be led forth in peace; the mountains and hills will burst into song before you, and all the trees of the field will clap their hands" (Isaiah 55:12).

The past two days we've discovered that: we have a reason to be strong in the Lord (because God has provided wine, water and milk for us). And, we have a reason to pray (for we can draw near to God because of his mercy and pardon). Today I want you to see that:

3. You Have A Reason to "Sing"!
"Burst into song…..clap their hands" (v.12).
 The mass exodus from Egypt was hurried and dangerous for Israel. This exodus from Babylon will be filled with joy, peace and singing on the way back to Jerusalem. But what are the reasons to sing and shout about? Why does Isaiah give us a reason to pause, celebrate, and express the joy of the Lord?

♦ We rejoice over the **"Ways" of the Lord**!
"For my thoughts are not your thoughts, neither are your ways my ways, declares the Lord" (v.8).
 This declaration has comforted millions in their journey with the Lord. Why? Because all of us have experienced things in life that were unplanned, uncomfortable and unexpected. All of us have been tempted to "second guess" the Lord and ask "why?". Yet God reminds us that: "As the heavens are higher than the earth, so are my ways higher than your ways and my thoughts higher than your thoughts" (v.9). God is reminding us right here; that He knows things that we don't know, can see things that we can't see, and is planning things that we can't plan!

♦ We can also rejoice over the **"Word" of the Lord!**
"So is my word that goes out from my mouth: It will not return to me empty, but will accomplish what I desire and achieve the purpose for which I sent it" (v.11).
 Isaiah reminds us that, as rain affects the earth that is hard and dry, so the Word affects our hearts that can be hard and dry. In other words, when the Word is sown into the heart, it will produce an intended result. And, although you may think that the Word has been sown in vain, it will be successful in producing a harvest!

♦ We can also rejoice over the **"Work" of the Lord!**
"Instead of the thorn bush will grow the pine tree, and instead of briers the myrtle will grow. This will be for the Lord's renoun" (v.13).
 Thorns and briers are symbols of desolation and uselessness. Fir and

Myrtle trees are symbols of beauty and usefulness. Isaiah is telling us, that under the gospel of Jesus, the Holy Spirit will affect great change in your heart and mine. What was once overrun with thorns and weeds, will be plowed, cultivated and permanently changed. And, this heart change will be God's great advertisement and drawing power to the world.

The Take-A-Way?
When our ways differ from God's ways, remember; there is always a bigger picture and you can trust God for "His way is perfect" (Psalm 18:30).

Nuf Sed!

"God's Glory Revealed"
Part I

"In all their distress he too was distressed, and the angel of his presence saved them. In his love and mercy he redeemed them; he lifted them up and carried them all the days of old" (Isaiah 63:9).

Isaiah 63 and 64 deal with the destruction of the enemies of God. Both chapters reveal how Jesus is the Mighty Savior! It is one great diary of how Jesus suffered to ensure our victory, how God has regard for his people, and how heaven wants to see answers to prayer on earth.

The seven chapters of Isaiah 60-66 describe God's glory to us. Isaiah uses the word "GLORY" 23 times in these chapters. We are given a clear revelation of what God's glory revealed means to us; how it is practically demonstrated in our lives today:

1. God's Glory Is Seen In His Power Over Sin!
"Who is this coming from Edom, from Bozrah, with his garments stained crimson? Who is this, robed in splendor, striding forward in the greatness of his strength? It is I, speaking in righteousness, mighty to save" (v.1).

Isaiah sees Jesus returning from the battle of Armageddon (Rev. 19:11-21). Edom is used to describe the nations that have oppressed God's people. Jesus is described as one treading in a wine press. Why? Because in ancient times, a wine press was a large hallowed rock. Grapes were placed in the rock for people to tread on. The juice ran out a hole in the rock and was caught in a vessel. When people crushed the grapes, juice would splash on their garments. Jesus is pictured here with his garments stained with blood, resulting from his victory over all enemies (Rev. 19:13). What does this picture of Jesus mean today?

Isaiah looks ahead and sees Jesus victorious over our enemies (the world, the flesh, and the devil). It's a picture of Jesus "mighty to save" (Isaiah 63:1).

"Blood spattered my garments, and I stained all my clothing" (v.3) is about Jesus! It's a reference to Jesus, how He has crushed sin's power to rule you like people crushed grapes in the wine press. The meaning here is unmistakable:

♦ Christ through His cross, has redeemed us from sin's penalty!
♦ Christ through His cross, has destroyed sin's power to rule us.
♦ Christ through His cross, has freed us from the ruling power of our flesh nature (just as Israel was freed from Moab's power).
♦ Christ through His cross, can "tread down" every fiery dart of the wicked one to lead you astray; But, not by your own power, strength and ability! We only win the war over sin and temptation when we look to Jesus! We can't win by trying harder and doing better! We only win when Jesus captures our heart, attention, focus and affection. His love will crowd out the idols and lesser gods of distraction!

The Take-A-Way?
Jesus has done for you what you could never do for yourself; His blood stained garments have truly paid it all!

Nuf Sed!

"God's Glory Revealed"
Part II

"Who led them through the depths? Like a horse in open country, they did not stumble" (Isaiah 63:13).

Jesus is revealed as our Mighty Savior, ready to save, in Isaiah 63 and 64. He is seen as the suffering one to ensure our salvation. We have a glorious picture of Jesus, the Christ, who crushed sin's power to rule us, like people crushed grapes in the wine press (v.2, 3). Yesterday we saw God's glory revealed in His power over sin. Today, notice:

2. God's Glory Is Revealed In His Care For His Own!

♦ "I will tell of the kindness of the Lord"(v.7).
♦ "Many good things he has done"(v.7)
♦ "In all their distress he too was distressed"(v.9)
♦ "The angel of his presence saved them"(v.9).
♦ "In his love and mercy he redeemed them"(v.9).
♦ "He lifted and carried them"(v.9).

Did Israel deserve God's goodness? Did they remain faithful to God at every turn? Was God's faithful care ever achieved (by works) instead of received (by grace)? Hardly so: "Yet they rebelled and grieved his Holy Spirit" (v.10). Israel vexed, or grieved, the Holy Spirit of God. God would then favor Israel's enemies and Israel experienced disaster after disaster. But in the midst of Israel's unfaithfulness, God was faithful again and again. So much so, that Isaiah reminds us of God's fatherly care for His own:

♦ God **Remembers** His Own!
"His people recalled the days of old.....He who brought them through the sea" (v.11).

While God was brokenhearted over Israel's disobedience, He did not forget that He had made a covenant with them. He remained faithful to His promise to be Israel's protector and provider! As God remembered Israel, so God remembers you!

♦ God **Renews** His Own!
"Where is he who set his Holy Spirit among them" (v.11).

Though God at times seemed to forsake Israel for their rebellion, He constantly renewed, strengthened and guided them through the wilderness.

♦ God **Rested** His Own!
"Like cattle that go down to the plain, they were given rest by the Spirit of the Lord" (v.14).

As cattle in the heat of the day found rest in the shade, so Israel found rest from their enemies.

♦ God **Responded** To Prayers From His Own!
"Look down from heaven and see from your lofty throne" (v.15).
"Return for the sake of your servants" (v.17).

Israel allowed Babylon to trample down the holy place and cause spiritual ruin. How? By disobedience and hardheartedness! Thus, Isaiah makes a desperate plea for God to "Return" (v.17).

The Take-A-Way?
If God has a perfect plan for your life, why would you ever want to step outside that plan through rebellion and disobedience?

Nuf Sed!

The "Grace" Of Christmas
Part I

"But made himself nothing, taking the very nature of a servant, being made in human likeness" (Philippians 2:7).

Christmas is around the corner! Because of the magnitude and meaning of Jesus' birth, we are dedicating the next 25 days to the greatest texts, themes and people surrounding the incarnation. There are so many relevant and practical lessons for you and me – from the Baby in the manger! We pray that God's Word will be timely and contextual where He finds you each day. Blessed Christmas season as we (daily) enjoy the journey.

In Philippians 2:5-11, Paul tells us how to do nothing out of selfish ambition or vain conceit. We learn how to consider others better than ourselves. We discover that humility is born in our hearts when we look at Jesus being born. Notice how Christmas reveals God's grace and melts the heart of all who believe. Paul gives us three revelations of Divine Compassion:

1. Christmas Reveals The Grace Of God (v.5-7)
"Who, being in very nature God, did not consider equality with God something to be grasped" (v.7).

This means that Jesus was equal with God the Father and fully divine in nature. He was crowned with glory and splendor, all sufficient, and in need of nothing. Yet, Jesus did not seize upon or pursue His position as equal with God. He did not eagerly seek to retain His heavenly place and position. He just wasn't hung up on status or titles. Jesus avoided arrogance, conceit, and wasn't bent on retaining His honor and glory. In fact;

♦ Jesus **"made himself nothing"** (v.7) which means:
Jesus was willing to be born, despised, rejected, and become "nothing" on our behalf. This means that Jesus volunteered to empty himself and give up His rights and rank in heaven for you and me (who did not deserve it). He emptied Himself, not of His deity but of His glorious privileges.

♦ Jesus took **"the very nature of a servant"** (v.7) which means:
Jesus was willing to condescend to a servant's role and perform the duties of a servant. He chose to advance others at the expense of Himself, cared less who got the credit, didn't need to be thanked for His service and took up His cross without complaint.

♦ Jesus was **"made in human likeness"** (v.7) which means:
Jesus assumed upon Himself a body like ours, willing to be born of a woman. Why? To be touched with what touches us, feel what we feel, and minister as

our faithful high priest. Not because we deserve it, but because of the Grace of God revealed at Christmas! Is there any more motivation needed (than this) to live our lives to honor His Name? Do we need any more incentive to humble ourselves under the mighty hand of God? Can anything melt our hearts like Jesus leaving heaven and coming to earth (for us)? I don't think so either!

The Take-A-Way?
How can we ever lift our hearts in pride, knowing that Jesus became poor so that we could become rich?

Nuf Sed!

December 2
The "Grace" Of Christmas
Part II

"And being found in appearance as a man, he humbled himself and became obedient to death – even death on a cross" (Philippians 2:8).

Yesterday we saw how Christmas reveals the amazing grace of God. Today, let's see the gift and the glory of God revealed in Paul's words to the Philippians:

2. Christmas Reveals The Gift Of God (v.8).
Three gifts of Jesus leap off the page in v.8. They are gifts that we could not merit or earn:

♦   I see Christ's **Humility**!
"He humbled himself" (v.8).
This means that Jesus refused to aspire to high honors and refused to yield to pomp and parade. Jesus refused to claim what He rightfully deserved; He did not demand that others wash his feet!

♦   I see Christ's **Obedience**!
Jesus, "became obedient to death" (v.8).
This reveals to us that Jesus yielded to the perfect will of God for his life. He submitted and surrendered to the Father's plan. Jesus literally obeyed the Father's design for our own redemption, and presented himself to take our sins away.

♦   I see Christ's **Sacrifice**!
"Even death on a cross" (v.8).
This is why we have Christmas Eve communion services. Why? Because Jesus was born to make a straight path to Calvary! Jesus was actually born to face suffering, shame and satisfy God's just demands. He was born to carry your sin and mine and deliver us from the slavery of sin.

3. Christmas Reveals The Glory Of God (v.9-11)
♦   There is a glorious **"Exaltation"**!
"God exalted him to the highest place" (v.9)
Because Jesus humbled Himself before the Father, God rewarded Him by exalting Him above all.

♦   There is a glorious **"Expectation"**!
"That at the name of Jesus every knee should bow" (v.10).
This reveals that God has given Christ supreme power and authority. How? One day, every creature in all the worlds and dimensions of being will bow

their knee to the Lord Jesus Christ.

♦   There is a glorious **"Exclamation"**!
"And every tongue confess that Jesus Christ is Lord, to the glory of God the Father" (v.11).

This means that God is going to see to it that every nation, tongue, language, person, race, color, creed, belief, religion, king, leader and authority – will confess that Jesus is exactly who He claimed to be – the Lord God of the universe! The day is coming when the Suffering Servant will be seen on the Throne of Glory! Christmas means that those tiny little feet in the manger, were formed to walk up Calvary's hill and purchase eternal life for you and me!

The Take-A-Way?
I can never feel arrogant or elite because I am only made holy by the work of another – Jesus!

Nuf Sed!

The "Glory" Of Christmas

"The Word became flesh and made his dwelling among us. We have seen his glory, the glory of the One and Only who came from the Father, full of grace and truth" (John 1:14).

Many years ago Solomon asked this question at the dedication of the temple: **"Will God really dwell on earth?"** (1Kings 8:27). God's glory had dwelt in the Tabernacle (Exodus 40:34), in the Temple (1 Kings 8:11), but departed when Israel became a disobedient people (Ezekiel 9, 10, 11). Then through the miracle of the virgin birth, God's glory came to earth again in the person of Jesus Christ, God's son. Remember now:

♦ Matthew wrote to the Jews, emphasizing how Jesus fulfilled the Old Testament prophecies.
♦ Mark wrote to the Romans, emphasizing Jesus as the Servant of Servants, ministering to the needs of people.
♦ Luke wrote to the Greeks, emphasizing Jesus as the compassionate Son of Man.
♦ John wrote to both Jew and Gentile, emphasizing Jesus as the Son of God.

The question is, how is the glory of God revealed in Jesus Christ? And, how was Jesus (the Word) made flesh to dwell among us? Discover today and tomorrow, The **"Glory"** of Christmas! Notice the four truths in John 1 that shed much light on the birth of Jesus:

1. Jesus Is Eternal (v. 1-3).

"In the beginning was the Word, and the Word was with God" (v.1). Did Jesus really exist with the Father before Christmas Day? "Father, glorify me in your presence with the glory I had with you before the world began" (John 17:5). How do we know that Jesus is eternal and divine? John gives us four reasons:

♦ **"In the beginning was the Word" (v.1)**.
Which means that Jesus existed in the indefinite eternity which preceded all time; the immeasurable past. The Logos cannot be said to have come into being at any specific moment. In other words, He always was!

♦ **"And the Word was with God"** (v.1).
Which means that Jesus was with God in the beginning before the world was made!

♦ **"And the Word was God"** (v.1).
Which means that Jesus (the Logos) possessed and eternally manifested the very nature of God, even before creation.

♦ **"Through him all things were made"** (v.3).
Which means that Jesus was the agent, or the efficient cause, by which the universe was made. In other words, it is Jesus who caused the transitions from what was not to what is!

The take-a-way?

Since Jesus always was, was equal with God before creation, is totally Divine in nature, and caused the world to come into existence – shouldn't it be easy to trust Him with your life and with your future?

Nuf Sed!

December 4
The "Glory" of Christmas
Part II

"From the fullness of his grace we have all received one blessing after another" (John 1:16).

Yesterday we learned that Jesus is eternal, was equal with God from eternity, is Divine in nature and caused the world to come into existence. Discover today how:

2. Jesus Is Life Giving (v.4).
"In him was life, and that life was the light of men" (v.4). The word "life" here is not just some conscious existence. It means, "the life of God expressed in human experience". It means that Jesus is declared to be the living God, is the source or the fountain of life, and is the source of life to the soul that was dead in trespasses and sin.

There are four essentials for human life: light, air, water and food. Jesus is all of these and more:
♦ He is the **light of life** and the Light of the world (John 8:12; Mal. 4:2).
♦ He gives us the **breath of life** (John 3:8; 20:22).
♦ He gives us the **water of life** (John 4:10; 7:37-39).
♦ He is our Food, the **bread of life** (John 6:35).

3. Jesus Is Supreme (v.5-13).
"The light shines in the darkness, but the darkness has not understood it" (v.5).

The words "has not understood" (v.5) do not mean to understand or comprehend. They mean, to overcome, overrule or overpower. In other words, Jesus shines bright in the darkness and the darkness of sin and satan cannot extinguish this light! The world can resist His light, but cannot put out His light! This means that, in spite of every power of darkness to stamp out God's presence in your life, darkness has no authority to control you any longer! Why? Because Jesus is supreme in His power over all darkness!

4. Jesus Is Accessible (v.14-18)
"The Word became flesh and made his dwelling among us" (v.14).

This is really the "Glory" of Christmas! We see how Christmas makes your life and mine meaningful today:
♦ **We know what Jesus did!**
He became incarnate (or assumed the nature of man). Jesus took on flesh and blood and experienced life in a human body. The invisible God expressed Himself in a human personality through the glorious incarnation!
♦ **We see who Jesus is!**
"We have seen his glory" (v.14), means majesty, dignity and honor has been expressed in Jesus' rank and character. This "glory" has been revealed

and seen in his miracles, teaching, resurrection and ascension.

♦ **We experience what Jesus does!**

"From the fulness of his grace we have all received one blessing after another" (v.16). This means that God's grace is not historic in nature, but something we can experience day after day. We receive God's grace and Divine life being poured into us as we humble ourselves before Him.

The Take-A-Way?

Fresh grace is available to us every day, but it's not achieved by works, it's received by faith!

Nuf Sed!

December 5
The "Visitation" Of Christmas

"Therefore the Lord himself will give you a sign: The virgin will be with child and will give birth to a son, and will call him Immanuel" (Isaiah 7:14).

Isaiah 7, 8, 9 are three chapters of one prophecy that detail the distress of Judah. It is an account of how Judah needed a ray of hope at a very dark time. It is a timely word for our hearts today.

Isaiah 7:1-9 is a message given to Ahaz. It is a great word of encouragement as two evil kings unite with an evil scheme to destroy God's people and Jerusalem. A message comes from God through Isaiah to the people. What's the message? "Keep calm and don't be afraid. Do not lose heart…..because of the fierce anger of Rezin…..have plotted your ruin" (v.3-6). Yet this is what the Sovereign Lord says: "It will not take place, it will not happen" (v.7). In other words, the Lord calms the worries and fears of his people with timely intervention. And, God's word came true concerning the two evil kings opposing God's people:

◆ Rezin himself was besieged and slain (2 Kings 16:9).
◆ Pekah was also dethroned and murdered (2 Kings 15:29, 30).
◆ The house of David escaped the crisis as well, and continued to occupy the throne of Judah.

Looking at Isaiah 7, I see three words that speak to you and me. They are timely, relevant and bring great encouragement to the soul this Christmas season:

1. God Keeps His **Promise**!
When the enemy said, "Let us invade Judah; let us tear it apart and divide it among ourselves" (v.6), God said, "It will not happen" (v.7). When the enemy came in like a flood to intimidate Ahaz, God gave a promise in perfect timing. The big deal about this is: the boldest promises of the Messiah have been given in the darkest hours of time (Genesis 3:15; Exodus 12:13; Isaiah 28:16; Jeremiah 23:5; Ezekiel 34:23). When things were at their worst, Jesus was the promised consolation!

2. God Brings His **Peace**!
What is the calming word to Ahaz in the face of danger?
◆ "Keep calm" (v.4) – or don't be afraid or disturbed.
◆ "Don't be afraid" (v.4) – or intimidated by what you see and hear.
◆ "Do not lose heart" (v.4) – or stay resolute and courageous.
So how is all of this healthy self-talk possible?

3. God Makes A **Visit**!
What does God tell Ahaz in his most needful hour? "The virgin will be with child and will give birth to a son, and will call him Immanuel" (v.14). When Ahaz is in danger from two kings stronger than himself, God promises a son

that will be a helper and deliverer from all enemies on earth. This Immanuel will come to earth for our salvation from the depravity of sin, and He will be our security through every season of life. Wow! Jesus really is present with us – in the secret place, the dwelling place, the market place, the holy place; in every place.

The Take-A-Way?
As God promised Ahaz "His" presence for suffering Israel during the forthcoming pain at the hands of Assyria, so God promises to be with you now, and His presence will be your joy and confidence!

Nuf Sed!

The "Gift" Of Christmas

"But you, Bethlehem Ephrathah, though you are small among the clans of Judah, out of you will come for me one who will be ruler over Israel, whose origins are from old, from ancient times" (Micah 5:2).

Micah 5:2 meets our greatest need and reveals the greatest gift of all time. Here's the setting:

The people of God are in great distress in Micah 5. In v.1 there is a siege and a smiting, and Jerusalem must collect itself and defend itself in battle. It is a picture of Israel suffering until the Messiah arrives. And, at the time of Zion's biggest void and deepest distress, God promises to send a Deliverer, King, Ruler and Savior who will meet the need of every human heart:

1. Jesus Is A Gift Of **Impartiality**!
"Though you are small among the clans of Judah" (v.2). Jesus was prophesied to be born within the tribal lot of Judah, six miles south of Jerusalem, in a town called Bethlehem. Bethlehem is called "small" in v.2. Jesus is not born on Hebron's royal mount or in Jerusalem's beautiful palaces. He is born in the little, humble and obscure place. Why? To reveal that He comes to the humble, contrite and lowly in spirit. Bethlehem means, "House of Bread". Ephratah means "fruitful and abundant". This reveals that Jesus comes for all, even those who feel unknown, unnoticed, and unimportant. He comes to be your fruit and abundant supply in the journey of life. Without partiality, Jesus receives you unto Himself!

2. **Jesus Is A Gift Of Love!**
"Out of you will come for me" (v.2), is all about the grace and love of God! "Out of you" (v.2) refers to Jehovah God who planned it all. It was the Father who drew salvation's plan; it was the Father who made a way for His justice to be satisfied. It was the Ancient of Days who, out of love, willed that His Son would be born and sacrificed as the ultimate gift!

3. **Jesus Is A Gift Of Power!**
"One who will be ruler over Israel" (v.2), refers to Jesus who is come to rule within our hearts. It means that Jesus has come to rule and govern over our desires, affections and temptations. It reveals that Jesus can subdue every distraction and sin that is not God's will for your life.

4. **Jesus Is A Gift Of Wisdom!**
"Whose origins are from old, from ancient times" (v.2). Jesus being born in Bethlehem is easy to grasp. But His origins from old and ancient times means that God had wisdom from eternity, and saw that we would need a Savior! In other words, it was God in His wisdom who knew that we would sin, could not redeem ourselves, and needed Christmas Day! In wisdom, the Father saw

us under the penalty of sin and unable to overcome sin, hell or the grave. In wisdom, Christmas means that God gave us the gift of eternal life in Jesus!

The Take-A-Way?
Christmas is not an afterthought or a surprise; it was God's plan when we could not help ourselves!

Nuf Sed!

The "Freedom" Of Christmas

"But when the time had fully come, God sent his Son, born of a woman, born under law, to redeem those under law, that we might receive the full rights of sons" (Galatians 4:4,5).

Paul the apostle had planted churches in Southern Galatia. After planting the churches, Paul made a return visit to strengthen the believers. What Paul discovered was, the Galatians had fallen prey to another gospel. What was this "other" (1:9) gospel? Teachers were perverting the Gospel of Grace and confusing believers. The Galatians were now being told to grow in the Lord by keeping the law of circumcision, rites, and ceremonies to please God. Teachers were actually promoting spirituality by the means of what you do, don't do, what leader you follow, and what group you belong to. Paul comes along and writes Galatians to reveal why the law was really given:
- It was given to reveal our sin (3:19).
- It was given to point us to Christ's coming (3:24).

Paul beautifully explains why Jesus was born in the fulness of time. We see how Christmas was God's idea to free us from the bondage that we could not free ourselves. Today and tomorrow discover the "Freedom" Of Christmas!

1. The Law Was A Problem! (v.1-3).

"What I am saying is that as long as the heir is a child, he is no different from a slave, although he owns the whole estate" (v.1). Teachers were bewitching new converts in Galatia (3:1). They were tricking them into thinking that keeping the ceremonial laws made them better Christians. Paul comes along and says: "As long as the heir is a child, he is no different from a slave, although he owns the whole estate" (v.1). This means, no matter how wealthy a father may be, his infant son could not enjoy his inheritance. Why? Because, "He is subject to guardians and trustees until the time set by his father" (v.2). Paul is simply saying here:
- Like a child was under their guardian, tutor or governor who took care of them (and)
- Like the same child was not yet able to enjoy their inheritance,

So you and I were under the law, "slavery" v.3, until Christ was born. We had a inheritance, freedom and salvation to come. But until Christ arrived, "we were children, we were in slavery" (v.3). All of this means that, under the law we live in frustration and bondage. Why? Because, before Christ, we can see ourselves but cannot change ourselves! We can see our weaknesses, but cannot overcome our weaknesses. We try harder to **achieve** our salvation, instead of simply **receive** our salvation. The problem under the law, before Christ, was:
- In v.1, we were children unable to enjoy the Father's wealth, and,

♦In v.3, we were in bondage to a system that produced no internal change.

The Take-A-Way?
Before Christ was born, we were in slavery to the law which exposed our sin but gave us no power over sin!

Nuf Sed!

December 8
The "Freedom" Of Christmas
Part II

"But when the time had fully come, God sent his son, born of a woman, born under the law, to redeem those under law, that we might receive the full rights of sons" (Galatians 4:4, 5).

Yesterday we looked at the problem of the law, how it revealed our sin but didn't give us power over sin. Discover God's answer to our dilemma:

2. The Lord Had A Plan All Along (v.4).
♦ **"But when the time had fully come"** means:
Jesus was born in Bethlehem in God's perfect timing, for Rome was expecting a deliverer. Old religions were dying and empty philosophies were fading. Alexander made the Greek language easy to be spoken. Spiritual hunger was everywhere and all major roads were connected to Rome.
♦ **"God sent his son"** means:
Jesus is God and all powerful! He has power over sin, satan, and death. He has power to rescue us from the law which could not save us.
♦ **"Born of a woman"** means:
Jesus was man as well as God. This means that Jesus could be our substitute and sacrifice. As a man, He could identify with every need we will ever have.
♦ **"Born under the law"** means:
Jesus was born to fulfill the demands of the law, to accomplish what we could not, and to supersede the law with the greater power of grace.

3. There Was The Purchase Of Our Liberty (v.5).
"To redeem those under the law, that we might receive the full rights of sons" (v.5).
You and I were under the law before Christ. We all have violated the law and deserved the penalty of the law which was death. But what did Jesus do? He "redeemed" us which means:
♦ To purchase by the paying of a price.
♦ To satisfy the law which we could not satisfy.
♦ To rescue us from the rule that crushed us and make us sons instead of slaves.

4. There Is The Provision Of Our Legacy (v.6,7).
The law cut off our approach to God, but Jesus made us sons and daughters, able to come near to God! This "Christmas Freedom" means:
♦ We've been **"accepted"**
"You are sons" (v.6) means that you have been fully pardoned through the merits of Jesus!

♦ We've been **"empowered"**

"God sent the Spirit of his Son into our hearts" (v.6) means the law was an external authority and could not change our hearts. But now, the Holy Spirit renews, quickens and empowers our inner man to follow Jesus.

♦ We've been **"delivered"**

"No longer a slave, but a son" (v.7) means we are no longer suppressed by ceremonial laws or slaves in servitude to sin. It means we are "heirs" which is someone who receives an inheritance because of another!

The Take-A-Way?

Christmas means "Freedom", freedom to have intimacy with God, freedom from slavery to sin, and freedom to call God, "Our Father".

Nuf Sed!

The "Increase" Of Christmas
Part I

"For to us a child is born, to us a son is given and the government will be on his shoulders…..of the increase of his government and peace there will be no end" (Isaiah 9:6,7).

Isaiah chapter 9 is a continuation of the prophecy from chapters 7 and 8. The prophecy is a collection of threats and promises. It denounces the sin of wicked Ahaz, yet it also offers a rainbow of hope in the storm clouds. On the one hand we see how a foreign invasion is about to cause trouble. Zebulun and Naphtali will be dishonored and Judah is in darkness under Ahaz. On the other hand, we see how the Redeemer will overcome darkness with light (v.2), restore Israel (v.3), be victorious like Gideon (v.4), defeat the enemy invasion (v.5), and give Isaiah and us great hope (9:6). The prophecy from God to Isaiah is clear:

♦ There is a nation groping in darkness in need of a deliverer, and,
♦ There is a great light that shines in the person of the Christ child!

The prophecy can only refer to Jesus! Isaiah sees Jesus rising in distant Galilee. Isaiah is given a picture that encourages your heart in a very strong way:

1. The Increase Of Christmas Is About A Person!
God shows Isaiah a picture of Christmas before Jesus is ever born: "For to us a child is born, to us a son is given" (v.6). This means that God declares the humanity of Jesus (a child), the deity of Jesus (a son is given), and the recipients of the blessing (unto us). In other words, it was for you that Jesus was born! It was for you that Jesus was conceived of the Holy Spirit! It was for you that Jesus was given on Christmas Day. And what would His name be called?

♦ **Wonderful** (which means One that is distinguished as a miracle Himself and a miracle worker).
♦ **Counselor** (which means One that is fitted to counsel, advise, and give direction to His people).
♦ **Mighty God** (which means One that is strong, powerful, and full of unlimited power).
♦ **Everlasting Father** (which means One who is eternal, always sovereign, and always in charge).
♦ **Prince of Peace** (which means One who brings peace with God through the work of the cross).

"Of the increase of his government and peace there will be no end" (v.7).
1. The word **"increase"** means that the work of Jesus in you will continue to be progressive and expanding and increasing within you.
2. The word **"government"** means to rule and reign within your heart (to

call the shots).

3.   The words **"there will be no end"** mean that God is unlimited in what He can do in you.

The Take-A-Way?

Jesus is not limited by space, time or your limitations, and is able to change what needs to be changed in you and me today!

Nuf Sed!

December 10
The "Increase" Of Christmas
Part II

"The people walking in darkness have seen a great light; of those living in the land of the shadow of death a light has dawned" (Isaiah 9:2).

Yesterday we saw that Christmas is about a **Person**, a person whose work "there will be no end" (v.7). Today we'll see that Christmas is also about a **Promise**! The promise is for everyone who has placed the government of their life on the shoulders of the Lord. What exactly is the Christmas Increase that Isaiah writes about?

1. There Is Light Instead Of Darkness!
"The people walking in darkness have seen a great light" (v.2). For Israel, it was a season of darkness! Assyria would come in and carry Israel away, there was a culture of immorality, and Israel was in the midst of an oppressive situation. There was a desperate need of Divine visitation. What happened to God's people in the darkness? They experienced a "great light" (v.2). In other words, Jesus came right into the dark region of Galilee to bring increase to His people. This means that Jesus can come right into the darkest circumstances and events of your life as well. It is Jesus who will bring peace and calm to your heart as you cast your cares upon Him.

2. There Is Joy Instead Of Sorrow!
"They rejoice before you as people rejoice at the harvest" (v.3). Israel was taken captive in Babylon. It seemed like their labor and seed sowing was in vain. Their size was decreasing because of war and deportation. And God comes along with a promise: The Christ child will reverse Israel's sorrow, will draw people to Himself, and will change everything because of the cross and the resurrection!

3. There Is Freedom Instead Of Bondage!
"You have shattered the yoke that burdens them" (v.4). This means that, as God delivered Israel in bondage to Babylon and Assyria, so the Christ of Christmas does the same today. The yoke, staff, and rod that was broken in v.4, means that Jesus was born to deliver us from the slavery and servitude of sin. You and I have been set free from the guilt, condemnation and control of sin's oppressive power!

4. There Is Life Instead Of Death!
"On those living in the land of the shadow of death a light has dawned" (v.2). The expression, "The Shadow of Death", is where all of us were before we met the light of the world. Sin and death cast a shadow over Israel and all of us. The Good News of Christmas is, light has overcome darkness and grace has overcome our sin! The Good News is, Jesus has done what is necessary

for you to enjoy this Christmas season! The "zeal of the Lord almighty will accomplish this" (v.7). You can't **achieve His grace** by works, but you can **receive His grace** by faith!

The Take-A-Way?
Our lives can be lives of decrease or increase, and only Jesus can bring the light, life and power that we need!

Nuf Sed!

December 11
The "Song" Of Christmas
Part I

"Simeon took him in his arms and praised God, saying: 'Sovereign Lord, as you have promised, you now dismiss your servant in peace. For my eyes have seen your salvation, which you have prepared in the sight of all people, a light for revelation to the Gentiles and for the glory to your people Israel'" (Luke 2:29-32).

There are five Christmas songs in the Book of Luke:
♦ In Luke 1:42, **Elizabeth** sings out.
♦ In Luke 1:46, **Mary** sings out.
♦ In Luke 1:68, **Zacharias** sings out.
♦ In Luke 2:13, **Angels** sing out.
♦ In Luke 2:29, **Simeon** sings out.

What are they all singing about? They are singing from their hearts, about the good tidings of great joy because a Savior is being born. But what is so special about Simeon's song? Discover the four reasons that Christmas puts a shout and a song in Simeon's heart:

1. Simeon Rejoiced In The Work Of The "Holy Spirit"!
"And the **Holy Spirit** was upon him" (v.25).
"It had been revealed to him by the **Holy Spirit**" (v.26).
"Moved by the **Spirit**, he went into the temple courts" (v.27).

Like the Holy Spirit drew the shepherds to Jesus, and drew the wise men to Jesus, and drew the angels to Jesus, the Spirit now draws Simeon to Jesus. But why now? Two reasons:
♦ The parents of Jesus were bringing in the Baby at this exact time, and,
♦ God had made a promise to Simeon that He would keep to Simeon:

"It had been revealed to him by the Holy Spirit **that he would not die before he had seen the Lord's Christ**" (v.26). In other words, Simeon is about to die, but the Holy Spirit told him years before that he wouldn't die until he had seen the baby Jesus! And, while Simeon is obeying God like any other day, the Holy Spirit leads Joseph and Mary to the exact place where Simeon is. Simeon has no idea that this is the day when his prayer will be answered. All he is doing is following the leading of the Holy Spirit by slipping into the sanctuary. He then discovers that God is keeping His promise!

The take-a-ways are clear to me:
♦ **God is doing something in your life today, but God is also up to something else!**
♦ **God knows more than you do so you can "rest well" and trust the leading of His Spirit!**
♦ **God is fully present in your normal everyday activities!**
♦ **At times God's work is invisible, but God is still working in ways unknown to you!** Nuf Sed!

The "Song" Of Christmas

"Sovereign Lord, as you have promised, you now dismiss your servant in peace" (Luke 2:29).

Yesterday we discovered how the Holy Spirit led Simeon into the temple at the exact time that baby Jesus was there. Why did this meeting take place? On one hand, Simeon was, "moved by the Spirit" (v.27) to go there. On the other hand, God sovereignly led Mary and Joseph there as well. Why? Because three legal ceremonies were required at the birth of Jesus. The **Ceremony of Circumcision** symbolized the Jews' separation from the Gentiles (Genesis 17:9-14). The **Ceremony of Redemption** was when a firstborn son was presented to God, acknowledging that the child belonged to God, who alone had the power to give life (Exodus 13:2, 11-16; Numbers 18:15-16). The **Ceremony of Purification** took place 40 days after the birth of a son, and 80 days after the birth of a daughter. The mother was ceremonially unclean and could not enter the temple, so Mary and Joseph bring a lamb for a burnt offering and a dove for a sin offering. The priest would sacrifice the animals and declare the woman to be clean. This is the setting of our text, when Simeon enters the temple. Notice what Simeon rejoices and sings about:

2. Simeon Rejoices In The "Salvation" Of The Lord!
"For my eyes have seen your salvation, which you have prepared in the sight of all people" (v.30, 31). Simeon acknowledges that regardless of what he's done, where he's been, who he is, and who he knows – there is only one way to be saved. He declares that Jesus is "destined to cause the falling and rising of many" (v.34). In other words, some will choose to trust Jesus (and rise) while others will choose to ignore Jesus (and fall).

3. Simeon Rejoices In The "Sacrifice" Of The Lord!
"A sword will pierce your own soul too" (v.35). Simeon tells Mary that her baby will be crucified because He's on a mission. He warns Mary that her heart will be broken because Jesus was born to be a sacrifice for sin. He prepares her somewhat for what lies ahead. He tells her that the baby she holds is part of a Master plan, to give His life as a ransom for us all.

4. Simeon Rejoices In The "Searching" Of The Lord!
"The thoughts of many hearts will be revealed" (v.35). Simeon rejoices in the fact that Jesus (the Christ child) will reveal the thoughts of your heart and mine. He (Jesus) will be able to search us, convict, us, turn the light on, and lead us to freedom. Simeon flat out celebrates the fact that Jesus can change us into His likeness!

The take-a-way from Simeon's encounter?

♦ **Jesus was born in our world to take us to His world! and,**
♦ **Jesus produces a song in the heart of those who trust him!**

Nuf Sed!

December 13
The "Providence" Of Christmas
Part I

"And having been warned in a dream not to go back to Herod, they returned to their country by another route" (Matthew 2:12).

Have you ever had your plans changed by a higher plan? Ever had your expectations delayed or put on hold? If so, I have two words for you, "You're Normal". In Matthew chapter 2, God gives us some practical wisdom to help us enjoy the journey.

1. Notice God's Providence At Work!
"After Jesus was born in Bethlehem in Judea, during the time of King Herod" (v.1).

Joseph and Mary lived in Galilee, and Mary was great with child in Galilee. Joseph and Mary had planned for Jesus to be born in Nazareth, in Galilee. But God had foretold 600 years before, that Jesus would be born in Bethlehem of Judea (Micah 5:2). So how did God get Joseph and Mary to move 80 miles from Nazareth to Bethlehem?

"In those days Caesar Augustus issued a decree that a census should be taken of the entire Roman world" (Luke 2:1).

How did God providentially move His plan forward? The Roman Emperor ordered a census in the middle of his reign. But why now? To force every Jewish male to the city of his father to record his name, family, property and occupation. This was God's way to get Joseph and Mary out of Nazareth and back into Bethlehem! But how can God use an ungodly ruler to fulfill Bible prophecy? God can do this because He is "all wise" and sees the beginning to the end. Notice the wisdom in this context:

◆ In **God's timing**, God can use people outside of your control to accomplish His will in your life!
(Caesar's decree overruled Joseph and Mary's expectation).
◆ In **God's timing**, God can change your immediate plans, to accomplish His long term plan in your life! (Sorry Joseph and Mary, but it's Bethlehem and not Nazareth).
◆ In **God's timing**, God can use people who don't know Him (Caesar Augustus) to promote His work in those who do know Him (Joseph and Mary).
◆ In **God's timing**, God will inconvenience your feelings and expectations to prepare you for greater service in the future. (Mary was sorely disappointed in moving until the Savior was born).

The take-a-way?

♦ **God is always in control, even when life seems out of control! and,**
♦ **God often leads us by indirect means!**

Nuf Sed!

December 14
The "Providence" Of Christmas
Part II

"An angel of the Lord appeared to Joseph in a dream. 'Get up', he said, 'take the child and his mother and escape to Egypt. Stay there until I tell you, for Herod is going to search for the child to kill him'"(Matthew 2:13).

Yesterday we saw that God's timing is always perfect. We discovered how God can use people outside of our control to accomplish His will in our lives. We learned that God can interrupt our plans because of His higher plan. We see in Matthew 2:1-23, that there is always a bigger picture and there is always an all wise God at work behind the scenes. Today, notice how it sometimes takes patience to cooperate with the providence of God.

2. Notice God's "Plan" Unfolding!
When Herod heard that the Messiah was being born, he was disturbed (v.3), he asked where Jesus would be born (v.4), he called a secret meeting with the wise men (v.7), he lied and said he wanted to worship Jesus (v.8). Herod actually wanted to kill Jesus because he was afraid that his reign was coming to an end. The good news is, even though the wise men and Joseph have no idea what Herod is up to, God knows and has a plan:
♦   In v.12, the wise men were warned in a dream not to go back to Herod.
♦   In v. 13, Joseph was warned by an angel in a dream to escape Egypt.
So, the plans of the wise men, Joseph and Mary were changed by God! And, sometimes your plans in life are changed by God. The reward of obedience in Joseph and the wise men was that God gave them Divine protection in their journey. Is obeying God always easy? Not hardly!

3. Notice The "Patience" Needed In This Story!
"Escape to Egypt. Stay there until I tell you, for Herod is going to search for the child to kill him" (v.13).

The stay in Egypt was six long years "on hold". The jurisdiction of Herod extended only to the River of Sihor, and beyond this river Joseph was safe these six years. Can we admit it, that "waiting patiently" is not always easy? Yet, it produces character and allows God to work out His sovereign plan. In v.22, Joseph was warned again and landed in a town called Nazareth. Why all this fuss to get Jesus back in Palestine? Because God had a plan all along, to provide a Savior that would die on a cross, so that we could receive this Christ of Christmas!

The take-a-way?
Just because you don't know where you are going, doesn't mean that you are going nowhere!

Nuf Sed!

The "Dayspring" Of Christmas

"Because of the tender mercy of our God, by which the rising sun will come to us from heaven" (Luke 1:78).

I love the song of Zechariah in Luke 1:68-79. It surrounds the detailed account of two babies being born:
♦ In v.13, the angel appears to Zechariah to announce the birth of John.
♦ In v. 31, the angel appears to Mary to announce the birth of Jesus.

Here's the context of the Song of Zechariah: Zechariah and his wife Elizabeth are a godly couple (1:5). They have no children but are seeking God in prayer (v.7). The priests drew lots to see which duties were to be done, and Zechariah was chosen to offer incense in the holy place in the temple (v.9). Then in (v.11) it suddenly happens: An angel of the Lord appears to Zechariah, and he is startled and surprised (v.12). The angel tells Zechariah that Elizabeth will bear a son and should be given the name John (v.13). Zechariah tells the angel that he's kind of old for this, but Gabriel confirms that God has spoken (v.19). In v.57, Elizabeth gives birth to John, and dad is filled with great joy and prophesied. And, Zechariah's song is filled with good news and saturated with sound doctrine. It's a message in song that speaks to us loud and clear. It lifts our spirits this Christmas season and reveals that:

1. Christmas Is About **Redemption**!
"Praise be to the Lord, the God of Israel, because he has come and has redeemed his people" (v.68).
   The word "Redeem" means, "To set free by paying a price". We learn here that it was God's idea to visit us in the person of His Son. It was God that condescended to free us from our sin. He paid a debt we could not pay.

2. Christmas Is About **Renewal**!
"He has raised up a horn of salvation for us" (v.69).
   The word "Horn" in scripture is symbolic of power, strength and victory (1 Kings 22:11; Psalm 89:24). It is a picture of an army about to be overcome, when help arrives to give victory. Jesus is our Helper and gives us strength to win in every spiritual battle.

3. Christmas Is About **Remission**!
"To show mercy to our fathers…...the forgiveness of their sins" (v.72, 77).
   The word "forgiveness" means remission, to dismiss and to send away. Zechariah sees all of us in debt and unable to pay the payment for our sin. He also sees Jesus coming in Bethlehem to be our sacrifice and satisfy God's wrath against us.

4. Christmas Is About **Rising**!

"The rising sun will come to us from heaven" (v.78).

The "rising" or "dayspring" refers to Jesus who will "shine on those living in darkness" and "guide our feet into the path of peace" (v.79).

The take-a-way in response to God's mercy?

My only response is, "to serve Him without fear in holiness and righteousness before Him all our days" (v.74, 75).

Nuf Sed!

December 16
The "Growth" Of Christmas
Part I

"'I am the Lord's servant', Mary answered. 'May it be to me as you have said'. Then the angel left her" (Luke 1:38).

L uke chapter one is an amazing revelation of Gabriel (the angel) visiting both Zacharias and Mary. Zacharias was told that John the Baptist would be born to his wife Elizabeth. Mary was also told that she would give birth:

"Do not be afraid, Mary, you have found favor with God. You will be with child and give birth to a son, and you are to give him the name Jesus.....his kingdom will never end" (Luke 1:30-33).

When Mary received the angel's news about what was soon to happen, she "was greatly troubled at his words" (v. 29). After this, Mary said, "How will this be.....since I am a virgin?" (v.34). Mary was then encouraged to believe by the miracle of her relative, Elizabeth, who would have a child in her old age. After Mary was told about Elizabeth, Mary responded in a remarkable way that teaches all of us. She was puzzled, single, not sexually active, and had never heard of this scenario before. Yet, after Mary was told that she would give birth to the Son of God, and that she should go see her cousin Elizabeth, Mary responded! And how she responded speaks to your heart and mine today:

1.   Mary Responded With A **"Surrendered Will"**!
"'I am the Lord's servant,' Mary answered. 'May it be to me as you have said'" (v.38).
    Even though Mary was young and would have to be somewhat secretive; Even though people would criticize her for being pregnant while still engaged to Joseph; Even though the spousal period was one year and adultery resulted in stoning; Mary surrendered her will to God's will! In other words:
♦   Mary was willing to give up her rights, and,
♦   Mary was willing to die to herself!
    When Mary said, "I am the Lord's servant" (v.38), she was saying that she was a bond slave or servant of God. Mary knew that a servant is someone who advances others at the expense of themself!

2.   Mary Also Responded With An **"Obedient Heart"**!
"At that time Mary got ready and hurried to a town in the hill country of Judea" (v.39).
    Mary obeyed God when three things were against her:
♦   She was an unwed mother and who would believe her story? (Luke 1:26; Matthew 1:18).
♦   She would have to face Joseph and risk his rejection from a broken trust

(Matthew 1:19-20).

♦ She faced the threat of being condemned to death for adultery (Deuteronomy 22:23).

Yet in the face of adversity and uncertainty, Mary obeyed God and trusted Him to work out all the details down the road. In fact, Mary "hurried" (v.39) and moved with haste to obey the will of God.

The take-a-way?

Don't put off until tomorrow what God has told you to do today!

Nuf Sed!

The "Growth" Of Christmas
Part II

"And Mary said: My soul glorifies the Lord" (Luke 1:46).

Yesterday we saw how Mary responded to the angel's news about her giving birth to Jesus. I call this the "growth" of Christmas because Mary's three responses help all of us to grow in the Lord. We looked at Mary's surrendered will and obedient heart. Today discover that:

3. Mary Responded With A **Grateful Spirit**!
    When Mary said, "My soul glorifies the Lord and my spirit rejoices" (v.47), she was magnifying God. The word "Glorifies" (v.46) means, "To declare the greatness of". The idea is habitual, or Mary continually rejoiced in the fact that God was in control of what she couldn't see. This passage of Luke 1:46-55 is known as Mary's song. It is a detailed account of Mary expressing her gratitude to God! It is a record of reasons why Mary is so grateful! We see what causes us to rejoice today:

1. You Can Rejoice In **God's Salvation**!
"My spirit rejoices in God my Savior" (v.47).
    Mary recognized that she was a sinner, could not save herself, but God was providing for her.

2. You Can Rejoice In **God's Grace**!
"For he has been mindful of the humble state of his servant" (v.48).
    Mary considered herself undeserving of God's grace because she was poor, obscure and unknown. This reminds all of us that while we were still sinners, Christ died for us" (Romans 5:8).

3. You Can Rejoice In **God's Power**!
"For the Mighty One has done great things for me – holy is his name" (v.49).
    God's power is seen in the conception of Jesus in the womb of Mary. "Holy is his name" (v.49) means that God is pure and without fault or mistake. If God could plant His Son in the womb of Mary, then surely God can be trusted with what's on your heart today.

4. You Can Rejoice In **God's Mercy**!
"His mercy extends to those who fear him from generation to generation" (v.50).
    Mary is so grateful because of God's mercy towards her – and all of us today. We are forgiven and have eternal life, only because of the mercy of God!

5. You Can Rejoice In **God's Justice**!
"He has scattered those who are proud in their inmost thoughts…..but has lifted up the humble" (v.51, 52).

Mary understands that Jesus will render justice, so we can leave matters in His hands.

6. You Can Rejoice In **God's Provision**!
"He has filled the hungry with good things" (v.53).

Mary sees the reward of those who are spiritually hungry and seek the Lord!

7. You Can Rejoice In **God's Liberty**!
"He has helped his servant Israel" (v.54).

Israel was enslaved by the Romans and needed deliverance. Mary testifies that Jesus liberates those who turn to him.

The take-a-way?
Christmas can birth in us a grateful spirit that overcomes every temptation to murmur and complain!

Nuf Sed!

December 18
The "Humility" Of Christmas
Part I

"This will be a sign to you: You will find a baby wrapped in cloths and lying in a manger" (Luke 2:12).

Today and tomorrow I want to look at how the manger speaks to us today. Here is the setting of Luke 2: Caesar Augustus made a decree while Herod was the ruler appointed by Rome. Caesar was the grand-nephew of Julius Caesar and was given the name "Octavian" which means "Venerable". He ruled Rome from 27 B.C. to 14 A.D. and came to power when Julius was assassinated. It was in the middle of his reign that Octavian ordered a census for military and tax purposes. This census called for every Jewish male to return to the city of his father to record his name, occupation, property and family.

In His great wisdom, God used Caesar's command to move Joseph and Mary 80 miles from Nazareth to Bethlehem. In Bethlehem, Jesus was born and placed in the manger, a feeding trough for cows. His birth drew the angels from heaven (v.8-14) and these angels made the first announcement to anonymous shepherds – who were outcasts in Israel. Jesus' birth drew the shepherds from the field, and "they hurried off and found Mary and Joseph, and the baby, who was lying in the manger" (2:16). I love the response of the fast moving shepherds:

♦ They **received** the message by faith (v.15).
♦ They **responded** with obedience (v.16).
♦ They **reported** the good news (v.17).
♦ They **rejoiced** in seeing Jesus (v.20).

But why was Jesus placed in the manger and what difference does it make today?

1. The Manger Reveals The **Humility** Of Jesus!
All of heaven was stirred when Jesus was born, yet there was no parade, kings palace or great show on earth. Why not? Why the birth and placement in a feeding trough for cows? It was all to reveal the humility, meekness, and lowliness of Jesus. It was to reveal His willingness to condescend. It was to show us that the way up is the way down in the Kingdom of God.

2. The Manger Reveals The **Grace** of Jesus!
"Do not be afraid. I bring you good news of great joy that will be for **all** the people" (v.10). All people means that whosoever will may come. The manger made it possible for everyone to approach Jesus. Anyone would feel comfortable to approach Him. No one would be afraid to draw near! No one would be intimidated or offended to shy away. The manger speaks to all of us – that we can come close and close the distance between His heart and ours!

The take-a-way?

"Though he was rich, yet for your sakes he became poor, so that you through his poverty might become rich" (2 Corinthians 8:9).

Nuf Sed!

December 19
The "Humility" Of Christmas
Part II

"You will find a baby wrapped in cloths and lying in a manger" (Luke 2:12).

Yesterday we learned how the manger reveals the humility and grace of Jesus. The feeding trough for cows shows us that Jesus is meek and willing to condescend for our benefit. It also reveals that all of us can draw near to Jesus without fear or intimidation. Today, notice three more ways that the manger speaks to our hearts:

3. The Manger Reveals The **Satisfaction** Of Jesus!
The place where Jesus was lying was prophesied by an angel. The angel told the shepherds that the Savior would be discovered, "wrapped in cloths and lying in a manger" (v.12). But why a manger?
♦   A manger was a feeding trough.
♦   A manger was where cattle were fed.
♦   A manger was where food was placed.
♦   A manger was where animals found their daily bread.
♦   A manger was where the survival lifeline was.
   Jesus said in John 6:35, "I am the bread of life. He who comes to me will never go hungry, and he who believes in me will never be thirsty". The manger held the bread (for the natural man). The manger also held the Bread of Life (for the spiritual man). The manger shows us all where real joy, peace, strength, and security is found!

4. The Manger Reveals The **Sacrifice** Of Jesus!
"Today in the town of David a Savior has been born to you; he is Christ the Lord! This will be a sign to you….,"(v.11, 12). What was the sign? Christ will be in a manger! Born and placed in a wooden trough, to one day die on a wooden cross.
♦   Jesus is willing to sacrifice in His birth – no crib.
♦   Jesus is willing to sacrifice in His life – no pillow.
♦   Jesus is willing to sacrifice in His death – no support.
   The manger fulfilled a prophecy of sorrow, sacrifice and love. It was all to cover your sins and mine! It was all to pay our debt and give us life beyond the grave.

5. The Manger Reveals The **Rejection** Of Jesus!
Mary, "placed him in a manger, because there was no room for them in the inn" (v.7). Neglected and turned away, rejected and ignored, Jesus was second to all the other guests at the inn. The manger reminds me that it's possible to reject the Savior, push aside His advance, resist His call, and crowd out His presence. But remember this about Jesus this Christmas season:
♦   There is no sinner that He does not love!

- ♦ There is no sin that He cannot forgive!
- ♦ There is no other way to be saved than through Jesus!
- ♦ There is no better time to be saved than right now!

The take-a-way?

Everything about the manger grows humility in our hearts, and humility will lessen stress in your life!

Nuf Sed!

The "Joy" Of Christmas

"Because Joseph her husband was a righteous man and did not want to expose her to public disgrace, he had in mind to divorce her quietly" (Matthew 1:19).

One of the great joys of the Christmas story, is how God intervened and led each step of the way. Somehow and for some reason I receive great comfort when I understand the wisdom and all seeing eyes of God. I think you will receive a calm assurance, that God will also lead you as you travel down life's journey. Take heart, rejoice and discover again: **You don't have to know where you are going, to be headed in the right direction!**

"After Jesus was born in Bethlehem in Judea, during the time of King Herod, Magi from the east came to Jerusalem and asked, 'Where is the one who has been born king of the Jews? We saw his star in the east and have come to worship him'" (Matthew 2:12).

The Magi, or wise men from the east, were learned men that dwelt in Persia and Arabia. In its original use, the term magi denoted three things: Philosophers, Priests and Astronomers. These men were devoted to astronomy, religion and medicine. They were held in high esteem by the Persian Court and were admitted as counselors to give advice. They were Gentiles yet interested in seeing Jesus the Jew. They were wealthy and brought free will offerings. They traveled a long distance – just to be close to Jesus! When Herod heard about the Magi visiting to worship this "King of the Jews" (2:2), "he was disturbed, and all Jerusalem with him" (v.3). Herod was troubled at Jesus' birth because he was afraid his reign was coming to an end. So Herod petitions the wise men, chief priests, and the scribes to find this Jesus so that he can thwart the plan of God. But notice how God intervenes; and recognize God's ability to lead you as you follw His plan for your life. He really does have a plan to lead those who follow Him! Never forget the following when you are tempted to worry about or fret over your future:
1. **God led** Joseph to take Mary home when he was planning to divorce her (Matthew 1:20).
2. **God led** the wise men from the east to baby Jesus (2:2).
3. **God led** them again as the star, "went ahead of them" (v.9) after visiting Herod.
4. **God led** them a third time, in a dream, to return to their country, "by another route" (v.12).
5. **God led** Joseph to "escape to Egypt" (v.13).
6. **God led** Joseph to "the land of Israel" (v.20).
7. **God led** Joseph to Galilee where it was safe (v.22).
   The joyful moral of this part of Christmas is, God still leads us even when we don't fully know all that's going on around us. What we know is:
♦ God will order our steps (Psalm 37:23).

- ♦ God will go before us (John 10:4).
- ♦ God will direct our path (Proverbs 3:6).
- ♦ God will sustain us in every season (2 Corinthians 12:9).
- ♦ God will finish what He started in us all (Philippians 1:6).

The take-a-way?
"Whether you turn to the right or to the left, your ears will hear a voice behind you, saying, 'This is the way; walk in it'" (Isaiah 30:21).

Nuf Sed!

December 21
The "Sadness" Of Christmas

"There was no room for them in the inn" (Luke 2:7).

Every year there is a sadness that surrounds Christmas. The sadness comes when you realize that so many people are missing the reason for the season. In the midst of all the shopping, spending, sales, parties, rushing, wrapping, tension and hurriedness, something is missing. What is it? It is the joy that Jesus and salvation bring to the soul! So many are so sad because they are missing the Lord who alone can satisfy and transform the heart. Without Jesus, Christmas is just another holiday to endure, tolerate and entertain. So who missed Christmas at Christmas?

1. The Innkeeper Missed Christmas!
It was census time in Bethlehem so the city was filled with people whose ancestry went back to Bethlehem. The innkeeper was very busy and pressed with customers. When Mary gave birth to Jesus, she wrapped him in cloth and laid him in a feeding trough for cows. Why? Because the innkeeper was too preoccupied, distracted and consumed with business. Busyness crowded Jesus right out of his schedule.

2. Herod Missed Christmas!
He pretended that he wanted to meet Jesus to worship him, but in reality he wanted no competition for his throne. He was a politician, had an army of his own, was ruthless in taking taxes from the people and was full of jealousy and insecurity. When tricked by the Magi, Herod became angry and had all the male children in Bethlehem under the age of two slain. He missed Christmas in preference to his own ambitions and was full of selfishness in his heart.

3. Jerusalem Missed Christmas!
The shepherds went back and told everyone in Jerusalem what they had seen concerning the child (Luke 2:17). Yet Jerusalem refused to visit Jesus, so close in Bethlehem. Jerusalem was the hub of religious activity and was busy with feasts, festivals and ceremonies. Caught up in all the external religious duties, Jerusalem was bent on earning their salvation through all the religious requirements. Jerusalem was religious but lost!

4. Nazareth Missed Christmas!
Nazareth was the home of Mary, Joseph and Jesus, yet Nazareth didn't recognize who Jesus really was. Nazareth was so familiar with Jesus that they missed the Savior. How sad to think, that it's possible to sing songs, decorate trees, and receive presents – yet be left unchanged this time of year.

5. The Romans Missed Christmas!
The Roman empire allowed their emperor to pretend to be God. In fact,

Caesar Augustus promoted emperor worship in the Roman provinces. Jesus just didn't fit into their system where idols were worshipped. Roman soldiers were everywhere in Bethlehem keeping law and order and overseeing the census. But the Romans missed Christmas because of their idols and lesser gods within their hearts.

The take-a-way?
May God help us to "Narrow Our Interests" and avoid crowding Jesus out of our hearts!

Nuf Sed!

December 22
The "Prophecy" Of Christmas

"But you, Bethlehem Ephrathah, though you are small among the clans of Judah, out of you will come for me one who will be ruler over Israel, whose origins are from old, from ancient times" (Micah 5:2).

Jesus was born in Bethlehem, the city of David, to fulfill Bible prophecy. He will also one day occupy the throne of King David; reigning as the Prince of Peace. When you examine what the Old Testament prophets wrote about Jesus' life and ministry, faith in the integrity of God comes alive. Every prophecy was fulfilled to the letter. Others remain to be fulfilled at Jesus' second coming. No impostor could have lived a sinless life and fulfilled every prophecy according to God's Word. Only Jesus proved to be the Son of God, born in fulfillment of scripture, born to be the Savior of the World! Let the truth below open your heart and remove all doubt. Remember why this devotional is in your hands today: "But these are written that you may believe that Jesus is the Christ, the Son of God, and that by believing you may have life in his name" (John 20:31).

Designation	O. T. Prophecy	N. T. Fulfillment
Birthplace – Bethlehem	Micah 5:2	Matthew 2:1
Born of a virgin	Isaiah 7:14	Matthew 1:18-23
Tribe of Judah	Genesis 49:10	Hebrews 7:14
Family of Jesse – David	Isaiah 11:1	Revelation 22:16
Would be in Egypt	Hosea 11:1	Matthew 2:13-15
Preaching deliverance	Isaiah 61:1-3	Luke 4:12-16
A prophet (Matthew 24)	Deuteronomy 18:15	Acts 7:37
The Light of the World	Isaiah 9:1, 2	Matthew 4:12-16
The Great Healer	Isaiah 53:4	Matthew 4:23, 24
The Good Shepherd	Isaiah 40:11	John 10:11, 14
The triumphal entry to Jerusalem	Zechariah 9:9	Matthew 21:1-11
Rejected by His own	Psalm 69:8	John 1:10, 11
Betrayed by a friend	Psalm 41:9; 55:12-14	John 13:18, 26
Betrayal price – 30 pieces of silver	Zechariah 11:12	Matthew 26:14-16
Silver purchased potter's field	Zechariah 11:13	Matthew 27:3-7
Beaten and spit upon	Isaiah 50:6	Matthew 26:67
Struck with a rod	Micah 5:1	Matthew 27:30
Silent under persecution	Isaiah 53:7	Matthew 27:14
Forsaken by His followers	Zechariah 13:7	Matthew 26:31, 56
Manner of His death	Zechariah 12:10	John 19:18, 34
Wounded hands and feet	Psalm 22:16	John 20:25, 27
Died among criminals	Isaiah 53:9, 12	Mark 15:27, 28
Buried with the rich	Isaiah 53:9	Matthew 27:57-60
Persecutors mocked Him	Psalm 22:7, 8	Matthew 27:39-44
His cry of agony – the very words	Psalm 22:1	Matthew 27:46
Given vinegar and gall to drink	Psalm 69:21	Matthew 27:34
His clothing divided by lot	Psalm 22:18	John 19:12, 24

None of His bones would be broken	Psalm 34:20	John 19:36
Body would not decompose in tomb	Hosea 6:2; Psalm 16:10	Acts 2:30, 31
He would ascend in triumph	Psalm 24:7-10	1 Peter 3:22
He would be our heavenly priest	Zechariah 6:12, 13	Hebrews 8:1,2;4:14

The take-a-way?

Christmas reveals that the Christ-child was born in fulfillment of scripture and is God's gift to all!

Nuf Sed!

The "Genealogy" Of Christmas

"Mary, of whom was born Jesus, who is called Christ. Thus there were fourteen generations in all from Abraham to David, fourteen from David to the exile to Babylon, and fourteen from the exile to the Christ" (Matthew 1:16, 17).

The genealogy of Jesus (Matthew 1:1-17) shows us that Jesus is the promised Son of David and the promised Son of Abraham. It also shows us, that in addition to Mary (v.16), four other women are listed among the list of men:

1. **Tamar** (1:3)
   - ♦ Tamar was Judah's widowed daughter-in-law,
   - ♦ She tricked Judah into sleeping with her to produce offspring to carry on her dead husband's name (Genesis 38).
2. **Rahab** (1:5)
   - ♦ Rahab was a Canaanite prostitute who lived in Jericho.
   - ♦ She harbored Israelite spies before Joshua's conquest of the city (Joshua 2).
   - ♦ She not only spared her family from destruction, but God made her part of the Messiah's ancestry.
3. **Ruth** (1:5)
   - ♦ Ruth was a foreigner in Israel when Israelites were commanded not to intermarry with other nationalities.
   - ♦ Ruth was privileged to become an ancestor of the Messiah (she was the great grandmother of King David). (Ruth 4:13-22).
4. **Bathsheba** (1:6)
   - ♦ Uriah's wife had an adulterous affair with David.
   - ♦ This led to David's murder of her husband, Uriah.
   - ♦ It also led to the birth of Solomon, an ancestor of the Messiah.

Why are these four unlikely women mentioned in Matthew's genealogy? Why were three of them Gentiles, and considered unclean by God's standard of Old Testament Law? Why list three women who were involved in illicit sexual relationships? Why are these four women in the genealogy of Jesus? I think it's a pretty clear message, and it's taught throughout the scripture:

- ♦ God is willing and able to forgive any sin whatsoever!
- ♦ God is bent on restoring people who don't deserve it (and none of us deserve God's Grace).
- ♦ God can do amazing things through people (men and women) who once were far away from Him.
- ♦ God is sovereign and will use anyone He desires to accomplish His purpose.
- ♦ God can use your pain and disappointments to accomplish His purposes in the future.

The reality is, something is going on in your life right now, but God is also mindful of something else. The Christmas genealogy teaches us that where sin abounds, grace much more abounds! Oh friend, don't miss this: It's not about your past sin or perceived self righteousness. It's about God's grace that can use you in your weakness as you lean upon Him. Be reminded this Christmas, that old things have passed away and Jesus is making all things new!

The take-a-way?
"God chose the weak things of the world to shame the strong...so that no one may boast before him" (1 Corinthians 1:27, 29).

Nuf Sed!

The "Worship" Of Christmas

"Where is the one who has been born King of the Jews? We saw his star in the east and have come to worship him" (Matthew 2:2).

Ever wonder how three wise men could travel over 1,000 miles to worship the Christ child? Ever wonder why they presented Jesus with gold, frankincense and myrrh? Ever wonder how they even found where Jesus was born? The scriptures reveal the majesty of this worship moment:

♦ The wise men from the east were from Chaldea, Persia or Arabia.
♦ The star they followed was not a fixed star (planet) or a meteor flash, but a supernatural phenomenon that appeared to lead the wise men to Jerusalem.
♦ The wise men traveled the distance for one reason, to worship Jesus. The word "worship" means to acknowledge the worth of, to give adoration, and to express reverence, awe and gratitude. True worship is unselfish; its end is the glory of God. But what is the meaning in the gold, frankincense and myrrh?

1. The **Gold** Speaks of **"Sovereignty"**.

The wise men brought their gifts to a child whom they understood was to be King of the Jews. But why the gold? Gold was a sign of royalty and was offered to kings.

♦ In Genesis 41:42, Joseph wears a gold neck chain.
♦ In Daniel 2:32, 38, King Nebuchadnezzar has a head of gold.
♦ In Daniel 5:7, 29, Daniel wears gold as a ruler.
♦ In 2 Samuel 12:30, Rabbah's king wears a crown of gold.
♦ In Psalm 21, the author of Psalm 21 wears gold.
♦ In Ecclesiastes 2:8, the King of Jerusalem is a collector of gold.
♦ In Esther 4:11, King Ahasuerus holds a golden scepter.

Gold was a gift fitted for a king because it represented the sovereignty of that king. It was symbolic of the sovereign rule of the one the gold was given to. This means that Jesus is sovereign, over all, and you can trust Him with your life.

2. The **Frankincense** Speaks Of **"Supplication"**.

Frankincense was a white resin (gum substance) taken from a tree. It was used on the altar of incense in front of the holy of holies. Incense was sprinkled on the coals and the sweet fragrant smoke rising heavenward was symbolic. It symbolized prayer being offered by the people and received by God. David prayed, "May my prayer be set before you like incense" (Psalm 141:2).

Giving frankincense to Jesus at His birth is telling us that Jesus our great intercessor is receiving our prayers. He longs to receive our adoration, petitions and supplication. It reminds us that it's okay to pour out your heart to God in prayer.

3. The **Myrrh** Speaks of **"Sacrifice"**.

Myrrh is a bitter substance taken from trees in Arabia. It was used for embalming the dead and symbolizes suffering and sacrifice. It means that Jesus is touched with the feelings of our infirmities and identifies with your pain and sorrow in life. It tells us, that, as Jesus was sustained by His Father in sorrow, so Jesus will sustain you as well.

The take-a-way?

The wise men worshipping are saying:

♦ **Gold means that you can trust in the sovereignty of God!**

♦ **Frankincense means that you can make supplication and pour out your heart to God in prayer!**

♦ **Myrrh means that you can be assured that God too is afflicted in your affliction!**

Nuf Sed!

December 25
The "Drawing Power" Of Christmas!

"When the angels had left them and gone into heaven, the shepherds said to one another, 'Let's go to Bethlehem and see this thing that has happened, which the Lord has told us about'" (Luke 2:15).

I loved playing with magnets as a child. I could never understand how a magnet had invisible drawing power to pull the other metals along. In the events of Christmas, I notice God's drawing power at work. See how this drawing power speaks to us today:

1.   The Birth Of Jesus Draws Mary and Joseph To Bethlehem (v.1-7).
God used the decree of Augustus Caesar to draw Mary and Joseph from Nazareth to Bethlehem (some 80 miles away).
♦   Bethlehem was the **birth** place of Benjamin!
♦   Bethlehem was the place of **death** for Rachel!
♦   Bethlehem was the **marriage** place of Ruth!
♦   Bethlehem was the place of **exploits** for David!
1. Like **Benjamin** it is our **birthplace** when we receive Jesus and are born again of the Spirit of God.
2. Like **Rachel** it is our **death place** when we die to our own will and the old selfish nature.
3. Like **Ruth** it is our **marriage place** when we make a vow and a covenant to be devoted 100% to putting Jesus first in everything.
4. Like **David** it is our **place of exploits** as we serve God and allow God to use us to bear fruit that remains.

2.   The Birth Of Jesus Draws Angels From Heaven (v.8-14).
After Jesus was born (v.7), something happened that involved angels:
♦   **The Shepherds** (v.8) were watching their sheep in the field. Shepherds were outcasts in Israel because their work made them ceremonially unclean. Their work kept them away from the temple for weeks at a time. Angels were drawn to the humble shepherds.
♦   **The Shining** (v.9) was from the glory of the Lord. The angels appearance was one of splendor, glory and intentionality.
♦   **The Salvation Message** (v.10) was the great announcement. The angels said that there is Good News (which is the message of salvation), to all people (which is the scope of salvation).
♦   **The Savior** (v.11) which is Christ the Lord, is the One who would provide for us what we could not provide for ourselves. Only Jesus can forgive and remove sin from our record!

3.   The Birth Of Jesus Draws The Shepherds From the Field (v.15-21).
"The shepherds said one to another, 'Let's go to Bethlehem and see this thing that has happened'" (v.15). The shepherds were determined to make the long

trip to find Jesus. They found Him and celebrated without reservation or hesitation. Why? Because gratitude filled their hearts for the gift of God's Son! In fact, they: "Returned, glorifying and praising God for all the things they had heard and seen" (v.20).

The take-a-way?
Mary and Joseph were drawn, the angels were drawn, the shepherds are drawn and you can be drawn closer to Jesus this Christmas season – closer than you've ever been before – Merry Christmas!!!

Nuf Sed!

"Ending The Year Intimate With God"

"Go up to the land flowing with milk and honey. But I will not go with you, because you are a stiff-necked people and I might destroy you on the way" (Exodus 33:3).

Exodus 32 and 33 is one great story of recovery and restoration because of God's grace and mercy. It's an account of Israel's failure and God's faithfulness. It's a record of intimacy reestablished between God and His people. Notice:

1. The "Grieving" Of The Lord Was Noticeable!
"I will not go with you…when the people heard these distressing words, they began to mourn" (33:3, 4).

The text reveals that Moses delayed to come down from Mount Sinai. While he delayed, the people became impatient and asked Aaron to make a new golden calf god out of gold earrings. God was grieved at the impatience and idol, and expressed His extreme disappointment. In fact, God said: "I will send an angel before you…but I will not go with you" (v.2, 3). In other words, God said that He was changing the way He would deal with Israel. He was opting out by withdrawing His visible presence. Instead, He would send an angel in His place. When the people heard this they mourned. Why? Because even angels cannot take the place of the Presence of God in your life! Thank God for angels, but all of us need the God of the angels most of all. So, Israel sinned, Moses was angry and God was grieved. Notice next:

2. The "Grace" Of The Lord Was Offered!
"Now therefore, I pray thee, if I have found grace in thy sight, show me now thy way" (Exodus 33:13, KJV).

After God withdrew His presence, Moses erected a prayer tent outside the camp. When Moses would go into the tent, the people would watch him and saw, "the pillar of cloud would come down and stay at the entrance, while the Lord spoke with Moses" (33:9). Here is the answer to intimacy restored with God:
♦ Moses asked God to be gracious and merciful with him and the people.
♦ Then God extended grace and mercy as Moses prayed: "They have made themselves gods of gold. But now, please forgive their sin" (32:31, 32).

3. The "Glory" Of The Lord Was Revealed!
"Then Moses said, 'Now show me your glory'" (33:18). The glory of God was revealed to you and me in three ways:
♦ It's found in a **place!**
"There is a place near me where you may stand on a rock" (v.21). That place is Jesus today.

♦ It's found in a **person**!
"I will put you in a cleft in the rock" (v.22). Jesus is the Rock; as Moses smote the rock and water came out, so Jesus was smitten, and His life blood flowed out.

♦ It's found in a **presence**!
"I will...cover you with my hand until I have passed by" (v.22). As Moses experienced the afterglow of God's presence, so Jesus clothes us with His glorious presence today!

The take-a-way?
As the new year approaches, why not draw near to God by His undeserved grace and experience the presence of Jesus continually.

Nuf Sed!

December 27
"Ending the Year with a Missionary Heart"

"If you wait for the perfect conditions, you will never get anything done" (ECC. 11:4, TLB).

Our text is an encouraging word for every laborer in the vineyard. It's also a warning against waiting for the "perfect" situations before we become missional and intentional. So, if you've ever wondered if your labor was in vain, you've ever been impatient while sowing seed and if you've ever been tempted to walk by sight and not by faith, this message is for you! Solomon gives us wisdom to honor God with a missionary heart; it's wisdom to make a difference!

I. The Bread Encourages Us (To Live **Unselfishly**)
"Cast your bread upon the waters" (V.1).

The bread that Solomon mentions here is an agricultural term. It's a reference to the farmer on the banks of the Nile River. Every year when the waters subsided, the farmer went forth upon the wetlands and scattered seed over the mud. Goats would trample the grain in the ground and the farmer knew that a harvest would be coming. And God says, "Cast your bread upon the waters" (V. 1) because we all have two choices in life:
♦ We can spend our lives on ourselves alone and use all of our seed for the moment (or)
♦ We can look long term and sow seed into the vineyard and reap down the road.

In other words, we can spend all of our resources (seed) on ourselves, or forego instant gratification for the days to come. I can keep all my seeds to myself or I can turn them into bread for the future. I can keep my life (and lose it in the end) or lose my life (and keep it in the end).

II. The Reward Encourages Us (To Live With **Patience**)
"...For after many days you will find it again" (V. 1). This means that we have a moral duty to discharge (or sow and give). And, we also have a guarantee from God that what we sow will germinate and multiply. "After many days you will find it again" (V.1) means: vegetation may be slow, but it's sure to come. This means that God never loses sight of your work, no work done in His Name is wasted and patience is required between the sowing and reaping.

III. The Warning Encourages Us (To Live With **Urgency**)
"If you wait for the perfect conditions, you will never get anything done" (V.4, TLB).

Here is the danger that faces us all: To look for the "perfect" and "ideal" circumstances before we invest and sow into the harvest. We can be a "fair weather" sower and procrastinate because of adverse conditions. We can make excuses, become distracted and refuse to risk. In other words, it's possible to be disengaged while waiting for a more "favorable day".

IV. The Unknown Encourages Us (To Live By Faith)
"You do not know the path of the wind, or how the body is formed in a mother's womb" (V. 5). In other words, you can't explain the wind and the womb process! And, just because you don't know the future, that shouldn't keep you from doing what you can do now. So, don't let what you can't do paralyze what you can do!

The take-a-way?
It pleases God when we sow seed in every season (both favorable and unfavorable).

Nuf Sed!

"Ending The Year Connected To Christ's Body"

"From him the whole body, joined and held together by every supporting ligament, grows and builds itself up in love, as each part does it's work" (Ephesians 4:16).

The expression of Jesus on earth is His bride, His church. The ultimate goal or will for the church is to make disciples (Matthew 28:18-20). A disciple is described in scripture as:

♦ A believer (Acts 16:30).   ♦A learner (2 Timothy 2:15).
♦ A follower (Matthew 16:24). ♦A witness (1 Peter 3:15).
♦ A reproducer after Christ's kind (Matthew 28:19.)

The purpose of growing healthy disciples is to see people go from consumers to contributors.

Spiritually healthy disciples love to give, serve and disciple others. Why? Because spiritually healthy people look beyond "events" to the "process" that builds strong people. Healthy believers want **spiritual substance** (not vanity fair), **internal change** (not just emotional highs), **lasting fruit** (not just frantic activity), **Christ-like character** (not entertaining performances), **God's Glory** (not ego gratification). And, God has given us two things to be healthy disciples:

1. We've been given **"grace"** (v.7) which means: God has distributed His gifts and grace to every believer to function somewhere in His body.
2. We've been given **"gifts"** (v.11) to lead, feed and protect the body of Christ:

♦ **Apostles** - those who go into virgin territory to plant a new body of believers.
♦ **Prophets** - those who proclaim God's Word to warn and awaken the body of Christ.
♦ **Evangelists** - those called specifically to bring unbelievers to decisions.
♦ **Pastors** - those called to assume responsibility for the spiritual welfare of a local congregation.
♦ **Teachers** - those gifted by God to clarify and communicate truth so that others can grow.

The end result of God's **"gifts"** and **"grace"** is something to behold.

1. You'll Be **"Prepared"** For Works of Service (v.12).
This means to perfect, equip, mature, restore, and make whole. It leads to the church body being built up, edified and growing healthy and strong.
2. You'll be **"Perfected"** (v. 13).
This word means to advance in godliness to become more like Jesus. True disciples don't want to be pampered and entertained, they want to advance in Christ-likeness.
3. You'll Be **"Protected"** (v.14).
"We will no longer be infants, tossed back and forth by the waves, and blown here and there by every wind of teaching" (v.14). God has given us spiritual

leaders to protect us from religious fads, trickery, fraud, manipulation, deceit and charlatans.

4. You'll Be **"Progressive"** (v.15).

And will, "grow up into him who is the Head, that is, Christ" (v.15). Walking in truth and love will help us to love no matter what and yet be truthful no matter what. This will help us to grow.

5. You'll Be **"Productive"** (v.16).

And see that the church "grows and builds itself up in love" (v.16). Notice God's Divine Blueprint:

♦ Each individual member grows and becomes obedient and fruitful.

♦ The church then becomes a coordinated team that is intentional and missional.

♦ The Lord then sees to it that the body increases and grows to minister to more people!

The take-a-way?

If we do our part in preparing and equipping people, God will do his part in giving the increase and rescuing more people!

Nuf Sed!

December 29
"Ending The Year Remembered By God"

"Can a mother forget the baby at her breast and have no compassion on the child she has borne? Though she may forget, I will not forget you" (Isaiah 49:15).

Isaiah 49 is all about Jesus (the Servant Of The Lord) and Israel (Jacob). The 26 verses read like a counselor reminding someone of some things we can forget. Jesus is seen before He was born (v.1) and also seen in His ability to speak and penetrate our hearts:

"He made my mouth like a sharpened sword...he made me into a polished arrow" (v.2).

This reveals how Jesus can cut through the veneer outer coating of our hearts, and purify and polish the heart he pierces. And, who of us doesn't need the Lord to speak to us when we are tempted to believe that our labor is in vain?

"I said, 'I have labored to no purpose; **I have spent my strength in vain** and for nothing. Yet what is due me is in the Lord's hand, and my reward is with my God'" (v.4).

If this devotion today finds you feeling that your labors for the Lord are in vain, think again! Allow the Word to correct your self-talk! Let the truth set you free from destructive thinking! Listen to what the Lord is saying to our hearts! It is the gospel; it is not good advice, it is Good News! It is God specifically saying, that you have been restored and remembered:

1. Jesus Restores You Because Of His Grace!
"To bring Jacob back to him and gather Israel to himself...because of the Lord, who is faithful...who has chosen you" (v.5, 7). It was God who recovered Israel to pure worship again. This is Jesus here, wanting to gather, restore, bring back and draw us close to Himself! The heartbeat of God is revealed: "This is what the Lord says...'Come out, and to those in darkness, Be free'! He who has compassion on them will guide them and lead them beside springs of water" (v. 9, 10).

And, if you're wondering how or why Jesus can restore you close to Himself again, here's why:

2. Jesus Remembers You Because Of The Cross!
"I have engraven you on the palms of my hands" (v.16). The word "engraven" means: "To cut into". It signifies permanence of memory. And, if you think that you don't deserve God's grace, you are correct! That's why (v.13) says, The Lord will have compassion (mercy) on his afflicted ones! In other words, at Calvary, Jesus paid it all! At Calvary, Jesus satisfied God's justice! At

Calvary, mercy rescued you and me! At Calvary, Jesus suffered in your place and mine! At Calvary, Jesus once and for all made the payment to free us from guilt and condemnation. And, at Calvary, like God delivered Israel from Babylon, so has God delivered you from sin's power.

The take-a-way?
Jesus paid it all so, "All mankind will know that I, the Lord, am your Savior, your Redeemer" (v.26).

Nuf Sed!

December 30
"Ending The Year Submitted To God"

"Yet, O Lord, you are our Father. We are the clay, you are the potter; we are all the work of your hand" (Isaiah 64:8).

Isaiah emphasizes the presence of God in chapter 64. He records the prayer from his heart and Israel's heart. He pleads for God to intervene because Jerusalem is desolate, the land lies in waste and God's people have been carried captive to a distant land. Isaiah appeals to God, the only One who can bring deliverance in the midst of difficult times. I love how God records Isaiah's appeal:

1. Isaiah Prays!
"Oh, that you would rend the heavens and come down" (v.1).
Here Isaiah prays that God would manifest his glorious presence and work noticeably with the fire of His Spirit. It's a prayer that God would be so tangibly present, that it would be, "as when fire sets twigs ablaze and causes water to boil" (v.2).

2. Isaiah Believes!
"Since ancient times no one has heard, no ear has perceived, no eye has seen any God besides you, who acts on behalf of those who wait for him" (v.4). This is a promise that God will show up for those who wait in faith, and believe, and trust in Him. It means that God takes notice when we align ourselves with his will instead of our own.

3. Isaiah Obeys!
"You come to the help of those who gladly do right, who remember your ways" (v.5).
Israel had sinned and was confronted with God's anger. When Israel turned back to God, their obedience was rewarded by God! This clearly shows us that God desires to bestow his favor upon those who trust him and do what He says.

4. Isaiah Repents!
"All of us have become like one who is unclean, and all our righteous acts are like filthy rags; we all shrivel up like a leaf, and like the wind our sins sweep us away" (v.6). "Do not remember our sins forever" (v.9). Isaiah writes that God has, "hidden your face from us and made us waste away because of our sins" (v.7). This is acknowledgment and godly sorrow because of offending God's holiness. And, humility gives us access to God while pride drives us further away from His presence.

5. Isaiah Submits!
"You are our Father. We are the clay, you are the potter; we are all the work

of your hand" (v.8). Israel was made up of individuals like you and me. All that God needed, was for Israel to submit to the Master Potter. I love the fact that the Potter never gave up on the clay (Israel).

The take-a-way?
God is preparing you (the clay) on the potter's wheel so that you can take it in the fire. But remember, his hand is always on the thermostat.

Nuf Sed!

"Ending The Year With Great Assurance"

"'For I know the plans I have for you', declares the Lord, 'plans to prosper you and not to harm you, plans to give you hope and a future'" (Jeremiah 29:11).

As we end this year and prepare for the next, my heart is drawn to the great "Hopeful Promise" in Jeremiah 29. More than any resolutions for the coming year, the following truth leads us to strong confidence in the plan that God has for you. And, God has a good plan for your days ahead.

Jeremiah 29 is a letter from God to His people who are captive in Babylon. In 597 B.C. the Babylonians began to deport the Jews to Babylon. These Jews would be taken captive, detoured from their hometown (Jerusalem), and be held in a pagan society for 70 years. Separated from their temple worship and service, they find themselves hemmed in by idolatrous Babylonians. And God has three things to say to His people, both then and now:

1.   God Is Sovereignly Over Your Detours and Delays (v.1-4).

"This is what the Lord Almighty, the God of Israel, says to all those I carried into exile from Jerusalem to Babylon" (v.4).

Who was it that allowed the Jews to be deported, exiled, detoured and delayed? It was God that allowed the uncomfortable season, all to accomplish His sovereign will. It was God that was working out His plan, though unknown to Judah. It was God who was at work behind the scene. Was it still painful? It was! Here's how it affected the hearts of Judah:

"By the rivers of Babylon we sat and wept when we remembered Zion" (Psalm 137:1).

"There on the poplars we hung our harps" (v.2).

"Our tormentors demanded songs of joy" (v.3).

"How can we sing the songs of the Lord while in a foreign land?" (v.4).

We all have two choices when we are tested: Hang our harps on the willow tree and resent our season, or trust that God will redeem our season and use it for His Glory in some way.

2.   God Is Actively Involved In Your Personal Development (v.5-7).

"Build houses and settle down; plant gardens and eat what they produce. Marry…increase in number…seek the peace and prosperity of the city to which I have carried you" (v.5-7).

While it would be easy to resist their pagan captors, Jeremiah says to make the best of it and let God help you to flourish where God has placed you. God, in fact, promises to give you increase right where He has put you! What's the lesson? The lesson is, God can cause us to flourish and grow where we are planted. He can sustain us, develop us, and use our detours for His glory. We can curse our pain and waste it, or we can reverse it and allow God to use it for our good.

3. God Has A Specific Plan For Your Future Destination (v.8-14).

"When seventy years are completed for Babylon, I will come to you and fulfill my gracious promise to bring you back to this place...to give you hope and a future" (v.10, 11).

Out of this Jewish remnant in captivity would be the group to return to Jerusalem (where Jesus would come from). In other words, God is telling us that nothing and no one can stop His will from being done in your life! God is clearly communicating that:

♦   Your present circumstances are known to the Lord! And,
♦   Your new year ahead is already known by your Maker!

The take-a-way?

Every detour, delay and disappointment can be used for our good when we humble ourselves and refuse to resist God's sovereign plan!

Nuf Sed!

Conclusion

What a joy it's been to share my favorite passages of scripture and part of my life's story with you. And, we all have a story, a history, and a testimony of God's goodness. Friend, you and I have a reason to be grateful! That reason is because God has not given us what we deserve. While all of us deserve judgment because of our sin, God in His mercy has laid that judgment on His sinless Son – Jesus. We all deserve eternal separation from God, but God in His grace has made it possible to be forgiven and accepted. It is my prayer that you will respond to God's grace and invite Jesus into your heart. If you are not absolutely 100% sure of your salvation, simply ask Jesus today to forgive your sin and put your trust in Him and His work on the cross. He will forgive you this very moment and forever change your heart for good. As Jesus becomes more beautiful than useful, you will never want to live without Him, nor will you ever be sorry for putting Him "first place" in your life.

So, until we meet one day on earth or in heaven, I leave you with the words of my wife, Eunhee. As we live life together, she tells people week after week this truth:

"You are beautiful, you are special, and you are loved!"

Nuf Sed!